Napoleon and the
Campaign of 1814

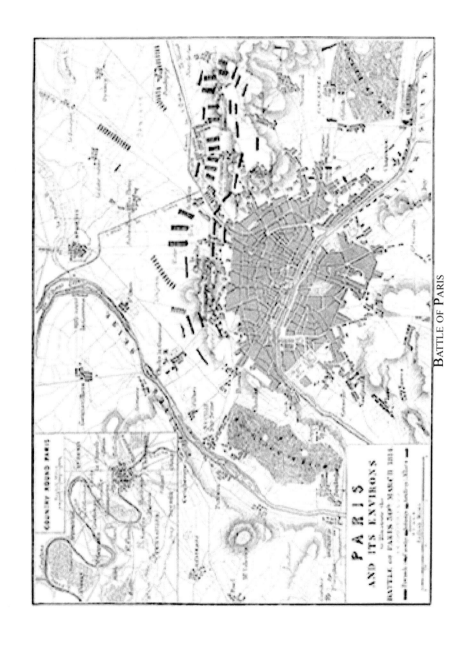

BATTLE OF PARIS

Napoleon and the Campaign of 1814

The Classic History of
the end of the Napoleonic epoch

Henry Houssaye

LEONAUR

Napoleon and the Campaign of 1814
The Classic History of the
end of the Napoleonic epoch
by Henry Houssaye

First published under the title
Napoleon and the Campaign of 1814

Leonaur is an imprint
of Oakpast Ltd

ISBN: 978-1-84677-774-5 (hardcover)
ISBN: 978-1-84677-773-8 (softcover)

http://www.leonaur.com

Contents

Translator's Preface

A hundred years have passed since the capture of Paris by the allies, but Napoleon's campaign in Champagne remains a masterpiece of defensive strategy, and the events connected with his first abdication have lost none of their interest. Henry Houssaye is recognized as being a leading authority on the latter portion of Napoleon's reign, and his vivid language describes both political and military matters in a way which invests them with unflagging interest and furnishes a graphic insight into the personalities of the leading actors in the events which he describes: his writing is not merely a dull catalogue of events, nor is it a partial and one-sided encomium on any one man, and for this reason Houssaye's volumes possess a peculiar interest both for the general reader and for the student of military history. The campaign of 1814 is one which has received little attention from English writers, and there should, therefore, be scope for a translation of the present volume into the English language.

R. S. McClintock.
Limerick, March 1914.

Preface

The campaign of 1814 in France, in which the courage of Napoleon's soldiers rivalled the genius of their leader, was divided into three distinct phases. The first phase lasted from January 25 to February 8, and was marked by the threatening advance of the allies. In vain had Napoleon conquered at Brienne, in vain had he held his own at La Rothière against three times his own numbers. His armies were in retreat, the situation appeared desperate, and the end of the war loomed near and inevitable. Napoleon felt himself powerless to stay the advance of the armies of Bohemia and Silesia, which had effected a junction with each other: he could no longer rely on his troops and could scarcely rely on himself. His one and only hope was that the enemy might commit a blunder.

The second phase, which was marked by a succession of victories, lasted from February 9 to 26. The whole feature of the campaign was changed: the allies had committed the strategic fault for which Napoleon had been watching, and, instead of advancing on Paris by converging lines, had moved apart and separated their armies. The Emperor threw himself upon Blücher, worsted him in four successive fights, then turned on Schwarzenberg and drove him back in retreat on Chaumont and Langres. On February 26 the hosts of the coalition were beaten and separated, the army of Bohemia retreating towards the east, and the army of Silesia committed to a flank march in which it risked annihilation. Napoleon had won ten battles in twenty days and restored the balance of the campaign; he had seized the initiative and hoped for victory.

The third phase of the campaign opened by the action at Bar-sur-Aube on February 27, and ended at the battle of Paris on March 30. In this phase the fortune of war turned against the Emperor, and his magnificent manoeuvres, combined with the heroic efforts of his soldiers, resulted only in Pyrrhic victories. There were, however, many alternations in the campaign, and many gleams of hope pierced the darkness. Three times the in-domitable genius of Napoleon was on the point of restoring the fight, and three times the allies were on the brink of disaster, but fortune was on their side and saved them from defeat.

This last period of the campaign is the least well known and the most dramatic, and it is principally with this period that the following pages deal: the narrative, however, has been carried on to cover the abdication of the Emperor, and the general his-torical developments have been described as well as the purely military events. The earlier phases of the invasion, also, have not been forgotten, and in the first chapters the reader will follow the fortunes of the allies from the Rhine to the Aube and will trace the slow retirements of Napoleon, pregnant with lightning counterstrokes; he will watch the laborious diplomacy of the Châtillon negotiations; he will see France ruined and stricken to the ground, torn by dissensions and conspiracies, pillaged by the Cossacks and the Prussians, and he will note how her submissive surprise changed to a fierce longing for vengeance.

For the purposes of this book only original documents have been made use of, and, with the exception of some half-dozen pages, no reliance has been placed on the writings of historians. It must not be understood that no histories have been consulted, for, if the archives of France and other countries have provided numberless documents, the German and Russian historians have also furnished a quantity of original material: Plotho's *Krieg in Frankreich*, for example, is, properly speaking, merely a collection of reports and orders.

Much time was required to classify and collate this mass of

documents but a keen critical sense was not necessary in order to distinguish between them, for though they were all equally authentic they were not all equally trustworthy. When an order written on the morning of a battle, at a time when the least error in the description of hour or place might lead to incalculable disaster, is found to differ from a report penned on the day following the action, there is not much difficulty in deciding which is correct: the same holds good between the correspondence and the memoirs of a minister, and between a confidential report and a publication in the *Gazette*. It is equally evident that a statement for or against the Empire carries varying weight according to whether it is written by a foreigner, a royalist, a republican, or a Buonapartist.

We have conscientiously sought for the truth. At the risk of clashing with every opinion, we have tried to omit nothing, to hide nothing, and to minimize nothing. But impartiality is not indifference: in this narrative in which we have seen, above all else, France stricken and wounded, it has been impossible not to feel pity for her and anger against her assailants. Without enlisting ourselves on the side of the Empire, we have rejoiced at the Emperor's victories and grieved at his defeats. In 1814 Napoleon is no more the Sovereign, he is the General, the first, the greatest, and the most resolute of the soldiers of France. We have rallied to his standard saying, with Godefroy Cavaignac's old countryman: "It is no longer a question of Buonaparte. The soil of France is invaded. We must fight for her."

H. H.

Paris, March 25, 1888.

CHAPTER 1

France at the Beginning of 1814

Disaster followed close on the heels of victory. The France of Napoleon, among her hundred and thirty departments, had numbered the department of Leman, with Geneva as capital, the department of Rome, capital Rome, the department of the Zuyder-Zee, capital Amsterdam, and the department of the Lower Elbe, capital Hamburg. She had counted as vassal states the kingdoms of Naples, Italy, Illyria, Spain, and the Confederation of the Rhine, which latter comprised the duchies of Berg, Hesse, Baden, Würtemberg, Bavaria, Westphalia, Saxony, and half Poland. At the period under review France, with her vast empire dismembered and her armies driven back, found the whole of Europe united against her, and saw the enemy's hosts to the eastward at the foot of the Vosges and the Jura, and to the southward on the near side of the Pyrenees.

The plains of Russia had swallowed up the Grand Army; the battles of 1813 had destroyed another Grand Army, and in the autumn of that year fresh decrees were issued calling another 796,000 men to the colours. The blockade of the Continent pressed heavily on the country, the fields were uncultivated, the factories closed, and business and public works were at a standstill; the deduction of 25 *per cent.* from all incomes derived from other than military sources, and the great increase of taxation, had brought scarcity to the rich and misery to the poor. The funds had fallen from 87 to 51 *francs*; the shares of the bank were quoted at half their former value, and the rates of exchange on notes were prohibitive. Cash was so scarce that it had been found necessary to postpone to January 1, 1815, the law which fixed the rate of interest at five or six *per cent.*, and everyone was free to lend at whatever rate he chose. In Paris nothing could be sold except foodstuffs. In the provinces the merchant vessels were unable to leave harbour, and in consequence the manufacturers had their warehouses full and the wine-merchants their cellars stocked; the latter, certainly, had debts owing to them from Germany, but there was no knowing when they would receive payment, and meanwhile they were forced to pledge their silver, their furniture, and their clothes.

Throughout the country bankruptcies were common. Numbers of men took to the woods to avoid the conscription, and they were there pursued by mobile columns, while bailiffs took possession of their parents' houses, and in some districts none but women and children worked in the fields. Meanwhile the Minister of the Interior published official instructions in the news- papers to the effect that women and children could advantageously take the place of men in field work, and that spade labour should be employed instead of ploughing, which had become impossible owing to the shortage of horses.

In this state of ruin and decimation the whole population of France had but one desire, namely, for peace; and this universal prayer rose to the steps of the imperial throne from city and from country, and even from the chiefs of the army themselves. Since the campaigns of 1808 and 1809, and especially since the retreat from Russia, France had been weary of war. The disasters of the Beresina and of Leipzig, and the march of the enemy's armies towards the frontiers, had awakened her from her dreams of glory in the same way that the massacres of the terror and the disorders of the Directory had scattered her visions of liberty. After twenty-five years of revolution and war France longed for rest, but the great majority of the country, amounting to four-fifths of the population, did not want the downfall of Napoleon, and did not even so much as think of it.

As a matter of fact, the old nobility and one section of the middle classes looked at things from a different point of view to the majority of the nation. Although many of them had become *partisans* of the empire, the nobles had never altogether lost hope; in the provinces the small secret meetings of royalists would adjourn indefinitely if the name of the chief of police were mentioned, and in the Faubourg Saint-Germain they carried on a guerrilla warfare of harmless epigrams. The liberals were a more serious danger because many of them were members of the legislative chambers, or held official appointments.

While the Emperor was master of the world their attitude had been one of obsequious grovelling, but when reverses came to him they blamed his cruel ambition, his mad dreams, and his despotic government. They railed at the servile attitude of the Senate, of which many of their own number were members; they arraigned the false nature of the representative institutions, in which they themselves had a share; they abused the tyranny of the administration, in which more than one among them had taken a leading part; and they accused the Minister of Police, whose hand they had all shaken, of employing the methods of the revolution, of issuing *lettres de cachet*, and of arbitrarily banishing and imprisoning numbers of people. This irritation on the part of the liberals was legitimate, but it was none the less tardy and inopportune: the deputies ought to have made their protests two years earlier; then they might have prevented aggression, whereas now they only paralysed the defence of the country.

The adjournment of the Chamber of Deputies, which took place on December 31, 1813, and the angry remarks which Napoleon addressed to the members at their farewell audience on the following day served to increase the discontent of the middle classes. The deputies who remained in Paris did not conceal the reasons for the adjournment, and repeated the Emperor's speech with many exaggerations. The same thing happened in the provinces, where numbers of the members returned during the first few days of January. In Bordeaux, Marseilles, and several other towns, Lainé, Raynouard and others distributed manuscript copies of the well-known report, and people drew the conclusion that it was in the Emperor's power to make peace but that he refused to do so, and they blamed his obstinacy, his pride, and his tyranny.

These opinions, which were beginning to hold sway in the drawing-rooms and shop-parlours of the towns, had not penetrated to the workshops nor to the country districts. There was naturally much suffering there, and the people longed for peace, but they did not on that account blame the Emperor; they hated war, but the man who was responsible for so many wars lost none of his popularity; they did not connect cause and effect, and failed to realize that war and Napoleon were synonymous terms. The peasants with the same breath cried "Down with the Taxes," and "Long live the Emperor."

In view of the law which permitted the purchase of substitutes for the conscription, the common people alone had paid for the glories of Napoleon with their blood, and yet they were the very people who had lost none of their faith in him. The correspondence of the *prefects* and the police reports of the earlier part of January, 1814, neither hide nor omit any detail of the prevailing misery and prostration, and give full accounts of the royalist placards, the desertions, the risings against the tax collectors, and the seditious speeches of the middle classes, but one searches in vain for any outburst of hatred or any threat against the Emperor from among the ranks of the common people; on the contrary there is much evidence to bear out Mollien's words:

> "The mass of the population had no knowledge of anything but the Emperor and the Empire."

Not only had the Emperor retained the affection of the people in spite of all his faults, but through all his defeats he was still looked upon as being invincible. When they timidly asked him to give them peace, they imagined that it lay in his hands and that he would dictate terms of truce to the allies; if he did not give them the peace which they longed for, it was because he was certain of victory.

The first of the immense levies ordered in the autumn of 1813 was carried out without difficulty; the Emperor called for 160,000 men of the years 1808 to 1814, and France, in spite of her exhaustion, gave him 184,000. The second levy (150,000 men from the conscription of 1815) met with no resistance either, except in a few departments of the west or south-west, but this levy could only furnish men of the average age of nineteen years, and, for that reason, was not pushed with energy. The administrative services, the recruiting offices, the clothing factories, and, above all, the arsenals, could not deal with so many men at once, and the Emperor preferred conscripts of twenty-five to those of nineteen. This levy of 1815 was begun immediately after that of the 160,000 men and was not nearly finished at the end of the war.

Difficulties began to be felt when a further order was issued to enrol 300,000 men. To raise another 300,000 men from the categories of the years 1800 to 1814 was like trying to squeeze a quart out of a pint pot. The men of the categories of the years 1800 to 1807 were now being drawn upon by the conscription for the second time. Those of the years 1808, 1813, and 1814 for the third time, and those of 1809 to 1812 for the fourth time! In addition to the normal levy of 150,000 men the categories of 1809 and of each of the three following years were being called upon to furnish a quarter of the abnormal levy of January 11, 1813, say 25,000 men, a seventh of the abnormal levy of October 9, 1813, 38,000 men, and a thirteenth of the abnormal levy of November 15, 1813, 24,000 men, making a total of 237,000 men; it was the wiping out of a whole generation.

The earlier levies had carried off first the bachelors, then the childless widowers; for the levy of 300,000 men they had to take those who were the support of their families, and even a certain number of married men. The conscription made slow progress; the registers were faulty and contained the names of men who had already been enrolled in former levies either as substitutes or as chasseurs and grenadiers of the National Guard.

The forests filled with defaulters. In certain towns only a quarter of the numbers summoned reported themselves to the officials. Also, while the levy of 160,000 men showed a surplus of 24,000 on January 31, that of 300,000 men revealed on the same date a shortage of 237,000; up to then only 63,000 conscripts, had been enrolled.

The National Guard was designed to form reserve armies, and the organization of this force proved even more unpopular and difficult than that of the active army. When the National Guard was once enrolled it was indistinguishable from the field troops, and this was, therefore, to all intents and purposes another conscription which fell almost entirely on the married men who had escaped the earlier levies, and on the men of over thirty-three years of age, who also, especially in the country districts, were almost all married.

The purchase of substitutes was allowed, but substitutes were costly, and, as almost all the unemployed workmen from the large industrial centres had already been engaged in this capacity, they were very hard to come by. In the middle classes numbers of men left the districts in which they were registered, and this movement became so common that the Government were compelled to refuse to issue passports until the contingents had been finally formed.

The peasants also were no more eager to serve; they were ready to defend their hearths and homes, but they did not want to rejoin the army. They were persuaded by the tears of their wives and refused to serve; there were riots and revolts, with the result that, by January 25, there were hardly 20,000 militiamen in the various camps of instruction. The so-called active National Guards rose, of course, to a larger number during the course of the campaign, but, even including those assembled at Lyons, the militia do not seem ever to have exceeded an effective total of 40,000 men engaged in active operations or organized and capable of taking the field; these numbers do not, of course, include the urban or sedentary National Guards of Metz, Strasburg, Paris, Rheims, Rouen, etc.

These various contingents of new levies amounted in the middle of January to an effective total of no more than 175,000 men who had joined the armies of the Rhine, of the North, and of the Pyrenees, or had arrived in the different depots scattered from Brittany to Rome, but, unfortunately, they were riot yet by any means ready for use. Before these recruits could be opposed to the enemy in the field they had to be trained, clothed, and armed. For the training there was no time, and in January 1814 four-fifths of the men were still learning their recruits' drill. The storehouses and arsenals of France proper did not contain sufficient material to clothe and arm them, for since 1811 Napoleon had depleted them to fill the depots of the frontier fortresses beyond the Rhine. There were arms at Hambourg, Stettin, Mayence, Wezel, and Magdebourg, but there were none at Metz or Paris.

During the last few years the muskets of the provincial National Guard had been called in, and these muskets, which were mostly in a bad state of repair, constituted almost the only resources of the last imperial army. Napoleon, it is said, kept continually repeating, "Why have they hidden the condition of the arsenals! From me?"

The state of the military divisions bears witness to the shortage of war material. In January 1814 there were a number of battalions which were complete in equipment and arms, but in the depots it was quite another story. Many of the soldiers were in the condition described by General Préval, commandant of the large cavalry depot at Versailles, who says, "There has just arrived here a squadron of light cavalry who are deficient of everything except waistcoats and breeches."

Only two men out of three, on an average, were dressed in uniform, and, more serious still, only one man in two was armed. The depot of the 1st Military Division (Paris) had 9,195 men present, and 6,530 muskets, and the depot of the 16th Division 15,789 men and 9,470 muskets. At Rennes, Tours, Perpignan, and in all the garrisons in the west, the centre, and the south, the state of affairs was worse still. For instance, the 5th Light Infantry had 545 men and 150 muskets, the 153rd of the Line 1,088 men and 142 muskets, the 142nd 324 men and 41 muskets, and the 115th 2,344 men and 289 muskets. Cavalry weapons also were deficient; the 1st Regiment of light cavalry had 202 sabres for 234 men, the 17th Dragoons 187 sabres for 349 men, and the 8th Cuirassiers 92 sabres for 154 men. There was also a shortage of horses, and in the large depot at Versailles there were 6,284 horses for 9,786 men.

The civil administration was charged with the clothing and equipment of the active sections of the National Guard, and the condition of the arsenals threw the further responsibility for the armament on their shoulders. These troops were no better furnished than the active army, and many men wore blouses and civilian caps, while almost all were clad in *sabots*; a few were given a military appearance by wearing a shako, a cartridge-belt, and a haversack.

In the course of the campaign the Emperor gave orders that the militia were to be clothed in the greatcoats and helmets taken from the prisoners of war, but these articles were found to be unwearable on account of the vermin with which they were infected. In the National Guard half the armament consisted of ineffective sporting weapons, which were obtained with difficulty by requisitions. Some battalions arrived at the points of concentration without any arms at all, and on February 16 1,000 National Guards armed themselves on the field of battle with muskets captured from the enemy.

The Emperor ordered fresh levies, doubled the taxes, devoted his private fortune to the various military departments, urged on the manufacture of arms, the construction of fortifications, and the supply of warlike stores: it was all in vain, both time and money were lacking. The difficulties were increased tenfold by the unexpected nature of the invasion. The hurried advance of the allies across the frontier in the first days of January surprised France in the very act of organizing the defence. This bold stroke on the part of the enemy stopped the recruiting and collection of taxes in one-third of the departments, threw the whole of

France into disorder, and compelled the victor of a hundred fights to stake his crown on the issue of a single battle.

The invasion struck terror into the hearts of the population of France, but it stirred up no determination to resist. In 1792 the abstract idea of the outraged fatherland had had great effect on the minds of a people rejuvenated by liberty, but in 1814 it failed to rouse a nation which had grown old in war and was weary of sacrifices and anxious for rest. To stir up the anger and hatred of the people there was needed the brutal and material fact of the foreign occupation, with its accompaniment of wrongs, of requisitions, pillage, violations, murders, and burnings.

At first the invasion absolutely failed to raise the courage of the nation and to give the Emperor a moral force on which he had the right to count, and of which he stood sorely in need: on the contrary, it only caused the public spirit to sink to still lower depths of depression. In some towns, such as Dôle, Chalon-sur-Saône, and Bourg-en-Bresse, the town guards received the Austrians with musket shots, but in most places the appearance of the allies was enough to cause an immediate submission. Epinal surrendered to 50 Cossacks, Macon to 50 hussars, Rheims to a handful of men, Nancy to the scouts of Blücher's army, and Chaumont to a solitary Würtemberg trooper!

Langres and Dijon proudly shut their gates, but the former capitulated at the second cannon shot, and the latter at the second flag of truce. In the country the cry of "Cossacks" was enough to send numbers of people flying to the woods, carrying their household goods and driving their cattle and pigs before them. Others trusted the proclamations of the allies, which promised respect for property and the strict maintenance of discipline, and these remained in their villages and tried to escape violence by the eagerness with which they complied with the demands of the soldiers and the requisitions of the officers.

Everywhere, it is true, the small French corps fell back before the overwhelming forces of the allies. Levies *en masse* had been ordered on January 4, but the generals appointed to command these levies in the frontier districts had not arrived before the enemy advanced, and the *prefects* and sub-*prefects*, in accordance with Napoleon's express orders, left the country in company with the last French troops. Without leaders, without organization, and almost without arms, the peasants could not oppose the march of 250,000 soldiers. It is true they had not the spirit to fight; their misery and the sacrifices they had made had crushed out all thoughts of resistance; their lands were untilled, and their children had been murdered by the enemy or were dead of typhus.

"The submission of the inhabitants encourages the allies," writes the Duc de Vicence [1] from Châtillon on January 31.

"There is no more spirit left in France," he says again on February 3.

"The inertia is the same everywhere," writes Marshal Mortier from Chaumont.

"Among the bulk of the people," says the Sub-*prefect* of Vervins, "there is only indolence and cowardice. They are without emulation or energy, and do not realize the disgrace of being invaded."

The news of the crossing of the Rhine was known in Paris and the surrounding departments on January 6 and 7. Before that date several copies of Schwarzenberg's manifesto had arrived, and this very clever document, which bore witness to the Prince's diplomatic powers, had the effect, not only of reassuring and so disarming the rural districts, but also of helping traitors to stir up a new and formidable feeling in the majority of the towns.

"The proclamations of the allies," wrote the Duc de Vicence on January 8, "are doing us more harm than their weapons."

The proclamation of Loërach, which bore the same general tenor as the Declaration of Frankfort, could be summed up in the words, "peace to France and war to Napoleon."

The malcontents were quick to make capital out of the distinction drawn by the allies between the country and the sov-

---

1 Caulaincourt, the Duke de Vicence, was the Minister for Foreign Affairs, and was Napoleon's plenipotentiary at the Congress of Châtillon

ereign: they compared this declaration with the action of Napoleon in dissolving the Chamber of Deputies, and they argued that, in bidding farewell to the representatives of the nation, the Emperor had himself announced his divorce from France.

In this tacit league between the liberals and the royalists, the former, who had no definite end in view, were animated only by malice and hatred, but the latter, who knew very clearly the goal for which they were striving, saw in the alliance a chance of gaining their ends. To the royalists the allies were not enemies, they were liberators.

"The *partisans* of the Bourbons," says Madame de la Roche-jacquelein, "never saw Napoleon undertake a war without hoping that he would be defeated."

To their disappointment, the French were always the victors; this time, however, they were beaten, and the hopes of the royalists began to rise. In the last few months of 1813, and in January 1814, secret meetings were held and displays of royalist sentiment were observed almost everywhere in France, though they could not anywhere be called serious.

There was nothing, however, which could be called a conspiracy, for organization was lacking, means of communication were difficult, and there were no recognized leaders. Bordeaux was the only place where so many as several hundred men obeyed the word of one chief. As a matter of fact, the royalists were far from numerous; but large numbers of people were unintentionally helping their cause by deploring the condition of France, by spreading alarmist reports, or by writing letters which gave only too true an account of the events in the theatre of war.

Many officials, even, by their despondency and lack of energy helped to add fuel to the flames; they felt the ground trembling under their feet, they thought of the future, and their anxiety to be on the winning side made them half-hearted in carrying out their duties. Throughout the half of France the *prefects* showed nothing but weakness; some fled from their districts before the troops had evacuated them, others failed to carry out the orders to arrest conspirators, and others again put off as long as possible the enforcement of the conscription and then carried it out without any energy.

"It is difficult to exaggerate the dissatisfaction which I feel with your *prefects*," wrote Napoleon to Montalivet. Some mayors purposely exhibited incomplete lists of men liable for the conscription; others abandoned their towns at the approach of the enemy; others, again, refused to issue arms to those men who wished to defend themselves; while some, whose action bordered on the treacherous, sent requisition orders in the name of the allies to villages which had not yet been occupied by them. At Lyons the inaction and cowardice of the *prefect*, the mayor, and the municipal councillors were made the subject of derisive street songs.

The lack of energy shown by the majority of the officials may be ascribed to despondency, a desire not to compromise themselves, and even to a natural fear of physical punishment; but a certain number hoped for the fall of the empire, like Lynch, the Mayor of Bordeaux, who conspired with Rochejacquelein, and Angles, the right arm of the Duc de Rovigo, who was embroiled in Dalberg's intrigues. The *prefect* of the department of the Somme stopped the departure of the conscripts, chose the officers of the National Guard from among the nobility, and appointed to a command a notoriously active royalist who was under observation from police head-quarters.

A highly placed employee of the *prefecture* of the Seine was guilty of a violent outburst against the empire in a public restaurant, and added, "My opinions are independent of the office I hold."

A government attorney had the audacity to say in a public place: "If the allies would offer one or two million *francs* for Napoleon's head, they would not have to wait long for it."

Although they were few in number, the royalists were full of activity. They set to work, first of all, to recall to the memory of Frenchmen the half-forgotten name of the Bourbons. Not a day passed but in some town or other notices were posted up or proclamations were distributed asserting that the allies were fighting for the Bourbons and would respect the houses of royalists, and promising that with the return of the legitimate king would come peace, reduction of taxation, and the abolition of conscription.

"Frenchmen," ran a proclamation of Louis XVIII, "you will hear from your king no word of reproach or complaint and no reference to what has passed. It is his will that you hear from his lips none but words of peace, of clemency, and of pardon . . . honours and dignities are the rights of all Frenchmen; the king can only reign with the consent of the nation and of the representatives of the people. . . . Receive these generous allies as friends, open to them the gates of your towns, forestall the violence which a criminal and useless resistance cannot fail to draw down upon you, and let their entrance into France be welcomed with joy."

"Frenchmen," we read in a proclamation of the Prince de Condé, "your rightful sovereign, Louis XVIII, has just been recognized by the powers of Europe. Their victorious armies are nearing your frontiers. . . . You will receive peace and pardon. The rights of property will be respected, the taxes will be reduced, and your sons will be restored to agriculture and to the arms of their parents."

With the mass of the people in the temper they were in at this time, the best arguments in favour of divine rights was the promise of peace, of educed taxes, and of an end to the conscription, and the *partisans* of the Bourbons had no need to devote their whole time to instilling in the minds of men an appreciation of these blessings. Before long, some of them, like Vitrolles and Polignac, went off to inform the allied staff as to the state of public opinion and the means of defence of Paris; some acted like Lynch, a count of the Empire, who invited the English to occupy Bordeaux, and others, like the Chevalier de Rougeville, who was "filled with zeal for the allies," or like the Chevalier Brunei, who "was ready to die for the Cossacks," became guides for the enemy's columns in their advance against the armies of France.

The Bourbons, on their part, did not remain inactive. Their hopes were raised by the reports which they received from France and by articles in the English and German newspapers advocating a restoration. The Prince Regent of England openly expressed his sympathy, and the other sovereigns, though they would make no definite promise, were certainly not discouraging. The princes took steps, therefore, to second the efforts of their supporters in person: on January 1 the Comte de Provence, already signing himself King of France, wrote the second proclamation of Hartwell; in the course of the month the Duc de Berri arrived in Jersey, where he was conveniently near to Brittany, and the Comte d'Artois and the Duc d'Angoulême took ship, the former to reach the Franche-comté *via* Belgium and Switzerland, and the latter to join Wellington's head-quarters to the north of the Pyrenees. The invasion had made it possible for them to enter France again.

The rebellious intrigues, combined with the inactivity of the officials and the news of the enemy's unchecked advance, served to depress the spirits of the nation arid to spread alarm and disorder. The greatest difficulty was found in raising conscripts and National Guards, for no one was willing to serve. The active contingent of Rouen was composed exclusively of substitutes and it was impossible even to find officers. There were numerous outbursts of feeling against the conscription, and in many departments each drawing of lots was the signal for a riot. At Toulouse a notice was posted up threatening to hang the first man who came forward to draw his number. On January 20, at the request of the *prefect* of Nantes, who expected a rising, the levy of 1815 was postponed for a fortnight.

The *prefect* of Maine-et-Loire wrote "there is danger of a general rising in the department," and the *prefect* of Calvados reported that at Caen things were ripe for a revolution. In spite of police, bailiffs, and mobile columns, the numbers of defaulters and deserters rapidly increased. A detachment of conscripts from the Lower Seine started 177 strong, but only 35 arrived at their destination. Though the soldiers were short of arms, the defaulting conscripts knew very well where to get them, and bands of 50, 200, or even 1,000 or 1,500 men overran Artois, le Maine, and Anjou, as in the times of the royalist risings, skirmishing with the troops, stopping the coaches, forcing the conscripts to join them, and robbing the tax-collectors' safes. Other smaller bands of defaulters robbed carriages and mail coaches on the Lyons, Marseilles, Toulon, and Montpellier roads.

The collecting of taxes met with as much resistance as the levying of conscripts. In Normandy great commotion was caused on January 12 by the report that the Government, in their extremity, intended to commandeer silver, jewellery, and cloth from certain individuals. In Gascony a former page of the Comte de Provence travelled from village to village urging the peasants not to pay the extra taxes.

At Marmande a notice was posted up that the tax-collectors would be hung in the presence of the English; but in many districts the populace did not seem inclined to await the arrival of the British, and the officials were threatened and ill-treated, and sometimes even their lives were in danger. The *prefect* of Angers writes that the collection of taxes was almost everywhere at a standstill. The result was that, although they had been almost doubled, the direct taxes only produced 33,743,000 *francs* in the first quarter of 1814, as compared with 75,500,000 in the same months of 1810.

The yield of indirect taxation was proportionally reduced; registration fees produced 13 millions instead of 25 millions, the Post Office 17,000 *francs* in place of 2,750,000, and at a Cabinet Council on January 25 it was stated that the Government had received 367,000 *francs* in one month in place of the ten millions which would have accrued in ordinary times.

At Paris Chateaubriand began to write his pamphlet *Buonaparte and the Bourbons*. The discontent increased, and in drawing-rooms, in restaurants, on the exchange, and in the half-empty theatres people expressed their fears openly, and the saying attributed to Talleyrand, that this was the beginning of the end, was constantly quoted. The chances of the Bourbons were discussed, and it was said that the allies intended to restore the former monarchy and to crown the King at Lyons, which was already in their hands. Cartoons of a Cossack handing the Czar's visiting-card to the Emperor were freely circulated, and one morning there was found fixed to the base of the column of the Grand Army a paper bearing the words "Pass quickly: it's going to fall."

While the common people, who had little to lose, dreaded pillage and incendiarism, the nobles awaited with less anxiety the arrival of the "restorers of the Throne."

The middle classes, and especially the women-folk, said over their teacups, "It is only in the *Gazette* that the Cossacks are described as badly behaved. When they arrived at Mâcon the allies gave fêtes and spent plenty of money. They are just what is wanted in Paris, where there is not a penny left, to restore gaiety and riches to the capital."

In spite of this talk, however, they buried their gold and silver in the cellars, and many people left Paris, following the example of the Duc de Rovigo's two daughters, whom he had sent to Toulouse with the valuable furniture from his mansion in the Rue Cérutti. That was certainly a curious way for a Minister of Police to reassure public opinion.

The newspapers published reports of successes gained by the garrisons on the left bank of the Rhine, and gave lurid descriptions of the weakness of the allied armies and of the patriotic enthusiasm of the country, and told of innumerable troops concentrating at Châlons. These tales deceived no one: on the contrary they only made people the more ready to believe the news spread by the alarmists and by the Germans living in Paris whom it had not occurred to the police to expel. Foreign papers, also, found their way into the capital in spite of the precautions which had been ordered, and these helped the Parisians to realise what was happening. All sorts of rumours were afloat: Murat had gone over to the enemy; a million men had crossed the Rhine; the allies were fighting for the Bourbons; Joseph had only been appointed to the Council of Regency in order to keep an eye on the other members, who were all in communication with the Austrians; if the emperor were victorious the National Guard would take steps to make him obey their wishes. Other sayings were more serious. Some people maintained that a conference was about to be held at which the Duc de Vicence would make peace, but the answer to this was given in the following terms, which carried conviction with them:

> None of the powers want peace; if there was one of them which had a leaning that way, it would immediately be opposed by Lord Castlereagh, who has joined the headquarters with the express purpose of preventing any negotiations.

> People said also, as if they were reading in the book of the future: "Paris is the allies' objective; to that they will direct all their efforts, for if they are once masters of Paris, the whole empire is theirs."

In vain the papers printed appeals to patriotism, in vain the barrel-organs were ordered to play the Marseillaise, which had been long prohibited; neither words nor tune awoke any echo in the public. In the borough offices there were ever- growing masses of requests for exemption from service in the Parisian National Guard, some of them recommended by the highest officials of the empire.

"The most healthy men declare that they are ill," writes Baron Pasquier. Three companies of artillery for the National Guard should have been formed from students of law and medicine, but when General Lespinasse arrived to enrol them he was received with such hooting that the organization of these companies was abandoned. It was said in Paris that the active army even would not fight, and instances were given of desertion, suicide, and wilful maiming on the part of young soldiers.

It was stated that a detachment of infantry when crossing the bridge over the Gironde at Bordeaux had thrown their arms into the river. Another story was current that while a battalion was marching along the Rue Saint-Denis on the way to the front, and someone shouted to the men that they were going to be butchered, the answer was returned from the ranks, "Nonsense: we're going to find a *louis*; at the first shot we shall go over to the enemy."

This story may not have been true; certainly the police report which tells it is not quite, convincing. One thing, unfortunately, which is not open to doubt is the lamentable condition of the recruits on their arrival at the main depot of Courbevoie. The conscripts were often without food or accommodation, and it was useless to complain to the overworked officers of the depot, who lost their heads among the crowds of recruits waiting to be organized and lacking every necessary.

In spite of all deficiencies, of the 50,000 conscripts who passed through the depot of Courbevoie in the space of three months, only one *per cent*, deserted. What a testimony to the honour of the soldiers of 1814! These poor youths, whose eyes filled with tears as they were dragged away from their desolate homes, were quickly transformed by the sight of the colours. From the bronzed veterans who had conquered Europe they learnt the noble self-denial and the cheerful fatalism which form the basis of the military spirit, and then one day, at a review, or before a battle, the Emperor passed before them and they came under the spell of his fascination; from that moment they fought, not from a sense of duty, not from patriotism, but solely for Napoleon.

The nickname of "Marie-Louises" was given to these poor little soldiers who had been hurriedly torn from their homes and formed into regiments, and a fortnight later were hurled into the thick of battle, and this name of "Marie-Louise" they wrote large in their blood across the page of history. Those *cuirassiers* who could hardly sit their horses and whose furious charge crushed five hostile squadrons at Valjouan, they were Marie-Louises.

Those cavalry were Marie-Louises of whom General Delort said, "No one but a madman would expect me to charge with such cavalry," and who burst through Montereau like a flood overthrowing the Austrian battalions massed in the streets.

It was a Marie-Louise who stood in his place immovable under a heavy fire, indifferent alike to the noise of the bullets and the sight of men struck down beside him, and who answered Marshal Marmont, "I would fire as much as anyone else, only I don't know how to load my musket."

It was a Marie-Louise who took General Olsufjew prisoner at Champaubert, and would hand him over to none but to the Emperor himself. The conscripts of the 28th Regiment at the battle of Bar-sur-Aube, with no weapon but their bayonets, held the woods of Lévigny against four times their own number, and they were Marie-Louises. The 14th Regiment of the Young Guard at the battle of Craonne remained for three hours on the crest of a plateau within close range of the enemy's guns while the grape shot mowed down 650 men out of 920: they also were Marie-Louises. The Marie-Louises went coatless in bitter frost, ill-clad and ill-fed they tramped barefooted through the snow, they scarcely knew how to use their weapons, and day after day they fought stern and bloody battles. Yet through the whole campaign they uttered no word of complaint, and in the ranks there was no murmur against the Emperor. Truly, France has the right to feel proud of her Marie-Louises.

Chateaubriand has said, "Such was my opinion of the genius of Napoleon, and of the courage of our soldiers, that I never dreamed it possible that a foreign invasion would be finally successful; I thought, however, that this invasion would make France realize so clearly the danger in which Napoleon's ambition had placed her that her people would themselves carry out their own redemption."

These opinions were wrong, and these hopes vain. If peace had been signed at Châtillon, no matter what the conditions were, France would have been freed from war, and her sons would have returned to their home and to their work: from such a France Napoleon would have had nothing to fear. Again, if the enemy had been driven back across the Rhine, the pride and enthusiasm of the nation over their new victories would have relieved him of all anxieties. In spite of the incitements to rebellion and the alluring promises of the royalist placards, in spite of the disasters and the prevailing misery, the majority of Frenchmen certainly neither desired the fall of the empire nor loved the name of the Bourbons.

How could the unknown king become popular? Even those who preached his return did not agree as to his identity, for some proclaimed the Comte de Provence, and others the Comte d'Artois, or the Duc d'Angoulême. Even though a certain number of people disliked the despotic rule of the Emperor, they were not on that account anxious to place themselves under the thumb of a king; and though people wished to gain liberty, they also wished to retain equality. The mass of the nation disliked the continual wars and the high taxes imposed under the empire, but they heartily dreaded a revival of the old-fashioned titles, of the local tyranny of the squires, and of the power of the priests. The peasants did not care a rap that the Chamber was dumb, the Senate servile, or Rovigo arbitrary, or that some books were prohibited and some persons banished by a simple administrative order.

In Paris the whole population was on the side of the Emperor. Three times during December and January Napoleon went on foot through the poorer quarters of the town; his calmness inspired the crowds with confidence, and he was received with cheers, while working-men pressed forward to offer him their services, and the only sign of disapproval was the silence of a few of the *bourgeoisie*. On January 25 the Emperor received the officers of the Parisian National Guard. These officers, who were not all by any means zealous supporters of the Government, were assembled to the number of nine hundred in the Hall of the Marshals. The Emperor appeared, and soon afterwards the Empress entered, accompanied by Madame de Montesquiou, carrying the King of Rome. The Emperor announced that he was going to place himself at the head of the army, and with the help of God, and aided by the valour of his troops, he hoped to drive the enemy across the frontier; then, taking the Empress by one hand and the King of Rome by the other, he said, "To the courage of the National Guard I entrust the Empress and the King of Rome my wife and my son," he added in a voice broken with emotion.

At these words the enthusiasm of the audience could no longer be restrained; the ranks were broken, and the officers spontaneously crowded round the royal group, while the eyes of many among them filled with tears. That evening an address to the Emperor was signed in the legions of the National Guard, though General Hullin, the Commandant of Paris, tried to prevent it for disciplinary reasons.

Among other protestations of loyalty and devotion the address contained the following characteristic words: "It is in vain that our enemies have tried to divide the nation. The fear of your genius fills them with hatred, but the vicissitudes of fortune have not destroyed the love and confidence of your loyal subjects."

On the following day the impression created by the Emperor's words was found to be so deep and lasting that some people set to work to counteract it, and tried to make out that the imposing demonstration in the Hall of the Marshals was nothing more or less than a well-staged theatrical scene.

The departure of the Emperor at four o'clock on the morning of January 25 to take command of the army restored the public confidence. Napoleon had been for so long invincible that people could not believe that he would fail to retrieve his fortunes now that France was invaded. It was said that all the odds were now on the Emperor, and it was reported that he had 200,000 troops at Châlons and that a secret treaty had been made with the King of Spain which would set free the veterans of Aragon and Catalonia.

On this latter point the public were well informed, for negotiations were set on foot at Valençay on November 19, by which the Emperor undertook to set Ferdinand VII at liberty and to recognize the integrity of Spain, on condition that Spain would remain neutral and would cease to harbour the English army. By this means the splendid troops of Soult and Suchet would be set free; but unfortunately mutual distrust and grave in- discretions caused such delays that Ferdinand did not set out for Spain till March 19, and at that date the Junta still refused to ratify the treaty which had been signed on December 11 between Napoleon and the captive of Valençay.

When the first reports were received of the battles of Saint-Dizier and of Brienne, which the newspapers described as great successes, the Stock Exchange rose by more than two *francs* in three days, and on February 1, when the first performance of *l'Oriflamme* was given at the Opera, the large and enthusiastic audience expected to see the Empress, King Joseph, and even the King of Rome, and to hear the great victory officially announced from the stage.

These hopes proved vain and fleeting. On the following day, February 2, the *Moniteur* caused uneasiness by speaking of the fight at Brienne as a mere rear-guard action, and on the 4th the news of the defeat at La Rothière and the retreat of the imperial army caused general consternation. Stocks fell to 47.75; the rates of exchange rose to 40 and 50 per thousand for silver and to 90 and 100 for gold, while many money-changers refused to give gold at any price. People crowded to the bank to change their notes, but by the decree of January 18 no more than 500,000 *francs* could be changed per day. At the pawnbrokers' the maximum price was fixed at twenty *francs*, no matter what the value of the article pledged.

The police could not deal with the demand for passports, and thirteen hundred were issued in one day; many shops were closed altogether, while those which remained open thought it wise to remove much of their stock. Masons found work, for their services were in great demand to make hiding-places in the walls, and, for fear communications should be interrupted by the enemy, people laid in provisions as for a siege. Potatoes rose to four times their former value, and the price of rice, dried vegetables, and salt pork doubled, with the result that the poor, who were brought face to face with starvation, threatened to sack the houses of the rich. The Government was extremely alarmed; the Empress ordered prayers to be said for forty hours at Sainte-Geneviève; King Joseph wrote letter after letter to the Emperor asking for instructions in case the enemy appeared under the ramparts of Paris, and the Director of Museums begged for leave to pack the pictures at the Louvre; a portion of the imperial treasure was loaded on to wagons in the courtyard of the Tuileries, and near the city gates one frequently heard the cry, "The Cossacks are coming; close the shops!"

The panic lasted for a week, and during that time all sorts of rumours were afloat. It was said that the French army was routed, Troyes burnt, and Marshal Mortier killed; 600 guns were reported to have been captured by the enemy, and it was said that the young soldiers had given way, and Napoleon had ordered his mounted grenadiers to cut them down. Rumour had it that the allies insisted on Napoleon taking the title of king, and surrendering Belgium, Italy, Alsace, Lorraine, and other frontier provinces; while it was confidently affirmed that King Joseph and the Empress were on the point of leaving for Blois or Tours. If any one dared to express doubts of the enemy's immediate entry into Paris he was suspected of being in the pay of the police, and in the Faubourg Saint-Germain the allies' arrival was definitely fixed for February 11, or at the very latest for the 12th.

On February 11 there arrived at Paris, not the allied army, but the news of Champaubert. The messenger from the imperial head-quarters reached Joseph as he was reviewing 6,000 of the Parisian National Guard in the courtyard of the Tuileries. The cheers of the militiamen were taken up by the crowd which was watching the review, and boundless enthusiasm was caused by the appearance of the little King of Rome at one of the palace windows dressed in the uniform of the National Guard; the crowd broke through the lines of troops and poured into the courts of the palace shouting "*Vive l'Empereur!*" At the Stock

Exchange the reading of the despatch evoked volleys of cheers, and in the boulevards, in the streets, and in the Champs-Elysées the sound of the guns of the Invalides, which had been so long silent, set every one talking of the battle and prophesying fresh victories to come.

"Not a single foreigner will recross the Rhine" was the general opinion, and on the terrace of the Tuileries the police had to save from the hands of the mob a man who was rash enough to assert that the war would have been much sooner ended if the enemy had entered Paris. In the evening at each theatre an actor read out the bulletin amid the frantic cheers of the audience, and at the Opera House there was an extraordinary scene of enthusiasm, all the chorus and supers thronging on to the stage and joining in singing "*La victoire est à nous!*" Paris was transformed, but the joy which burst forth this day was very natural; for six months no victory had been won, and under the Empire this was novel experience.

The bulletin of Champaubert was followed by those of Montmirail, of Chateau-Thierry, of Vauchamps, Nangis, Montereau, and Troyes. Every day a fresh victory increased the enthusiasm of the Parisians, and their confidence in the Emperor's success became so great that they believed Schwarzenberg had escaped total defeat by retreating to the Aube.

On February 16 a first column of 5,000 Russian and German prisoners entered Paris and passed along the boulevards escorted by grenadiers of the National Guard. The whole population, warned by the papers, turned out to meet them, and even the Stock Exchange was deserted. The Russian generals, who rode without their swords at the head of their troops, were received with cries of "*Vive l'Empereur! Vive Marie-Louise!* Down with the Cossacks!"

In the Rue Napoleon (Rue de la Paix) and in the Place Vendome the people, by their shouts of "*Vive la Colonne!*" uttered a protest against the design imputed to the allies of destroying that monument, and at several places the demeanour of the crowd became insulting and threatening, and the escort had to force a passage. The miserable plight of the rank and file, however, roused feelings of pity and put an end to such outbursts. Their clothing was so ragged that it no longer suggested a uniform, and with their heads wrapped in dirty bits of cloth for want of hats, and with cooking-pots on their backs, they looked more like a gang of gipsies than a convoy of prisoners of war.

As they passed they stretched out their hands to the crowd and pointed to their open mouths, and people ran to the provision shops, so that before long bread, food, money, and clothes were distributed to these unfortunate wretches, who acknowledged them with barbaric cries and gestures of thanks. On February 17, on the 18th, and on every day for a week, fresh columns of prisoners marched through Paris, until 12,000 in all had passed, arousing the same sympathy and receiving the same charity, and inspiring confidence in the ultimate triumph of the Emperor.

This confidence increased when it was seen that the Russian and German prisoners were on very bad terms with the Austrians. The former said that their defeats were due to the slowness of the Austrians, and the latter replied that it was Blücher's mad presumption which had led the army of Silesia to well-merited disaster. They called each other "Cossacks" and "*Sauer-kraut* eaters," and from insults they passed to threats, and from threats to blows, so that General Hullin ordered them to be kept apart both on the march and in camp. From these quarrels the conclusion was drawn that the armies and the staffs, as was actually the case, were not quite at one, and hopes rose high in consequence.

Paris now felt safe, and those individuals who had sent away their furniture to the country or hidden their money in their cellars came in for plenty of chaff, and the supplies which had been laid in during the panic were distributed among the wounded and the prisoners. Even if business was still slack, people at any rate began to amuse themselves, and numbers paraded the boulevards in fancy dress at Shrovetide, and the last balls at the opera were very gay affairs. The Palais-Royal was brilliant as of old, and dances were held in the public saloons, while the ordinary daily events of literature and art again became topics of conversation. M. Denon, who was Director of Medals as well as Curator of Public Museums, no longer worried about saving the pictures from the Louvre; on the contrary, he was fully occupied in engraving a medal for the battle of Champaubert. The theatres were filled again, and many people went to them in the uniform of the National Guard; in fact, it was the fashion for men to wear uniforms as it was for women to make lint.

In the daytime there were other sights to be seen: there were reviews to be watched, and troops marching through Paris, and finally, on Sunday, February 27, there was the presentation to the Empress of the colours captured at Champaubert, Montmirail, and Vauchamps one Austrian, five Russian, and four Prussian. For this ceremony the whole of the garrison of Paris was massed on the Place du Carrousel and the escort of the captured colours was formed of detachments of the National Guard, the Imperial Guard, and of the Line, under General Hullin, the commander of the 1st Military Division.

Ten officers of different arms carried the ten standards; the troops presented arms, and the drums sounded a raffle. The Empress, surrounded by ministers and high officials, received the colours in the Throne-room; they were presented by Clarke with a high-flown speech containing references to Charles Martel and the Saracens, and to this Marie-Louise made the following beautiful and simple answer: "I cannot look on these colours without emotion; they are in my eyes pledges for the safety of our country."

There is no doubt that a number of people did not consider these victories decisive, and expected sooner or later to see Napoleon driven back on Paris, but in face of the new attitude of the populace they dared not utter these thoughts in public. The alarmists were silent, and there is unassailable evidence to prove the change in public opinion caused by the battles of Champaubert and Vauchamps. The Baron de Mortemart writes to the Emperor on February 24:

"A most astounding change has come over Paris. The stupor in which I left it has given place to delight and enthusiasm, and the most unbounded confidence is felt."

General Hullin, who was not a man who would let himself be under any illusion, says in one of his reports: "The temper of the populace is good and becomes daily better."

The Pefect Pasquier, who was even less of an optimist than Hullin, says, on February 16: "The enthusiasm has never been more ardent or more widespread."

Even enemies bear witness to the transformation which had come over Paris, and an English officer, who was a prisoner on parole, says: "A sudden change has taken place in public opinion; from the deepest dejection the Parisians have passed to the most unbounded confidence."

The Spaniard Rodriguez, in a book which from first to last is nothing but a diatribe against the Emperor, says: " From this moment gaiety and lightheartedness, which are never long absent from Paris, began to assert themselves again and to make themselves seen in society, in the public spectacles, and everywhere else."

Finally, there is another witness which is not less convincing, namely, the Stock Exchange, which is unswayed by sentiment or by altruism. The funds since January 8 had oscillated between 48 and 50 *francs*, and on the news of the defeat of La Rothière on February 4 had fallen to 47.75; on receipt of the news of the battle of Champaubert on February 11 they rose to 56.50, and up till March 3 they stood between 57 and 54. This rise is a proof of renewed confidence in the fortune of Napoleon, that divinity to whom the ancients would have erected altars.

No one was convinced by the argument that the Emperor's successes only postponed his fall. If that had been the opinion of the Stock Exchange, the victories of Napoleon would have caused a fall in prices, because those victories would have been looked on as putting off the final success of the allies, or, in other words, postponing peace. In common with the whole of France, the Exchange wished for peace, but, in common with the whole of France, she hoped for a glorious peace, and believed that the Emperor's victories were already forcing such a peace on the allies.

While these victories restored the courage of Paris and of the provinces, the crimes of the Russians and Cossacks roused the inhabitants of the invaded departments to fury. When the allies crossed the Rhine they published most reassuring proclamations, and for the first few days they maintained good discipline, but very soon the inhabitants were exasperated by the boasting words and the offensive manners of the officers, who announced that they had come for the purpose of muzzling France.

At Langres, in addition to feeding the troops, the town had to supply at two days' notice 1,000 shirts, 1,000 pairs of gaiters, 500 white cloaks for the cavalry, 500 brown cloaks for the infantry, and 2,200 pairs of trousers, of which 1,000 had to be of sky-blue cloth. Three weeks afterwards the towns of Langres, Chaumont, and Vassy were taxed to the extent of 26,000 *ells* of cloth and 50,000 *ells* of linen, in addition to requisitions on individual parishes. Vicq, with a population of scarcely 1,000, had to supply to the Russians in one week, 560,000 lb. of bread, 28,000 lb. of meat, 360 bottles of wine or brandy, 40,000 lb. of potatoes, forage and oats in proportion, and finally, 650 cords of dry wood and 500 lb. of candles. At Chaumont the famous Radetzky, then a major-general, earned the reputation of an ogre, for he required for his table every day 30 lb. of beef, a sheep, half a calf, six turkeys, geese and chickens, ten bottles of champagne, ten bottles of Burgundy, three of liqueurs, with pies, tarts, etc., in addition.

Through all the occupied territory it was the same: Troyes was taxed by Prince Hohenlohe to the tune of 150,000 *francs* in silver, 18,000 cwt. of flour, 12,000 bottles of wine, 3,000 bottles of brandy, 1,000 oxen, 18,000 cwt. of hay, and 344,000 rations of oats; in La Marne the cellars were emptied, in the department of the Aisne the enemy took 6,000 horses, 7,000 horned cattle, and 40,000 sheep. In addition, the allies claimed as their right the unpaid contributions for 1813, and those Duc for the current year. The tax collectors as well as the other officials were obliged to serve the allies as they had served the French Government; and as a number of functionaries had fled, the generals appointed in their place other persons who were bound to undertake the duties imposed on them under pain of immediate transportation to a fortress or immediate death.

The invading army was fed and even clothed free of cost by means of requisitions, but that was not enough to satisfy the soldiers; as the allies penetrated farther into the country, and especially after their first reverses, their march was marked by fire, pillage, and rape. The local traditions say that the Prussians committed more atrocities even than the Cossacks, but after a careful study of authentic documents it would seem that there was not much to choose between them; for pillage and violence the Prussians and Cossacks ran a dead heat, the Bavarians and Würtembergers came in second, and the Austrians and Russian regulars were not much behind.

General York one day said to his officers, "I thought I had the honour to command a Prussian corps, but I find I only command a band of brigands."

It must be admitted that the soldiers often acted contrary to the proclamations and orders of their generals, and that their officers made efforts to restrain them; for instance, Blücher in his proclamation of March 13 states that several pillagers had been executed, and Pugiat also says that four soldiers were condemned to death, but pardoned at the request of the Mayor of Troyes; he adds, however, "If all those guilty of pillage had been shot, Schwarzenberg would have left his whole army at Troyes."

Unfortunately the glowing proclamations and stern orders of the generals were printed in French, and the Cossacks and Kalmuks did not understand that language, while the members of the Tugenbund pretended to have forgotten it. Among this crowd of men of different nationalities, also, animated largely by mutual jealousies, written safeguards were of no value, and the authority of officers commanded little or no respect. After the battle of Fère-Champenoise the wife of a French colonel, who had been killed in the action, fell into the hands of the Cossacks; Sir Charles Stewart's *aide-de-camp* who tried to rescue her was half killed, and the unfortunate woman was never heard of again.

A less tragic story is told of the mayor of a town near Pont-sur-Yonne, who was summoned before a general, and was relieved of his boots by the sentry at the door of the general's room, with the result that he had to go in bare-footed.

The Prince of Metternich pretended to be much affected by the miseries caused by the campaign, and wrote to Caulaincourt: "The Mesgrignys are lucky enough to have me in their home, a great piece of luck indeed, because I don't eat them. War is an unpleasant thing, especially when 50,000 Cossacks and Baskirs take part in it."

The officers of one army attributed all the excesses and acts of violence to the troops of the other armies, and refused to intervene when their own soldiers were not at fault. At Moret the mayor asked an Austrian general to stop the pillaging of the town by the Cossacks and received the answer, "They are Russians, I have no authority over them."

At Chaumont the Grand Duke Constantine was moved by the tears of a gardener whose home was being robbed to go and order away the looters; he recognized the Austrian uniform, however, from a distance and remarked with a laugh, "Ah, these are the soldiers of your Emperor's father-in-law; I am not in command here."

On occasions, however, towns and villages were looted at the express orders of the generals. The soldiers were told that pillage was authorized for two hours, four hours, or a whole day, and the soldiers, naturally, always took more than their allowance. Troyes, Epernay, Nogent, Sens, Soissons, Château-Thierry, and more than two hundred towns and villages were literally sacked. "The allied generals," as eye-witnesses said, "look upon looting as a debt which they owe to their men."

Sometimes the soldiers rushed upon their quarry with savage yells, sometimes they set to work calmly and methodically, and sometimes they deigned to laugh. One of their favourite amusements was to strip men and women naked and drive them with whips out into the snow-covered country. Another favourite pastime was to take the village mayor, priest or doctor, to grip his nose in pincers and drag him round and round the room, or again in a college the head master would be stripped naked and flogged in the courtyard before the assembled scholars.

These were simple games, fit to while away an hour's leisure. When, however, after a victory or a defeat, or even without these excuses, the Cossacks or Prussians entered into a town or village, a farm or country house, they brought every form of horror in their train. They were not content with searching for loot, but deliberately strove to cause ruin and desolation: they had drunk their fill of wine and brandy; their pockets were full of jewellery (five watches were found on the body of a Cossack), their haversacks and holsters were filled to overflowing with knick-knacks of all descriptions, and the wagons which followed their columns were laden with furniture, bronzes, books, and pictures. This did not satisfy them, and what they could not carry away they set to work to destroy; they broke windows and glass-work, they smashed panelling, tore down hangings, set fire to ricks and barns, burnt ploughs, broke down fruit trees and dug up vines, they made bonfires with furniture, broke tools, threw the chemists' bottles into the gutters, and stove in casks of wine and brandy.

At Soissons 50 houses were burnt to the ground, at Moulins 60, at Mesnil-Sellières 107, at Nogent 160, at Busancy 70, at Vailly and Chavignon more than a hundred, and at Athies, Mesbrecourt, Corbény, and Clacy the whole towns were destroyed. True to the Muscovite traditions, the Cossacks began by smashing the pumps, and the light of the burning houses lit up scenes of horror which do not bear description. Sabre and bayonet were freely used against men, and some were tortured, flogged, or roasted until they revealed the hiding-places of their valuables.

The priests of Montlandon and Rolampont were left for dead. At Bucy-le-Long the Cossacks roasted the legs of a servant named Leclerc who had been left in charge of a country house, and as he still refused to speak they filled his mouth with hay and set it on fire. At Nogent a cloth-merchant named Hubert was set upon by a dozen Prussians who pulled on his arms and legs till he was almost torn into pieces, and a kindly bullet ended his sufferings, and at Provins a baby was thrown upon the fire to make its mother speak.

A woman of eighty was wearing a diamond ring, and as it fitted tightly and could not easily be drawn off, her finger was chopped off with a sword. In the canton of Vandeuvre alone the number of people of both sexes who died as a result of violence was estimated at five hundred and fifty. If the injuries and violences inflicted on men were serious, they were trivial in comparison with the brutal outrages inflicted on the unfortunate women of the occupied territory, and neither youth nor age offered any safeguard against the lust of the allied soldiers.

At Château-Thierry, Sacken's Russians began to pillage during February 12, and York's Prussians carried on the work during that night and the following morning. As they had done at Moscow, the Russians opened the prisons and let loose the inmates; they broke into houses, hospitals, colleges, convents, and churches, murdering, violating, and looting; they stole the plate from the churches and turned their lances against the priests and nuns; the outrages committed on the inmates of the convents and schools and on the inhabitants generally will not bear describing, and numbers of people were murdered.

At Montmirail the Cossacks arrived on the fair day, when the streets were full, but everyone fled at the sight of the troops. The commander of the Cossacks announced that people could go about their business without fear, and he then evacuated the town. An hour later the Cossacks returned to the number of four or five hundred and charged the crowd, using their lances and sabres freely and trampling numbers of people under their horses' feet, after which they dismounted and began to make arrests. One man was stripped naked and tied in a chair with his feet in a basin of melted snow, and was set in the street to watch his home being pillaged. The Cossacks also took fifteen of the leading men of the town, stripped them naked and gave them each fifty lashes with the knout. There then followed the scenes of violence, outrage, and loot which invariably accompanied the occupation of a town by the invaders.

At Sens the pillage lasted for nine days, from February 11 to 20, and during the whole of this time the town was in possession of a raging mob who broke into all the houses and churches, bent on loot and outrage. A supreme touch of irony was added by the hereditary Prince of Würtemberg, a well-known dandy, who as he left this town of Sens, where he had presided over the pillaging, as a last act requisitioned twenty-four pairs of white gloves.

The barbarous behaviour of the allies exasperated the population, reconciled the most hostile to Napoleon, and roused the most peaceful to resistance. A professor named Dardenne, an ardent Republican, wrote from Chaumont: "You may well wonder at the changeable nature of my opinions. You know how much I dislike the savage soldier who has hitherto guided the destinies of France. . . . Well, the sight of my country at the mercy of these odious Cossacks fills me with a shame which so masters all my other feelings that I now pray for the success of Napoleon's arms."

General Allix wrote from Auxerre: "The people are becoming more and more exasperated, and the *partisans* of the enemy dare not open their mouths."

Finally, the *prefect* of Seine-et-Marne summed up the general feeling in these words: "The people will forget past wrongs and will make further sacrifices if only they can be revenged on the Cossacks."

The peasants who were so cruelly disabused of their trust in the proclamations cried out that they were ready to hunt the enemy like wild beasts, and this was no vain threat. Large numbers armed themselves with pitchforks, old fowling-pieces, or with muskets picked up on the battlefields, and attacked the enemy whenever they were found in small parties or when they were retreating. At Montereau and Troyes in the latter part of the battles, the inhabitants hurled tiles or pieces of furniture on to the head of the Austrians and shot them from behind the shutters or from the man-holes of cellars. At Château-Thierry some workmen brought boats to the soldiers of the Guard regardless of the Prussian bullets; during the sack of Soissons a servant girl wounded two Prussians who offered her violence, and a butcher posted himself at the foot of some cellar steps with a cutlass and killed the looters as they came down into the darkness. Along the lower Marne the villagers arrested 250 Russians and Prussians in four days.

The day after the battle of Champaubert a boy of thirteen years old brought two Russian grenadiers as prisoners to the outposts of the 6th Corps. On the road from Chaumont to Langres a party of peasants handed over to Oudinot 400 soldiers whom they had captured at the battle of Bar-sur-Aube. Between Montmédy and Sézanne for a distance of one hundred miles as the crow flies the villages were completely deserted by their inhabitants, who were carrying on a guerrilla war in the woods, and through the whole of the north-east of France the peasants were organized in companies of *partisans* or gathered at the alarm signal to fight shoulder to shoulder with the regular troops.

The parish priest of Pers, near Montargis, became a leader of *partisans*, and at the head of a dozen men armed with double-barrelled guns he defended his village or laid ambushes and held up convoys: as chief of the band he rode on horseback with his cassock tucked up, a sword at his side, and a musket slung across his shoulders, but at the least sign of the enemy he leapt to the ground, and in order to encourage his men he always fired the first shot.

Near Piney, the farm of Gerandot was known as the Cossacks' tomb: they were given a hearty welcome and provided with as much drink as they wanted, and then, while they were drinking their brandy, the farmer, with his servants and labourers, shot them through the windows; none ever came away from Gerandot to tell the tale of what happened there. A young widow who lived in a large, isolated house near Essayes took in sixty Cossacks and made them all drunk, and then during the night

44

with the help of her servants she set her house on fire. Near Bar-sur-Ornain the peasants murdered a Prussian general who had remained behind with a small escort.

A gamekeeper of Sauvage, named Louis Aubriot, saw opposite his house four Prussian dragoons, two on horseback and two dismounted; he rushed out, and with two shots from his gun brought down the mounted men and then attacked the two dismounted ones with the butt-end, with the result that one dragoon was killed and the other three taken prisoners. In the village of Vailly there was an old soldier of herculean strength who was known as the "Throat-cutter of Vailly," and who disdained to attack less than three men at a time: he used to offer to guide small parties of the allies who had lost their way, and would kill them on the way.

At Presles a servant girl killed, with a pitchfork, two Cossacks who were sleeping in a barn. At Crandelain the villagers attacked a Cossack outpost during the night and killed every man, and for a long time in the neighbourhood of Laon the peasants would not use the wells because so many bodies had been hidden in them.

Whole volumes could be filled with the savage acts of the allies, and the no less savage reprisals of the peasants. During the night of March 7 to 8, the inhabitants of Paissy, Ailles, and Quiches, men and women, finished off the Russian wounded on the battlefield of Craonne. In explanation, though not in excuse, of this hideous massacre it must be said that two days before these same peasants had abandoned their villages at the approach of the Cossacks, and taken refuge in the quarries in the mountain-side, and the Cossacks had tried to smoke them out, with the result that several children were suffocated, though the adults survived, thanks to a ventilating shaft.

The captured allied officers admitted that their men were terrified by the rising of the peasants: the hostile detachments no longer dared to billet themselves in the villages, but had their requisitioned supplies taken to their bivouacs, and for fear of being murdered by the country people the stragglers surrendered to the French outposts. The woods, streams, ponds, and sunken lanes became the scenes of murders, and bands of from ten to three hundred men, armed with shot-guns, forks, or axes, lay in wait to attack detachments or scattered at the approach of large forces. A German historian says that large escorts were required for convoys, and a hundred troopers had to accompany each dispatch rider. The country-side was roused, and waged relentless war on stragglers, *vedettes*, and patrols.

CHAPTER 2

The First Battles

At first the march of the allies into France was nothing but a military promenade. They crossed the Rhine between December 21 and January 1, in twelve or fifteen columns, on a front extending from Basle to Coblentz, and drove back without difficulty the small French forces scattered along the frontier. Marmont, Victor, Macdonald, and Ney had at most 46,000 combatants, while Schwarzenberg, commanding the army of Bohemia, and Blücher, commanding the army of Silesia, had nearly 250,000 soldiers in the first line.

In face of such overwhelming numbers, the marshals could only retreat, fighting and skirmishing as much as possible, but avoiding a serious engagement in which they would have been uselessly compromised. [1] With the exception of Dôle, Châlons, Tournus, Bourg, and Sain-Jean de Losne, the unfortified towns surrendered at the first summons, and, taught by the precepts of Napoleon, under whose orders many of them had served, the allied generals did not wait to lay siege to the fortresses: such places were turned and invested by a small force while the main armies of the allies pushed straight on into the heart of France.

On the extreme left Bubna seized Geneva and advanced on Lyons by the Jura and the valley of the Saone. In the centre Schwarzenberg's various columns, passing by Dôle and Auxonne, Montbéliard and Vesoul, Remiremont and Epinal, Colmar and Saint-Dié, reached Dijon, Langres, and Bar-sur-Aube. On the

---

1 The composition of the opposing armies is given at end of chapter.

right Blücher's two corps passed through Lorraine and marched on Vassy, Saint-Dizier, and Brienne. On January 26 almost all the troops of the allies were concentrated between the Marne and the upper Seine.

On this day the Emperor set out from Châlons in the hope of preventing this concentration and attacking the Prussians before they had effected a junction with the Austro-Russian army. He found Blücher at Brienne and defeated him with loss, but Brienne is not far from Bar-sur-Aube, and the field-marshal fell back on Schwarzenberg's army. The latter set his masses in motion, and on February 1 the battle of La Rothière was fought, in which the French held their own for eight hours against three times their numbers, and made such an impression on the enemy that they succeeded in effecting their retreat on Troyes the following day by the only available bridge at Lesmont.

The result of this battle filled the allies with joy. They had captured 50 guns and 2,000 prisoners, and 4,000 dead or wounded Frenchmen littered the plain, but it was not these trophies or these hecatombs which raised their spirits to such a height: they themselves had had 6,000 men mown down by the grape shot; but they had overthrown Napoleon in fair fight on the soil of France; the charm which had been broken at Leipzig had not been restored, and it was again proved that the Emperor was not invincible. In face of the enormous forces which they had available, the Emperor was as good as beaten unless he were invincible.

Alexander congratulated Blücher with the words, "This victory places the crown on all our others," and Sacken ended up his report with the words "From this day Napoleon is no longer a dangerous enemy, and the Czar can say, 'I give peace to the world.'"

Their heads were turned by this easy victory, and the allies imagined that nothing could now stop them, and they had only to go forward and dictate terms of peace at Paris. They flattered themselves that the last French army was not only in retreat, but dispersed and scattered to the four winds. The officers made appointments for a week in advance in the garden of the Palais-Royal, and the Czar said to General Reynier, who was being released in consequence of an exchange of prisoners of war, "We shall be in Paris before you."

A council of war was held in the castle of Brienne on February 2, and it was resolved to march at once on Paris. In order to give Blücher, "the hero of La Rothière," the satisfaction of operating independently, and in order also to facilitate the supply of their large armies, the allied generals decided to advance on two lines.

The army of Silesia, after being joined by the corps of York, Kleist, and Kapzéwitsch, who were coming up from the Rhine, was to move along the valley of the Marne, while the army of Bohemia would advance to Troyes, and from there march by both banks of the Seine. Such was the confidence and blindness of the allied sovereigns and their advisers that they neglected all strategic considerations and concerned themselves only with the self-esteem of their generals and the comfort of their night's lodgings.

The veteran Blücher, who always showed the characteristics of a colonel of Hussars, started off at once. On February 3 he was at Braux, on the 4th at Sompuis, and on the 6th at Goudron, throwing forward the corps of York and Sacken to Chateau-Thierry, followed at an interval of two days' march by the corps of Kleist and Kapzéwitsch. During this time Schwarzenberg, with his usual dilatoriness, moved solemnly on Troyes.

Instead of vigorously pressing the French army and driving it back on to that town, he hesitated, issued counter-orders, and let himself be imposed on by the vigorous reconnaissances of a few bodies of cavalry, with the result that the Emperor had time to rest his soldiers, to bring up fresh troops, to reorganize his army, and, in fact, to restore order among the prevailing chaos. The Emperor did not evacuate Troyes till February 6, and then his retirement to Nogent was quite unmolested. If Schwarzenberg had been bold enough to attack Troyes from the east and south he might have finished the war with a single blow.

The Emperor was now in the most critical situation. His reception at Troyes was most depressing, and his entry into the town was not greeted with a single cheer: the streets were empty and the houses shut up. The army was so short of supplies that some men actually died of hunger, and the population would give no help as they were keeping everything to meet the requisitions which the enemy would impose on them. The only direction in which the people exerted themselves was to encourage the desertion of the conscripts, who were worn out with fatigue, hunger, and defeat, and a large number, amounting to some 6,000, left the ranks.

It was not only the troops who were in a state of stupor, but the staffs of the commands, and even the Emperor's immediate entourage. Napoleon was the only man in the army or in the whole country who did not despair: certainly, during these few days, his letters betray great uneasiness and show a lack of confidence. He gave his brother Joseph instructions as to the eventual abandonment of Paris: he ordered Prince Eugène to evacuate Upper Italy and General Miollis to abandon Rome; Marshal Suchet and Prince Borghese were to abandon Barcelona and Piedmont respectively, and he authorized Caulaincourt, his plenipotentiary at the Congress of Châtillon, to accept the allies' terms. Many restrictions, however, were added to these orders, which were liable to alteration if matters improved, and he did not forget to utter exhortations to courage and appeals to confidence.

Meanwhile the Emperor reorganized his divisions, altered their positions, and planned fresh manoeuvres: he issued orders for the armies of Lyons, of the Pyrenees, and of the Netherlands, and looked into the military and political situation of Paris: he entered into all details of armament, equipment, supplies, and administration; he filled vacant commands, signed decrees for publication in the press, reprimanded his ministers, and among so many grave anxieties he found time to write to Joseph, "Keep the Empress amused; she is dying of consumption."

To judge from the extraordinary calmness of the Emperor,

one would think that France was not invaded, and that he was on the point of undertaking a distant expedition with two hundred thousand soldiers!

The allies looked upon the campaign of France as already finished, but in Napoleon's eyes it was only just beginning. The dilatoriness of Schwarzenberg left the Emperor full liberty of movement, and meanwhile Blücher rashly embarked on a flank march across Napoleon's front while his four corps were spread out at more than a day's march apart. During the night of February 7-8, when the Duke of Bassano came to the Emperor to get him to sign some dispatches for Châtillon, he found him stretched on the ground studying his maps, on which the positions of the troops were marked by flags.

Napoleon hardly turned his head, and said, "Ah! There you are. I am busy at present with something quite different. At this moment I am engaged with Blücher."

On the following day Napoleon issued his orders. Marshal Victor, with Oudinot in second line, was to remain at Nogent to hold the passage of the Seine against the Austrians and Russians, while Marmont's corps and the Guard, with Grouchy 's cavalry, were to advance by Sezanne to attack the army of Silesia, which was moving on the main road from Châlons to Paris. The Emperor did not hurry matters, and was most careful to make no false movements. For two or three days past he had been contemplating his magnificent manoeuvre, but before setting it in motion he wanted Blücher to be hopelessly compromised. Napoleon himself did not leave Nogent till February 9; he spent that night at Sézanne, and at 9 a.m. on the 10th he joined Marmont's corps before the defiles of Saint-Gond, and sent his columns forward to the attack.

Olsufjew's division of Langeron's corps was driven from position to position past Champaubert and was almost annihilated: the French captured more than 2,000 prisoners, including Olsufjew and two other generals, besides fifteen guns, some colours and baggage, and hardly 1,500 men escaped: the delighted soldiers called the wood of Champaubert the "enchanted wood."

Napoleon's fine strategic movement had succeeded. The long column of the army of Silesia was cut in two, and the Emperor had interposed his army between Blücher, who was coming up from Châlons, and Sacken and York, who were driving Macdonald back on Meaux. These two latter generals had just heard of the march of Napoleon's army, and they turned about and moved in all haste on Montmirail. The Emperor forestalled them there, and his victory was as complete as it had been the previous day at Champaubert. With the loss of 4,000 men the Russians retired, or rather fled, by the road to Château-Thierry. The French followed them, and on the following day, the 12th, they defeated them again, killing or capturing 3,000 men, driving them into Chateau-Thierry and thrusting them in disorder behind the Ourcq.

Meanwhile Blücher, imagining that his two lieutenants had disposed of the imperial army, was quietly continuing his march. On February 12 he was at Bergeres, and on the 13th he reached Champaubert, after driving back without difficulty the corps of Marmont, which the Emperor had left to watch the movements of the Prussians. The Emperor was warned, and left Chateau-Thierry during the night of the 13th-14th: at 8 o'clock he was at Montmirail, and ordered Marmont, who was continuing his retreat, to attack the enemy as he emerged from Vauchamps. The Prussian advance guard was vigorously charged; and being taken by surprise was driven in confusion into Vauchamps and out again on the opposite side. Behind Marmont's troops Blücher saw the whole guard advancing, and the dreaded cry of "*Vive l'Empereur!*" rising from ten thousand throats fell like thunder on his ears.

He decided to retreat, and for two hours his troops, formed in squares placed chequerwise, steadily endured the fire of Drouot's artillery and the furious charges of the cavalry of the Guard. However, by a magnificent turning movement Grouchy with the cavalry of the line got behind the enemy to the far side of Fromentière; he ordered the charge, and his 3,500 horsemen burst their way into the middle of the mass of 20,000 Prussians, throwing them into disorder and panic: they met with practically no resistance, and carved bloody furrows through the German squares. Blücher, Prince Auguste of Prussia, and Generals Kleist and Kapzéwitsch were knocked over by the fugitives, and came a dozen times within an ace of being captured, killed, or trampled under the horses' hoofs. The pursuit lasted far into the night. Blücher lost 6,000 men, and, as often happens in battles which quickly degenerate into routs, the action was costly only for the vanquished, and the loss of the French army amounted barely to 700 men.

The Emperor's intention was to pursue Blücher as far as Châlons, and finally to dispose of what remained of the army of Silesia; he would then turn southwards through Vitry, and fall upon the rear of the army of Bohemia. He received dispatches, however, which told him that the Austro-Russians had pressed their advance, driving back Victor and Oudinot, and pushing their advance guards to Provins, Nangis, Montereau, and Fontainebleau. Paris was in danger, or, rather, Paris appeared to be in danger.

As a matter of fact, the news of Blücher's defeat had a most disconcerting effect on the head-quarters staff of the allies, and plunged them into doubt and uncertainty. Jomini, who was consulted, was in favour of a direct advance on Paris; but General Knesebeck, the official adviser of the King of Prussia, whose word was always law, would not hear of an advance, and expressed the opinion that Blücher had been beaten because he had marched on Paris. The advance was, therefore, suspended, and the various corps of the allies were ordered to remain stationary on February 15th, 16th, and 17th, "in order to await the development of Napoleon's manoeuvres," to quote Schwarzenberg's order.

Napoleon did not carry out the manoeuvres he had contemplated, and during the battle of Vauchamps he altered his plan. In order to cover Paris he had to abandon his former objective, the pursuit of Blücher's army; but, on the other hand, the slipshod dispositions of the army of Bohemia, which was scattered over a length of nearly fifty miles, exposed this army to the fate of the army of Silesia. On February 15 the Emperor reached Meaux, and on the following day his army arrived at Guignes, after a forced march in which some of his infantry were carried in commandeered wagons, and at this place the guard effected a junction with the corps of Victor, Oudinot, and Macdonald.

On the 17th the army advanced from Guignes. At Mormant, Victor's corps, which was leading, overthrew and routed 8 battalions and 24 squadrons under the command of Count Pahlen, and two hours later this corps had another successful engagement at Valjouan, with Lamothe's division, which was driven back on Donnemarie. Victor continued his march towards Montereau; on the plateau of Surville he drove in the Prince of Würtemberg's outposts, and his main body halted for the night at Salins. Meanwhile, Macdonald in the centre advanced on Bray, Oudinot, on the left, on Provins, and the Emperor arrived at Nangis with the Guard.

The Emperor severely blamed Victor for not having occupied Montereau on this day. If he had seized the bridge on the 17th, the Emperor would have crossed on the following day, cut off the retreat of Bianchi's corps, and taken in reverse the corps of Wiggenstein and De Wrède which were at Bray and Nogent. The army of Bohemia would, in all probability, have suffered the same fate as the army of Silesia. But Victor had been marching and fighting the whole day, and only arrived in front of Montereau between 6 and 7 o'clock in the evening.

It seems doubtful if he could have captured this position from 14,000 Würtembergers by means of a night attack, more especially as the following day 4 divisions of infantry, 2 divisions of cavalry, and a large force of artillery took six hours to dislodge the Prince of Würtemberg. We must either conclude that the Emperor imagined Montereau to be occupied only by a detachment from de Wrède's corps and not by the whole of that of the Prince of Würtemberg, or else that he had other cause of complaint against Victor, who had shown weakness and carelessness in the defence of Alsace.

It may be remarked that if one of the Emperor's lieutenants deserved blaming during these glorious days it was Macdonald. If this marshal had advanced from La Ferté-sous-Jouarre to Château-Thierry on February 10 and 11, as he should have done, he would have cut off the retreat of the routed corps of Sacken and York, not a man of which would have escaped. However, Victor was relieved of the command of his corps, but he did not remain long in disgrace. Fain tells how the marshal came to the Château de Fréville and said to the Emperor, "I have not forgotten my old trade. I will shoulder a musket and find a place in the ranks of the Old Guard."

The Emperor immediately gave him command of the two divisions of the Young Guard which had been recently formed, and had a strength of 10,000 bayonets.

The Austro-Russian army was everywhere driven back, and the leading troops, which had reached Fontainebleau and Nemours, were in danger of being cut off. Schwarzenberg took alarm, and sent Count Paar to the imperial head-quarters with a letter for Berthier.

"Having received intelligence," wrote Schwarzenberg, "that preliminaries of peace were signed at Châtillon yesterday on the basis of the conditions proposed by the Duc de Vicence and accepted by the allied sovereigns, I have countermanded all offensive movements against the French army. Your offensive operations, however, are being continued, and I suggest that they should cease equally with mine."

In this letter Schwarzenberg was lying freely. He knew perfectly well that the peace preliminaries had not been signed, and if he had suspended his advance it was not on account of news from Châtillon, but under the pressure of Napoleon's movement. The Emperor was not deceived, but saw clearly that these false assurances were only meant to lead up to an armistice, under cover of which the Austro-Russians could concentrate in a less exposed position.

"An absurd proposition," he wrote to Joseph, "which would make me lose all the advantages of my manoeuvres." The Emperor let his indignation have full play in his letter to his brother, but he was careful to hide it from Schwarzenberg, and kept Count Paar waiting for three days at the outposts before he sent an answer.

Meanwhile, Napoleon continued his advance. On February 18, Gerard, with the 2nd Corps, which, owing to Victor's disgrace, had come under his command during the battle, and Pajol with his cavalry, dislodged the Würtembergers from the plateau of Surville, followed them across the bridge of Montereau, and drove them into the country between the Seine and Yonne. On the same day Macdonald drove Wrède back to Bray, Oudinot forced Wiggenstein's outposts back towards Nogent, and Allix obliged Bianchi to evacuate Nemours.

This was more than enough to make Schwarzenberg decide on a prompt retreat. He immediately sent back his baggage to Bar-sur-Aube, and concentrated all his troops at Troyes, very relieved to have escaped with nothing worse than a fright and three forced marches. The French army was delayed by false movements on the part of Macdonald and Oudinot, which resulted in a block at the bridges over the Seine, and lost contact with the enemy. It was not till the afternoon of February 22 that the heads of the columns reached the plain of Troyes, and at the same time on the left flank Boyer's brigade drove the advance guard of the Russians out of Méry. Blücher had collected his scattered troops at Châlons, and had started towards the Aube on the 19th in order to effect a junction with Schwarzenberg.

The main allied army was formed up in order of battle in front of Troyes, with its right flank resting on the Seine and its left on the village of Saint-Germain. It was too late for the Emperor to attack on the 22nd, especially as all his troops had not yet arrived, but the prospects for the following day looked bright. Napoleon's movement to the Seine had only half succeeded, because of the seven corps of the army of Bohemia five had escaped him. At last Schwarzenberg had halted, and the Emperor, whose troops were full of confidence and eagerness, would dispose of him at a single blow in a bloody and decisive battle. The Austro-Russians were certainly in greatly superior strength, but the bad position they had taken up, with their backs to a river, neutralized the advantages of numbers, and further, they were in a state of considerable demoralization. The Emperor was not the least afraid of the army of Silesia, which threatened his left flank. The bridge at Méry had been destroyed, and the left flank was guarded by veterans drawn from Spain. It would take Blücher twenty-four hours to force the passage of the river, and in that time Napoleon would have beaten Schwarzenberg, and the army of Silesia would be in great danger of being beaten in turn and driven back into the river.

Unfortunately Schwarzenberg held the same views as Napoleon; he realized the great danger of fighting in front of Troyes, and was not so afraid of public opinion as to be ready to sacrifice his magnificent army to the glory of France. At 4 o'clock on the following morning the allied army began its retreat towards the Aube, leaving only a screen of troops in front of Troyes, and at 11 o'clock the Prince of Neufchatel received fresh proposals for an armistice. The allied army of 150,000 men was not prepared for a trial of strength with the Emperor's 70,000.

The Czar, the King of Prussia, Knesebeck, and others wished to accept battle, while Schwarzenberg, Lord Castlereagh, Nesselrode, Toll, and Wolkonsky counselled retreat. The Emperor of Austria, who had few ideas of his own, agreed with Schwarzenberg, and during the night of February 22 and 23 Schwarzenberg took upon himself to order a retreat. It is only justice to the Austrian general to say that this decision, which seemed at first to be unnecessarily cautious, proved to be the salvation of his army. In war, as in other matters, it is necessary to choose times and seasons, and on this day the morale of the allies was not good enough to justify a battle.

This is the reason why Thielen says: "Schwarzenberg, on his own responsibility, and against the advice of others, made two manoeuvres which crowned the campaign with success. The first was on February 23, when he retreated to Troyes, and the second was on March 20, when he attacked the French at Arcis-sur-Aube."

In the morning the order for the retreat, which was already in progress, were ratified by a Council of War held at the King of Prussia's quarters at 8 o'clock, at which it was decided to take up a position behind the Aube. On the preceding day Count Paar had come back from the French outposts bringing a letter from Napoleon to the Emperor of Austria, and also one from Berthier for Schwarzenberg. These letters were carefully worded, and though their tone was somewhat threatening yet they hinted that an agreement was not impossible.

The Council of War decided that a fresh flag of truce should be sent to the imperial head-quarters to ask again for a suspension of hostilities. To judge by their appearance, the allied troops were not making a strategic movement, but were in full retreat after a lost battle; they were half-starved and half-frozen, worn out by forced marches and snowy bivouacs: they were demoralized by their defeats and by this retreat of seventy miles, which seemed likely, as the officers said aloud, to come to an end only on the farther side of the Rhine. In these circumstances a purely military armistice, which would in no way bind the diplomats at Châtillon, offered great advantages to the allies, who urgently needed time to restore order in their army and to give their troops several days' rest in good quarters.

The Emperor received Schwarzenberg's messenger in a wheelwright's shop at Chartres, where he had spent the night. The Prince of Lichtenstein expressed the greatest admiration for the courage of the French troops and the genius of their leader, and concealed none of the difficulties of the allies. These confidences put the Emperor in a genial temper, and he asked whether it were true that the war had become dynastic and that the allied sovereigns intended to reinstate the Bourbons.

To these questions, and to some justifiable representations as to the princes being allowed to be in France, Lichtenstein answered that all these reports were false, that Austria would have no hand in such schemes, and that the allied sovereigns had only one object in view, namely, the restoration of peace. Lichtenstein was doubtless sincere in these statements, but he was not a clear-sighted man: he was dismissed by the Emperor, who promised to send a general officer to the outposts on the following day to negotiate for an armistice.

The Emperor expected to enter Troyes that day without striking a blow, but the town was still occupied by a part of De Wrède's corps. An assault was on the point of being delivered when this general sent a letter to Napoleon saying that he would evacuate the place on the following morning, but that if the attack was not immediately stopped he would set fire to the town. The Emperor, who chose to save the town rather than to capture the Bavarians, immediately counter- ordered the attack and spent the night in the suburb of Noues.

When he entered the town on the morning of February 24 the spontaneous enthusiasm of the populace formed a striking contrast to the cold silence with which he had been received twenty days before. The exactions of the allies and the recent victories of the Emperor had worked a great change in the feelings of the people. Not even on his triumphant returns from Austerlitz and Jena had his reception been more enthusiastic and more sincere. The Emperor could hardly force his way through the crowds of people who were trying to touch his boots and his hands.

Among the cries of "*Vive l'Empereur!*" however, others of "*À bas les traîtres!*" could be distinguished. During the occupation of the town by the allies, two ex-aristocrats, the Marquis de Vidranges and the Chevalier Gouault, had been very active. Not content with wearing the white cockade and the Cross of St. Louis, and with trampling a tricolour flag under foot in the middle of the street under the eyes of the Prussians, these men had printed a thousand copies of Louis XVIII's proclamation, and had distributed them through the town; they had also presented the Czar with an address in favour of the restoration of the Bourbons.

Vidranges, the more active of the two, had left Troyes to join the Comte d'Artois, but his accomplice, Gouault, paid for the crimes of both and for those of many others even more guilty than himself. He was denounced by popular clamour, arrested and tried before a military commission, and was shot in the corn market less than an hour after the promulgation of the sentence. He died bravely, wearing the Cross of St. Louis, crying "Long live the King!" and himself giving the command to fire. It is said that if his execution had been less hurried the Emperor would have pardoned him.

The allies had only asked for an armistice with the idea of gaining a respite, and they hoped that hostilities would be suspended as soon as the emissaries met at Lusigny. Napoleon naturally saw the matter in quite another light. The situation was favourable to him, and in order to reap the full advantages from it he must be able to continue his advance. General Flahaut reached Lusigny in the afternoon of February 24, and announced that the negotiations would not interrupt the military operations, which would continue till the armistice was definitely concluded.

As a matter of fact, on this day Gérard and Oudinot pursued the Bavarians on the Bar-sur-Aube road as far as Montieramey, and Macdonald drove back the Austrian rear-guard towards Bar-sur-Seine. The allies were hotly pressed, and it was evident that they would be compelled either to fight a battle or to abandon the line of the Aube as they had abandoned that of the Seine two days before It is true that Blücher, who was in occupation of Méry and Anglure, on the flank of the French, kept asking for instructions and offered to make a diversion so as to relieve the pressure on the main army; but, in the south, Bubna, who was being driven back on the Ain by Augereau, was clamouring for immediate reinforcements.

On February 25, at 8 o'clock in the morning, the three sovereigns held a further Council of War at Bar-sur-Aube, and summoned to the council-board Schwarzenberg, Metternich, Lord Castlereagh, Nesselrode, Hardenberg, Radetzky, Diebitsch,

Wolkonsky, and Knesebeck. At the request of the King of Prussia, the Council was held in the room of the last-named general, who had been suddenly taken ill, "for" as William said, "we cannot do without Knesebeck's advice."

An agreement was easily come to as to the necessity for sending reinforcements to Bubna; it was resolved that the Prince of Hesse-Hombourg should assume command of the 1st Army Corps, the 6th German Corps, and the 1st Division of Austrian reserves, and should immediately leave the army of Bohemia and march towards the Saone with the object of stopping Augereau's advance, relieving Geneva, and opening up the line of communication through that town.

The next point to be discussed was the question of the defence or the abandonment of the line of the Aube, and on this point the discussion was brisk and at times almost violent. Schwarzenberg protested that the army had already suffered heavy losses in battle and in the forced marches, and was about to be further reduced by the detachment of the troops under the Prince of Hesse-Hombourg against Augereau; as a result, he maintained there was no option but to retreat. Schwarzenberg's advice was opposed by the Czar, who was always in favour of energetic action and who had been fired by Blücher's letters.

With some heat he expatiated on the advantages of a battle in which the army of Bohemia posted behind the Aube should contain Napoleon in front, while the army of Silesia attacked him in flank, but he was in the end overruled by the Council. Alexander, however, next demanded that the order to retreat should not extend to Blücher's army, but that the field-marshal should be left at liberty to carry out whatever movement he might wish, whether it be to attack the French or to march on Paris. Schwarzenberg did not at all like the idea of Blücher's embarking on a flank march similar to that undertaken at the beginning of February, and likely to result in similar disasters, and would have preferred to see Blücher either in close touch with the army of Bohemia or halted in a position of readiness behind the Marne.

The Czar, however, carried his point by declaring that if the Council decided against him a second time he would withdraw the corps of Wiggenstein and all the Russian reserves, and would attach them to the army of Silesia. The King of Prussia, who was described by a citizen of Troyes as the Czar's chief *aide-de-camp*, said he would do the same with his Royal Guard. It was decided that the army of Bohemia should retire to Langres and should there make ready either to accept battle in the event of Napoleon's continuing his advance, or to resume the offensive if Blücher should draw the French against himself.

As to Blücher, he was to be left untrammelled, but as his army was now reduced to 48,000 men the Council decided, on the suggestion of the Czar, that he should be given command of Winzingerode's corps, then in the vicinity of Rheims, and of Billow's corps, which was beginning to arrive from Belgium. Lord Castlereagh undertook to write to Bernadotte to tell him that, in the general interest, the Council of the Coalition had found it necessary to reinforce the army of Silesia by the corps of Billow and Winzingerode, which had hitherto belonged to the army of the north, but that to make up for this loss Bernadotte was to be given the chief command over the Hanoverian, English, and Dutch troops who were operating in the Netherlands.

On the following day, February 26, the whole of the Austro-Russian army had crossed the Aube. Barclay de Tolly marched from Chaumont on Langres, Würtemberg on Blessonville, Gyulai on Arc-en-Barrois, and Wiggenstein occupied Colombey. During the afternoon De Wrède's corps, which formed the rear-guard, was driven by Oudinot and Gérard's troops from the bridge of Dolancourt and from the suburbs of Bar, and Macdonald advanced on Ferté-sur-Aube and compelled the Austrian garrison to evacuate Châtillon. Blücher, whose troops had crossed the Aube at Anglure on the two preceding days, commenced to march on Paris by the main road through Coulommiers.

On February 26 the general position of the armies was as follows: Napoleon, in occupation of Troyes, had under his own hands 74,000 men and 350 guns, concentrated between the Seine and the Aube.

In front of him the main allied army, reduced to some 120,000 men, was retiring on Chaumont and Langres. On the Emperor's left, Blücher, with 48,000 men, was undertaking a most danger-ous flank march, for he was in danger of being attacked in the rear by Napoleon, while being held in front by Marmont and Mortier, whose corps had been reinforced to a strength of more than 16,000 men. [1] On the Emperor's right, General Allix, one of the most energetic officers in the army, was defending the line of the Yonne with 2,000 soldiers and a number of peasants. Each day there arrived at Paris from all parts of France parties of recruits and of details, and each day there marched out from Paris battalions, squadrons, and batteries to join the various ar-mies. Finally, National Guards were being organized in every province, and in the theatre of war armed peasants were laying ambushes, defending villages, attacking small parties of the en-emy, capturing convoys, and pursuing stragglers.

In the south, Augereau, who had 28,000 men in the army of Lyons, had at last made up his mind to take the offensive against the 20,000 Austrians under Bubna and Lichtenstein. He had formed his troops into two columns, the left of which had driv-en the enemy across the Ain. while the right column marched on Geneva, and had commenced to invest the town on February 26. Augereau had express orders to retake Geneva, and to place himself across the Bale-Langres road, so as to sever Schwarzen-berg's communications, a magnificent manoeuvre planned by the Emperor, which could have been easily carried out by the exercise of a little resolution and promptitude.

In Spain, Marshal Suchet had 15,000 men concentrated at Figueras, and about 23,000 in occupation of Barcelona, Toledo, and other places, and with these he held in check the 55,000 Anglo-Spanish troops under Lord Bentinck and Copons. He was only waiting for the treaty of Valençay to be ratified by the Cortes in order to bring into France these magnificent troops,

1 See note, end of chapter

bronzed by the fire of a hundred battles.

In the Pyrenees Soult's 48,000 men, massed at Bayonne and Orthez, detained behind the Adour and the two Gaves Wellington's main army of 72,000 English, Spanish, and Portuguese.

Across the Alps, on the line of the Mincio, was Prince Eugène. With 48,000 men he threw on to the defensive Bellegarde's 74,000 Austrians, and forced Murat's Neapolitans to retire.

On the old northern frontier, General Maison, with 15,000 men, was opposed to 30,000 Germans and Prussians under the Prince of Saxe-Weimar and General Borstell. This French general handled his troops with great ability, and by dint of rapid movements misled the enemy as to his real strength and avoided a pitched battle.

In the Netherlands French garrisons occupied Maestricht, Bergen-op-Zoom, Antwerp, and Niew-Diep, and were holding out against the attacks of Graham's English, Valmöden's Saxons, and the Prince of Orange's Dutch troops.

In the Rhine Valley and in Germany the Emperor's troops held Glogau, Custrin, Magdebourg, Wursbourg, Petersberg, Hamburg, Wezel, Mayence, Luxembourg, Strasbourg, Neuf-Brisach, Phalsbourg, Landau, Hüningen, Belfort, Metz, Saarlouis, Thionville, and Longwy. These fortresses, being well supplied and held by good garrisons, defied both assault and blockade.

From the Oder to the Aube, from the Mincio to the Pyrenees, the enemy's forces were everywhere held in check.

Forces of the Allies

Showing approximate strength at the beginning of January
Army of Bohemia (also called the Grand Army). Commander, Prince of Schwarzenberg:

*1st Corps (Colloredo)	15,708	men
*2nd (Prince Aloys Lichtenstein)	12,708	,,
3rd (Gyulai)	14,732	,,
4th (Prince of Würtemberg)	14,000	,,
5th Bavarian (De Wrède)	34,200	,,
6th Corps (Wiggenstein, afterwards Rajewsky)	21,066	,,

*Light Div. (Bubna and Moritz Lichtenstein) 11,240 ,,
*6th German Corps (Bianchi)   13,250 ,,
*Austrian Res. (Prince of Hesse-Hombourg)   18,500 ,,
Grand Russ. and Pruss. Res. (Barclay de Tolly) 38,696 ,,
Platow's Cossacks   6,000 ,,
            Total   200,100 ,,
*Detached to form the army of the South on February 25.

Army of Silesia. Commander, Field-Marshal Blücher:
Prussian Corps (York)   19,560 men
Russian (Sacken)   19,400 ,,
Olsufjew's (afterwards Kapzéwitsch's) Russians
(detached from Langeron's Corps)   5,697 ,,
Korff's Cavalry (detached from the same corps) 2,000 ,,
            Total   46,657 ,,

Grand total of allies who entered France in the first fortnight
of January: 246,757 men.
    To these must be added the following forces:
    (a) For the army of Bohemia:

Prohaska's Division   9,000 men
Doring's Würtemberg Division   10,600 ,,
8th German Corps (Hochberg)   10,330 ,,

These troops only entered France in February.
    (b) For the army of Silesia:

Kleist's Prussian Corps   20,000 men
Langeron's Russian Corps (less the troops already
enumerated and those left before Mayence) 19,500 ,,

Kleist's Corps crossed the frontier at the end of January and
Langeron's, in several portions, during February and March.

4th German Corps   12,000 men
5th   ,,   ,,   9,320 ,,

These corps did not enter France.
    (c) The army of the North. Commanded by Bernadotte.
Bülow's Corps (Prussian)   30,000 men

Winzingerode's Corps (Russian)	30,000	,,
Prince Weymar's Corps	23,000	,,
Walmöden's Corps	15,000	,,
Swedish Corps	23,000	,,
Duke of Brunswick's Corps	32,000	,,

Only the corps of Bülow and Winzingerode, reduced to a total of 42,800 men, entered France, in the month of February.

(d) The second-line armies comprised the Russians under Beningsen and Rostowsky, Prussians under Tauenzien, with Austrian reserves, etc. These various troops, estimated at more than 300,000 men, laid siege to the fortresses in Germany or remained in garrisons and took no part in the invasion.

(e) The army of Italy (Bellegarde) 74,000 men, operating against Prince Eugène.

(f) English, Spaniards, Portuguese, and Neapolitans, 160,000.

To sum up, the Austrians, Prussians, and Russians invaded France in the beginning of January with 245,000 men, and the fresh troops which crossed the frontier between the end of January and the beginning of March, including Wellington's 72,000 English and Spaniards, would have raised the number to 420,000 without making any deduction for losses.

If to these figures are added the second-line and reserve troops and the armies of the Netherlands, Spain, and Italy, the numbers must have amounted to more than a million men.

The French forces amounted, by the middle of February, to 650,000 men, including the armies of Catalonia, of the Pyrenees, of Italy, of the Netherlands, the garrisons of the fortresses on both sides of the Rhine, and all the depots of France and Italy, but not including the National Guards.

It is unnecessary to remark that on both sides these are paper numbers, and give the total strength of the forces without deducting losses due to battle, desertions, sickness, etc.: these numbers can certainly be reduced by a quarter or even by a third, and the number of effectives under arms in the whole of Europe may be taken at 400,000 for the French and 750,000 for the allies.

French Army
As organized on February 26
Napoleon:

7th Corps (Oudinot)	17,028	men
11th ,, (Macdonald)	8,797	,,
2nd ,, (Gérard)	6,257	,,

1st Division of the Young Guard (Meunier)

and 2nd ,, (Curial) 2,244		
and Boyer's Spanish Brigade 1,912		
(Ney)	4,156	,,

1st Provisional Division of the Young Guard"
    (Charpentier)
and 2nd Provisional Division of the Young Guard
    (Boyer de Rebeval)

(Victor)	12,556	,,

1st Division of the Old Guard (Friant)	6,600	,,
1st Division of the Parisian Reserve (Arrighi)	3,430	,,
Grand Park (Sorbier) and Res. Guard Artillery	2,000	,,
Total infantry	60,824	,,

Roussel's Cavalry Division	2,174	men
2nd Cavalry Corps (Saint-Germain)	2,380	,,
5th (Milhaud)	3,351	,,
6th (Kellermann)	3,819	,,

2nd Division Guard Cavalry (Exelmans)

and 3rd ,, ,, ,, (La Ferrière)		
(Nansout)	3,168	,,
Total cavalry	14,892	,,

Total under Napoleon	75,716	men

Marmont:

6th Corps (Ricard and Lagrange's Divisions)	3,685	men
1st Cavalry Corps (Bordessoule)	2,403	,,

Mortier:

Defrance's Gardes d'Honneur 913 ,,
2nd Division of the Old Guard (Christiani) 2,422 ,,
1st Division Guard Cavalry (Colbert) 909 ,,

Reinforcements sent from Paris to the two marshals on February 28:

3rd Provisional Division of the Young Guard (Porret
     de Morvan) 4,879 men
Provisional Cavalry Division (Boulnoir) 1,026 ,,
One Company of Artillery 150 ,,
        Total for the two marshals 16,507 men

CHAPTER 3

The Châtillon Negotiations

It might seem that the prospects of peace would have been brightened by the change which had come over the fortunes of the war, or, to speak more accurately, by the triumphs of genius over numbers. Napoleon had won several victories, but he was still in a critical situation: the allied sovereigns were still on French territory, but their beaten and demoralized armies were in full retreat. It would have appeared that both sides should have been ready to make concessions, but, as a matter of fact, an agreement was farther off than ever. The glamour of Montmirail and Vauchamps and the hope of further triumphs prevented Napoleon from accepting the terms dictated by the allies, and they, in turn, in spite of their reverses, had made up their minds to refuse the Emperor's proposals.

It is doubtful whether the allies really wanted peace when they opened negotiations at Prague: it is more doubtful whether they wanted it at Frankfort, but there is no doubt whatever that they did not want it when they sent their plenipotentiaries to Châtillon. If nothing beyond the will of the allied sovereigns had been consulted, the comedy known to history as the Châtillon negotiations would never have taken place. From the moment their armies crossed the French frontier they had tacitly agreed on the overthrow of Napoleon. The only difference of opinion was as to the form of government to be set up in France. England wished to restore the Bourbons; the prospect of making Marie-Louise Queen of France appealed to the fatherly instincts of the Emperor Francis; but under the influence of Metternich and Schwarzenberg he rejected the idea. In common with the Emperor of Austria and the British Government, the King of Prussia was ready to agree to a restoration, provided that his army might satisfy their revenge by steeping France in blood and fire.

The Czar was not in principle opposed to the restoration of the Bourbons, but he considered their return impossible for the reason that France did not want them. Alexander was swayed partly by a vague liberalism and partly by personal friendships, and had no definite plan in his mind; at one time he favoured making Bernadotte Emperor, and at another he proposed summoning an assembly of deputies who should be free to decide the destinies of France: he even would not have minded seeing a republic proclaimed. The Czar, however, was dominated by one fixed idea: Napoleon had entered Moscow, and the Czar wished to enter Paris; he wished to ride into Paris at the head of his guard, with drums beating and colours flying. His mind was not filled with the dreams of blood and fire which haunted the brains of Blücher and of the members of the Tugenbund, but he wished to show himself in his glory and in his magnanimity to Paris and to the whole world.

In view of these projects the allied sovereigns were not anxious to enter into negotiations the success of which would only upset their plans; but for the last three months the ministers of the coalition had been proclaiming their desire for peace. On November 9, at Frankfort, they had officially proposed to treat on the basis of the natural frontiers of France; on November 25 they had officially announced that they were ready to enter into negotiations; and on December 1 in the Declaration of Frankfort they had proclaimed that the first use which the allies had made of their victory was to offer peace to Napoleon. After this a refusal to negotiate would exasperate the whole of France and shock the public opinion of Europe, which wanted peace as much as France did.

At last, on January 29, the Czar gave way to the representatives of Castlereagh and Metternich and agreed to open negotiations, but on the basis that France should revert to the frontiers she possessed in 1789, which was very different to the terms offered at Frankfort. It was further stipulated that military operations should not be interrupted, and the Russian plenipotentiary, Razumowsky, received from the Czar secret instructions to drag out the negotiations as much as possible. Caulaincourt, the Duc de Vicence, who had been waiting for three weeks at the hostile outposts, was at last informed that the plenipotentiaries would meet at Châtillon.

The allies risked little by entering into negotiations. Only two months earlier Napoleon had hesitated to allow his empire to be reduced to the natural frontiers of France, and they knew very well that he would never consent to give up the left bank of the Rhine. The sovereigns of the coalition realized that it was necessary to destroy the root of the evil, and they meant the negotiations to fail.

Napoleon at any rate was not deceived. He, like the allies, embarked on the negotiations in order to show that he was peacefully inclined, but, like the allies, he believed that an agreement was impossible. He was ready to treat on the basis proposed at Frankfort, but guessed that the allies would insist on harder terms. Napoleon, therefore, had offered to negotiate on terms which he knew would be refused by the allies, who in their turn were only willing to treat on terms which the French could not accept. It was a comedy on both sides, planned and carried out with the sole object of deceiving public opinion.

The Congress opened on February 4, but at the first meeting the only business done was to adjourn to the following day. On February 5 the plenipotentiaries of the allies announced that they were instructed to treat for peace in the name of united Europe, that they would only treat conjointly, and lastly, that the maritime code would not form a matter for discussion. Caulaincourt, on behalf of Napoleon, agreed to these conditions and requested that they should immediately set to work. At this point, however, Razumowsky objected that his credentials were not in order, and the conference was put off till the following day, but was again postponed for a day on account of Razumowsky's credentials. When the next meeting was held, on February 7, the representatives of the allies announced as their terms that France must be reduced to the frontiers existing before the Revolution, " with the exception of modifications made for mutual convenience," and that she must abandon all influence beyond her future frontiers. The Duc de Vicence remarked that these conditions differed greatly from those proposed at Frankfort, and Razumowsky and Stadion had the face to reply that they did not know that the allied courts had ever made such propositions to the Emperor of the French.

It has frequently been stated that on this day Caulaincourt held in his hand the choice of peace or war, because if he had immediately accepted the terms offered by the allies, hostilities would have come to an end. This is not the case, however. The truth is that on this day the Duc de Vicence did not feel that he was invested with wide enough powers to allow him to sign such a treaty without discussion and practically with his eyes closed. It is true that he had received on February 4 a letter from Napoleon, who had just lost the battle of La Rothière, saying, "As soon as the allies announce their conditions you are free to accept them," to which, however, were added the words, "or to refer them to me."

He had received the well-known letter from the Duc de Bassano, dated February 5, which ran,

His Majesty directs me to tell you that he gives you carte blanche to carry the negotiations to a conclusion, so as to save the capital and avoid a battle on the result of which would turn the last hopes of the nation.

But on the very day on which he had received this *carte blanche* he also received a further letter from the Emperor: "You should agree to the terms if they are acceptable," wrote Napoleon, " but if not, we will take the chances of a battle and run the risk of losing Paris and all that that will involve."

The receipt of these contradictory orders, and the uncertainty as to what constituted "acceptable" terms, could not fail to embarrass the Duc de Vicence. However, the governing consideration was the fact that the full powers, although evidently authorized by Napoleon, were conveyed by Bassano, while the other letter was written throughout by the hand of the Emperor. Caulaincourt, therefore, could only be guided by Napoleon's last letter, "agree to the terms if they are acceptable."

It was obviously impossible for him to consider as "acceptable" the terms characterized by Thiers as an "indecent proposition," and he could not have forgotten the words of Napoleon, "The most adverse fortune of war would never make the Emperor consent to ratify a treaty which would be dishonourable to him and insulting to France." Under the circumstances all the Duc de Vicence could do was to refuse in principle terms which differed so greatly from those proposed at Frankfort, and to ask in the most moderate language that the plenipotentiaries should give full details of their proposals. In this way Caulaincourt gained time to write once more to the Emperor. The moderation of Caulaincourt's tone alarmed the allied representatives, who feared that he might agree to the conditions without delay, and they, therefore, also felt the need of further instructions.

Caulaincourt could not have accepted the terms offered by the allies on February 7 without proving false to the wishes expressed by the Emperor. Even if he had offered to conclude peace on the spot the allied representatives would not have consented. On February 6 Razumowsky had received a letter from Nesselrode, which said,

> His Majesty entirely approves of the way you have spun out the negotiations, and hopes you will continue to do so. Since the victory of La Rothière delay is increasingly necessary.

The clause in the proposed terms suggesting modifications in the frontiers for mutual convenience would have furnished the representatives of the allies with a pretext for endless discussions, during which they could have easily put forward fresh claims, while Caulaincourt's counter-proposals could have been refused or referred to the sovereigns, and either alternative meant delay.

At Châtillon the Duc de Vicence was alone, and often had no information except false news told him by the allies, who caused the diplomatic messages to be delayed to such an extent that couriers took six days to go and return from Napoleon's headquarters. He was disturbed by the retreat of the French armies, and wished to arrange for an immediate armistice, but when he approached one of the plenipotentiaries on the subject he was roundly told that whatever he proposed he would not obtain a suspension of operations. Caulaincourt then determined to ask the Prince of Metternich to act as mediator, and wrote to him on February 9 asking his good offices to obtain an immediate armistice.

"On these conditions," he wrote, "I am ready to negotiate on the basis of the frontiers obtaining before 1789, and to hand over as pledges some of the fortresses of which this sacrifice will deprive France."

Caulaincourt was offering a good deal, but an armistice would not have definitely pledged Napoleon's word as to the territories to be handed over, and by giving up some fortresses on the left bank of the Rhine Napoleon would have regained the use of a veteran army. Finally, if the conditions should prove unacceptable, Napoleon would be free to denounce the armistice, and take the field with a larger and better-organized army. Caulaincourt's letter ought at any rate to have been considered by the allies because it contained an offer to negotiate on the terms proposed by the allies themselves, and volunteered to hand over fortresses as a pledge of good faith.

On the very day on which this letter arrived at Troyes, February 10, the plenipotentiaries handed to the Duc de Vicence a note, couched in very curt terms, informing him that the congress was postponed *sine die*, on the pretext that the Emperor of Russia wished to consult with the allied sovereigns as to the object of the negotiations. This note had been drafted some days before, but the plenipotentiaries had hesitated to present it, and had only been persuaded by Razumowsky's threats of retiring from the Congress. Caulaincourt returned a dignified and carefully reasoned reply to this most unexpected communication, but at the Czar's head-quarters the Duc de Vicence's protestations received little attention. The armies of Silesia and Bohemia were in full march on Paris, and Alexander had determined to break off negotiations for fear that peace might be signed before he could make his triumphal entry into Paris.

Caulaincourt's letter, however, was a source of concern to Metternich, to the Emperor of Austria, and to all the allied ministers except the Russian, for, however badly disposed they were to Napoleon, Lord Castlereagh, Metternich, and Hardenberg hesitated to break off the negotiations. On the one hand, the conciliatory attitude adopted by Caulaincourt, and the tone of depression which underlay his letter, seemed to indicate that peace might possibly be arranged on the basis of the terms proposed by the allies; on the other hand, however, Napoleon might be beaten and in retreat, but he was not yet absolutely crushed, and his genius might still carry his arms to success.

A treaty of peace which reduced France to the frontiers of 1789 would more than accomplish all the avowed objects of the war, but then there remained the secret object, the dethronement of Napoleon, and to insist on this involved a risk of sacrificing all the great advantages which they were on the point of gaining at Châtillon. The doubts of the ministers were solved by the determination of the Czar to continue the war, and had it not been for the defeats suffered by Blücher the conferences at Châtillon would certainly never have been resumed.

Lord Castlereagh undertook to try to persuade the Czar of the necessity for reopening negotiations, but all his arguments both verbal and written failed to produce any effect on Alexander, who maintained that the only course was to continue the war, and to act more vigorously than they had hitherto done.

While not giving up hope of persuading the Czar, the ministers met at Troyes on February 13 in order to discuss several points, the principal among which were the answer to be given to the Duc de Vicence, the policy to be pursued towards the Bourbons and towards Napoleon, and the measures to be adopted in case Paris were captured.

These points were put to the Czar in writing, and he took up his pen and at once gave the following replies:

1. An armistice will be refused, and all the other propositions will automatically fall to the ground.

2. The policy hitherto adopted will be pursued. The powers will not pronounce in favour of the Bourbons, but will leave to the French the choice in this matter: they will not prevent the Bourbons from displaying activity outside the territory occupied by the allied forces, but they will not encourage them and will avoid any appearance of so doing.

3. The state of public feeling in the capital will guide the allies in their action. H.M. the Emperor considers that the members of the different corporate bodies and men of mark and leading should be summoned, and this assembly should be invited to express its opinion as to the person it considers most suitable to be placed at the head of the Government.

It will then be possible to estimate both the support which Paris will be likely to give to the selected party and also the effect which this party will have on the army which remains with Napoleon. If Paris does not pronounce against the Emperor it will be better to make peace with him.

4. The local and municipal authorities of Paris should be retained, and a governor should be appointed who would have a general control over them. H.M. the Emperor considers that as Russia has been the most inveterate opponent of the common enemy, a Russian should be selected as governor.

In this extraordinary document the Czar evinced the greatest political sagacity and described with marvellous foresight the events which were about to take place.

As a result of the Conference of Ministers Castlereagh and Hardenberg drew up a report which recommended that the proposals of the Duc de Vicence should be accepted and that peace should be concluded on the basis of the frontiers of 1789. To this report the Czar replied by a very long note in which he again asserted his desire to continue the war and gave it as his opinion that the probability of success was still on the side of the allies, and that the fall of Napoleon was most necessary and was the greatest example of justice which could be given to the world.

In face of Alexander's determined opposition Hardenberg was ready to waive his own opinion and even to retire from the counsels of the allies lest his presence might endanger the good relations of Russia and Prussia. Lord Castlereagh, however, had the tenacity of his race and did not consider himself beaten: on February 14 he went to Pont-sur-Seine, where the Czar had gone as much with a view to escaping from further discussions as to hasten the march of the army of Bohemia, and he again urged upon Alexander the necessity for reopening the negotiations at Châtillon.

"We must make peace," he insisted, "before we are forced to retreat to the Rhine."

The Czar lost his temper and replied in a loud tone of voice: "My lord, that would be no peace: that would be merely an armistice which would give us only a few days' rest. You must understand once for all, that I shall not always be willing to march my troops four hundred leagues to help you. I shall make no peace so long as Napoleon remains on the throne."

Lord Castlereagh retired without having obtained anything. On the following day, however, the fourth defeat suffered by Blücher induced Alexander to change his opinion and the ministers were informed that the Czar consented to the renewal of negotiations. At the same time, however, Alexander sent fresh instructions to Razumowsky, bidding him to continue causing as much delay as possible.

The plenipotentiaries met again on February 17, but the events of the last ten days did not tend to promote agreement. The representatives of the allies were much perturbed by Napoleon's victories, and with the exception of Razumowsky, were ready to make a sincere effort for peace on the terms of the frontiers of 1789, but Caulaincourt, on the contrary, had definite orders to refuse these terms. The day after the battle of Montmirail, Napoleon had revoked the *carte blanche* which he had given, directing that nothing was to be signed without reference to him, and had stated that there could be no lasting peace except on the Frankfort terms.

Caulaincourt, however, was still in favour of peace and looked upon Napoleon's success as merely temporary, and he, therefore, listened to the allies' proposals without revealing his new instructions. The plenipotentiaries adopted a high tone and refused to grant an armistice on the grounds that a preliminary treaty would be a more effective way of reaching the desired goal: they then read out a draft treaty on the lines proposed in principle at the meeting of February 7. To this the Duc de Vicence replied that the document which had just been read was of such importance that he could not give an immediate answer; he would, therefore, propose a further meeting when he should be in a position to discuss the matter.

This reply of Caulaincourt's was very judicious: he had been taken in by Metternich's friendly assurances, and believed that peace could be obtained on the terms put forward by the allies, and he hoped to be able to induce the Emperor to accept these terms. He might have pointed out to the plenipotentiaries that Napoleon's recent victories should have caused them to moderate their terms, but to do so would have risked breaking off the negotiations a second time, and this he wished of all things to avoid.

Napoleon took the draft treaty much less calmly than Caulaincourt, to whom he wrote on February 19, "I am so moved by the infamous proposals which you send me that I feel it is a dishonour to have put myself into a position which renders them possible. I wish to deliver my own ultimatum, and as soon as I reach Troyes I will send you a counter-proposal which you will present."

The Emperor was in no hurry to present this counter-proposal, which he intended to base on the Frankfort terms. He realized that the ministers of the allies would not agree to these terms and he wished, before presenting it, to enlist the Emperor of Austria on his side; the army of Bohemia was beaten and Schwarzenberg was asking for an armistice, so the present moment appeared a suitable one for the purpose. On February 21, therefore, he wrote a letter to Francis I, in which endearments were mingled with threats: he proudly announced his unalterable determination to yield no territory and alternately implored and summoned the Emperor to make peace on the Frankfort terms.

This letter increased the uncertainties of the allies, who pressed their demand for an armistice. Napoleon could not refuse a suspension of hostilities without giving the lie to the yearnings for peace which he had expressed in his letter, and the emissaries met at Lusigny on February 24; General Flahaut represented the French army and Generals Duca, Schouvalow, and Rauch that of the allies. The soldiers had a better chance of coming to an agreement than the diplomats, but unfortunately Napoleon had insisted on two conditions, the first of which was that military operations were not to be suspended, and the second that the preamble of the protocol should state that the plenipotentiaries had met at Châtillon in order to negotiate a peace on the Frankfort terms.

Military emissaries had no power to agree to this preamble, which would have been binding upon the plenipotentiaries at Châtillon, and on the following day Flahaut abandoned the point. Other difficulties arose, however, in connection with the districts to be occupied by the two armies, and each side put forward extravagant claims. Flahaut and Duca were both anxious for peace, and deplored the restrictions imposed by their respective instructions: General Duca begged the French representative to get concessions from Napoleon. "In God's name," he wrote, "let us bring the hostilities to a close. I assure you that the Emperor of Austria and the British Government wish to make a peace which will be consonant with the honour of France."

"General," said he again, "we are not diplomatists: we are two soldiers. I have proved to you that I hope for peace, and I assure you that such is the wish of my Emperor, but our powers go no further than I have told you. You must answer yes or no. What difference does a little territory more or less make in an armistice? If only your Emperor would give a little more help to the cause of peace!"

In his letters to the Emperor, Flahaut did not dare to give any advice, but his opinions were fairly evident, and Napoleon decided to make some very reasonable concessions. Flahaut announced these concessions on the 27th, but they were not enough: the fact is that an armistice could only have been obtained by accepting the impossible conditions of the enemy's staff. On the 28th the allied emissaries offered these conditions a second time to Flahaut, and this time the offer took the form of an ultimatum. The negotiations were broken off, but for the last three days the time and trouble of Flahaut and Duca had been wasted, for we find the King of Prussia stating in a letter to Blücher on February 25 " No suspension of hostilities will take place."

In the Council of War held in General Knesebeck's quarters at Bar-sur-Aube on February 25, the allied sovereigns had not confined their deliberations to the military question. After having decided that the army of Bohemia should retire to Langres, that Blücher's army should move forward, and that an army of the South should be formed, they then went on to discuss the line to be adopted as regards the negotiations which were on foot at Lusigny. The refusal of Napoleon to suspend hostilities during the negotiations at Lusigny rendered the proposed armistice useless to the army of Bohemia, and, further, this army had managed to avoid a battle and to make good its retreat across the

Aube. A sudden reaction, also, had taken place in the feelings of the English and Austrians, who for some days had been inclined towards peace: Napoleon's letter had at first alarmed the allies, but seventy-two hours had passed since its arrival, and in that time their main army had escaped the enemy. The Emperor's arguments were forgotten, and the only part of his letter to be remembered were his haughty threats and his declaration that he would make peace on no other terms than those of Frankfort.

A treaty of peace which should leave to France her natural frontiers was very far from being the intention of any of the allies. If Castlereagh and Metternich had opposed the wishes of the Czar for four days in their desire to see the negotiations resumed, it was because they feared that further victories of Napoleon might drive the allies across the Rhine. It went much against the grain to grant peace at all, and they were determined that this peace must brand Napoleon with humiliation and condemn France to feebleness. Europe must regain all the territory which she had lost since the Revolution, and if she could not yet do so, the allies would continue the war at whatever risk.

The Emperor Alexander had been over-ruled on the military question, and the Council had decided that the army of Bohemia should retreat, but he gained his own way in the matter of diplomacy; he was empowered to decide upon the line of demarcation to be insisted upon in the proposed armistice, and this was equivalent to breaking off the negotiations. As regards the Congress of Châtillon it was decided that the plenipotentiaries should press the French representative to give a definite answer, and that they should allow him a very short time in which to agree to the preliminary treaty which had been presented to him on February 17; at the end of this time the negotiations should be considered as being broken off.

The fourth meeting of the Congress was held at Châtillon on February 28, and the representatives of the allies began by expressing their astonishment that Caulaincourt should not have yet replied to their proposals, which were based on an offer made by him to Prince Metternich on February 9. They went on to declare that any further delay would be looked upon as a refusal to negotiate on the part of the Imperial Government, and they added that they could entertain no proposals which contained any essential divergence from the offer made by the French plenipotentiary.

Caulaincourt, who had not yet received Napoleon's counter-proposal, replied that the allies could not justly complain of the delay, because they themselves had postponed the sittings of the Congress nine times without cause, and, further, that they could not claim the right to avail themselves of the offer which had been made confidentially to Metternich, because that offer had been conditional on an immediate armistice, and this the allies had refused. The plenipotentiaries disdained to reply to these arguments, and insisted again that the Duc de Vicence should name the date on which he would give his answer. Caulaincourt objected in vain that in so important a matter he could not bind himself to a definite date: he was obliged to fix March 10 as the latest date by which the reply would be given.

Lord Castlereagh had recovered from the alarm into which he had been thrown by Napoleon's letter to the Emperor of Austria, but he was afraid that another effort in the same direction might succeed in detaching Austria from the coalition: he desired therefore to bind the European alliance more closely together by a new treaty, and he found a pretext in the necessity for putting on a proper basis various financial arrangements which had originated in lack of funds among the continental powers.

This treaty, which was the origin of the "Holy Alliance," was signed on March 1 at Chaumont, to which place the allied staff had moved from Bar-sur-Aube. The contracting Powers bound themselves for a period of twenty years, during which they each undertook not to treat individually with France; England guaranteed for the whole period of hostilities an annual subsidy of 150,000,000 *francs*, to be divided between Russia, Austria, and Prussia, and each of these powers undertook to carry on the war with a contingent of 150,000 men.

CHAPTER 4

The Battle of Bar-sur-Aube

Napoleon was very sceptical as to the prospects of an armistice, and when the negotiations began at Lusigny he remained at Troyes and disposed his army with the intention of pursuing the Austro-Russians across the Aube. His orders for this move had been issued, when on the morning of February 25 he received a letter, dated the preceding evening, from Marmont, who said that Blücher was marching on Sezanne, and that he would delay him as much as possible. The Emperor suspended his movement, but until the night of the 26th–27th he hesitated to believe that Blücher was really marching on Paris. In view of the failure which had attended the march of the Prussians on Paris three weeks before, it was improbable that Blücher would attempt a similar move again, and it was more likely that his forward march was intended to cover a retreat on Châlons.

At all risks, however, the Emperor took steps so as to be in a position to profit by Blücher's rashness in case the movement towards Paris should be carried too far, and on February 26 Ney, Victor, and Arrighi were directed on Arcis, Méry, and Nogent respectively. By the following morning there was no further possibility of doubt as to Blücher's objective, and there was no longer any fear that Napoleon would be committing a false move by following the Prussians: by 7 o'clock in the morning the Emperor had definitely made up his mind, and at midday he left Troyes with his guard.

The manoeuvre of the middle of February was about to be

83

repeated, with the difference that instead of attacking the flank of the army of Silesia, the Emperor was now aiming at its rear, while the head of the Prussian columns was engaged with the united forces of Marmont and Mortier.

In order to detain the army of Bohemia behind the Aube the Emperor left behind a force of 40,000 men, composed of the 2nd, 5th, and 6th Cavalry Corps, and the 2nd, 7th, and 11th Corps (Gerard, Oudinot, and Macdonald). This force was placed under the supreme command of Macdonald. The army of Bohemia was demoralized and in retreat, and there was not much chance of its assuming the offensive unless Schwarzenberg were to become aware of Napoleon's departure, and this the Emperor hoped to be able to hide from him. Macdonald and Oudinot were directed to use every means to create the impression that the Emperor was still with them: his quarters were prepared near Bar, and his arrival there was announced for the following day; while they were not to commit themselves beyond the Aube, the marshals were to conceal from the enemy that they were acting on the defensive, and in case they were attacked the soldiers were to shout "*Vive l'Empereur!*" The Duc de Vicence also was pressed into the service, and was instructed to send all his couriers to Bar.

In spite of these precautions, twenty-four hours before the Emperor left Troyes, and eighteen hours before he had made up his mind to do so, the King of Prussia was informed that the move was imminent. Frederick William was at Colombey-les-deux-églises with Schwarzenberg when, at midday on February 26, he received a dispatch from the head-quarters of the army of Silesia informing him that the Emperor was preparing to follow Blücher with the bulk of his force, and had detached against the army of Bohemia a force of two or three corps only.

This news was, to say the least, premature, and Blücher's announcement can only have been founded on presumption, for on February 25, on which day this letter was written, not a single Frenchman had yet crossed the Aube. It seems likely that this dispatch was a device of Blücher's to induce the army of

Bohemia to take the offensive: the old marshal feared that Napoleon might attack him, and a movement on the part of the Austro-Russians would compel the Emperor to concentrate all his forces between Troyes and Bar; and the army of Silesia would then be free to advance on Paris without anxiety as to its rear.

At the council of war which had been held at Bar-sur-Aube, it had been decided that the army of Bohemia should resume the offensive as soon as Napoleon should turn against Blücher, and the King of Prussia drew attention to this decision when he communicated Blücher 's dispatch to Schwarzenberg. In common with all the generals of the allies, Schwarzenberg was afraid, not of the French army, but of Napoleon, and the power of the initiative came back to him as his distance from the Emperor increased. The Emperor certainly was justified when he said, "I have 50,000 men and myself: that is 150,000."

The various corps of the army of Bohemia were turned about, and a general attack was ordered for the following morning. The Count de Wrède even made a vigorous attack that evening on Bar, where Gérard's two divisions had just arrived, but the Bavarians were hotly received, and retired in disorder with the loss of more than 200 men.

This attack argued further offensive movements on the following day, and the country people reported a general movement of the Austrians towards the Aube. The prisoners, however, all said that the retreat was being continued, and Oudinot disposed his troops as if the enemy were a hundred miles away. Leval and Rothembourg's divisions and the 2nd Cavalry Corps bivouacked along the road between Montier and Ailleville, facing towards Bar, which was occupied by Gérard's corps. Oudinot's troops were crowded in the narrow valley on the right bank of the Aube, with the river on their right and the heights of Vernonfays on their left: their rear, also, was exposed, because Pacthod's division and the 6th Cavalry Corps had not yet crossed the bridge of Dolancourt.

Napoleon had intended that the line of the Aube should be defended, and that the river should not be crossed. Oudinot had not complied with Napoleon's wishes, and had placed his troops in a position which was equally unsuitable for attack or defence: he apparently realized this, for during the night he made the whole of his artillery recross the Aube and park at Magny-le-Fouchard, eight miles from the main portion of his troops.

The marshal ought either to have withdrawn his whole army across the river, or to have retained his artillery, summoned the 3,000 horsemen of the 3rd Cavalry Corps, and occupied the heights of Vernonfays with one division. One of the brigadiers of the 7th Corps seriously stated that Oudinot sent back his artillery because they would have been an embarrassment in case of attack: artillery is frequently a cause of embarrassment, but the absence of guns on the field of battle is a most serious danger.

On the morning of February 27 the army made no preparations for battle, although both the outposts and the country people reported the presence of the enemy. The marshal was not convinced that attack was imminent until after ten o'clock, when a cavalry reconnaissance was made against his left flank by Count Pahlen's Cossacks. Oudinot at last issued his orders, and Leval's division moved off towards the dominating position of Vernonfays, which should have been occupied on the previous day.

These fine regiments climbed the slopes and drove back the heads of some Russian columns which were advancing across the plateau, but the enemy's infantry re-formed in rear of their cavalry and soon 48 pieces of artillery opened fire on the French: Leval had not a single gun with which to reply. Three times the veterans of the Spanish wars assailed the Russian masses and forced them backwards, and three times they were shattered by grape shot and forced to abandon the ground they had won. The King of Prussia stood calmly in the thick of the fire in spite of Schwarzenberg's appeals, and watched with admiration the heroic attacks of Leval's troops. "These charges," he said, "are among the finest feats of arms I have ever seen."

Oudinot was on the horns of a dilemma; a general attack would have been risky, and a retreat would have been dangerous.

He hesitated to support Leval for fear lest the whole of his troops might be committed and no reserve be left to cover his retreat. As a result, Rothembourg's division and Saint-Germain's cavalry did nothing, and Pacthod's division remained on the left bank of the Aube. Kellermann's cavalry division marched towards the sound of the guns, crossed the river without orders and made three charges against the Russian batteries on the heights of Vernonfays, but they were unsupported by Oudinot. The whole of the artillery of the 7th Corps remained at Magny-le-Fouchard, and, instead of calling them up, Oudinot asked Gérard to lend him some guns. This general, who was defending Bar against De Wrède's Bavarians, sent one battery, but they were quickly crushed by the powerful Russian artillery.

By 4 o'clock in the afternoon Oudinot found that his centre was powerless against an enemy who was constantly being reinforced; his right was hard pressed and his left was threatened by Pahlen's cavalry. He decided to retire, and the troops retreated slowly, from point to point, and crossed the Aube by the bridges of Dolancourt and Bar. Gerard evacuated Bar the same evening, and on the following day the two corps were concentrated between Magny-le-Fouchard and Vendeuvre. They had lost 2,500 of the best troops in Napoleon's army, except Friant's division of the Old Guard: the allies had lost barely 2,000 killed and wounded.

When, during the battle, the soldiers found themselves fighting without artillery they cried out that they were betrayed, and this belief persisted for some time among the peasants of the Aube. This, of course, is absurd, but it cannot be denied that Oudinot displayed a lack of both foresight and resolution which cannot be too severely blamed. Good positions were open to him, but he placed his troops in an impossible situation: he had at his disposal a force almost equal to the enemy, but he so ordered matters that the three brigades of Spanish veterans and Kellermann's cavalry, in all 7,200 muskets and 3,800 sabres, were for five hours opposed without artillery to 26,000 Austrians and Russians.

It was useless for the troops to hope to deceive the enemy by shouting "*Vive l'Empereur!*"When the battle was fought after this fashion it was evident that Napoleon was not in command.

Oudinot's retreat completely uncovered Macdonald, who, on February 27, was marching from Fontette to La Ferté-sur-Aube. Luckily the boldness of his advance-guard entirely deceived the Prince of Würtemberg's troops, some of which, in accordance with Schwarzenberg's order of the day, had been pressed across the river with the object of resuming the offensive.

The Würtembergs recrossed the river and postponed their attack till the following day, but by that time Macdonald was no longer within reach. Reconnaissances which he had sent towards his left, in order to get into touch with Oudinot, reported the presence of the enemy's troops, and Macdonald concluded that the 2nd and 7th Corps were retiring on Vendeuvre and Troyes: as he did not wish to remain in the air he also retired on Troyes through Bar-sur-Seine, and during this march his rear-guard was often engaged with the enemy, who followed closely. Macdonald reached Troyes on March 3, and effected a junction with Oudinot's and Gérard's corps, which thenceforward came under his command.

Napoleon received the news of Oudinot's defeat on March 2: he was then at La Ferté-sous-Jouarre, in the middle of his operations against Blücher, with whom he hoped to try conclusions within the next two days. The reverse at Bar-sur-Aube was enough to irritate Napoleon, but not enough to make him alter his plans. Even if the French army had abandoned the line of the Aube, it was still holding that of the Seine, and Schwarzenberg's usual caution made it likely that the allies would require at least a week to drive Macdonald's three corps away from that river. By that time Napoleon, having exterminated Blücher, as he expressed it, would be ready to fall on the flanks or the rear of the army of Bohemia. Without being too much upset by the advance of the Austro-Russians, therefore, Napoleon sent instructions to his lieutenants to dispute every inch of the ground, and he himself continued his pursuit of the army of Silesia.

CHAPTER 5

Blücher's March on Paris

The initial stages of Field-Marshal Blücher's bold move were carried out with great success. On February 24, before the receipt of orders from general head-quarters, he had on his own initiative crossed the Aube at Baudement, Anglure, and Plancy. On February 25 he received letters from both the Emperor of Russia and the King of Prussia, who not only authorized him to assume the offensive, but warmly encouraged him to do so. "Your operations cannot fail to have the most beneficial effect," wrote the Czar.

"The issue of the campaign is in your hands; the happiness of the nations depends on your success," said Frederick William.

What pleased him more than these good wishes was the news that Bülow's Prussian corps, 16,900 strong, and Winzingerode's Russian corps, 26,000 strong, were for the future placed under his command. The Czar enclosed orders for these two generals, who were then at Laon and Rheims respectively. Blücher lost no time in forwarding these orders to his new subordinates, together with his own instructions, and he then immediately put his army in motion. He imagined himself as already in Paris, for he believed that only Marmont's small corps was in a position to bar his progress, and this handful of men could offer no serious resistance to his army, whose numbers reached the imposing total of 48,000 men. [1]Blücher certainly expected to have to fight

---

1. Made up as follows: York, 14,288; Kleist, 9,800; Sacken, 13,700; Kapzéwitsch, Rudzéwitsch, and Korff (subordinates of Langeron), 10,000 or 11,000.

a considerable force under the walls of Paris, but he counted on being joined by Winzingerode and Bülow before that time.

Other reinforcements also were on the way; the Comte de Langeron had left Mayence, on Blücher 's pressing orders, on February 2, and on the 24th was at Vitry; and his subordinate, the Comte de Saint-Priest, who also was a French exile in the Russian service, was at this time in Lorraine. Blücher believed that if only a portion of these troops joined him in time he would be strong enough to attack Paris, while the reinforcements on the way would protect his rear against any move on the part of Napoleon. Further, in order that he should have nothing to fear from the Emperor, he dispatched a letter to the King of Prussia telling him that the imperial army was preparing to follow the army of Silesia. Blücher assumed that Schwarzenberg would take the offensive on the receipt of this letter, and in that case it was probable that Napoleon would be forced to concentrate all his troops to oppose the army of Bohemia.

On February 25, then, Blücher set off, having Marmont as his tactical objective and Paris as his strategical. In the afternoon the head of his columns attacked Marmont's small corps on the heights of Vindey, behind Sézanne. The French retired step by step, covered by mobile artillery, which checked the constant charges of the hostile cavalry. On the 26th Marmont reached La Ferté-sous-Jouarre, closely followed by the Prussians under Kleist and York, while Sacken and Kapzéwitsch's Russians marched direct on Meaux by the main Coulommiers road.

At La Ferté-sous-Jouarre Marmont was joined by Marshal Mortier, whom he had summoned from Soissons, and the two marshals had now a force of over 10,000 men. On February 27 they were at Meaux, determined to defend the right bank of the Marne at all costs. After one attack the Russians retired, and Blücher, abandoning the idea of forcing the passage of the Marne in the face of the two marshals, brought his troops during the night of the 27th-28th to La Ferté-sous-Jouarre. They there crossed the river and marched towards the Ourcq so as to take in rear the French posted in front of Meaux.

When the Russians retreated Marmont guessed Blücher's plan, and he left his position on the morning of the 28th and, in company with Mortier, marched on Lizy-sur-Ourcq. Kleist's Prussians, however, Blücher's leading corps, had already crossed the Ourcq and were in a strong position behind the Thérouanne stream. The marshals attacked, and, after an hour's fierce fighting, the Prussians gave way and retired a distance of five miles along the road to La Ferté-Milon. The night had now come, and Mortier proposed remaining till the following day in the position they had won. Marmont, however, with truer strategic insight, pointed out that their success would be thrown away unless they occupied the right bank of the Ourcq before morning. Mortier, therefore, moved to Lizy and Marmont advanced to beyond the village of May, which Kleist had passed in his rapid retreat.

On the following morning Blücher's whole army had reached the Ourcq, and he made ready to pass the river which barred the road to Paris. His vanity could not permit, nor could his fiery nature understand, that a handful of French should hold a puny stream against an army of 50,000 men commanded by himself.

The allies made three simultaneous attacks: Sacken was directed on Lizy, while Kleist on the left bank of the Ourcq and Kapzéwitsch on the right bank attacked Marmont 's position at May and at Croüy. Both the Prussians and Russians were repulsed, thanks largely to a reinforcement of 6.000 men which reached the marshals from Paris during the night.

Blücher wished to renew the attack on the following day, but during the night of March 1 and 2 he received news which compelled him to completely alter his strategic plans and forced him to give up the offensive and to retreat as fast as possible. Napoleon was approaching by forced marches. The Emperor had left Troyes on February 27, and on the 28th had reached Sézanne; on March 1 he was at Jouarre with his advance- guard at La Ferté-sous-Jouarre, and on the morning of the 2nd he himself was on the Marne. His army numbered about 35,000 combatants. He had with him Victor and Ney's four divisions of the Young

Guard the 1st Division of the Old Guard under Friant, Boyer's Spanish Brigade, Arrighi's division, and 6,000 horsemen under Nansouty and Roussel. If Blücher had not had the foresight to destroy the bridge of La Ferté, Napoleon would have struck the rear of the army of Silesia in full retreat on March 2.

"If I had had a bridging train," he wrote on this day, "Blücher's army would have been lost."

As a matter of fact, as soon as he heard of Napoleon's march the field-marshal's sole idea was to escape as soon as possible from the clutches of the Emperor's army. He says so openly in his general order dated March 2:

> As the Emperor Napoleon marching from Arcis was at Sézanne on the 28th, and it is not certain whether he will cross the Marne at Meaux, La Ferté, or Château-Thierry, and as in these circumstances it is of the first importance that we should effect a junction with Generals Bülow and Winzingerode, the army will march as follows: York's corps *via* La Ferté-Milon and Ancienville to Oulchy, where it will take up a position behind the Ourcq, facing Château-Thierry; Sacken's corps on Ancienville; Langeron's corps on La Ferté-Milon; Kleist's corps on Bourneville and Marolles; baggage on Billy.

Blücher was in retreat, and as he did not know whether the French columns might not overtake him on the following morning, he placed his troops in positions which would, if necessary, be suitable for a battle.

When he wrote that York should face Château-Thierry, and that the other troops should bivouac behind the Ourcq, he indicated that he would accept battle if Napoleon were to press him too closely or if he himself should receive reinforcements.

Blücher's hopes lay in the arrival of reinforcements. On February 25 the Field-Marshal had sent orders to Bülow and Winzingerode to march at once on Paris, the former by Villers-Cotterets and Dammartin, and the latter by Fismes, Oulchy, and Meaux; on the 28th he had received a letter from Winzingerode telling him that his instructions would be carried out. According to Blücher's calculations Winzingerode ought to reach Oulchy on March 1 or 2, and Bülow on this date should be on the left bank of the Aisne. If then the army of Silesia could effect a junction at Oulchy with the two corps of Winzingerode and Bülow, Blücher would be in a position to fight with all the advantages of numbers on his side. But hour by hour these golden hopes faded in the minds of Blücher and of his advisers Gneisenau and Müffling. If these corps were within one day's march of the army of Silesia, how was it that nothing was known as to their movements or present position?

For three days Blücher had been without any news of them, and several staff-officers who had been sent out to search for the missing corps had given no sign of life. As a matter of fact one of these officers had sent off a message on March 1 from Braine announcing that the two corps were in that neighbourhood; but this message had not arrived at its destination, for the Cossack dispatch rider had lost his way and been taken prisoner in the forest of Villers-Cotterets.

The movements ordered by Blücher were carried out on March 2, but not without interference on the part of the enemy. In order to hide the retreat of the army Kleist made a reconnaissance in force towards May. Marmont was not deceived; he warned Mortier that the allies were retreating and asked for his immediate co-operation. The two united corps briskly repulsed Kleist's Prussians and pursued them at the point of the bayonet. At midnight the head of Marmont's troops reached La Ferté-Milon, which Blücher had just evacuated. On the following morning a large number of the allies were still on the left bank of the Ourcq at Neuilly, and Marmont lost no time in attacking them vigorously. The enemy, however, brought 24 guns into action, and under cover of their fire the rear-guard succeeded in crossing the Ourcq. Marmont had his horse killed under him by a cannon-ball.

Although the allies were all concentrated behind the Ourcq during the morning of March 3, the situation of Blücher's army had not much improved, for Napoleon also had crossed the Marne at La Ferté-sous-Jouarre, and was marching in pursuit of the army of Silesia. The Emperor's advance-guard reached Rocourt and La Croix on this day, and their left was in touch with Marmont's cavalry. "We are in touch with the enemy," wrote Berthier to the corps commanders, " tomorrow there will be a battle."

As we know, Blücher had hoped to find Winzingerode's corps at Oulchy, where he arrived during the night of March 2 and 3; but as a matter of fact he found no trace of that general there. Under these circumstances there were four courses open to the Field-Marshal. The first was to remain behind the Ourcq and there await Napoleon's attack; this had been Blücher's idea on the previous day, but he had then counted on receiving reinforcements which had failed him. The second course was to hasten his retreat, to march to the Aisne by the shortest road and cross that river either at Soissons or by a bridge of boats.

But Blücher knew that Soissons was occupied by the French, and he could not expect to capture that place in one day. He could not, either, make a bridge of boats and cross his army over the river in one day; one day, however, was all the start he had ahead of Napoleon, and if the army of Silesia were to waste forty-eight hours in front of the Aisne it could not escape a battle. The third course was to reach Laon by Villers-Cotterets and Vic-sur-Aisne, but this movement was excentric. The fourth alternative was to escape the French by moving towards the north-east; he would have to march up the Aisne as far as Berry-au-Bac and cross the river there by the new stone bridge; but this course also threatened to bring Blücher into contact with Napoleon, who was manoeuvring so as to turn the left of the allies if they remained in position behind the Ourcq or to cut off their retreat to Rheims or Berry-au-Bac if they should move in that direction.

Blücher's army was in a terrible state of exhaustion. In the last seventy-two hours the troops had fought three battles and had made three night marches, and for a whole week there had been no issue of rations. Several cavalry regiments, notably the Lithuanian Dragoons, had not been able to unsaddle since February 22; many horses were foundered and almost all had sore backs. Some of the artillery trains had stuck in the muddy roads, and the drivers had been forced to abandon and blow up the ammunition wagons. The infantry were worn out and hungry, barefooted and in tatters; they straggled along the roads grumbling against their leaders and living by means of pillage.

With his army in this condition, and without the reinforcements he had expected, Blücher could not accept battle at Oulchy. Soissons was closed to him and there remained only a retreat by Berry-au-Bac. Blücher did not yet know that Napoleon was moving towards Fismes, but he hesitated to commit his whole army to the perils of a flank march. After some consideration, he decided on a middle course and determined to cross the Aisne, if possible, at several points: the baggage, the artillery, and a portion of the infantry were to cross at Berry-au-Bac; the other troops would use a bridge of boats which was to be built between Soissons and Vailly.

On March 3, therefore, at 6 o'clock in the morning, the corps commanders were ordered to move their baggage on Fismes and their troops to Buzancy, where they would receive further orders. The movement of the baggage was to begin at midday, but the infantry were not to march until 3 or 4 o'clock; the cause of this delay was that it was absolutely necessary to give the soldiers half a day's rest. At the same time as he issued these orders to Gneisenau, Blücher sent a staff officer to ascertain where it was possible to build a bridge across the Aisne. The Field-Marshal himself intended to go early to Buzancy in order to decide on the site of the bridge and to issue definite orders for the passage of the river.

Hardly had these orders, which clearly reflected Blücher's embarrassment, been received by the corps commanders, when the Field-Marshal received news of his two lieutenants. At 7 a.m. a courier arrived post-haste bringing the following letter from Winzingerode, dated from a bivouac in front of Soissons at 5 a.m. on March 3:

"I understand that your Excellency is retiring by Oulchy. Soissons being occupied by the enemy, and an attempt to take the place having failed yesterday, I cannot but think that your Excellency will move on Rheims *via* Fismes. Under these circum- stances I think it is advisable that I should move the greater part of my infantry across the Aisne at Vailly, where Bülow has made a bridge. I myself, with one division of infantry and the whole of my cavalry, will remain in front of Soissons until daybreak, and if there are no fresh developments in the meanwhile I shall then march on Fismes."

This news was very far from being what Blücher had expected. His definite orders of February 25, enjoining a march on Paris by Fismes and Oulchy, had not been carried out. On February 27 Winzingerode had learnt of Napoleon's advance, and he considered that in these circumstances it was necessary for Blücher to have his retreat over the Aisne made secure. Now the most suitable passage over the Aisne for the army of Silesia was the bridge at Soissons; he had, therefore, written to Bülow suggesting that he should march from Laon to Soissons while Winzingerode himself moved there from Rheims: that fortress would be attacked on both sides of the river and taken in twenty-four hours, and they could then both march if necessary to Blücher's assistance. Bülow had agreed to Winzingerode's plan; on March 1 the two generals had set out, and on the 2nd they had invested Soissons; on the 3rd, however, as we have seen, this town had not surrendered, as the commander of the Russian corps, despairing of capturing the place in time, was preparing to raise the siege.

Certainly this news was sufficient to surprise and irritate Blücher, and Muffling tells us that he was very angry. Winzingerode had not carried out his instructions and had not effected a concentration with Blücher at Oulchy; he had not captured Soissons, the possession of which place would to a certain extent have justified the failure to carry out his orders; also, although he knew the dangerous situation of the army of Silesia, so far from collecting all his troops and hurrying to the rescue, he was dividing his force and sending it off in opposite directions. There was nothing to cause a change in Blücher's plans, and at 11 o'clock he went to Buzancy in order to decide where the bridge should be thrown.

The siege of Soissons was being raised; Billow's corps was on the far side of the Aisne; Winzingerode's troops were being scattered on both sides of that river; the army of Silesia was being pressed by Marmont and its flank was threatened by Napoleon: it was impossible for Blücher to hide from himself the extreme peril of his position, when, at midday, he received at Buzancy a letter from Bülow telling him that Soissons was captured and that the line of retreat was open to him.

"I do not doubt," wrote Bülow, alluding to the French garrison having been allowed to march out with the honours of war "I do not doubt that your Excellency will prefer the immediate possession of this place, which is of such importance at the present juncture, to a chance of capturing the garrison, and I flatter myself that the news I have to convey will be welcome to you. It seems to me all the more important as I can hear a brisk cannonade in progress."

The capture of Soissons was indeed important, and this event altered the whole complexion of affairs.

CHAPTER 6

The Surrender of Soissons

Soissons commanded the main road from Paris to Mons, and was considered an important strategical point. If the place had been well fortified and defended by a good garrison it would have been able to hold out for a long time, because the hills which dominate it from all sides, and which in 1870 made the town a shell-trap, were beyond the effective range of the guns in use in the beginning of the nineteenth century.

Unfortunately the old fortifications of Soissons were in an absolutely useless condition. All the outer works had been destroyed, and the maintenance of the ramparts was the business of the town council, who only maintained them in so far as they helped in the collection of the *octroi* duties. Only those breaches which might have let through a smuggler were repaired; the curtains had no banquettes, and the counterscarp had in many places fallen into the ditch, a great part of which was filled up and used as kitchen gardens.

It was only in the middle of January 1814 that any steps were taken to put Soissons in a state of defence. A commission of generals was sent from Paris, and began the works most urgently needed. The breaches were repaired, banquettes and embrasures were constructed, the counterscarp was revetted, some houses were burnt close outside the ramparts, and two outworks were built in front of the Rheims gate. A garrison was allotted, consisting of 4,000 conscripts and National Guards with eight field-pieces. In spite of these works, and largely owing to the lack of discipline of the garrison, Winzingerode captured Sois-soson February 14. General Rusca was killed, and a panic set in among the troops, who escaped along the Compiègne road. Winzingerode took possession of the town, but on February 16, on hearing of Blücher's defeats, he evacuated it and retired on Rheims, and Soissons was reoccupied by Mortier on February 19.

Napoleon was surprised and annoyed that the Russians should have been able to capture Soissons so easily, and gave orders that the town should be put in a thorough state of de-fence. The Minister of War sent a Colonel Müller to Soissons to inspect the place. His report made it evident that Soissons had been captured owing to the neglect of some simple precautions, and that the place could be put in a state of defence in a few hours, and that the first necessity was to appoint an able and determined commandant.

The Minister's choice fell upon Brigadier-General Moreau, who was not particularly able and who was absolutely lacking in determination. On February 11 he had defended, or rather had made preparations to defend, Auxerre against the Austrians, and had imposed upon the Minister, who believed him to be a thunderbolt of war, and charged him to defend Soissons with the same energy and vigour as he had displayed at Auxerre. As a matter of fact Moreau's vigour and energy at Auxerre consisted in his having assured thirty Austrian troopers who summoned him to surrender that he would defend the town to the death, for on the following day, when 2,000 Austrians appeared, he abandoned the town without even waiting for a flag of truce, which was received by the civil authorities.

This general assumed command of the garrison of Soissons, which was small in numbers, but composed of seasoned troops; 80 troopers, 140 artillerymen, and a Polish battalion 700 strong were allotted to the town, which was armed with 20 guns. There was also a town guard of 300 men, and a brigade of the National Guard, composed of 2,550 men who had already seen fighting, was expected to arrive in a few days to complete the garrison;

by some mistake, however, this brigade, which was at Orleans, was not ordered to march until February 28, and did not arrive at Soissons in time. Moreau and his staff made haste to put the place in a state of defence; he pulled down the houses which overlooked the ramparts at the Laon gate, and with the débris he constructed a parapet; he built up the new breaches, deepened the ditch, and placed obstacles on the eastern front, which formed a pronounced salient; a strong palisade was also built on the bridge over the Aisne.

It seems, however, whether it was from lack of time and labour or from want of initiative and energy, Moreau did not carry out to the full the instructions of the Minister of War. A certain number of houses in the suburbs which would have afforded shelter to the enemy's sharp-shooters were neither pulled down nor burnt. The Minister of War had expressly enjoined that the bridge should be prepared for destruction; Moreau merely wrote several times asking that 400 lb. of powder should be sent for the purpose, and as the powder did not arrive he took no further steps in the matter.

Like many others, Moreau thought that he had plenty of time available, even when Soissons was already surrounded with enemies. On March 1 he wrote to the Minister of War to ask for 400 lb. of gunpowder, and on the 2nd he wrote again to ask for reinforcements; but these dispatches do not show that Moreau was at all concerned at the approach of the enemy. He mentions as facts of no importance that a party of Prussian hussars had been captured and that General Bülow was reported to have arrived in the department of the Aisne and to be near Laon. Within less than an hour of having written this letter Moreau was to learn from personal observation where Bülow was.

At 9 a.m. on March 2 the outposts reported the simultaneous arrival of two hostile columns: Winzingerode's Russians were coming from Rheims and Bülow's Prussians from Laon. It has been mentioned that these generals had planned a concerted march upon Soissons, and they arrived under the walls of the town with admirable punctuality at the hour agreed upon.

While the small garrison was hastening to the ramparts the enemy ostentatiously deployed their forces within sight of the town; Winzingerode's corps took post across the Rheims road, with its right on the Aisne, and Bülow massed his troops in the plain of Croüy, to the north-east of Soissons.

The first shot was fired from the fortress, and at 10.30 a cannon-ball scattered a group of Russian horsemen who were passing within 300 yards of the Rheims gate. Winzingerode sent a flag of truce, but, as it was not received, the enemy's batteries opened fire. The defenders replied vigorously, and succeeded in dismounting three of the attackers' guns, but in spite of the skill and gallantry of the French this artillery duel was one-sided: forty guns were firing against the town, which could only reply with twenty, most of which were of small calibre.

By midday several of the French guns had been dismounted, and there had been some casualties among the artillerymen. The fire lasted until about 3 o'clock, at which time a strong Russian column crossed the little stream of the Crise and developed an attack against the ramparts. Some volleys of grape and a hot musketry fire checked the assailants, and Kozynski, at the head of 300 Poles, sallied out from the town and drove the enemy at the point of the bayonet into the suburb of Rheims; here the Russians rallied, but a fresh charge drove them clear of the houses into the open country. A short time later the enemy made a second attack with equal lack of success. The bombardment was resumed, and lasted till 10 p.m. Both artillery and infantry had behaved well, and the little garrison of Soissons lost twenty-three killed and 123 wounded. The enemy had also lost heavily, but owing to the number of his troops his loss did not seriously weaken him.

Meanwhile Winzingerode and Bülow had heard the sound of guns in the direction of the Ourcq, and were far from being easy in their minds. Matters were not going as they had hoped. The resistance offered by the garrison forced them to give up the hope of capturing the place by a *coup de main,* as they had done on February 14; and, on the other hand, twelve hours' continued bombardment had not succeeded in making a breach.

The wall was hardly damaged, and even when it was de-stroyed the earth behind would be found to be frozen as hard as stone; the rampart would need another twelve or thirty-six hours' bombardment before a breach would be practicable. At the earliest the assault could not take place before March 4, and then it might not succeed. Under the prevailing conditions, when the possession of the bridge was urgently needed, it was necessary to capture the place at once. The two generals thought that perhaps negotiations might give the town into their hands, and Bülow consequently sent a flag of truce.

Captain Mertens appeared at the gate of Croüy and demand-ed to be taken to the governor. Moreau received him in his private room, but broke off negotiations as soon as he heard Mertens's terms. Instead, however, of dismissing the envoy in a way calculated to show his determination not to receive a second messenger, he merely said to him, "I cannot reply to ver-bal propositions made by an officer who brings no credentials." Mertens understood this to be an invitation to him to come back with fuller powers, and within an hour he was back again, bringing the following letter from Bülow:

> Your Excellency has desired that I should write to him on the subject of a proposition which I had made verbally through one of my *aides-de-camp*. I am quite willing to make this second attempt in order to prove to your Excel-lency how much I desire to avoid useless bloodshed and to spare Soissons the terrible fate of a captured city. I propose to your Excellency, in concert with the Commander of the Russian army, that we should draw up a capitulation according to terms which circumstances permit us to gain for ourselves and to grant to you. I count upon receiving your reply before daybreak.

An energetic officer who was determined to resist would not have received the envoy a second time. As we have seen, Soissons was not yet in a desperate situation: the ramparts were almost untouched, and the garrison, which had only lost a tenth of its numbers in twelve hours' fighting, had displayed the greatest gallantry; supplies were abundant, and before morning the embrasures could have been repaired and the dismounted guns again rendered serviceable.

Further, during the evening the sound of guns had been heard from the direction of the Ourcq; and this fact, which was of such importance to the besieged town, ought to have made him reject the idea of an early surrender. At any rate he could, without danger, have put off the negotiations till the following day, and he would thereby have gained eight hours of darkness during which there was little to fear from the enemy; if on the following morning it had appeared impossible to continue the defence, it would then have been time enough to negotiate for a surrender. Moreau proved himself, if not actually guilty, to be at any rate unwise, in receiving the hostile envoy for the second time.

Captain Mertens was a diplomatic and skilful talker. He began by praising the courage of the garrison and of its commander. Then he pointed out the small number of French troops, the weakness of their artillery, the large perimeter to be defended, and the bad state of the fortifications; and he ended by pointing to the numbers of the allies, in which matter he had no need to exaggerate. Finally Mertens said that honour was satisfied, and that the commandant of the place would incur the gravest responsibility if he persisted in a useless defence, which would only expose the town to be pillaged and burnt after the inevitable assault. Moreau, as in duty bound, replied at first by the usual formula that rather than surrender he would be buried beneath the ruins of his ramparts.

The Prussian, however, was not the least disconcerted by these brave words, which were contradicted by Moreau's obvious hesitation and irresolution; he replied by lavishing fresh praise on the gallantry of the garrison, and informed Moreau that his brave troops would be allowed to march out with all the honours of war and that they would be free to rejoin the French army and to fight again under happier conditions.

It is probable that if the proposed terms had been too hard if, for instance, they had insisted on the garrison becoming prisoners of war or of surrendering their arms Moreau would have resisted to the last. The conditions offered, however, were such as to make Moreau weigh against each other the doubtful advantages of a hopeless defence and the certain gain to the French armies of a prompt capitulation. Within two, or at most three, days Soissons would certainly be captured by assault, and the survivors of the garrison would be made prisoners. Would it not be better to abandon this place, which was bound to be lost in the end, and to save to the Emperor a thousand seasoned soldiers who would be of the greatest service to him?

This argument was the emptiest of sophistries, but the Governor of Soissons allowed himself to be swayed by it. Moreau had been sent to Soissons in order to hold the town, which was a place of strategical importance, and not in order to preserve a handful of soldiers for the field army. His orders were to defend Soissons, and it was not his business to criticize them; his duty was to carry out his orders to the letter, and on this point the regulations enjoined that "he should exhaust every means of defence; he should pay no attention to intelligence communicated by the enemy, and should oppose the besiegers' insinuations as stoutly as his attacks."

The fact that he had heard the sound of guns during the day ought to have nerved the governor to the most determined resistance. It seems, indeed, as if the sound of this cannonade had been sent in order to remind the general of the following extract from a decree of Napoleon's dealing with the defence of fortresses:

> The governor of a fortress must remember that he is defending one of the main avenues of our empire and one of the bases of our armies, and that the postponement of the fall of a fortress by a single day may be a fact of the first importance to the defence of the State and the safety of the army.

When a soldier begins to have doubts as to where his duty lies, he is in imminent danger of considering nothing but his own interests. Moreau was a brave man under the Empire no one reached the higher ranks unless he was a brave man but he was not a hero, and he did not relish the idea of sacrificing himself for a cause which he, in common with many other generals of the time, regarded as lost. He considered that an honourable capitulation which would save the town from the horror of pillage and preserve a fine body of troops for the Emperor, would suit his personal interest and would cast no reflection upon his honour as a soldier.

Moreau asked for a delay of some hours in order to call together the council of defence; Captain Mertens raised no objection to this delay and returned to the Prussian lines. It then occurred to Moreau to climb to the top of the Cathedral Tower, in order, as he put it, "to verify the reports he had received as to the enemy's strength."

When we remember Moreau's attitude during the negotiations and consider his character, we cannot help coming to the conclusion that, when he climbed those 354 steps in order to examine the enemy's positions for the last time, the commandant of Soissons was more anxious to find some justification for a prompt surrender than to see whether a further defence might not be possible. Moreau's guilty imagination showed him many things which did not exist; he writes:

> At this moment I saw shells set the town on fire in several places, and I could make out wagons laden with scaling ladders ready for the assault.

In view of the truce agreed upon between the general and the Prussian representative, it is most unlikely that the bombardment had been reopened at this moment, and it has been shown elsewhere that the besiegers were not yet preparing for an assault. Further, Moreau states that he climbed the tower at dawn; at the beginning of March dawn is not till after 5 a.m., and at 3 o'clock Moreau had returned from the Cathedral and was presiding over the council of defence. It seems certain, then, that Moreau can have seen nothing from his observatory except the light of a few bivouac fires.

After having returned from the Cathedral, Moreau assembled the council of defence, laid before them Bülow's letter, and explained his view of the situation. Each member of the council was invited to state his opinion, and Colonel Saint Hillier, the chief engineer, as the junior member, replied first. He started by asking Colonel Strols, the commander of the artillery, how much ammunition was left, and received the reply that there were three thousand rounds of gun ammunition and two hundred thousand musket cartridges.

Saint Hillier then gave it as his opinion that the defence should be prolonged; the enemy had not effected a breach, and it would probably take them two days to do so, and, even if the garrison had suffered some loss, it was still strong enough to hold out and was in good spirits; further, they had heard that evening the distant sound of guns, which probably indicated the approach of a relieving army: it was their bounden duty, then, to prolong the defence for at least twenty-four hours, and in his opinion it was possible for them to do so. Saint Hillier was afterwards blamed by the court of inquiry because he lacked the courage to say openly the whole of what he thought; he realized that there was probably some connection between the cannonade which they had heard and the eagerness with which the allies desired an immediate surrender, and though he appreciated the fact that the surrender of Soissons might have the most serious effect on the general course of operations, yet he did not suggest this point of view to the council.

Colonel Kozynski, who commanded the infantry, and who had been wounded during the sortie on the previous day, warmly supported Saint Hillier's opinion that they ought to hold out to the last extremity. Colonel Strols, who spoke next, was also in favour of resistance, but he spoke without enthusiasm and without conviction. Colonel Bouchard, the commandant of Soissons, was the only member of the council in favour of surrender.

General Moreau was a weak man; an hour ago he had been won over by the specious words of Mertens, and now he was fired by the determination of the majority of his council. Saint Hillier again insisted that whether they negotiated or whether they fought, they must at any rate hold out for not less than twenty-four hours longer. Moreau and his council agreed, and it was decided that they should ask for time for consideration. Bouchard drafted a reply to Bülow, and the council began to disperse.

Saint Hillier was the first to leave the room, and had hardly gone when a fresh envoy was announced. This time it was Colonel Lowenstern, who had left the Russian cantonments at 1 o'clock, and had found great difficulty in gaining admittance to the town. All the members of the council except Saint Hillier were still present, and Moreau reopened the meeting, and introduced the envoy. Lowenstern had brought the following letter from Winzingerode:

"Before ordering the assault, and in hopes of saving Soissons from the horrors of pillage and massacre, I suggest that you should surrender the town to the united army of North Germany. Military honour does not demand a resistance against such an overpowering force, and the responsibility for the inevitable results of such a resistance must rest with the commandant of the fortress."

This summons, with its suggestions of immediate assault, of pillage, and of massacre, threw Moreau once more into alarm, and made Colonel Strols uneasy; as to Colonel Bouchard, he had already declared himself in favour of surrender. In the absence of Saint Hillier, Kozynski found himself alone in recommending resistance, and as he was a foreigner his advice did not carry much weight. Lowenstern saw the effect produced by the letter, and lost no time in saying: "In two hours we shall be in the town, cost what it may. Consider, gentlemen, that in a battle quarter is given to the conquered, but after an assault all are put to the sword. Soissons and its inhabitants will become the prey of our soldiers."

Moreau then took Lowenstern aside and told him that he was ready to capitulate, provided that the town was not pillaged or called upon to pay any indemnity and that the garrison was allowed to march out with their arms and effects. Lowenstern was ready to grant any conditions, provided that the town was evacuated; he went back to the Russian head-quarters, and returned almost at once with the following letter from Winzingerode:

> General, I agree to your proposals, subject to the stipulation that our troops shall at once take possession of the gates on the Rheims and Laon roads. You will leave the town, taking with you two guns with their ammunition wagons, and the transport which belongs to the troops; you will march not later than 4 p.m. by the road to Compiegne.

Moreau laid this letter before the council of defence, which passed a resolution to the effect that:

> In view of the weakness of the garrison, the lack of resources of the fortress, and the strength of the besiegers, resistance was obviously impossible, and, in consequence, the enemy's proposals ought to be accepted.

The advice of the council in no way relieved Moreau of responsibility. A council of defence is purely consultative; the regulations were definite on this point:

> The governor, after hearing the opinion of his council, will formulate his plan on his own responsibility, without being obliged to follow the voice of the majority. He will adopt the boldest and most determined proposal unless it is absolutely impracticable.

Far from adopting the boldest and most determined proposal, that given two hours earlier by Saint Hillier, who was not present at this last meeting of the council, Moreau lost no time in telling Lowenstern and Mertens that he was ready to sign the capitulation.

Meanwhile the day had come. The troops began to be

alarmed by the passing of the envoys, and the silence of the enemy's guns; they began to suspect that the town was going to be surrendered; and as their suspicions grew, murmurs of indignation were heard, not only from the soldiers, but also among the civil population. Suddenly, at about 9 o'clock on the 3rd, a furious cannonade was heard from the direction of the Ourcq. This sound caused an outburst of rage and despair. People realized that the Emperor was at hand, and demanded that the negotiations should be broken off, or the capitulation torn up if it had been already signed.

At this moment the signatures had only just been placed to the capitulation. Difficulties had arisen as to the number of guns to be taken by the garrison; Moreau wished to take six, and Winzingerode had said two. Negotiations were in danger of being broken off when Lowenstern took upon himself the responsibility of agreeing to Moreau's request. Moreau had barely signed his name when the sound of artillery was distinctly heard; Moreau grew pale, and grasped Lowenstern's arm: "I am lost, you have deceived me. The battle is approaching, Blücher is in full retreat, and the Emperor would have driven him into the Aisne if I had not surrendered. I am a lost man, the Emperor will shoot me."

Lowenstern admitted that he was touched by the General's grief: "I could not, however, say much to comfort him," he says; "he would have made a fine figure in history if he had held out, but he thought of nothing but saving his troops."

When Lowenstern returned to the Russian head-quarters with the capitulation in his pocket, Winzingerode threw his arms round him and embraced him. When Lowenstern apologized for having allowed the French to take the six guns, General Woronzoff, who was present, and who had heard the cannonade, exclaimed: "They may take all their guns and my own too, as long as they only go."

In accordance with the terms of the capitulation, the Poles had to hand over the gates on the Rheims and Laon roads at once; and they were so exasperated that they were with difficulty restrained from attacking the allies who came to relieve them. At about 3 o'clock Winzingerode, who was impatient to take possession of the town, entered Soissons at the head of two battalions; as he entered the Rue des Cordeliers he found himself face to face with Kozynski's Poles. "You still here," he said to the colonel, whose arm was in a sling.

"We do not leave till 4 o'clock," replied Kozynski, "and if you don't retire at once, we'll fire on you."

Winzingerode, pulling out his watch, replied, "That is true"; then turning to his officers he said, "About turn, gentlemen."

At 4 o'clock, however, the town had to be evacuated; the troops with their artillery and baggage marched with drums beating in front of the enemy's staff, which saluted them as they passed. When Winzingerode saw the small number of French he asked Moreau why the main body of his division was not following his advance-guard. "Those are all the troops I have got," replied Moreau. Winzingerode's words were an unconscious tribute to the bravery of the small garrison of Soissons.

The allies did not wait for the French to leave in order to make use of the advantages which the capitulation gave them. At midday Bülow began the construction of a second bridge under the guns of the town opposite the Rheims suburb. This bridge was completed during the night, and a third bridge was commenced on the following morning, the 4th; so the allies had in all, counting the bridge at Soissons, four bridges available in the neighbourhood of the fortress.

At midday Blücher, having heard of the capture of Soissons, issued fresh orders; he gave up the idea of building a bridge across the Aisne, and, on Müffling's advice, directed his baggage to move on Soissons instead of on Berry-au-Bac; and the corps commanders were also ordered to march direct upon that town. Blücher arrived there himself, with Sacken's advance-guard, between 4 and 5 o'clock in the afternoon of the 3rd.

Winzingerode and Bülow visited the Field-Marshal, expecting to be congratulated on the success they had just gained. Blücher, however, was angry that his orders had not been carried out, and was also annoyed that the turn of events had placed him under an obligation to his two subordinates; he received the two generals very coldly, and did not deign to mention the capture of Soissons. Bülow had his revenge for this reception, for when he saw the exhausted and disorganized troops marching behind Blücher, he said out loud and without a smile, "A little rest will do no harm to these gentry."

Although night was falling, the troops began at once to cross the Aisne by the Soissons bridge, and the passage continued during the whole of the following day and the succeeding night, by means of this bridge and the other three temporary ones. Winzingerode's troops crossed first, followed by the corps of Sacken and York; then came Kapzéwitsch's troops, the command of which was assumed by Langeron, who arrived during the night; Kleist's corps came next, and finally the rear-guard, composed of cavalry and horse artillery. On the morning of March 5 there remained on the left bank of the Aisne two regiments of infantry and six of Cossacks; the majority of the Cossacks crossed at Berry-au-Bac, and the remainder, with the infantry, managed, with great difficulty, to get across at Vailly.

Meanwhile Napoleon and Marmont, who did not know of the surrender of Soissons, had continued their march in pursuit of Blücher's army. On March 4 the Emperor arrived at Fismes with the Old Guard, Ney's corps, and the cavalry of the Guard, thus blocking the road to Berry-au-Bac, while one brigade of cavalry advanced towards Rheims, from which it drove the enemy during the night. On the left, Marmont and Mortier crossed the Ourcq at 6.30 a.m., and their cavalry pursued the Russian rear-guard to within five miles of Soissons. When they reached Hartennes the marshals learnt of the capitulation, and Marmont stopped the pursuit and wrote to Berthier as follows:

This regrettable event, which deprives us of the success we were on the point of achieving, is bound to alter the Emperor's plans. Consequently it seems to me no longer necessary to move my whole force to Soissons, I will await the Emperor's further orders here.

It was from this letter that Napoleon, during the night of March 4-5, learnt that Soissons had capitulated. The Emperor was furious. On the following day he wrote to the Minister of War as follows:

> The enemy's situation was desperate, and we were in hopes that we should today reap the reward of several days' fatigue, but the treason or the folly of the commandant of Soissons has given this fortress to the enemy. . . . Arrest this scoundrel and the members of the council of defence; bring them before a commission of generals, and, by God, see that they are shot within twenty-four hours on the Place de Greve. It is time to make an example. See that the sentence, and the reasons which prompt it, are made public.

The members of the council were soon released, but Moreau was tried before a commission of generals, who recommended that he should be brought before a court-martial on a charge of having failed to do his utmost to defend the place. Luckily for Moreau, who was liable to the death penalty, the report of the commission was dated March 24, only five days before the allies reached Paris. In the chaos and demoralisation which ensued the matter was not pressed. Moreau was released by the Provisional Government, and lost no time in espousing the cause of the Bourbons. He was given further command, and died in retirement in 1828.

The Emperor's anger was natural; he himself said that the capitulation of Soissons saved Blücher's army; Marmont was of opinion that the fate of France and the issue of the campaign turned upon Soissons holding out for thirty-six hours; and Thiers has stated that, next to the battle of Waterloo, the capitulation of Soissons is the most disastrous event of French history. These opinions are perhaps exaggerated, but it cannot be denied that the surrender of this town saved Blücher's army from disaster. This conclusion is drawn from French documents, and is also borne out by the majority of Russian and German papers.

As a matter of fact, Blücher would never admit that he was in great danger; to do so would have been to confess that his march on Paris was rash, and that he had been saved by his subordinates, one of whom was a Russian. Although the Russians and Prussians were allies, they were not on the best of terms, and Blücher, as commander- in-chief and as a Prussian, was not at all disposed to admit his indebtedness.

As we have seen, the Field-Marshal received Bülow very coldly; later on he expressed to the King of Prussia his dissatisfaction with the terms of his report on the capitulation, and he complained in no measured terms that Winzingerode had not carried out his orders; he asserted that instead of dallying in front of Soissons, "a miserable hole of a place," of no importance, he ought to have joined him at Oulchy; Blücher added that although he was separated from Bülow by the Aisne, and was ten or twelve miles distant from Winzingerode, yet his situation was not dangerous. Even if his rear was pressed by Marmont and Mortier, and his flank threatened by Napoleon, yet the marshals were not strong enough alone to carry through an attack against him, and he had a day's start of the Emperor. It was open to him then to escape the French, either by a bridge of boats or by Berry-au-Bac. These arguments are advanced by Müffling, Clausewitz, and Blücher's apologists.

Some of Napoleon's letters give the impression that, on the afternoon of the 4th, before hearing of the surrender of Soissons, he had given up hope of bringing Blücher to battle to the south of the Aisne, and was heading so as to intercept him at Laon. This may possibly have been the case, but, even so, it does not much affect the question of the danger to Blücher's army. If Soissons had not surrendered on the 3rd, Blücher would have retreated towards Berry-au-Bac, and would have encountered Napoleon's advance-guard at Fismes on the afternoon of the 4th.

If, on the other hand, he had thrown a bridge of boats across the river above Soissons, he would have been attacked in this neighbourhood by Marmont, and Napoleon would have moved towards the sound of the guns, and would have fallen upon the Prussians in the act of crossing the river. It is well to bear in mind that, thanks to the capitulation, the crossing of the river was carried out over four bridges, and began at 5 p.m. on the 3rd and was completed during the morning of the 5th; if the town had not surrendered, it would not have begun till the morning of the 4th, and only two bridges would have been available; consequently, on the evening of the 4th two-thirds of Blücher's army would still have been on the left bank of the river.

It is worth while examining Blücher's claim that he was twenty-four hours ahead of Napoleon. On the afternoon of the 3rd the main body of the army of Silesia was at Oulchy with its rear-guard on the Ourcq; the main body of Napoleon's army was at Château-Thierry and the advance-guard at Rocourt. Château-Thierry is fifteen miles from Oulchy and Rocourt is three miles from the Ourcq. As far as distance goes, therefore, Blücher was hardly eight hours ahead of the French, and he was likely to lose this advantage as he had to make a detour through Fismes to Berry-au-Bac, and Fismes is almost as far from Oulchy as it is from Château-Thierry.

We must remember, however, that at 4 p.m. on the 3rd the Prussian army was about to resume its march after a halt of nearly twenty-four hours, while the French had covered a long distance that day before reaching their halting-place at Bezu 4½ miles north of Château-Thierry. From this point of view it would seem that Blücher had twenty- four hours' start, but, on the other hand, his army would have been forced to bivouac at Braine after a night march of more than 20 miles and would probably not leave that place till 4 p.m. on the 4th; Napoleon, after a night's rest at Bezu, had ordered his troops to march on Fismes at daybreak, and would consequently have reached that place at the same time as Blücher.

It seems, then, that in the event of the Prussians moving on Berry-au-Bac, Blücher was very far from having the twenty-four hours' start which he had claimed. As a matter of fact, Napoleon's advance-guard was near Braine on the 4th and the Emperor himself was at Fismes on the evening of that day; also a baggage column which had left Oulchy for Berry-au-Bac at midday on the 3rd and had not received the order redirecting it on Soissons, was attacked by French cavalry between Fismes and Braine on the afternoon of the 4th. It is certain, therefore, that the army of Silesia could not have reached Berry-au-Bac without being attacked by the French. The battle would have taken place on the plateau of Fismes, and Blücher's army, exhausted and demoralized as it was, would have been exposed to the simultaneous attacks of Napoleon and Marmont: there can be little doubt as to what would have been the result.

General Moreau does not deserve to be called a traitor, but his criminal weakness had all the consequences of treason. If he had exhausted every means of defence, as the regulations ordained, he could have held out for a day longer. Saint Hillier, the chief engineer of the fortress, said that this was possible, and the court of inquiry agreed with him. If the resistance had been prolonged for twenty-four hours, Blücher could not have escaped Napoleon. Winzingerode's letter to Blücher, dated 5 a.m. on the 3rd, proves that if the place had not capitulated that day the siege would have been raised.

Even if Bülow and Winzingerode had changed their minds and had captured the place by assault on the morning of the 4th the army of Silesia could not have avoided a battle. Bülow could not have told Blücher on the 3rd that the bridge of Soissons was open to him, and consequently Blücher would have marched on Fismes and Berry-au-Bac; he would have heard of the capture of Soissons on the 4th when he was between Braine and Fismes. It is very unlikely that Blücher, who would have known of Napoleon's approach, would have exposed his army to the danger and loss of time inseparable from a countermarch. Most probably he would have continued his march and attacked Napoleon's advance-guard on the plateau of Fismes. A decisive action would then have taken place on the plateau of Fismes and all the chances would have been in favour of Napoleon.

It has been said that one should never leave one's last round unfired, because there is always a chance that it may kill the enemy, so Moreau's last round fired on the morning of March 4 from the crumbling ramparts of Soissons might perhaps have altered the whole course of the campaign.

Chapter 7

The Battle of Craonne

Since the Russian campaign Napoleon had been used to strokes of unexpected bad luck; he met them without depression of spirits or loss of resolution, and his genius never failed to devise fresh strategic combinations to replace those which had gone wrong. The loss of Soissons was a great misfortune, but the Emperor did not consider it an irretrievable disaster; he had not succeeded in bringing Blücher to book on the near side of the Aisne, but he would catch him on the far side of the river.

Napoleon knew that Winzingerode's corps had arrived to reinforce the Field-Marshal, but he believed this corps to be no stronger than it had been at the first capture of Soissons, about 15,000 men. He believed that Bülow's corps was still near Avesnes, and he expected to be able to force a battle before it could join the army of Silesia. Napoleon was afraid that Blücher might make an obstinate defence on the left bank of the Aisne, and he ordered several bridges to be extemporized so that he would not need to force a passage at Berry-au-Bac

Blücher meant to dispute the passage of the river, but he expected Napoleon to attack near Yenisei or Missy; he had not thought it necessary to occupy Berry-au-Bac in force, and had drawn up his troops with his right at Fontenoy and his left at Vailly, with some cavalry posts as far as Berry, where the bridge was defended by some regiments of Cossacks with a few infantry and a couple of guns. At 11 a.m. on March 5 Napoleon learnt from a cavalry reconnaissance that the bridge at Berry could be captured without difficulty. He immediately altered his plans, and the corps commanders were ordered to stop the construction of the bridges and to march at once to Berry-au-Bac, where the whole army would cross. Nansouty, with the Polish lancers and the 2nd division of Guard cavalry, was ordered to seize the crossing; the Cossack *vedettes* posted on the left bank retired across the bridge at a gallop, with the Poles close on their heels.

The attack was so sudden and so fierce that the enemy had no time to man their defences; both cavalry and infantry fled through the village, leaving their two guns and 200 prisoners in the hands of the French. Prince Gagarine was captured by an old sergeant of dragoons, a veteran of Egypt and Italy with twenty-three years' service, who was decorated by the Emperor on the following day. The passage was now open; Ney's corps crossed first, followed by the Old Guard under Friant, and took post between Berry-au-Bac and Corbény, with Nansouty's cavalry in advance. The other troops followed, and they were not all across until the 7th.

It was only on the evening of the 5th that Blücher learnt that the French had captured the bridge and were moving so as to intercept him at Laon, and he then decided to try to surprise Napoleon by a vigorous attack on his left flank. Several roads led towards the plateau of Craonne, which overlooked Napoleon's line of march between Berry-au-Bac and Corbény; the corps of Winzingerode, Sacken, Kleist, and York, with Langeron's cavalry, were directed on Craonne; Bülow was placed in reserve at Laon, and Rudzéwitsch, with all Langeron's infantry, remained at Soissons. On the 6th Blücher himself started for Craonne, but before he arrived there he found that his plan could not be carried out. Winzingerode had been lacking in energy, and had not succeeded in occupying in force the forest of Corbény, or the village of Craonne, which stood on the eastern edge of the plateau, and Napoleon, hearing of the enemy's movement, had occupied the village with two battalions of the Young Guard, while on the right Ney had driven back the advanced Russian troops.

If this move on the part of the French had disconcerted Blücher, Napoleon, on the other hand, found his plans upset by the allies' advance on Craonne. The Field-Marshal was forced to abandon the hope of attacking the French on the march in open country, and Napoleon had equally to give up his design of marching straight on Laon. The two commanders simultaneously adopted new roles: Blücher determined to await attack on the plateau, while Napoleon made shift to overwhelm the allies where he had found them. Blücher was lucky in finding that he had an unexpectedly strong defensive position.

Between the parallel valleys of the Aisne and the Ailette there rises a long plateau of varying width, stretching from the neighbourhood of Corbény on the east to the far side of Soissons on the west. At its eastern extremity there juts out into the plain a salient, which rises to a height of nearly 500 feet above the level of the valley; this salient is known as the small plateau of Craonne, and is joined to the main plateau by a neck which is only 150 yards wide, on which stands the farm of Hurtebise. The only road on to the main plateau leads past this farm, which is slightly below the level of the two summits. Behind the neck, the north and south sides of the plateau are very steep, falling on the north towards the valley of the Ailette, and on the south towards the valley of Foulon, the head of which is so precipitous that it is known as the Trou d'Enfer.

Seeing that the plateau could only be attacked from the narrow neck, Blücher decided that it was not necessary to occupy it with his whole army; a force of 30,000 men, supported by a strong body of artillery, would be sufficient, and the remainder of his troops would be available to make a turning movement to take the French in the rear. Count Woronzoff, one of Winzingerode's subordinates, was ordered to defend the plateau with 16,300 infantry, 2,200 horsemen, and 96 guns, and this force was supported by Sacken's three divisions of 13,500 men.

A force of 10,000 cavalry with 60 light guns was obtained by massing the remainder of Winzingerode's cavalry with that belonging to the corps of Langeron and Yorck. This cavalry corps, together with Kleist's corps, was placed under Winzingerode's orders, and he was directed to cross to the north of the Ailette, and to make a wide turning movement through Festieux, so as to attack Napoleon in the rear on the following day.

While Blücher was issuing these orders, fighting was going on on the little plateau. When the two battalions of the Guard had driven the Russians from the village of Craonne, one of the battalions had advanced on to the open plateau, where it had been charged by Paulowgrad's hussars and driven back again into the village. Meunier's small division, led by Ney in person, had captured the abbey of Vauclerc in the valley of the Ailette, and had followed the retreating Russians as far as the farm of Hurtebise; this place had been captured and recaptured three times, when Ney decided at 7 o'clock to evacuate it. Meunier's division bivouacked to the south of the Ailette, and Boyer's brigade at Bouconville.

Napoleon's head-quarters were between Berry-au-Bac and Corbény, and in this neighbourhood were the bivouacs of the 1st and 2nd Divisions of Guard cavalry, Roussel's cavalry division, Friant's Old Guard, and Boyer de Rebeval's and Curial's divisions. Strong outposts were on the Laon road and on the little plateau. Part of the artillery with Charpentier's and Arrighi's divisions had not yet crossed the bridge. Marmont and Mortier were still far away, Mortier at Cormicy and Marmont at Braine, for they had not received the order to rejoin the Emperor till the afternoon of the 5th, at which time they were in front of Soissons, and had just made an unsuccessful attack on the suburbs, losing 800 men.

In the evening Napoleon prepared his attack for the following day; he had maps, but according to his custom he wished to supplement them with local information. The postmaster of Berry-au-Bac said that M. de Bussy, the Mayor of Beaurieux, who had formerly served as an officer, was the very man for the purpose; Napoleon, who had a marvellous memory for names, remembered that he had had, in the artillery regiment of La Fere, a comrade of the name of De Bussy; a cavalry escort was sent to the Mayor of Beaurieux, and he arrived in the middle of the night. After a friendly greeting Napoleon explained to him his plan of attack. The Emperor intended to make an artillery demonstration against the neck of Hurtebise in order to make the Russians think that he was preparing a frontal attack. During this bombardment Ney's troops were to climb the slopes of the plateau behind Hurtebise and fall upon the enemy's left flank, while Nansouty's cavalry, with some batteries of light artillery, were to climb the plateau from the southward and make a vigorous demonstration against the enemy's right.

The Emperor expected that the Russians would find themselves out-flanked on both wings. De Bussy pointed out that the route laid down for Ney's column was too much to the eastward, and that the proper direction of his attack was through the village of Ailles. The Emperor agreed, and sent fresh orders to Ney. De Bussy was reinstated in the army with the rank of colonel of artillery, and was directed to guide Nansouty's cavalry on the left flank. The reports received during the night were to the effect that the bulk of the Russian troops were moving towards the rear, and Napoleon was under the impression that there was nothing in front of him but a rear-guard, which he would be able to disperse without difficulty.

On the following morning, March 7, at about 8 o'clock, the Emperor rode up to the small plateau in order to examine the enemy's position. On the main plateau the Russians had already formed up in three lines of battalion columns: the first line, fourteen battalions strong, stretched across the road opposite the farm of Hurtebise, and 1,200 yards distant from it, with its left on the edge of the plateau, and its right overlooking the valley of Foulon. The second line was composed of seven battalions, and the third of nine, and they were drawn up 500 and 1,000 yards respectively in rear of the first line.

The farm of Hurtebise was occupied by 800 men with two squadrons in support. On the right of the first line Paulowgrad's Hussars, with four regiments of Cossacks, were ready to charge any attackers who might climb the southern slopes of the plateau. Some two miles in rear of the third line were massed Sacken's 4,000 cavalry, and the remainder of his corps formed the general reserve. Thirty-six guns commanded the neck, and were supported by twelve more posted farther to the southward; on the left wing eighteen guns were trained on the valley of the Ailette, and a reserve of twenty more were posted between the second and third lines.

There had been a hard frost during the night, and the ground was very slippery; the artillery horses could not keep their feet, and the leading French batteries did not reach the little plateau till between 9 and 10 o'clock. In his impatience to engage the enemy's attention, the Emperor ordered fire to be opened at once; the Russian batteries replied, but very little damage was done on either side, for the distance of 2,500 yards was beyond the effective range of the guns of the period.

Blücher had spent the night at Braye, and was at this time on the plateau ready to assume the offensive as soon as the sound of Winzingerode's guns should tell him that the turning movement was taking effect. At 10 o'clock he learnt from an orderly that the main cavalry column, which, according to his calculations, ought to have arrived at Festieux, had not yet left the valley of the Ailette. Blücher immediately left Sacken in command, and hurried off to hasten Winzingerode's march.

At the moment when Blücher left the plateau, Ney, hearing the sound of the guns, launched his columns to the attack. On the right Boyer's brigade marched on Allies, and on the left Meunier's division, supported by Curial's, moved under the cover of woods to the foot of the slopes, and commenced the steep ascent. The French advance was reported by skirmishers who lined the crest of the plateau, and the Russians opened a hot fire of musketry and artillery against the attacking columns. Ney's soldiers succeeded in reaching the plateau, but were soon driven off, and re-formed a short distance down the slope ready for a fresh assault. At the extreme right of the enemy's line, the 1st and 2nd Divisions of Guard cavalry were climbing the slopes, moving in single file along steep paths, and progress was slow.

At this time the Emperor had only Friant's division available, and the moment had not yet arrived for the employment of these veterans, whom he spared much more than he spared himself. At last Victor arrived with Boyer de Rebeval's division of the Young Guard. The Emperor ordered him to work round the northern slopes beyond the farm of Hurtebise, and to prolong the left of Ney's troops, who had already attempted a second assault. The Russian garrison of the farm were in danger of being cut off, and retired to the main plateau, after having set fire to the buildings. The thick smoke from the burning barns allowed Boyer de Rebeval's division to deploy without much loss, and to reach the edge of the plateau. The neck being now clear, Napoleon ordered forward four batteries which took post on Boyer's left. The artillery opened fire, but the gunners were untrained, and suffered heavily from the fire of the better-served Russian guns.

The enemy, however, were shaken by Ney's repeated attacks, and Woronzoff drew back his left wing. Victor took advantage of this move to advance his division about 1,000 yards to the farther side of a small copse, known as the Marion Wood. During this advance Victor was severely wounded in the thigh and the command devolved on Boyer de Rebeval: this general found his division exposed in the open to the concentrated fire of the whole Russian army, and he did not dare either to advance or to retire; an advance would have thrown his division to no purpose against an overwhelming force of the enemy, and a retirement to the shelter of the wood would have involved a serious risk of panic.

The conscripts were already much shaken and would have broken on the slightest provocation. The general did not even dare to deploy his division, but kept his battalions in mass under the close fire of the Russian guns. The young soldiers behaved better than might have been expected, but they lost terribly; the 14th Light Infantry lost 30 officers out of 33, and the regiment was mown down like a field of corn.

At last reinforcements crossed the Hurtebise neck; they consisted of Sparre's brigade of dragoons whom Grouchy sent forward as soon as they arrived. The dragoons came out from behind the corner of the Marion Wood and charged the guns on the enemy's left; the artillerymen were sabred and the twelve guns captured. While Grouchy was capturing this battery, at the other end of the line Nansouty had succeeded in forming up Colbert and Exelman's divisions of cavalry and threw them against the enemy's right; they overthrew the Cossacks and Paulowgrad's hussars and charged two Russian battalions, who were driven back almost to Paissy; men and horses were mingled in an inextricable disorder and would have been driven into a precipitous ravine had not one of the reserve batteries suddenly opened fire and checked the advance of the French.

Woronzoff's centre was still intact, but he had abandoned the advanced post of Hurtebise, his right flank was driven in, and his left was with difficulty holding its own against the charges of Grouchy's dragoons supported by Ney and Boyer's infantry. Woronzoff's orders were to hold his ground to the last so as to gain time for the development of Winzingerode's flank attack. A counter-attack was imperative.

On the right the Russian battalions and squadrons, rallying under the fire of the reserve artillery, drove back Nansouty to the heights overlooking Vassoigne. On the left two regiments of infantry attacked Grouchy's dragoons with the bayonet; the cavalry were driven back on to the battery which they had just captured and were forced to abandon the guns; as they re-formed in front of Boyer's division, Grouchy and Sparre were wounded almost at the same moment, and finding themselves without leaders the dragoons remained inactive under the Russian grape shot. Woronzoff sent forward a fresh brigade from the third line, which advanced with the bayonet against these squadrons; the dragoons fled and carried back with them Boyer's infantry.

The panic spread to Ney's young soldiers, and they too broke and fled, in spite of the exhortations of the marshal, who used the flat of his sword freely in his efforts to stem the rout. Both horse and foot fled in disorder into the valley of the Ailette, and the main plateau was almost entirely abandoned. For the fifth or sixth time the French were driven from the heights which they had captured with such heavy loss.

For some time past the Emperor had been receiving constant appeals for reinforcements from Ney and Boyer. "We can hardly hold out any longer," said Boyer. "Many guns have been dismounted and there are so many wounded that our infantry fire is negligible." The fault was that Ney had launched his attack the moment he heard the first guns and before Napoleon had collected enough troops, and no reinforcements had yet reached the field of battle. At last, at 1 o'clock, La Ferrière's cavalry division, Charpentier's infantry, and the reserve artillery reached the small plateau, and the decisive moment arrived.

La Ferrière's division crossed the neck of Hurtebise at a gallop and threw themselves against the centre of the enemy's line; they were driven back, but their furious attack had gained time for Charpentier's division to come up in line with Boyer's shattered battalions, which were re-forming in front of the Marion Wood. At the same moment Ney's troops again seized the edge of the plateau on the right, and on the south the three cavalry divisions, 4,500 strong, advanced in line.

Finally, amid the cheers of the whole army, 72 guns of the guard and reserve artillery issued at a trot from the Hurtebise neck and passed through the intervals between brigades; the guns came quickly into action in front of the infantry and opened fire on the Russians, and at the same time Napoleon himself arrived in the line of battle.

The Russians now stood in urgent need of a diversion on the part of Winzingerode's troops. If the Russian cavalry had arrived they would have been reported by the Polish lancers who were in observation on the Laon road, and they would have been opposed by Roussel's 2nd brigade, in occupation of Corbény, and by Arrighi's division and Marmont and Mortier's corps, which were by this time between Berry-au-Bac and Craonne. It seems very probable, then, that Blücher's manoeuvre would not have obtained the result which he had hoped from it, namely, the overthrow of the French army.

As a matter of fact, the diversion never took place, for the bad state of the roads made it almost impossible for the turning force to arrive in time. Winzingerode had not shown sufficient energy, and the route which he was ordered to follow was not the shortest possible.

When Blücher learnt during the morning that Winzingerode was still some twelve miles away from where he expected him to have arrived, he hurried off at once to hasten the march of the column, but where Winzingerode, whom Blücher described as the greatest bungler in Europe, had not succeeded, the Field-Marshal had also failed. The muddy lanes of the Ailette valley, where the frost had had little effect, and the slippery roads on the surrounding hills, proved difficult for the cavalry and impassable for artillery. To make matters worse, Kleist's infantry also arrived in the valley, and all these troops were jumbled together in a fearful confusion.

Finding that all his efforts were in vain, and hearing the guns on the plateau, Blücher saw that Winzingerode's flanking movement was bound to be too late; he decided to concentrate his army at Laon, and sent orders to Sacken to retire. This order reached Sacken at 1.30, and he sent it on to Woronzoff on the field of battle. That general at first replied that, as he had already held out for five hours, he felt confident of being able to stand his ground till nightfall, and this would involve less loss than a retreat across the open plateau without the aid of cavalry. Sacken sent him peremptory orders to retire and added that he would send forward his 4,000 horsemen to cover the movement.

The French by now had formed line across the plateau parallel to the Russians, who, as they retired, found themselves under a heavy artillery fire from the front while their right was threatened by the French cavalry and their left by Pierre Boyer's Spanish veterans who were vigorously attacking the village of Ailles and the heights overlooking it. Whether Woronzoff wished it or not, he would have been forced to retire. At first the retreat was carried out in very good order; the Russians retired slowly in squares, carrying off their dismounted guns and some of their wounded. One Russian brigadier, General Ponset, who had not yet recovered from a wound received at Leipzig, refused at first to retreat, and when General Wuitzch, the commander of the first line, galloped up to see why his order was not being carried out, he exclaimed; "I will die where I stand, but I will not retreat an inch."

General Wuitzch replied with the utmost calmness, "If your Excellency wants to die here I have no objection, but I must insist that your brigade retires at once."

One regiment even, instead of retiring, dashed forward against the French guns, and narrowly escaped being captured.

The French attacks were pressed more vigorously as the retreat went on. The threatening attitude of the French cavalry forced Woronzoff to retreat rapidly to the high ground in front of Cerny, a mile and a half from his first position. At this place he put 24 guns in line and for some time kept the French in check. Although the plateau narrowed at this point, the Russian right was exposed to the attacks of the French cavalry, who easily overpowered Woronzoff's few squadrons. Luckily Sacken's 4,000 horsemen arrived in time to succour this flank by means of frequent charges.

Thanks to this diversion, the Russian infantry was able to continue the retirement in good order, but they tried in vain to make a fresh stand at Cerny. Sacken's cavalry were driven back, but rallied behind a line of 36 guns which that general had established some 1,500 yards behind Cerny. Woronzoff withdrew his infantry to either side of this line of guns, which succeeded in checking the French cavalry.

In less than half an hour, however, the Russian guns were reduced to silence and the French advance continued. While the bulk of Woronzoff's troops continued to retire along the plateau, several battalions moved down a hollow road which led into the Ailette valley; they suffered heavily and were nearly headed off by one of Ney's divisions, but succeeded in joining General Langeron's force in the valley. On the plateau the French drove the enemy back as far as the main road to Laon, when darkness put an end to the pursuit.

Thus ended the fierce and bloody battle of Craonne; some positions were only captured after six assaults; neither guns nor prisoners were taken, and one quarter of the men engaged were killed or wounded; the Russians lost 5,000, the French 5,400 men, and among the wounded were Victor, Grouchy, and seven other generals.

Napoleon's correspondence agrees with the *Moniteur* in describing the battle of Craonne as a great victory, in which the French defeated the whole Russian army, capturing guns and prisoners, and placing many men hors de combat, with a loss of only 800. The majority of French historians, among others Thiers, say that Napoleon with 30,000 men captured a formidable position defended by an army of 50,000.

The Russian and German historians, on the other hand, give a very different account, and describe the battle as merely a rearguard action, in which Woronzoff with 15,000 held at bay twice that number of the enemy, and only abandoned his position on Blücher's express orders. They describe March 7 as being a most glorious day for the Russian arms and the battle as being a "notable victory."

To describe the battle as a notable victory is ludicrous. The stubborn defence of a defile, followed by an orderly retreat, is not a thing to be ashamed of, but the loss of a formidable position to an enemy of equal numbers, followed by a rear-guard action extending over eight miles, cannot be described as a victory. The Russians also assert that the defenders of the plateau numbered 15,000, and the attackers 30,000. The truth is that Napoleon had 20,000 men actually engaged against 22,500. The opposing forces, then, were practically equal, and there were not two Frenchmen to three Russians as believed in France, nor one Russian to two Frenchmen as the Russian historians claim.

When Woronzoff received the order to retreat he had lost very little ground. For this reason the Russian general thought himself justified in claiming that he retired because he was ordered to and not because the French forced him to do so. When we remember the different events of the battle, however, there is no doubt that Woronzoff would anyhow have been forced to retreat. Between 2 and 2.30, before he ordered the retirement, the Russians were already beginning to give way.

The French attack, which had hitherto been disjointed, was at this time becoming general; the Emperor was throwing into the fight 72 guns and 10,000 fresh troops, and the infantry of Ney, Boyer, and Charpentier and Colbert's, Exelman's, and La Ferrière's cavalry were deploying on the plateau while the Old Guard was close at hand ready to take part in the battle. Woronzoff was forgetting that he had been opposed by only 6,000 troops at first, increased before long to 10,000, and that now a reinforcement of 10,000 men had just reached the French, and that whereas at first he had been defending an almost impregnable position, from this time onwards the battle was to take place on open ground.

There is no doubt that the Russian resistance would have been more stubborn if they had not been ordered to retire, and it is possible that the retreat might have been put off for a couple of hours, but from the moment when the French army formed line upon the plateau the battle was virtually won.

CHAPTER 8

The First Day of the Battle of Laon

"As false as the official account of a battle" was a common phrase during the latter days of the Empire. It was not Napoleon's vanity, however, which made his dispatches deviate so far from the truth. After the glorious days of Montmirail and Vauchamps he wrote to the Duc de Rovigo, " You must have lost your heads in Paris to say that we were one against three; I make a point of saying that I have 300,000 men; the enemy believes this to be true, and we must lose no opportunity of saying so.

This is the way in which you, by a stroke of the pen, throw away all the results of my victory. You must know that this is not a question of vainglory, and that one of the first principles of war is to exaggerate one's strength. It is not easy, however, to impress this fact upon poets, whose only desire is to flatter me and to pander to national pride." In the same way it was not with a view to magnifying his own achievements that on the day following the battle of Craonne Napoleon ordered it to be generally given out that he had beaten all that remained of the Russian army; he hoped by this means to relieve public opinion and to deceive Schwarzenberg, who was not in communication with Blücher.

But Napoleon did not deceive himself, and he saw quite clearly that only one portion of the allied army had been engaged at Craonne. He was led to believe that the stubborn defence of this position was intended by Blücher to hide either a retreat on Avesnes or a fresh movement on Paris *via* Laon, La

Fère, and the right bank of the Oise. Even before the battle the abandonment of the line of the Aisne had made him think that Blücher was trying to slip away. In either case, whether Blücher was retreating to the north or whether he was advancing on Paris, Laon would have been selected as a point of concentration and not as a defensive position; it would therefore only be occupied by a rear-guard, and might be captured by a *coup de main*, or at any rate by an assault.

Napoleon no longer had hopes, as he had had a week earlier, of being able to "exterminate the army of Silesia." The heavy losses which the French had suffered at Craonne, when they were opposed by only a part of Blücher's army, showed that it would be no easy task to beat the united forces of the enemy. If, however, he could seize Laon, defeat the enemy's rear-guard again and drive Blücher away from his line of operations, it would be a not unsuccessful result of the campaign; he would have freed Paris, driven off the Prussians, and alarmed the allies, and he would then be able to rally the garrisons of the north-eastern fortresses, and with this reinforcement he would fall upon the right flank of Schwarzenberg's army, while Augereau attacked their left *via* Bourg and Vesoul.

There were two roads which the Emperor could use to reach Laon; the Soissons road which approaches Laon on the south-west, and the Rheims road which leads into the town from the north-east. On the evening after the battle of Craonne the bulk of the Emperor's army was on the former road and Marmont's corps on the latter, and the Emperor decided to use both roads. This was a dangerous manoeuvre, for it violated the principle of strategy that concentration should be effected beyond reach of the enemy. It was quicker to move in two columns, however, and Napoleon did not expect to find Blücher in force at Laon.

The orders were issued during the morning of March 8. Marmont was given the command of the right column, which consisted of the 6th Corps, the 1st Cavalry Corps, and Arrighi's division, a total strength of about 9,500. Roussel's dragoons and the whole of the guard, with Mortier's divisions, formed the left column, which was commanded by the Emperor in person. These troops, after deducting losses, amounted to only 27,000 men. Colbert's cavalry, which led the advance, drove back the enemy's rear-guard as far as Etouvelles. At this place the road ran across marshy ground which was impassable to cavalry, and the defile was defended by four regiments of Russian infantry with twelve guns.

The French cavalry were checked, and halted until one of Ney's divisions should clear the way. The marshy ground, however, presented great difficulties to the deployment of infantry, and Ney retired to Urcel to wait for further orders. According to his usual custom the Emperor questioned the local inhabitants, and he learnt from them of a road which led round the right side of the defile. Gourgaud, a squadron leader and one of the Emperor's orderly officers, was ordered to turn the position with two battalions of the Old Guard and 300 cavalry, while Ney's infantry were to attack it in front; as soon as the defile had been captured, Roussel's dragoons and the whole of the Guard cavalry were to move forward at a trot and try to rush the town of Laon.

The attack took place at 1 a.m. and proved successful; the Russians were surprised and were bayoneted in their sleep, and only one regiment escaped to Laon. Whether it was that the large body of Guard cavalry took too long to concentrate or that the narrow road was blocked, it was nearly 5 o'clock before the cavalry moved forward; they reached Laon before daybreak, but the enemy were on their guard; the dragoons were received with a salvo of grape shot and retired beyond artillery range.

Laon was not open to a surprise. Blücher was tired of retreating, and had made preparations to defend the town. Whatever Woronzoff's opinion was, Blücher considered the battle of Craonne to be a reverse, and wished to have his revenge at Laon, which was a formidable position, and suited to the large army which he commanded.

The hill of Laon rises in the middle of a large plain to a height of some 300 feet above the Ardon stream which flows at its foot; the plain is wooded and slightly undulating to east and west of the town, and to the north it is absolutely level and bare, the open cornfields extending as far as the eye can reach.

The top of the hill is flat, and the sides fall at an angle of 45 degrees; the plain is irregular and affords several natural bastions separated by deep ravines, and the slopes are planted with patches of wood, vineyards, and gardens, separated by stone walls. Five roads approach the suburbs which stand in the plan, and the town itself is only reached by narrow and steep paths. In 1814 the ramparts of the old town were in a very bad state of repair; there was a continuous *enceinte* following the outline of the hill, but it was in a crumbling condition and there were many breaches. The town, then, was not exactly a strong fortress, but the hill was a formidable position and constituted an extraordinarily strong *point d'appui* for an army.

The defence of the plateau was entrusted to General Bülow, whose corps numbered 17,000 men: he scattered his infantry by battalions and even by companies in various posts on the southern and western slopes. These posts were connected by chains of skirmishers and were capable of giving mutual support. A strong reserve occupied the town, and two detachments, each of two battalions, occupied the suburbs of Ardon and Semilly. A portion of the cavalry watched the main roads and the remainder was massed in reserve on the north of the hill near the suburb of Vaux. Fifty guns were in position on the hill covering the exits from Ardon and Semilly.

To the west of Laon, Winzingerode's corps formed the right wing; the infantry were deployed in columns of regiments, the front being at Clacy, and the artillery was in advance of the infantry with the cavalry in third line. To the east, the corps of Kleist and Yorck formed the left wing, which was slightly drawn back and faced the roads leading to Athies and Rheims. Yorck's infantry faced Athies, which was held by an advance post of two battalions, and Kleist's infantry were drawn up across the Rheims road.

The bulk of the artillery was on the left and the cavalry was massed to the left rear of the infantry. Two regiments of hussars were watching the Rheims road near the village of Eppes, and four kilometres farther to the front five squadrons under Colonel Blücher, the son of the Field-Marshal, were in occupation of Festieux.

The Russians under Sacken and Langeron, who had only rejoined the army at 10 a.m. *via* Coucy, and the garrison of Soissons, were in reserve to the north of the town, between the suburbs of Vaux and La Neuville. The total number of Blücher's army amounted to 84,000 men. The reserve was completely hidden from the assailants by the hill, and the left wing could not be seen by the French advancing from Soissons, nor the right wing by those advancing from Rheims.

The inhabitants of Laon thought that the enemy were going to continue their retreat. They had no definite news of the battle of the 7th, but the arrival of the mass of Russians and Prussians made them think that the allies had had the worst of the fight. Blücher's army certainly seemed innumerable, but the morale of the troops did not appear to be of the highest; also, as the whole of the baggage and the majority of the troops were halted at the foot of the hill and close to the Avesnes road, it looked as if Blücher was preparing for a retreat. The town was in terror, for a state of siege had been declared and a bombardment was expected, but even under these conditions the genius of Napoleon imparted a certain measure of confidence.

There is no doubt that the French were mistaken as to the intentions of the Field-Marshal, but although he was determined to make a desperate stand at Laon, Blücher did not neglect the possibility of his being forced to retire. The Cossacks had captured a Hanoverian named Palm, who was attached as a clerk to the Emperor's staff, and this man said that Napoleon was advancing at the head of 60,000 or 70,000 men, and that he was followed by two of his marshals with a further 20,000. Müffling placed little reliance on this report, but Gneisenau, the chief of the staff, who was always prone to exaggerate Napoleon's strength, was somewhat alarmed and imparted his fears to the old Field-Marshal. Certainly the possibility that Napoleon might arrive with 90,000 men was bound to cause Blücher some anxiety.

It snowed hard all night, but stopped at 6 a.m., and when the day of March 9 broke the ground was covered with one of the dense fogs which are common in the damp, marshy valley of Laon. Ney's corps was the first to arrive on the field of battle, followed by that of Mortier; the troops deployed opposite the town on either side of the road, Mortier on the right and Ney on the left. During this deployment the two marshals, hoping to surprise the enemy under cover of the fog, sent forward Porret de Morvan's division against Ardon and Pierre Boyer's brigade against Semilly. Boyer seized the suburb at the point of the bayonet, and the Prussians were driven back to the slopes of the hill; Clausewitz asked for reinforcements and made a successful counter-attack; the French re-formed, seized the position again, but were once more driven out, and until 11 o'clock Semilly was alternately taken and retaken. Porret de Morvan was more successful, and his division drove back the Prussians to the foot of the hill, which was over 1,000 yards distant from the suburb.

Under cover of the fog a company of the Young Guard climbed up a steep path and reached the crest of the plateau near the old abbey of St. Vincent; at this height the fog was very thin and these adventurous spirits were soon attacked by a whole battalion and came down the hill quicker than they went up. De Morvan's division fell back to Ardon and remained in occupation of that suburb. Meanwhile the Emperor, blinded by his pre- conceived ideas, believed that the town had been occupied by the French advance-guard.

On the day of the battle of Craonne the Emperor reached the field of battle in front of his troops and was busy in inspecting the enemy's positions by 8 in the morning; on the 9th, however, midday still found him at Chavignon, five miles away from Laon. At this hour the Emperor learnt of the resistance which his marshals had encountered, and moved forward with the remainder of his troops.

Blücher's intention was to deliver a vigorous counter-stroke as soon as Napoleon's attack had developed, and, until that moment arrived, his corps commanders were directed to maintain a defensive attitude. The Prussian staff was gathered on the ramparts at the foot of an ancient tower named Madame Eve, and were anxiously waiting for the mist to rise and show them the French army. Towards 11 o'clock Blücher was able to make out Ney and Mortier's weak battalions deployed in front of the hill.

The very weakness of these troops caused uneasiness in the mind of Blücher's staff; the Emperor could not propose to attack the formidable position of Laon with so small a force; these must be only a part of the French army, making a demonstration, while the real attack came from another direction. From which direction was this attack coming, and with what force would it be delivered? Napoleon was capable of the boldest and most unexpected manoeuvres, and as far as numbers went he seemed to be able to create men. What if the prisoner Palm had told the truth, and Napoleon had really 90,000 men? Blücher was in grave doubt and hesitated to give the order to attack, and towards midday his uneasiness was increased by the receipt of a message from his son which reported that a strong hostile column was advancing on Laon through Festieux.

At this moment Müffling so says Müffling, who always attributes good advice to himself suggested that it would be well to crush the left wing of the French deployed in front of Semilly. This would force them to show their hand; if they retired it would mean that they meant to move towards their right to join the troops coming from Festieux; if they held their ground stubbornly it would mean that the Festieux troops were intended to move to the westward.

Blücher approved of Müffling's suggestion and ordered Winzingerode to attack the left flank of the small French corps with one division of infantry and the whole of his cavalry and light artillery. While this movement was being carried out the staff kept their field-glasses anxiously glued upon the battle. At the approach of Winzingerode's troops, Boyer, who had been fighting the whole morning in Semilly, withdrew his brigade because his line of retreat was threatened. A column of Russian infantry had almost reached the road when Ney collected some squadrons and drove it back to Clacy, and at the same time a French cavalry brigade repulsed some Cossacks who were attempting a turning movement against the French left. At this very moment the Emperor arrived at the front.

Both Blücher and Müffling were satisfied as to the intention of the French; they evidently wished to remain in possession of the ground to the north of the Ardon stream, and their objective must be the southern spur of the hill. On this supposition it was of importance to retake Ardon so as to cut the communications of the French with the Festieux column, which was obviously destined to make the main attack, and probably comprised the bulk of the Emperor's army. On Blücher's orders, Bülow sent forward against Ardon Krafft's brigade, which consisted of nine battalions and four squadrons.

After a brisk fight the Prussians captured Ardon and drove back Porret de Morvan's division, which retired toward Leuilly. Krafft's brigade was advancing in pursuit when it was stopped by an order from the Field-Marshal. Blücher had been assailed by fresh doubts; was it likely that Napoleon's two wings would be so widely separated unless there was a centre column to connect them with each other, and was there not, then, a third French column advancing from Bruyeres? Until the situation should be cleared up Blücher determined to postpone a general attack, and sent Müffling to reconnoitre the Bruyeres road and to try to ascertain the strength and intentions of the Festieux column.

The column advancing from the direction of Rheims was Marmont's force, which was six hours late in arriving on the field of battle. He had not marched on the previous day, although he had received two distinct orders to do so. He had occupied the village of Aubigny the night before, but the bulk of his troops had not left Berry-au-Bac until the morning of the

9th. He reached Festieux soon after 10 a.m. and halted there till midday.

"The fog," he explains, "was very thick. Until it cleared I could not risk committing my troops on the immense plain."

It has been pointed out that if Marmont was afraid of committing his troops to the plain he could have moved along the plateau to his left and reached the Roman road which led straight through Bruyeres to Laon. It would have taken some time to climb the steep sides of the plateau, which is some 300 feet high, but he could have borne to his left and reached the Roman road by skirting the edge of the high ground.

In this way he would run no danger of stumbling upon the enemy's cavalry in the fog. Marmont's orders did not lay down what road he was to follow beyond Aubigny, but directed him to keep in touch with the Emperor; he was therefore free to move to his left, and should have marched towards the sound of the Emperor's guns which he heard at Festieux. Marmont's main fault, however, was his delay in leaving Berry-au-Bac. His memoirs make it clear that after the fall of Soissons he had given up hope, and his only object was to obey his orders literally but without zeal. It does not follow, however, that Napoleon would have won the battle if Marmont had arrived before Laon at 8 a.m. instead of after 2 o'clock.

The fog cleared and the troops advanced. Colonel Blücher's squadrons retired without fighting, and Marmont moved forward to within 1,200 yards of the enemy's front opposite Vaux and Athies. He brought twenty-four guns into action against Athies, while other guns engaged the Prussian artillery. Athies was soon abandoned by York's infantry, whose left flank was threatened by the resolute advance of a brigade of Arrighi's division. Whether it was with a view to delaying the occupation of the village by the French, or whether, as Blücher asserts, the inhabitants had fired on them, the Prussians set fire to Athies before leaving it; they did so methodically, after removing the sick and infirm inhabitants, and the whole village was burnt to the ground.

During the fire, which only burnt itself out at about 6 p.m., Arrighi's young soldiers pursued the Prussians, but were soon driven back by artillery fire. From this time onwards the enemy, whose serried masses were visible to Marmont, showed no sign of yielding his ground. It has been said that York's first retirement was made with a view to drawing Marmont into a trap, but we must remember that Blücher had ordered his corps commanders to be content with holding their ground until the time for a general counterstroke should arrive. Eppes and Athies were merely advanced posts, and not part of the main position, and a resolute defence was not intended.

From his post on the hill Blücher could see the fight at Athies, but, owing to a strong westerly wind he could hardly hear the sound of the guns. Certainly, then, the Emperor, who was farther off still, could not distinguish the sound of this fight above the noise of his own and the Prussian artillery, and of course he could not see what was happening in the plain of Athies. His position at Chivy is only about five miles as the crow flies from Athies, but the view is limited by houses and woods, and was also impeded by the smoke of the battle.

While Marmont was attacking Athies Napoleon knew nothing of his movements, especially as the marshal, in spite of definite orders, had made no attempt to communicate with him, and all the messengers sent by the Emperor were captured by Cossack patrols. Napoleon could not press his attack until he knew that Marmont had arrived, and delay was dangerous.

In order to engage Blücher's attention, the Emperor ordered further attacks to be made on the southern suburbs. Boyer once more succeeded in capturing Semilly, and a charge of Roussel's dragoons helped Porret de Morvan to retake Ardon. At last, at about 4 o'clock, Victor's two divisions, henceforth under Charpentier's orders, arrived by the Soissons road, and the Emperor sent them against the village of Clacy, which was occupied by several Russian battalions supported by guns.

Clacy stands in the middle of a marsh, and can only be reached, by one narrow road. Some skirmishers moved along the edge of the marsh and engaged the enemy with a brisk fire, and meanwhile Montmarie's brigade attacked the position in front. The attack was so sudden that the Russians were surprised and left 250 prisoners in the hands of the Young Guard. Encouraged by Charpentier's success, Ney tried to drive the enemy back to La Neuville, but he was checked by the Russian guns. On the other flank Boyer's brigade and Porret de Morvan's division were both driven out of the suburbs after desperate fighting, in which General Porret de Morvan was severely wounded.

It was now past 5 o'clock, and the night was at hand. The Emperor determined to break off the battle till the following day, when he relied on Marmont's co-operation. The troops bivouacked along the front of battle, except Friant's Old Guard and a portion of the cavalry, which were a few miles in rear. Strong cavalry detachments were placed at a distance of some three miles on either flank of the army.

At Athies the battle had ceased at about 6 p.m. After the capture of this village Marmont had made no further advance. He says that he came to the conclusion that Napoleon was beating the air; he could see in his immediate front the whole of Kleist's and York's corps, and on his right were Ziethen's numerous squadrons, while farther off, in reserve, he could distinguish the Russian troops of Sacken and Langeron. Marmont was wise not to come to grips with so strong an enemy, but he was in the air in the middle of a plain and in the presence of four times his own numbers, and he would have done better still if he had withdrawn his corps as far as Eppes, or even to the defile of Festieux, but apparently he never thought of doing so.

His troops bivouacked where they had fought; the infantry and artillery were between Athies and the Rheims road, and the cavalry to their right rear. Arrighi's young soldiers, who had just been under fire for the first time, were the most exposed; they had behaved well, but they had no experience of protecting themselves in the presence of the enemy. The gunners, who were for the most part sailors, were fine men and skilful at their own branch of gunnery, but knew nothing about service in the field, and instead of limbering up and parking their guns they left them in action. Marmont admits that he had noticed the complete lack of experience of his troops, but he nevertheless took no steps to see that proper measures of security were taken. He spent the night at the castle of Eppes, three miles from Athies, trusting to Providence to protect his army.

CHAPTER 9

The Surprise of Athies

Blücher had remained on the defensive for the whole day through the fear of seeing the French centre appear from the direction of Bruyeres. When Marmont's troops had opened fire on the Prussian positions in the afternoon the Field-Marshal sent Müffling to discover the strength and the dispositions of this force. Müffling arrived on the left wing at the time when Athies was being burnt, and he clearly saw the small number of the attackers; he came to the conclusion that there was little chance of a third French column arriving so late in the day, and he returned to Laon to tell the Field-Marshal that he could safely risk an attack on Marmont's corps.

The head-quarters staff of the army of Silesia were not the only people who came to this conclusion. When York was leaving the field of battle he asked Ziethen, the commander of the cavalry, whether he thought he could successfully attack the right flank of the French. Ziethen was prepared to make the attempt, and when Kleist was consulted he proved to be equally ready to assume the offensive, and the Count of Brandenburg, one of Yorck's *aides-de-camp*, was at once sent off to Blücher to ask for his permission. Neither York nor Müffling, however, can claim the sole credit for this idea.

From the top of the hill Blücher had summed up the situation as accurately as they had done, and he ordered Sacken and Langeron to support Yorck and Kleist, and sent an *aide-de-camp* to order York to attack at once. Blücher's *aide-de-camp* crossed both Müffling and Brandenburg on his way.

When he received the order York assembled his generals, and gave them his instructions. Some time was needed to form up the troops for the attack, but there was no immediate hurry, and it was better to wait for night, when darkness would increase the chance of a surprise.

Those of Marmont's soldiers who were not worn out with eight hours' marching and four hours' fighting were scattered among the neighbouring farms searching for food; the majority, however, were numb with cold and weak from want of food, and were sleeping the sleep of utter exhaustion round the bivouac fires. At 7 o'clock the Prussians in four columns moved silently into the plain. Prince William's division entered Athies without firing a shot. Arrighi's soldiers were surprised, and offered hardly any resistance; some were killed or captured, and the others fled towards the remainder of the troops, closely followed by the Prussians.

Before the alarm reached them the veterans of the 6th Corps were attacked by Kleist's column, which had marched rapidly across the fields between Athies and the Rheims road, and the artillery found themselves assailed by Horn's troops. The gunners defended themselves as best they could with butt and sabre; some tried to bring the guns into action, but in the darkness the fire had no effect, and in a very short time the men were killed, and the guns seized by the Prussians.

While the French centre and left were being so vigorously attacked, on the right the massed cavalry of Yorck and Kleist's corps, more than 7,000 strong, crossed the stream of Chambry and fell upon the bivouac of Marmont's 2,000 horsemen. The French were charged just as they were in the act of mounting; they had not time to form, and fled in a confused mass towards the Rheims road, exchanging sabre cuts with the pursuing Prussians. Some battalions of the 6th Corps which were beginning to rally received the mixed mass of French and Prussian cavalry with murderous volleys. The confusion was terrible, the French and Prussians were everywhere mingled, and in the darkness it was impossible to distinguish friend from foe, the more so as York's soldiers shouted "*Vive l'Empereur!*" in hopes of deceiving the enemy.

Marmont hastened up from Eppes, forcing his way through the mass of fugitives and the debris of the cavalry, but when he reached his troops he found himself unable to restore order. Luckily at this terrible moment there was an unexpected diversion. At 6 p.m. Colonel Fabvier had been sent with 1,000 infantry and two guns to open communications with the Emperor; on hearing the noise of battle he turned back, and realizing what was taking place he resolutely attacked General Kleist's right flank. The Prussians were surprised, and driven back beyond the Rheims road. Fabvier then held the line of the road, and served as a rallying-point for the fugitives. Marmont took advantage of this diversion to restore a certain amount of order among his troops, and to start them off towards Festieux in two columns, the infantry on the road and the cavalry moving parallel to it.

Thanks to Fabvier's counter-attack it was possible to make a more or less organized retreat. For three hours the columns had to cut their way with the bayonet through the masses of cavalry which barred the road and harassed the flanks, while the Prussian infantry followed close behind the rear-guard, and fired volleys at regular intervals.

"I shall never forget that march," says Marmont. "Bugle-calls were heard, and the enemy halted and fired at us for some minutes; then all was silence until the bugles again heralded a fresh outburst of fire."

During this slow and disastrous march some of the enemy's cavalry, accompanied by artillery, were sent on ahead to cut off the retreat of the French at the Festieux defile. If this movement had succeeded Marmont's whole corps would have been destroyed, but the danger was averted by the presence of mind and determination of a handful of soldiers. A detachment of 125 infantrymen of the Old Guard had arrived during the night at Festieux with a convoy of clothing from Paris.

They learnt of the marshal's retreat, and these veterans realized the danger in which the army was placed; they seized their arms, and took post at the entrance of the defile, where they kept the Prussian squadrons in check till Marmont's column arrived.

At Festieux the danger was over: a rear-guard was left there and the main body went into bivouac between Corbény and Berry-au-Bac. The Prussians left their cavalry and a strong detachment of infantry near Festieux, and the remainder of their troops halted between Eppes and Athies. On the following day Marmont's corps concentrated at Berry-au-Bac; 700 men had been killed or wounded and 2,500 captured; 45 guns and 120 wagons had fallen into the hands of the enemy, and Marmont had only 8 guns left.

Meanwhile, as soon as Blücher had ordered the attack he returned to his quarters, as certain of success as a general can ever be. At 9 o'clock, as he was just finishing his supper, an *aide-de-camp* announced that the surprise had succeeded, and that Marmont had been driven back in disorder; at 10 o'clock, as he was going to bed, a second *aide-de-camp* reported that the enemy had been unable to re-form and that success was certain.

Blücher was delighted, and finally, at 11 o'clock, a third *aide-de-camp* arrived with the news that the enemy had been routed and were being hotly pursued on the Festieux road. Blücher immediately sent for Gneisenau and Müffling to discuss the plans for the following day.

The orders for March 10 were sent during the night to the corps commanders; Yorck and Kleist were to pursue Marmont to Berry-au-Bac, Winzingerode and Bülow were to drive back the Emperor's army towards Soissons, while Langeron and Sacken were to march *via* Bruyeres and the Craonne plateau so as to cut off Napoleon's retreat at L'Ange Gardien.

CHAPTER 10

The Second Day of the Battle of Laon

The French outposts did not hear the noise of the battle of Athies; the wind was still blowing from the west, and spasmodic firing was going on all the night. The Emperor had gone back to Chavignon, and during the night of March 9-10 he knew nothing of the disaster which had befallen Marmont. At the very time when the 6th Corps was retiring in utter route on Festieux, Napoleon was framing orders as to its share in the general attack which he intended to make at dawn on the following day.

Napoleon intended that Charpentier and Boyer's divisions, supported by Ney and Friant's corps, with the three divisions of cavalry and the reserve artillery, should issue from Clacy and drive the allies towards La Neuville; Mortier with Porret de Morvan and Christiani's divisions and Roussel's dragoons were to form the centre of the army, and to hold themselves in readiness to support the attack. On the right, Marmont was to manoeuvre so as to threaten the road from Laon to Avesnes.

On March 10, between 4 and 5 a.m., Napoleon's horse was standing ready, and he was just pulling on his boots, when the officer on duty brought to him two dismounted dragoons who had escaped from the battle of Athies and had just found their way to Chavignon. These two men described the fight and said that Marmont's troops were routed, and that the marshal himself was either killed or captured. At first the Emperor would not believe the story, and sent off all his orderly officers to search for news, but before long, reports of reconnaissances confirmed the tale and placed the defeat of Marmont beyond doubt; it was ascertained, however, that Marmont had not been killed and was rallying his troops in the neighbourhood of Corbény.

This news was of a nature to make the Emperor hesitate. Without Marmont's co-operation the success of his proposed attack seemed very doubtful, and, further, it was likely that the enemy had withdrawn troops from Laon to attack the 6th corps, and a vigorous attack might capture the town. In any case if Napoleon held his ground the allies would be obliged to concentrate, and would be unable to pursue Marmont. The Emperor decided to remain in front of Laon during the day, and to be guided by circumstances in the choice between an offensive or a defensive attitude. In spite of the resistance they had met with on the following day, and in spite of the defeat of Marmont, the Emperor and his subordinates still held to the idea that Blücher was ready to evacuate Laon.

In accordance with the orders issued at midnight from the Prussian head-quarters, four corps of the allies marched at daybreak. When Yorck and Kleist, who were pursuing Marmont, had passed Festieux, and Langeron and Sacken in their move to intercept the Emperor's retreat had reached Bruyeres, each of these generals received a sudden counter-order. In the early morning Blücher was attacked by a sudden fever and was unable to leave his bed; he had been unwell for the last couple of days, and the whole day spent upon the exposed ramparts of Laon had proved too much for him.

The Field-Marshal felt that he was incapable of directing the operations, and handed over the command for the day to his chief of the staff. Gneisenau accepted this responsibility with misgivings, and his heart failed him when he learnt from the reports of the outposts that the French were not retreating, and seemed to be preparing to attack.

"The orders today must be changed at once," he said to Müffling, "the proposed plan of operations is too risky and may end in disaster. Bülow and Winzingerode are not strong enough to resist Napoleon, and the other four corps must be recalled at once."

Müffling was in despair and tried in vain to alter Gneisenau's decision. By this counter-order Gneisenau abandoned a strategic manoeuvre which might have resulted in the total destruction of the French army in favour of the certainty of a slight tactical success. If prudence is the first military virtue, Gneisenau was certainly a good general.

At about 9 a.m. Winzingerode, who was in front of the village of La Neuville, received orders to drive the French out of Clacy. This village had been put in a state of defence and was occupied by Charpentier's division; two of Ney's divisions were in the right rear of the Clacy marsh, and Pierre Boyer's brigade was in occupation of the outskirts of Semilly; the remainder of the French army was deployed on both sides of the Soissons road.

Woronzoff was charged with the attack on Clacy, and after a bombardment he sent forward one division against the village; Charpentier held his fire until the Russians were in a solid column on the narrow road which led to the village, and then, at 200 yards' range, he checked them with grape and musketry fire. A second attack, supported by a useless cavalry charge across the frozen marsh, met with no better success.

Two more Russian divisions were thrown into the fight, and between 12 noon and 2 p.m. five separate assaults were beaten back. Ney's guns gave valuable help by enfilading the Russian columns, but unfortunately they also caused some loss to Charpentier's troops. The Emperor had come to Clacy, and was examining the field of battle from the church tower, and he is said to have sent an *aide-de-camp* to Ney to tell him to correct the aim of his guns.

Gneisenau saw that the attacks were unsuccessful, and ordered them to be supported by some of Bülow's battalions from the garrison of the hill. The Emperor saw these Prussian troops moving and thought that the enemy had at last begun to evacuate Laon. In order to hasten their retreat he directed Charpentier to drive the Russians back to La Neuville while Ney attacked Semilly and Mortier assailed Ardon. These three points were strongly occupied, and the French were repulsed. To the west of Semilly, however, one battalion succeeded in reaching the lower slopes of the hill before being driven back by the Prussian guns. This general attack was not altogether without result, for the allies were alarmed and remained on the defensive for the rest of the day.

The bloody repulse of so many attacks showed that victory was impossible, but Napoleon could not make up his mind to abandon the plain of Laon. Possibly the heavy losses only increased his usual tenacity, and Generals Drouot and Belliard were sent one after the other to the front edge of the small wood of Clacy to examine the Russian line and to report whether it could be outflanked. When neither could hold out any hope, the Emperor at last reluctantly determined to retire to Soissons, which had been reoccupied on March 9 by a small French garrison.

The cannonade was kept up to impose on the enemy, and at nightfall the army commenced its retirement. Charpentier and the cavalry moved *via* Anizi, and Mortier and Friant by the main road. Ney, who was always first in the advance and last in the retreat, was to hold his ground until the following day with his own corps, two of Charpentier's battalions, and Roussel's dragoons; he wrote to Berthier:

"A handful of men cannot successfully carry out a retreat in the face of an army. This duty should have been assigned to the Old Guard itself."

The night passed quietly, and it was not until March 11 that the Russians attempted to interfere with the retreat. A party of cavalry succeeded in capturing some prisoners from Charpentier, and on the main road Czernischeff's Cossacks, supported by guns and 1,500 infantry, set out in pursuit of Ney. The last detachment of the rear-guard was composed of two battalions under Colonel Sémery, who determined to prepare a surprise for the Cossacks.

He hid his leading battalion in a wood which bordered the road and allowed the rear battalion to march through them. The Cossacks passed through the wood in pursuit and fell into the ambush. After this the Russian cavalry maintained a respectful distance of nearly two miles from Ney's rear-guard. The army was not further molested, and concentrated at Soissons in the afternoon and evening of March 11.

At Laon the French had lost more than 6,000 in killed, wounded, and prisoners, but for two whole days the Emperor had imposed on the enemy with a handful of men, and on the third day he had marched away from the field of battle as if there was no enemy in the neighbourhood. The presence of Napoleon always acted like Medusa's head in sapping the strength of the enemy. If Blücher had resolutely hurled his enormous forces against him, a terrible disaster would have overtaken the little French army.

The allied corps commanders were exasperated by the counter-order issued on the morning of March 10, and they did not hide their discontent from head-quarters. Woronzoff declared that it had been a great misfortune; Sacken lost all self-control, and said to Müffling:

"Listen, General, up to now I have always respected the Field-Marshal's decisions, but for the last four days he has lost his head. What was the reason for counter-ordering the plan which would have allowed us to crush Napoleon?"

It was not only the loss of this opportunity which exasperated the Russian generals. Mistrust and jealousy reigned supreme among the allies. The Russians maintained that Gneisenau had abandoned the attack in order to spare the Prussian troops who were in first line. At Craonne the Russians alone had been engaged, and Blücher had been so much impressed by their losses that he had announced that at the next battle the Russians would be in reserve; now Gneisenau stopped the proposed operations just as the Prussians were about to become engaged.

York thought he had other grounds for complaint; he was on bad terms with Gneisenau, and imagined that the chief of the staff had recalled him to Laon in order to deprive him of the honour of completing Marmont's defeat. Yorck was too proud to indulge in recriminations and kept away from head-quarters. On the 10th, towards midday, his corps took up its position between Vaux and Athies, and he spent this day among his troops supervising disciplinary measures and distributing bread to the unfortunate inhabitants of Athies, whom his soldiers had pillaged the previous day.

As he went on his rounds during the night he saw a woman on her knees; he rode up with his *aide-de-camp* to drive away what he took to be a ghoul engaged in robbing the dead. The woman, however, who was a French *vivandière* of the 6th Corps, drew herself proudly up and said, "I suppose I have the right to bury my husband."

On the following day fresh orders were issued by Gneisenau, by which Corbény was allotted as quarters for Yorck's corps. Now Corbény had been more ravaged than any other district in the neighbourhood, and this order was more than the old general could bear; he issued his instructions as to the march and cantonments, and then, without warning a soul beyond his *aide-de-camp*, he got into a carriage and started for Brussels. Yorck's departure raised a considerable amount of feeling at head-quarters and throughout the whole army. Blücher's officers wished to have Yorck brought before a council of war, but they did not dare to suggest this to the Field-Marshal.

It was first of all proposed that Blücher should write a letter pretending to believe that York had suddenly been taken ill, and hoping that he would return shortly and resume the command of his corps. Yorck's friends knew that this letter would not alter his determination, and they persuaded Blücher to consult only his own feelings in composing his letter to Yorck. The Field-Marshal had been attacked by a form of ophthalmia, and could hardly see; he wrote these three lines in large letters:

My old comrade, history would be ashamed to relate a thing like this between us two. Be reasonable and come back.

Prince William of Prussia also wrote to Yorck a letter which honoured both himself and the general to whom it was addressed.

> The departure of your Excellency has given the most profound grief to all of us who were happy enough to be under your orders. We know your generous character, and we hope that you will not abandon us. Prussia has never had greater need than now of generals such as he who gave the signal to cast off the foreign yoke. As your fellow-countryman and your subordinate, as the grandson, the son, and the brother of your Kings, I pray that you will come back to us.

As the result of these two letters Yorck came back and resumed his command.

In the army of Bohemia there was much jealousy and distrust between the Russians and Austrians; this ill-feeling also reigned in the army of Silesia, not only between Russians and Prussians, but even between Prussian and Prussian. When Langeron saw that Blücher was ill and almost blind, and had lost the strength of both mind and body, he was afraid that he, as the senior general, would have to assume the responsibilities of the commander-in-chief, and, as he left the Field-Marshal's room, he cried out, "For God's sake, whatever happens, let us take that corpse along with us."

CHAPTER 11

Retreat of the French Armies

On February 27 Napoleon had started from Troyes with all his former confidence, determined to annihilate Blücher, but since that time not a day had passed without some misadventure. The advance into the country lying between the Marne and the Aisne had promised excellent results, but it had only ended in the retreat of the small French army, after having lost more than a third of its numbers in the forced marches and the bloody battles of Craonne and Laon. The Emperor said that the Young Guard was melting like snow in sunshine.

In Champagne, Macdonald had been driven from the line of the Aube, and had also been forced to abandon the line of the upper Seine. After the fighting of February 27 and 28 at Bar-sur-Aube and La Ferté-sur-Aube he had expected to be able to maintain himself at Troyes in accordance with the Emperor's orders, but Oudinot had already rendered defence difficult by his faulty dispositions.

His first line was formed by Gérard's corps at the Guillotiere bridge, and Rothembourg's division on the plateau of Laubressel; in second line were Saint Germain's cavalry at Saint-Parre-aux-Tertres, and Leval's strong division with Kellermann's cavalry at the Saint Hubert bridge; Amey and Pacthod's divisions were in reserve at Troyes. The army had been disposed on so narrow a front that the enemy were able to occupy Bouranton and so turn the first line.

As he had done at Bar-sur-Aube, Oudinot made no use of his

reserve, and his cavalry, which were only five miles away, did not stir from their bivouacs. Gérard and Rothembourg were vigorously attacked in front and flank, and retired on Troyes.

Macdonald was suffering from rheumatic gout, and could hardly mount his horse, and, on assuming command during the night of March 3 and 4, he found all the troops in retreat. Troyes was threatened with an attack on three sides, from the right bank of the Barse and on both banks of the Seine. The place was hardly tenable, but Gérard was ordered to hold it during the whole of the 4th with a view to protecting the retreat of the army.

The allies appeared before Troyes at 8 a.m., and Gérard resisted until the afternoon, when, in order to save the suburbs from being burnt, he asked for an armistice, and was permitted to leave the town. On the following day, March 5, almost all the allied troops concentrated at Troyes, and Macdonald's three corps assembled near Nogent. On March 6 Macdonald crossed to the right bank of the Seine and blew up the bridge of Nogent, and on the 7th he established his head-quarters at Provins. Thus, in one week, Oudinot and Macdonald had lost 6,000 men and had yielded over 60 miles of ground to the enemy.

On the Swiss frontier Augereau had been no less fortunate, arid had shown even less skill. Macdonald, or rather Oudinot, had neglected the ordinary precautions and had made tactical mistakes, but the defence of the Aube and the Seine against three times their own numbers was a very difficult operation. Augereau, on the contrary, had only got to march straight forward with his 28,000 men, and he could not have failed to defeat the opposing force of 19,000 Austrians, who were split into three detachments. He had been slow and undecided, however, and his behaviour, which almost amounted to disobedience, was responsible for the failure of the great strategical operation which the Emperor had planned.

The orders of Napoleon and of Clarke were precise and formal. Augereau was ordered to recapture Geneva, and after occupying it with a strong garrison to march rapidly on Vesoul by the

Bale-Langres road, so as to cut the communications of the army of Bohemia. Augereau made a thousand excuses for remaining at Lyons. The Emperor repeated his orders again and again with no effect. On February 18 the Minister for War wrote to him:

> The Emperor bids you forget that you are fifty-six years old, and remember only the glorious days of Castiglione.

Napoleon wrote him a letter full of the most burning eloquence which would have stirred the most apathetic.

> "My cousin," he said, "can it be that you are not on the move within six hours of having received the first troops from Spain? Six hours' rest would have been enough for them. I won the battle of Nangis with a brigade of dragoons which had not unsaddled their horses since they left Bayonne. I charge you to march within twelve hours of receiving this letter. If you are still the old Augereau of Castiglione you will obey this order; if your sixty years weigh upon you, hand over the command to the senior of your generals. Our country is in danger; she can be saved only by courage and energy, not by useless delay. Be in the forefront of the fight; in this crisis it is not enough to follow the methods of the last few years; we must show the spirit and determination of '93."

It was not till February 28 that Augereau left Lyons to advance to Geneva, to which place Generals Dessaix and Marchand had driven back Bubna's Austrians. On March 8 his army was between Lons-le-Saulnier and Morey, within one day's march of Geneva, when Augereau, as if he had already captured the town, stopped his movement and marched on Vesoul. He had, however, lost a fortnight at Lyons, and a new army under the Prince of Hesse-Hombourg was arriving by forced marches to oppose him.

On March 4 the French were attacked at Poligny by General Wimfenn. A week earlier Augereau would only have found in front of him three isolated divisions, but now he was opposed by a whole army. The whole of the Austrian troops, however, were not yet in line, and if Augereau was the man he had been he would have been able to drive them back across the Doubs, but he was afraid for the safety of Lyons, which appeared to be threatened by the enemy's right, and which he had neglected to put in a state of defence; he had constructed no works there, and had not even brought up from Avignon the 80 guns which were intended for the armament of the town.

Marchand and Dessaix's divisions remained in observation of Geneva, and Augereau collected the remainder of his troops at Lyons, where he arrived on March 9. Thus the whole plan was ruined by the negligence and lack of energy of which Augereau had been guilty, and a magnificent manoeuvre which would have dealt a crushing blow to the enemy had utterly failed. Even if Augereau were to defend Lyons successfully, his troops would from henceforward be of no use in the field.

From the north and from the Pyrenees the news was equally gloomy. On the Belgian frontier General Maison had been driven back from Tournay to Courtray, and from there to Lille. Marshal Suchet was still in Catalonia, waiting for the ratification of the treaty of Valençay; he was to all intents and purposes a prisoner, and could take no share in the main operations of the campaign. Marshal Soult was losing ground; until the middle of February he had kept his army concentrated behind the Adour, the Bidassoa, and the Gaves, and from here, supported by the entrenched camp at Bayonne, he had held Wellington's Anglo-Spaniards in check.

Unfortunately, on February 22 Soult was deceived by Wellington's clever manoeuvres, which aimed at drawing the French away from Bayonne, and he left this position, which was the key of the lower Pyrenees. On February 27 a battle was fought at Orthez; after an obstinate defence in which each side lost about 2,500 men, the French retired towards Mont-de-Marsan. Two days later Soult changed the direction of his march and moved on Tarbes. Bordeaux was uncovered, but Soult believed that the English would not dare to enter the Landes while he was on their flank. He was right, and Wellington followed him towards Tarbes and Toulouse, but Soult's calculations were upset by treason.

The Bourbons had always had a numerous and active following in Bordeaux. In 1796 the royalists founded a secret society under the name of the Philanthropic Institute. In 1799 they took up arms, and were dispersed by the troops. In 1806 they tried to deliver Ferdinand VII, and in 1807 the imperial police foiled another plot. Correspondence was carried on with London under the guise of a commercial firm, Henri & Co.; in these letters the word "indigo" meant "Bourbon," and "cargo of cotton" implied "expeditionary force."

The disasters of the campaigns in Russia and Saxony raised the hopes of the royalists. In the autumn of 1813 eight companies of Royal Guards were organized, with a full complement of officers, and, what is more extraordinary, with as many men in the ranks as there were officers. In the beginning of 1814 the royalists gained a recruit who was worth as much as all the eight companies put together; this was a first-class scoundrel named Lynch.

Lynch had been first of all Mayor of Bordeaux, then a Count of the Empire, then a Chevalier, and finally, on January 8, 1814, he was made an officer of the Legion of Honour. In fact, as he himself admits, he had always been well treated by Bonaparte, and in his speeches he was never tired of expressing his devotion to the Emperor. When he was Mayor of Bordeaux he may not have said to his officials, in the words of the catechism of 1807. that "one was bound to render to the Emperor love, taxes, and military service under pain of eternal damnation," but he at any rate lost no opportunity of reminding them of "the glory and favours of Napoleon the great."

Towards the end of 1813 he changed his mind; the Empire was threatened and it was time to abandon the Emperor. Lynch, however, took care to show no relaxation of zeal. In Paris, where he had gone in November 1813, to give fresh proofs of his loyalty, he finished his speech to the Emperor with these words.

"Napoleon has done everything for the French, the French will do everything for him." A short time afterwards he asked Polignac to include him among the chiefs of the royalist party in Médoc. At Bordeaux he presented colours to the National Guard on January 20, and said to them, "If the enemy approaches Bordeaux I shall be the first to set an example." A few days before this he had said to La Rochejacquelein, "I, the Mayor of Bordeaux, hope to have the honour of being the first to proclaim Louis XVIII."

It was one thing to desire a monarchical revolution, and another thing to carry it out. There were at Bordeaux a special commissioner, a *prefect*, and a divisional general, and none of these were inclined to favour the plans of the royalists. A small garrison would have found no difficulty in dealing with the armed rising on the part of the eight companies of the Royal Guard, and the bulk of the population were opposed to the Bourbons. Although Bordeaux had been ruined by the continental blockade, the great majority of the inhabitants were attached to the Emperor, and Lynch saw that he could not proclaim Louis XVIII without the help of Wellington's red-coats.

When the Duc d'Angoulême arrived at Wellington's headquarters, the Marquis de La Rochejacquelein embarked secretly for Saint Jean-de-Luz and unfolded the plans of the royalists. Wellington, however, refused curtly to have anything to say to the matter. The road to Bordeaux was open to him, and he clearly understood the advantages which the allies might have gained from the royalist intrigues, but so long as the sovereigns were treating with Napoleon, Wellington refused to help those who were conspiring for his fall.

On March 6 another messenger was sent to Wellington to tell him that the garrison and all the officials had evacuated Bordeaux. Wellington still had scruples, but after some hesitation he ordered Marshal Beresford to move on Bordeaux with three divisions of infantry, a cavalry brigade, and some artillery. Wellington's hesitation, and the doubts which he entertained as to the success of the operation, bear out the statement of one of the royalist leaders that without the efforts of the Bourbon party the English would not have entered Bordeaux for another month.

Meanwhile Lynch's messenger returned to Bordeaux with the news that the English were coming. The departure of the *prefect* and the general had left Lynch master of the city, and he laid his plans carefully. It was announced that the whole of the English army was coming, but the fact that the Duc d'Angoulême was also expected was not made public; the National Guard was sent to the ordinary posts without ammunition, and the Royal Guards were ordered to turn out with their arms concealed and with white cockades in their pockets ready to be put on as soon as the signal was given; at the same signal the banner of the Bourbons was to be hoisted on the cathedral tower.

On the morning of March 12 an English flag of truce arrived. By means of a stratagem Lynch outwitted the only Bonapartist magistrate who was popular enough to have caused trouble, and he rode out to meet Beresford, and welcomed him to the town over which the *fleur-de-lis* was now flying.

The English and the royalists entered Bordeaux amid the acclamations of the Bourbon sympathisers; the great majority of the inhabitants were surprised by the suddenness of the revolution and overawed by the presence of the English, and before long numbers of them began to side with the royalists; when the Duc d'Angoulême arrived a couple of hours later, he was led in triumph to the cathedral to hear a *Te Deum*, after which Louis XVIII was proclaimed from the steps of the Town Hall.

The following day the enthusiasm for the Bourbons waned. Many of the employees of the municipality refused to serve any longer, and Marshal Beresford left the town with two-thirds of his force. Lynch was left without police and without money, and had reason to fear that the Duc d'Angoulême might be assassinated, and that a counter-revolution was hatching. Nevertheless the Bourbons had been proclaimed at Bordeaux, and this fact had great effect throughout France and at the headquarters of the allied sovereigns. The serious events at Bordeaux were not known in Paris till March 16; but during the previous fortnight there had been many grounds for fear. Up till March 2 public opinion confidently expected either a decisive victory in Champagne or the signing of an honourable peace at Châtillon. It seemed as if the theatre of war had already receded to the frontier; Paris was calm and confident, and life went on as usual. During March 3 and the following days news was received of the defeat at Bar-sur-Aube, the retreats of Macdonald and Soult, and of the rupture of the negotiations at Lusigny; there was an absolute dearth of news as to the Emperor's movements, and a feeling of alarm began to spread. There was a slump on the Stock Exchange; but although there was no panic such as there had been after the battle of La Rothière, the enthusiasm inspired by the Emperor's subsequent victories had vanished.

The general public were anxious; but a much more serious state of alarm prevailed among the members of the Government, who were better informed as to the progress of the Emperor and as to the paucity of his resources. In Paris it was still believed that the victor of Austerlitz and Jena was in a position to gain a battle, and to force a peace upon his enemies; in the Tuileries, on the contrary, the general opinion was that the Emperor would be forced to purchase peace at the expense of the utmost humiliation.

On February 21 King Joseph had written to the Emperor that everyone would be content with a peace which would give France her natural frontiers; now, however, he prayed and begged him to abandon the natural frontiers, and to make peace on any terms.

"There would be no dishonour in a peace," he wrote, "which would not involve a surrender of any of France's ancient territory. And, Sire, if you will give up the idea of being an extraordinary man, and be content to be a great monarch, you will become the father of your people." Again he wrote, "The only remedy is peace, and with as little delay as possible. It will not be your fault if the terms are bad, for they will have been demanded by every class of society."

On March 2 the Emperor ordered his brother to assemble the Council of the Regency to record their opinion on the negotiations. The Council unanimously decided that the terms offered by the allies must be accepted. The minutes of the meeting were forwarded to Napoleon, and at the same time Joseph wrote as follows:

> Sire, all the members of the Council appear to have been of one mind. They considered the enemies' proposals to have been most unjust, and they expressed an absolute confidence that your Majesty's instructions to your plenipotentiary will result in the acceptance of terms such as they realize your Majesty would consent to in the last extremity. They generally agree in thinking that it is better that France should be reduced to the territory which she possessed before 1792 rather than that the capital should be exposed. They look upon the occupation of the capital as the end of the present regime and the beginning of great misfortunes. An early peace is indispensable, no matter what the terms may be. You will be spared to France, and it will be the same France as that which astonished Europe. You saved France once before, and you will save her a second time by signing an early peace, and by saving yourself with her. Whether your Majesty has won a victory today or not, peace is absolutely necessary: that is what everyone here is thinking and saying.

Napoleon answered his brother by announcing the victory of Craonne, and by sending him instructions on military matters; there was no mention of peace. The letter in which the Emperor had ordered the Council to be assembled contained these words:

> I do not want formal advice, but I am very glad to hear what people think.

This was tantamount to saying that unless his ministers agreed with him he would take no notice of any advice they might give.

Some of the ministers were much annoyed that their advice had so little weight with Napoleon; they did not hide their irritation, and blamed the Emperor's obstinate blindness. Joseph, no doubt, also spoke among his own entourage of the necessity of peace and of Napoleon's stubbornness. Among the ministers and the members of the Senate and of the Council of State the opinion gained ground that Napoleon himself was the chief obstacle which lay in the way of peace.

Some members of the Senate were so misled by their fears as to form a design of deposing the Emperor on the grounds of madness. There would have been no danger in broaching this proposal to Talleyrand [1]; but they had the audacity to unfold the plan to Joseph, telling him that he alone, with the Empress, was able to obtain peace, and giving him hope that he would be appointed regent during the long minority of Napoleon II. Weak opportunist as he was, the ex-King of Spain showed no displeasure when he heard these flattering insinuations; but loyalty and good sense soon reasserted themselves in his mind.

He allowed the conspirators to speak, but he showed them that he would prevent their taking action. Joseph was troubled by the unrest in the departments of State; and he formed the idea of gaining some advantage for both France and the Emperor from the prevailing anxiety. In concert, we had almost said in complicity, with Cambacérès he conceived the idea of presenting to Napoleon an address in favour of peace, to be signed by the members of the Council of the Regency, the ministers, the Senate, and the Council of State. By this means the Emperor's will would be forced, and he would be relieved of responsibility, while his legitimate pride would not be offended; the great warrior would not have yielded to the fortune of war, but the sovereign would have bowed to the will of the people.

But Joseph knew his brother, and realized that Napoleon's character was too upright to be satisfied with such a sophistry,

---

1 Talleyrand, the Prince de Bénévent, had formerly been Bishop of Autun: he was excommunicated, and became Napoleon's Foreign Minister. In 1814 he was Vice-Grand- Elector of France.

and that his autocratic spirit would refuse to yield. He realized that this address was in danger of meeting with a very unfavourable reception, and he hesitated to set the matter on foot without the Emperor's knowledge. The mission of broaching the subject to Napoleon was entrusted to Baron Meneval, a confidential secretary of the Emperor's, who had been left with the regency as the man whom Napoleon most trusted. Faithful servant as he was, Baron Meneval hid none of the circumstances from the Emperor, but displayed the utmost tact in his letter.

As Joseph feared, the Emperor was more than surprised. This projected address was in fact on the same footing as the famous report of Laine, only it was rather worse. When the enemy was on the Rhine, Napoleon had permitted no remonstrance from an elected Chamber; and now that the allied army was on the Seine he certainly would not tolerate orders, however disguised, from a body nominated by himself. Joseph thought that this address would save Napoleon: as a matter of fact it would have made it equally impossible for him either to negotiate or to fight.

The coalition would have gained incalculable strength from a manifesto accusing Napoleon of being the only man who did not wish for peace, and denouncing him as a public enemy. The Emperor answered Meneval: "If an address is presented to me asking for peace I shall look upon it as an act of rebellion."

Napoleon did not stop there; he wrote to both the Ministers of War and of Police.

"I do not approve," he said to the Minister for War, "of King Joseph having around him any military or civil functionary. Such people have a special leaning towards factions. My intention is that the majority of the *aides-de-camp* who have been in Spain should be employed with the army and King Joseph must find others."

The Emperor's letter to the Minister for Police was more outspoken and couched in a different tone.

You can tell me nothing of what is happening in Paris.

There is the matter of the address, of the Regency, and of a thousand absurd intrigues which might all have been conceived by an idiot like Miot. These people do not know that I am cutting the Gordian knot as Alexander did. They had better remember that I am the same man that I was at Wagram and at Austerlitz; I will have no intrigue in the State; there is no other authority than mine, and in case of a crisis the Regent alone has my confidence. King Joseph is weak, and lets himself be involved in intrigues which might be dangerous to the State; they will certainly be dangerous to him and his advisers if he does not quickly mend his ways. I am displeased that I should have learnt all this through a channel other than you. Either you are inefficient or you are serving me no longer. You must know that if I had been presented with an address contrary to authority, I would have arrested the king, my ministers, and all those who signed it. I will have no people's tribune; it must not be forgotten that it is I who am the great tribune.

Both the military and the political situations had changed for the worse, and in the region of diplomacy the outlook also was less favourable. The Congress at Châtillon was engaged in its fifth sitting; a fresh treaty of alliance had been signed at Chaumont; the negotiations for an armistice at Lusigny had been broken off and the main Austro-Russian army had resumed the offensive; less than ever, therefore, could the Duc de Vicence hope to induce the allies to moderate their terms. He continued, however, to think that peace was possible, provided France would make every sacrifice, and he wrote many respectful but despairing letters to the Emperor, asking him to formulate counter-proposals.

"Fear has united all the sovereigns," he wrote; "we must make sacrifices and we must make them at once. We must yield to united Europe. The more I consider what is past, the more convinced I feel that there is no help unless we do submit counter-proposals which modify the Francfort terms. They only want a pretext in order to break off the negotiations."

This last dispatch was dated on March 6, and reached the Emperor at Braye on the evening of the battle of Craonne. Fain says that this letter made more impression on the Emperor than did the advice of the Council of the Regency; this may be so, but it achieved no result. The Emperor did not make a counter-proposal, and only replied to the Duc de Vicence's courier that he did not wish by any act of his own to add to his humiliations.

This was hardly an answer; Napoleon had promised his plenipotentiary to make counter-proposals, and he now refused to do so on the grounds that he was not bound to invite humiliations. To this strange verbal response of the Emperor's Bassano added a long letter of explanation.

> "His Majesty," he wrote, "cannot make peace on more onerous terms than the allies are prepared to grant. Their first proposal cannot be their ultimatum; if this were the case the negotiations would necessarily be broken, for the Emperor cannot consent to such conditions. We must arrive at a positive ultimatum."

There is no doubt, however, as to the allies' ultimatum, which was that France should revert to the frontiers of 1789. The Emperor was much too clear-sighted to have any illusions on this point; the only doubt he could have had was whether the allies were ready to make peace even on these conditions.

When they entered France the allies were certainly not prepared to consent to these terms, but the defeats of Blücher and Schwarzenberg had greatly upset them. The importance of these battles as regards the final issue of the campaign has been denied; the sudden change of front on the part of the ministers of the coalition, however, and the resumption of negotiations on February 17, showed that the allies' confidence of victory had been shaken.

At the beginning of March their anxiety was not at an end, and they might perhaps have been ready to agree to a peace. Lord Liverpool said so in Parliament and Metternich and Prince Esterhazy frequently assured the Duc de Vicence of their pacific intentions. This, however, proves nothing; Lord Liverpool's utterance was purely political; Metternich was deceiving the Duc de Vicence and Esterhazy was the dupe of his sovereign.

A much more pertinent fact, however, was the patience shown by the plenipotentiaries at Châtillon; if they had given up all idea of peace, the Duc de Vicence's procrastination would have been a good enough pretext for breaking off the negotiations on March 10. Unfortunately, if the allies were patient they were also unjust; they had increased their claims with their victories, but they would not permit Napoleon to do likewise. The glorious days of February had only given the Emperor the possibility of a humiliating peace; Napoleon, however, was not in a hurry to seize his advantage; on March 8 he had just won the battle of Craonne and he believed that Blücher was in retreat. Contrary to King Joseph's opinion, he did not believe that the game was up.

On March 10 the Duc de Vicence had no counter-proposals to place before the Congress, and in order to fill the gap he read a long memoir on the question. He maintained that the allies' proposals were contrary to the letter and the spirit of the Frankfort terms: contrary to the letter because they now wished to deprive France of some territory which was to have been left to her; contrary to the spirit because, after insisting on the maintenance of the balance of power, they now wished to destroy this balance by placing France in a position of inferiority as regards the other Powers.

He pointed out that Europe was very different from the Europe of twenty years before; the last partition of Poland, the fall of the Venetian republic, and the treaties of Tilsit, Vienna, and Abo had secured to Russia, Prussia, and Austria the equivalent of the territories which France had gained by conquest, and which they now, nevertheless, proposed to take from her. As for

England, the conquest of India had doubled both her wealth and her power. The Duc de Vicence advanced the best arguments in the world, but there w r as no question of convincing the allies, whose minds were made up.

This memoir was for the benefit of posterity, and was not the distinct and explicit reply which the plenipotentiaries had demanded. They listened with bad grace, saying that they were being laughed at, and that after a delay of ten days there was no reason why the Emperor should not have replied to their proposals. They were on the point of closing the meeting, when Caulaincourt, for fear that negotiations would be broken off, announced that the Emperor was ready to surrender his claims over all countries outside France, and to recognize the independence of Spain, Italy, Switzerland, Germany, and Holland.

To tell the truth, this was no concession, for although the Duc de Vicence had made no formal announcement, none of the plenipotentiaries had any doubt on these points. The allies, however, were not free from anxiety. The staff had no news of Blücher, and though Macdonald had been driven beyond the Seine, Schwarzenberg did not dare to advance any farther. The plenipotentiaries thought that they would not be justified in high-handed measures, and they decided that another meeting should be held on the 13th, and Caulaincourt felt that this would be the last sitting of the Congress.

CHAPTER 12

The Victory of Rheims

The imperial army was in retreat on Soissons; Macdonald was retiring on Provins, Soult on Toulouse, and Augereau on Lyons; the conspirators at Bordeaux were on the point of proclaiming Louis XVIII; Paris was in despair; the Regency was in trouble, and the plenipotentiaries were ready to break off negotiations. Anyone but Napoleon would have felt himself to be beaten. But the Emperor was not subject to fits of depression; and even if he had been, the varied duties of commander-in-chief would have left him no time to indulge in gloomy thoughts. He found in activity the cure for despondency. On March 11, at 3.30 p.m., the Emperor rode into Soissons; at 4 o'clock he wrote orders for the disposition of his troops, and at 5 o'clock he was on the ramparts inspecting the works with the new commandant of the fortress, Colonel Gérard.

March 12 was employed in a reorganization of the army. [1] Some reinforcements had arrived; 2,400 cavalry from the Versailles depot, 1,000 infantry of the 122nd Regiment of the Line, some artillery detachments, and finally the Vistula regiment, which had formed part of the garrison of Soissons, and had received thirty crosses of the Legion of Honour for its gallant conduct in the defence. Ney and Victor's corps were dissolved; the four divisions which composed them, and also Porret de Morvan's division of Mortier's corps, were amalgamated into two new divisions of the Young Guard, commanded by Char-

1. See table end of chapter.

pentier and Curial. Mortier was given the command of these two new divisions, and retained in addition Christiani's fine division of the Old Guard.

Ney's command was reduced to Pierre Boyer's brigade, augmented by the Vistula regiment and a battalion of the 122nd. A division, composed of a brigade of heavy cavalry under General Mouriez, and a brigade of light cavalry under General Curély, was formed out of the cavalry which had arrived from the depot; this division, which was known as the composite division, was commanded by General Berckheim, and with Roussel's 2,000 dragoons formed General Belliard's command. The Emperor retained under his immediate orders the three divisions of Guard cavalry, commanded by Colbert, Exelmans, and Letort, who replaced La Ferrière, wounded at Craonne. The three divisions of Guard cavalry were under the command of Sebastiani, in place of Nansouty, who had been invalided.

When he reorganized his army Napoleon did not yet know in which direction he was going to march. He was evidently quite undecided, when he received news which would have been a blow to any other commander. The Comte de Saint-Priest, a subordinate of Langeron's, had recaptured Rheims, which had been occupied since March 5 by a small garrison under General Corbineau.

On February 27 Saint-Priest had reached Saint-Dizier with a portion of the 8th Russian Corps, and in accordance with Blücher's orders had remained there with a view to assembling the other troops coming from the Rhine and to maintaining communication between the army of Bohemia and the army of Silesia. On March 4 he learnt that Blücher was hard pressed by Napoleon, and that Rheims was threatened; he marched in the direction of this town, but found it already occupied by the French.

The Russian general halted at Sillery to await the arrival of other portions of his corps; meanwhile some Cossacks rode up to the suburbs and demanded that the town should be surrendered, failing which it would be burnt to the ground. Corbineau had only 100 cavalry, 50 *gendarmes*, and 1,000 National Guardsmen, but he refused to surrender the town. The Russians remained quiet until March 11, by which time they had been joined by Pantschulidsew's division and 5,000 Prussian *landwehr* under General Jagow. On the morning of the 12th Saint-Priest attempted a surprise, and attacked the town in three places. The small garrison was driven from the gates; the National Guard dispersed to their homes, and the remainder of the garrison escaped to Chalon-sur-Vesles, where they joined Defrance's Gardes d'Honneur.

The occupation of Rheims by the Russians re-established communication between the armies of Bohemia and Silesia. This was a serious matter, but Napoleon knew how to reap advantage from the blows of fortune; without delay he issued his orders. On the 12th at 6 p.m. Berthier wrote to Marmont, who after the surprise of Athies had retired first to Berry-au-Bac and then to Fismes; he was ordered to march on Rheims at daybreak on the following day.

"You will form the advance-guard," added Berthier, " the Emperor will follow you with a portion of his troops."

Ney's small corps, Friant's division, the Guard cavalry, and the reserve artillery, who were more than forty miles distant from Rheims, began their movement the same evening. The Emperor himself left Soissons at daybreak on the 13th.

Blücher's dispatches had announced to Saint- Priest "the total defeat of the French at Laon, where the Emperor had sacrificed the remains of his army."

This general, therefore, was in no anxiety. He wished to give two or three days' rest to his troops, and, relying on Blücher's statement that the French army was scattered, he cantoned his army in comfort, in a depth of sixteen miles, from Rosnay to Beaumont.

During the morning of the 13th Bordesoulle's cavalry, which formed Marmont's advance-guard, met a hostile cavalry patrol a mile from Rosnay; the patrol galloped away without firing a shot and the French lancers trotted into Rosnay, where two battalions of *landwehr* were having their dinners. A number of Prussians were sabred before they could seize their arms; the others formed square and succeeded in reaching Orme, where they took up a position behind the walls of the cemetery; here they were able to defy the charges of the cavalry, but as soon as they saw Ricard's infantry approaching they surrendered at discretion.

Slight resistance was met with in the other villages; at Gueux General Jagow escaped on a barebacked horse, and at Tillois some infantry were surprised in bed and fought in their shirts. The heads of the French columns were able to advance to within two miles of Rheims almost without striking a blow, and there Marmont halted in accordance with the Emperor's instructions.

The fugitives warned Saint-Priest that the French army was approaching; he, however, refused to believe it and ascribed the alarm to an attack by guerrillas; he felt so safe that he gave no orders for a concentration. Between 1 and 2 p.m. the general went out of Rheims, and he was able to distinguish artillery along the front of the French troops; he decided therefore to form up his force in front of the town. Marmont had been ordered by the Emperor to await his arrival, and he allowed the allies to occupy the heights of Sainte Geneviève, where they formed up in two lines, with their right resting on the Vesle and the cavalry covering both flanks.

If the Comte de Saint-Priest had thought he was going to be attacked by Napoleon he would not have remained where he was, for he had plenty of time to retire either to Berry-au-Bac or to Châlons, but he was deceived by Marmont's inaction and thought the marshal had only a few thousand men. Saint-Priest had 15,000 men, and he reasoned that either the French would be daunted by the position he had taken up or would make an attack and be crushed. One of his subordinates, who was less blind than his general, asked him in which direction they should retire in case it should prove to be Napoleon who was in front of them.

Saint-Priest replied, "Oh, *monsieur*, why should we think of retiring as long as we have life?"

The Emperor arrived upon the ground about 4 o'clock. He saw that the enemy's right was resting on the Vesle and his left extended for some distance. He decided therefore to make a frontal attack. The masses of the allies were shattered by a furious cannonade, and Marmont's infantry advanced in two columns on either side of the road; Bordesoulle's lancers and *cuirassiers* and Colbert's and Defrance's light horsemen and Gardes d'Honneur marched upon the wing, and Ney, Friant, and Exelmans' remained in reserve.

From the number of the assailants and the vigour of the attack Saint-Priest came to the conclusion that Napoleon was present, and he was beginning to give orders for a retreat, when he was mortally wounded. The Russians and Prussians gave way in disorder and retired on the suburb of Vesle; they were pressed by the French cavalry, who made some gallant charges; the 3rd regiment of Gardes d'Honneur under General de Ségur charged right through the retreating mass and reached the ramparts of the town, where, however, they were surrounded by the enemy and with difficulty evaded capture.

Night had come; Marmont's infantry captured the suburb, but neither sap nor gun had any effect upon the iron gate, which was covered by an advanced outwork, and fighting went on at this point until past 11 o'clock. During the assault on the ramparts, which were defended by five Russian regiments, the remainder of the enemy's troops evacuated the town by the Berry-au-Bac and Neufchatel roads. Burning with impatience, the Emperor strode up and down beside a bivouac fire; he had hoped to capture the whole of Saint-Priest's troops in Rheims and he realized that they were escaping. Towards midnight the French at last forced their way into the town, where fighting went on till 2 a.m.; the Emperor entered after the leading infantry among Bordesoulle's *cuirassiers*, who were advancing at a trot to sabre the retreating Russians in the streets.

Suddenly the noise of the musketry and the clatter of the

horses' hoofs were drowned in shouts of "*Vive l'Empereur!*" every window was lit up in honour of the Emperor's victory. A crowd assembled and escorted him in triumph to the Town Hall, where, among the notables, he recognized General Corbineau, who had remained in the town in disguise after the entry of the Russians.

The following morning the Emperor sent for Marmont, whom he had not seen since the disaster of Athies. In his report on the action the marshal had tried to excuse himself, but the facts were against him. As soon as Napoleon saw him he burst out into reproaches which the marshal took very much to heart. Soon, however, the feelings which the Emperor had always entertained towards his former *aide-de-camp* gained the upper hand, and he spoke to him like a master to his favourite pupil and finished by asking him to dine. Marmont's conduct during the battle of Rheims, in which no other troops than his had been engaged except Colbert and Defrance's cavalry, was sufficient to blot out, for the day at least, the memory of his culpable negligence at Athies.

It was a complete victory: 4,000 infantry and 4,000 cavalry had overthrown 15,000 of the enemy; they had captured a town, had taken twelve guns and 3,000 prisoners, and killed or wounded more than 3,000 men. The French loss was only 700. The Emperor was much impressed by the death of the renegade commander of the allies, who had been killed, like Moreau at Dresden, by a French cannon-ball, and on March 14 he wrote to King Joseph, "General Saint-Priest has been mortally wounded. The remarkable thing is that he was hit by the same gun-layer who killed General Moreau. The hand of Providence is clearly seen."

By the occupation of Rheims the Emperor placed himself on the line of communication between the two allied armies, and the capture of the town had in consequence a great moral effect. The victory of March 13 raised the courage of the French troops and correspondingly depressed the allies. Blücher had claimed to have destroyed Napoleon's army, and now this army had descended like a thunderbolt upon Saint-Priest and was in a position to menace the flank of the Austro-Russians.

Blücher was the first to get into trouble. He wasted the first two days after the battle of Laon before making up his mind to take advantage of his victory. On March 13 all his troops resumed the offensive. Sacken advanced on Soissons, York on Berry-au-Bac, Kleist on Pont-à-Vaire, and Bülow on Noyen and Compiegne. A brisk engagement took place at Croüy between the Russians and one of Mortier's divisions which was covering Soissons, and on the following day, the 14th, Blücher, on hearing of the capture of Rheims, recalled his different corps and concentrated them between Laon and Corbény. The order to retreat did not reach Bülow's advance-guard until after they had appeared before Compiègne.

They summoned the town to surrender, and the commandant made the following short and ironical reply, "I will surrender the town when his Majesty the Emperor gives me the order to do so." On receipt of the order to retreat, Bülow retired at once to Laon.

Blücher was half blind from ophthalmia and was weakened by fever, and was, therefore, a prey to every fear. In common with most of his generals, he feared that Napoleon might make a fresh attack by Berry-au-Bac or that he might move through Rethel and Montcornet, for it was rumoured among the allies that the garrisons of the fortresses were on the march to join the imperial army.

> "This terrible Napoleon," said Langeron, "we expected him to appear anywhere. He had beaten us all, one after another; we always feared his daring, his rapidity, and his brilliant combinations. We could hardly devise a plan before it was baffled by him."

On March 7 Napoleon had published two decrees, known as the decrees of Fismes, in which he called upon all French citizens to take up arms and harass the enemy. It is doubtful to what extent these decrees were obeyed, but their publication had the effect of alarming the allies, and Blücher felt uneasiness at the prospect of a general rising of the peasants. He had replied to the decrees by authorizing pillage and by burning the village of Athies, and had published a proclamation to the effect that each commune would be held responsible for acts of guerrilla warfare committed within its boundaries, and that any peasant found in possession of arms would be shot.

These threats failed alike to reassure Blücher or to intimidate the guerrillas; ambuscades, attacks on convoys, and murders at isolated farms continued just as if Blücher had not spoken, and the day after he issued his proclamation the peasants of the Oise harassed Bülow's troops as they were returning to Laon. Schwarzenberg issued a similar proclamation, and it is worthy of remark that it opened with the words, " Frenchmen, you are being incited to rebellion."

The old Field-Marshal had still another cause for uneasiness. Bernadotte had been at Liège since the beginning of March, and he and his 23,000 Swedes had made no move, and Blücher imagined that the Prince of Sweden was only waiting for a sign from Napoleon to attack the rear of the army of Silesia. There is no doubt that Bernadotte had received an emissary from King Joseph, and although he had come to no arrangement with the French the allies doubted his fidelity.

He was very much annoyed that they had taken away from him the command of Bülow's and Winzingerode's corps, and he nourished a secret hope that he might be appointed sovereign of France; for this reason he was not at all anxious to figure as an invader of his former country, and he had decided not to cross the frontier. By a subtle distinction Bernadotte appeared to think that the French would forget that he had fought against them on the banks of the Elster as long as he had refrained from fighting them on the banks of the Seine.

Blücher's fears, however, were imaginary. It was unreasonable to count upon the co-operation of the Swedes, for Bernadotte had written to the allies to say that he was not in a position to make any active movement, but there were no grounds for fearing an attack from him. The Prince of Sweden was too clever to compromise himself by offensive action on either side, and his object was to husband his strength until the campaign had been decided.

If the allies were to win, he would remain a claimant for the throne of France, and could advance as excuses for his inaction his scruples as to invading his native country, which he aspired to rule. If, however, the French were to win, he might perhaps attack the allies as they retreated; in either case he had hopes of gaining compensation in Finland as a reward for his neutrality. Blücher was not able to see through Bernadotte's double-dealing and his anxiety was acute; he rightly thought that he was safe in the strong position of Laon, and he could not make up his mind to leave it.

If Blücher had been checked in mid-career by the capture of Rheims, the effect produced on the cautious Schwarzenberg was proportionately greater. From March 5 to 11 his operations had been carried out with his usual slowness. He had captured Troyes on the afternoon of the 4th, and during the following days he had only pushed his advance-guards as far as Nogent, Sens, and Bray, while his reserves remained at Chaumont.

He was deaf to the impatience of the Czar, who had wished to march in pursuit of Napoleon after the battle of Bar-sur-Aube, and he paid no attention to the jokes and criticisms of the Russian and Prussian staffs. Schwarzenberg behaved as if he was faced by an enemy of twice his own strength.

There were two courses open to him: with his 120,000 men he might have routed Macdonald's 30,000 and then have marched direct on Paris, or he might have left a few divisions to contain the marshal while he himself moved so as to crush Napoleon between the armies of Bohemia and Silesia. If Schwarzenberg had adopted one or other of these plans he would quickly have brought the campaign to a glorious issue.

In addition, however, to the political reasons which have been ascribed to him without much grounds, military considerations were enough to prevent Schwarzenberg from adopting a determined offensive. He had no news of Blücher, and if the Field-Marshal had been beaten, to advance against Napoleon's victorious army would have been to invite a check, or possibly a disaster.

"I have no news, and I confess that I am in dread," wrote Schwarzenberg. "If Blücher has been defeated I dare not fight a battle, for if I were to be beaten what a triumph it would be for Napoleon, and what a humiliation for the sovereigns, who would re-cross the Rhine at the head of a routed army!"

As to pushing straight on to Paris, Schwarzenberg considered this would be risky until he had news of Blücher's operations. In addition, supplies were becoming scarce; a movement on Paris would lengthen the line of communications, and increase the difficulty of protecting convoys against guerrillas, and would involve a danger of starvation. These considerations would certainly not have stopped a resolute and enterprising soldier, but Schwarzenberg was neither resolute nor enterprising.

Macdonald was agreeably surprised by the enemy's delay, and he seized the opportunity to reorganize and rest his troops. Several of his subordinate officers were much discouraged.

"I will do my best," he wrote to Clarke, "I do not require to be urged; I wish I could infuse some of my own zeal into others."

Every evening Macdonald expected that the following day would bring an attack, but day after day passed in quiet.

It was not until March 11 that Schwarzenberg made up his mind to drive Macdonald away from the right bank of the Seine. The 12th and 13th were employed in preparatory movements. On the 14th Wrède bombarded Bray and Gyulai, and the Prince of Würtemberg occupied Sens and Nogent in force, and meanwhile Rajewsky, who had succeeded Wiggenstein in command of the 6th Corps, crossed the Seine at Pont and advanced on Villenoxe.

On the evening of the 14th Schwarzenberg received a dispatch from General Saint-Priest dated from Sillery on March 11, which announced Blücher's victory at Laon and Napoleon's retreat on Soissons. This news was of a nature to encourage the Austro-Russians, and on the 15th and 16th they adopted a vigorous offensive. The French, however, stood firm.

They had maintained almost all their positions, but Macdonald considered it imprudent to defend the passage of the Seine any longer, now that his left flank was turned, and he ordered Amey to evacuate Bray and Gérard to retire on Provins. On the 16th Macdonald retired again, and took up a position behind Provins with all his troops: the right of his infantry was at Donnemarie and the left at Cucharmois, covering Nangis and the road to Paris; the whole of his cavalry was massed at Rouilly, blocking the road to La-Ferté-Gaucher. He wrote to Clarke:

> My left has been turned and I have been obliged to evacuate Provins. I will contest every step of the ground, but I am in urgent need of help.

Macdonald had nothing more to fear from the enemy. During the evening of the 16th Schwarzenberg ordered his corps to abandon the offensive; he had heard of the battle of Rheims and had received reports that French troops were near Châlons. The following letter, written by an *aide-de-camp* of the Czar, who was attached to Rajewsky's staff, expresses the anger which the Russians felt at this sudden change of plan.

> If the folly of the Austrians is not assumed, as I fear, the terrible lessons which we are forcing the enemy to give us will at last open people's eyes as to this Viennese scum. I am furious on account of what we are doing, and still more on account of what we are failing to do.

This fiery *aide-de-camp* would probably have been less furious if he had known that Napoleon was arriving by forced marches on the flank of the army of Bohemia, whose corps were scattered over a depth of fifty miles.

FRENCH ARMY

As reorganized after the battle of Laon

Napoleon:

1st Division of the Old Guard (Friant)	
Reserve Artillery	6,800
Sebastiani's Cavalry:	
1st Division Guard Cavalry (Colbert)	
2nd ,, ,, ,, (Exelmans)	
3rd ,, ,, ,, (Letort)	4,200
*Lefebvre-Desnoettes' Cavalry	1,500
*Henrion's Division of the Young Guard	3,000

Ney:

Defrance's Gardes d'Honneur	800
Rousseau's (late Boyer's) Brigade	2,250
*Janssen's (afterwards Lefol's) Division	2,900

*Joined the army before the battle of Arcis-sur-Aube.

Belliard:

[1]Roussel's Dragoons	1,880
Composite Cavalry Divisions (Berckheim) (Mouriez' Heavy and Curély's Light Brigades)	1,800

Mortier:

1st Division of the Young Guard	(Charpentier)	
2nd ,, ,, ,, ,,	(Curial)	
3rd ,, ,, ,, ,,	(Christiani)	600
Grouvelle's Light Cavalry		600

Marmont:

Ricard's Division	
Lagrange's Division	
Arrighi's Division	4,000
Bordesoulle's Cavalry	1,800

The troops under Macdonald (2nd, 7th, and 11th Corps, and the 2nd, 5th, and 6th Cavalry Corps) were not affected by the re-organization.

---

1. Left with Marmont and Mortier on the Aisne.

CHAPTER 13

Napoleon's Advance to the Aube

When Napoleon marched after Blücher on February 27 he had outlined the whole plan of the campaign in his mind. He would crush the army of Silesia and drive its remnants beyond the Oise; he would then march towards the north-eastern fortresses, assemble their garrisons, and fall upon the rear of the army of Bohemia with 10,000 sabres and 40,000 bayonets; at the same time the Austro-Russians would be engaged in front by Macdonald and on their left flank by Augereau.

This was a magnificent strategic conception, and with good luck it was not impossible of execution; but everything had gone against Napoleon; the capitulation of Soissons had saved Blücher, and the successful resistance of the army of Silesia at Laon, combined with the retreat of Macdonald on Provins and of Augereau on Lyons, made the proposed movement risky in the extreme. Before the Emperor could reach the fortresses and collect their garrisons the armies of Bohemia and Silesia might have pushed back Macdonald and Mortier and advanced on Paris, and by the time he had begun his movement against the rear of the Austro-Russians Paris might already be in the hands of the allies. Napoleon knew how cautious Schwarzenberg was, and he was certain that if Blücher was beaten he would not advance alone upon Paris. But with Blücher unbeaten the conditions were different. If Schwarzenberg knew that Napoleon was beyond the Meuse he might make a combined movement with Blücher and march rapidly on Paris, even at the risk of parting with his line of communications. The Emperor found himself under the necessity of temporarily giving up his plan. It was essential that he should remain behind the Aisne, where he could contain Blücher and overawe Schwarzenberg, and where he would be within two long marches of Paris. On March 10 he wrote to King Joseph:

"It is difficult for me to go anywhere else until I have been able to compromise the army of Silesia."

The recapture of Rheims, which the Emperor rightly thought would intimidate Blücher and Schwarzenberg, caused him to modify his ideas and directed his thoughts towards his original plan. With some slight modifications, this plan had again become possible. Macdonald's dispatches warned the Emperor that the army of Bohemia was so near Paris that there was not time for him to collect the garrisons of the fortresses; it might be possible, however, to surprise Schwarzenberg, to beat one or two of his corps in detail, and then, when the Austro-Russians were in retreat, he would be free to march into Lorraine.

In order to be ready to act as advanced and flank-guards, Colbert was sent to Epernay and Ney to Châlons, and at the same time the Emperor again ordered the governors of the fortresses to take the field and join him. On the morning of the 15th Napoleon explained his plan to Marmont, who writes as follows in his *Memoirs*:

"The Emperor told me that after having beaten the Austrian army he proposed to march to the eastward, collect almost all the garrisons of the fortresses, and manoeuvre on the enemy's rear; during this time he would leave me in front of Paris in order to defend the capital."

It was on the morning of March 14, that is to say, eight hours after he had entered Rheims that the Emperor conceived the idea of moving against Schwarzenberg, but it was not until the 17th that he made up his mind as to the point on which his attack should be directed. He might march towards Provins or Meaux so as to join Macdonald in front of the enemy, or he might march by Fère-Champenoise and Arcis-sur-Aube on

Méry, or on Troyes, so as to attack the flank or rear of the Austro-Russians. In the opinion of the Emperor the first plan was the safer, but he chose the second "because it was the bolder of the two."

Marshal Ney had entered Châlons almost unopposed on March 15 and captured a considerable quantity of supplies; he was now ordered to march on Arcis. General Berckheim, who was at Fismes with the composite cavalry division, was ordered to join the army at Fère-Champenoise. Fresh instructions were sent to Marmont and Mortier, who were directed to pivot on Soissons and Rheims and to devote all their attention to keeping Blücher behind the Aisne; if they could not succeed in this they were to retire towards Paris, disputing the ground as they went. Including the garrisons of Soissons and Rheims, the marshals had at their disposal more than 20,000 men.

Mortier was the senior of the two, and was given command of the two corps, but Berthier wrote confidentially to Marmont:

"The Emperor has confidence in your ability; you should direct the operations, but you should let it appear that you are co-operating with Mortier and not that you are in command. This will require tact, but it is not beyond your powers."

The marshal's troops were made up as follows:

Under Marmont:
Ricard's, Lagrange's, and Arrighi's Div.	4,000	effectives.
Bordesoulle's Cavalry	1,800	,,

Under Mortier:
Christiani's, Charpentier's and Curial's Div.	8,500	,,
Roussel's Dragoons	1,880	,,
Grouvelle's Light Cavalry	600	,,
Garrison of Soissons	2,800	,,
Garrison of Rheims	1,500	,,

Feeling confident that Blücher would undertake nothing, at any rate for several days, the Emperor left Rheims on March 17; he had with him the Old Guard, Letort's and Exelmans' divisions of light cavalry, and the reserve artillery. This handful of men would, however, shortly be joined by others, for at Epernay the Emperor would pick up Colbert's cavalry division, and at Fère-Champenoise he would be joined by Berckheim. Ney was to march on a parallel road from Châlons, and he had lately been reinforced by the arrival of Janssen's division from Mézières; in addition, General Lefebvre-Desnoettes was on the march from Paris with a column of all arms. If these various detachments should all arrive, the Emperor would have 15,000 bayonets and 8,000 sabres. With these 23,000 combatants Napoleon was about to attack Schwarzenberg's 100,000 men. Boldness is not the same thing as rashness, and it must be remembered that the Austro-Russians were already engaged with the 30,000 men under Macdonald, who was prepared to assume the offensive in co-operation with the Emperor.

On March 17 the Emperor reached Epernay. The brave inhabitants of this little town received Napoleon with unbounded enthusiasm; they produced the contents of their cellars which they had succeeded in defending against the attacks of Cossacks, and for several hours the good wine of Champagne made the soldiers forget their weariness and the generals their anxieties.

At dawn on the 18th the Guard marched towards Fère-Champenoise, while Ney advanced from Châlons towards Mailly. In the afternoon Sebastiani's cavalry drove back Kaizarow's Cossacks, who were protecting the enemy's left flank, and Ney's cavalry were engaged with Frimont's Uhlans. In the evening the infantry were at Fère-Champenoise and Mailly with the cavalry of the Guard to their front.

At Fère-Champenoise the Emperor learnt that the negotiations of Châtillon were on the point of being broken off. There had been another sitting on March 13 and the representatives of the allies, who had heard of Blücher's victory, demanded a definite answer; some of them even thought that the Congress ought to be closed at once because Caulaincourt's reply was not satisfactory. The Duc de Vicence managed to obtain a delay of thirty-six hours, and he gave the Emperor a full account of the meeting, finishing his letter in the following words:

I am informed that the allied Governments have given definite orders; they have drawn up a notification that the Congress is broken off, and if I do not reply to their proposals this notification will at once be presented to me. I will give them counter-proposals, but they will be merely the Frankfort terms in another form. If we do not make concessions we must abandon the negotiations.

The thirty-six hours came to an end and Caulaincourt had received nothing from the Emperor except a dispatch from Bassano minimizing the importance of the battle of Laon. On March 15 the French plenipotentiary had nothing to produce except a counter-proposal based on a letter from Napoleon written on March 2. This proposal differed very little from the Frankfort terms, and the allies received it in stony silence; they refused to enter into a discussion and announced that they could make no immediate reply, but that they would propose a further conference. From the attitude of the allied plenipotentiaries, Caulaincourt came to the conclusion that the next meeting would find them still unwilling to discuss his proposals and that they would then declare the negotiations at an end; he was of opinion that the only way to prevent a rupture was to accept the allied terms in their entirety.

On March 17 Napoleon yielded to Caulaincourt's representations to the extent of giving him authority to concede enough to prevent a rupture; this short note was accompanied by a more detailed letter from Bassano, who suggested the cession of Antwerp. The bearer of these two dispatches, in spite of his diplomatic character, was refused permission to pass through the allied lines at Nogent and did not succeed in reaching the Duc de Vicence till March 21, two days after the negotiations had been definitely broken off. Even if this messenger had arrived earlier the result would have been the same. The military situation was causing the allies some anxiety, but they would certainly not have consented to modify their ultimatum.

As we have seen, Caulaincourt did not receive the courier in time, and on March 18 he had no further proposals to present to the meeting. As he had feared, the allied representatives refused to discuss his counter-proposals; they read a long declaration in which they protested their sincere desire for peace and laid at Napoleon's door the blame for the failure of the conference. "The allied powders," they concluded, "consider that the Châtillon negotiations have been terminated by the French Government."

Caulaincourt considered that he ought to refute these allegations, and requested that the signature of the protocol might be postponed till the following day. On March 19 he presented his reply and, after a discussion, the plenipotentiaries definitely separated. The comedy was ended and the curtain was rung down on the Congress of Châtillon.

Napoleon expected this result and it did not disturb him; on the previous day he had been equally unmoved by the news of the proclamation of Louis XVIII at Bordeaux. He anticipated such a result from the manoeuvres in which he was engaged that he looked upon everything else as of minor importance. The plots of the royalists and the ultimatum of the diplomatists were of small account when he was on the point of falling upon the flank of the enemy's main army. He counted on victory to defeat, not only the enemy, but also the treason of his own subjects.

As at Nogent on February 9, Napoleon believed that he was on the point of overthrowing the enemy. His march towards the Aube had struck terror into the heart of the allies. The headquarters at Troyes were in a state of disorder which presaged a retreat. Both officers and men said they were surrounded and would have to cut their way out towards the Rhine; they believed that the peasants of the Vosges had risen *en masse* and that the Swiss had sided with the French and were advancing under the leadership of Napoleon's generals. The inhabitants of Troyes expected an early deliverance. In spite of his confidence and obstinacy, the Czar himself was staggered. He had meant to go to Arcis in order to follow the movement of the army on Provins, but when he learnt that the French had occupied Châlons he determined not to leave Troyes.

Prince Wolkonsky wrote on the 18th to General Toll, who was with Schwarzenberg at Pont-sur-Seine:

> We are remaining at Troyes to avoid having to come back again if Napoleon marches on Arcis. His Majesty thinks it is better to go direct from Troyes to Bar-sur-Aube. In a word, we don't know what is going to happen or where we ought to go. I am in a quandary; in the name of heaven give us some comfort.

Schwarzenberg was in no condition to comfort the Czar. The orders and counter-orders which he issued on the 16th, 17th, 18th, and 19th bear witness to the confusion of his mind. On the evening of the 16th, as we have seen, Schwarzenberg suspended his advance against Macdonald; for the 17th he had ordered the following moves:

> The 5th Corps will concentrate at Arcis; the 6th Corps will move on Méry; the 4th Corps will be between No-gent and Pont; the 3rd Corps will occupy Troyes, and the Guard and reserve will remain at Brienne.

This was clearly a retreat. On the 17th he issued the following orders for the 18th:

> The 5th Corps will advance from the Aube towards the Marne, covering the front Ramerupt Allibaudière; the 6th Corps will march on Charny; the 4th and 3rd Corps will be echeloned between Pont-sur-Seine and Joigny; the Guard and reserves will occupy Pougy, Lesmont, Donnement, and Dommartin. Head-quarters will be at Arcis.

This was not a concentration, it was a dispersion. Schwarzenberg wished to detain Macdonald behind the Seine at Joigny, Pont, and Villenoxe where Pahlen's cavalry still was, while he offered battle to Napoleon beyond the Aube. He scattered his troops in an immense semicircle on a front of 75 miles.

By occupying such an extended front he gave Napoleon an

opportunity of piercing his line and beating in detail several of the corps of the army of Bohemia. The Emperor could not have hoped that the allies would have adopted a formation so favourable to the success of his manoeuvre. Unfortunately the Czar, who was much alarmed by the approach of Napoleon, realized the mistake of the Austrian commander-in-chief. Ever since the beginning of the campaign Alexander had been annoyed by Schwarzenberg's slowness in advancing, and now his slowness in retreating filled him with alarm. Schwarzenberg was less timid than irresolute, and his hesitation was equally conspicuous in a retreat as in an advance.

On March 17 Napoleon was still believed to be at Rheims, and on this day the Czar noticed with concern that Schwarzenberg's left was beyond Sens, while his right was on the far side of the Aube. On the 18th the danger became acute, and Alexander was actuated by fear rather than by strategy in asking the commander-in-chief to come and speak to him. Schwarzenberg was ill in bed, for in this terrible winter campaign no commander kept his health except Napoleon. He sent one of his *aides-de-camp* to the Czar, who was not satisfied, and started in a coach for Arcis. At 6 o'clock in the evening he reached the head-quarters, and meeting General Toll in the ante-room he said to him angrily, "What is happening? do you wish to ruin the army?"

Toll replied: "Your Majesty will be able to judge for yourself as to the indecision of the generals. I have done my best to point out the danger of our position. It is an excellent thing that your Majesty has come in person."

While they were talking the Czar and his *aide-de-camp* had gone into another room, where they found Radetzky, Langenau, and the principal officers of Schwarzenberg's staff.

"Well, gentlemen," said Alexander, "what do you propose to do in this crisis?"

The generals replied that they must wait for news from the advance-guards which were engaged with the French.

Toll rightly thought this answer unsatisfactory, and exclaimed,

"Every minute is precious; the only way to avoid a disaster is to concentrate all our troops between Troyes and Pougy, and to make Wrède's corps recross the Aube and defend the bridge of Arcis."

The movement which Toll suggested was not a mere concentration to the rear with a view to giving battle in a new position; it was clearly the beginning of a retreat. Toll wanted Wrède to dispute the crossing at Arcis in order to protect the flank of the columns which would have to retire from Nogent, Pont, and Méry. The Czar agreed with his *aide-de-camp's* suggestion, as it involved an immediate retreat; then, with his plan cut and dried, he went into Schwarzenberg's bedroom. Alexander pointed out to the Field-Marshal the dangers which the length of his front involved, and they both agreed as to the necessity of concentration. Fear is sometimes a good counsellor.

Verbal orders were immediately sent to the corps commanders, and at 8 p.m. Schwarzenberg dictated the following dispositions for the next two days:

On the 19th the 6th, 4th, and 3rd Corps will march on Troyes; the 5th Corps will retire to the left bank of the Aube; the Guard and reserves will mass behind the Voire; head-quarters will be at Pougy. On the 20th the 6th, 4th, and 3rd Corps will march on Vendeuvre, and the 5th on Brienne; the reserves will concentrate at Trannes; head-quarters will be at Bar-sur-Aube.

This was more than Toll had asked for; he named Troyes as the first point of concentration, and Schwarzenberg was retreating direct on Bar. In one moment Schwarzenberg had changed from sublime assurance to the depths of cowardice. At 6 o'clock he had proposed to hold Macdonald behind the Seine and to fight a battle with Napoleon between the Marne and Aube; at 8 o'clock his only thought was to escape from his two opponents and to make his 100,000 men retire 25 miles before half that number of French troops.

Napoleon foresaw that the news of his march would alarm

Schwarzenberg and would lead him to make a false movement, but he did not expect so hurried a retreat. Until the evening of the 18th he believed that almost the whole of the army of Bohemia had crossed the Seine, and was engaged with Macdonald in the neighbourhood of Villenoxe, Nogent, and Provins, and he expected to be able to cross the Aube at Arcis, and find himself in Schwarzenberg's rear. When he reached Fère-Champenoise at 4 p.m. he learnt that the army of Bohemia had begun to retreat, and that a portion of it was collected at Arcis and Plancy. If he were to attack the troops at Arcis, he would lose a day and night and not capture the crossing; the Emperor, therefore, determined to take a short cut and cross the Aube at Boulages, and the Seine at Méry. He hoped to be able to cross the two rivers unopposed, and to be in time to attack the enemy's rear-guard as it retreated to Troyes. At the worst, if this country had been already abandoned, he would effect his junction with Macdonald.

On the morning of the 19th the Emperor marched on Boulages with the Guard cavalry and composite cavalry in front, followed by the Old Guard and the artillery. According to his orders, Ney moved to his right and marched on Plancy via Villers and Champfleury. Macdonald had failed to assume the offensive the previous day, and left Vulaines this same morning, moving on Lechelle, Sourdun, and Bray.

Sebastiani's cavalry soon encountered Kaizarow's Cossacks and drove them back to the Aube. The Cossacks had posted their light artillery on the left bank and tried to dispute the passage. While the sappers restored the bridge of Plancy, the lancers and dragoons forded the river in face of the enemy's fire and pursued the Cossacks as far as the village of Pouan. At 3 o'clock the Emperor moved forward from Plancy with the 3rd division of Guard cavalry and the composite cavalry division and marched rapidly to Méry. The Prince of Würtemberg's rear-guard, which was marching from Nogent to Troyes, attempted to defend the crossing at Méry, but with no better result than at Plancy; the French cavalry forded the Seine and fell upon the Würtembergers, who fled towards Troyes and lost a number of prisoners and a bridging train.

At 7 p.m. all the corps of the army of Bohemia were in retreat, except Kaizarow's Cossacks and Wrède's rear-guard, who still held the right bank of the Barbuisse and the town of Arcis-sur-Aube. The Emperor spent the night at Plancy, and all his troops were in the neighbourhood of that village except Berckheim and Letort's divisions, which remained at Méry. Macdonald reached Villenoxe and reported from there that "the enemy's retreat has been so rapid that we have been unable to keep touch with his rear-guard." The Austrian retreat had certainly been very rapid, but there is no doubt that Macdonald's march had been extremely slow.

The weakness of the enemy's resistance at Plancy and Méry and the direction of his retreat agreed with the reports of the troops and of the peasants in indicating that the army of Bohemia was retreating by forced marches through Troyes on Brienne or Bar-sur-Aube. The Austro-Russian retreat had been more rapid than the Emperor's attack, and their sudden abandonment of the line of the Seine prevented the Emperor's movement being completely successful. The essential part of the operation, as a whole, however, was not compromised.

His march towards the Aube was only a preparatory manoeuvre; this march had not been rapid enough to end in a flank attack, but it had succeeded in relieving the pressure on Paris and Napoleon had joined Macdonald, driven back Schwarzenberg and deceived Blücher. A week ago the Emperor had not had time available to enable him to march towards the fortresses and come down upon the rear of the army of Bohemia, but now it seemed that this manoeuvre was possible.

Schwarzenberg's fright had saved his army from a partial defeat, but if the approach of a handful of men towards his flank had caused the commander-in-chief to fall into such a panic, it is easy to imagine what his state of mind would be if the Emperor were to fall upon his rear with a force of 90,000 men, composed of his own army augmented by the garrisons of the fortresses and troops under Macdonald, Marmont, and Mortier.

No possible movement ever escaped the Emperor, and he doubtless considered the question of pursuing the enemy towards Troyes, but he did not decide to do so. The Austro-Russians had effected their concentration and had more than twice his own numbers in line. The opportunity of attacking them had passed, and the Emperor determined to march through Vitry towards the eastern fortresses.

There were two roads which led from Plancy to Vitry; one *via* Salon, Fère-Champenoise and Sommesous, the other through Arcis, Mailly, and Sompuis. These roads were of equal length, and under the circumstances each had advantages and disadvantages. The first was the safer because the road led at once away from the enemy, but a movement by this road would appear to be a retreat and might restore Schwarzenberg's confidence and induce him to advance again on Paris.

By moving up the Aube to Arcis, however, there would be a risk of meeting the enemy's rear-guard, but a more likely result would be to frighten Schwarzenberg and to make him concentrate and remain stationary for some days. It is almost unnecessary to say that Napoleon's bold strategy made him adopt the second course. Also Sebastiani's cavalry was already in front of Pouan, halfway to Arcis, in touch with the Cossacks, and if they were to retire and cross the river at Plancy the Austrian staff would soon know of it, for in presence of the Cossacks it was impossible to keep any movement secret.

The orders for the march were issued on the morning of the 20th; Ney, Sebastiani, and Letort were to move to Arcis by the left bank of the Aube and to take up a position in front of that town; Defrance, Friant, and Drouot were to move by the right bank to a position opposite Arcis and were to be ready to march on Vitry in the afternoon or during the night; Macdonald was ordered to march his three corps on Arcis by the right bank "without tiring his troops too much"; and finally, orders were sent to Marmont and Mortier to rejoin the Emperor *via* Châlons.

During the morning of March 20 Napoleon wrote to the Minister of War:

"My movement has been perfectly successful; I will neglect Troyes and will march in all haste to the fortresses"; and as he was about to mount his horse he wrote to him again: "I am starting for Vitry."

Berthier's orders were very clear and precise and they bear out the Emperor's letter; there can be no doubt that Napoleon intended to march to Vitry and that he had no thought of pursuing the enemy. His movement, he says, or rather, the first part of his movement, "has been perfectly successful."

He was ready to sacrifice everything in order to make the success complete, and for this reason he ordered Marmont to uncover the road to Paris. Napoleon certainly found that Blücher would not dare under the circumstances to advance alone on Paris; the Emperor's usual sagacity was not at fault here, but, no matter what Blücher did, the Emperor would not have altered his resolution.

He had been unaffected by the news of the capture of Bordeaux, he contemplated with perfect calm the capture of Paris, where every preparation had been made for moving the Government. He looked upon the loss of the capital as a mere accident of war and as of small importance as compared with the destruction of the enemy's main army. The imperial head-quarters would henceforth be the capital of the Empire.

CHAPTER 14

The First Day of the
Battle of Arcis-Sur-Aube

The Prince of Schwarzenberg was not chary of orders and
counter-orders. He would sometimes lay down three different
dispositions of his troops in one day, and then alter the third on
the following day. It would have been a miracle if he had remained constant for twenty-four hours to the orders which he
issued on the evening of the 18th. On the morning of the 19th
he learnt that Wrède's rear-guard had recrossed the Aube at Arcis without having been molested by the French, who had been
marching towards that town the previous day; he concluded that
Napoleon was moving on Brienne and he determined to oppose him on the line of the Voire.

The troops received orders to concentrate between Lesmont
and Braux, facing towards Dommartin and Donnement, but
during the afternoon Kaizarow's report on the fighting at Plancy was received; instead of marching on Brienne as Schwarzenberg imagined, Napoleon had crossed the Aube below Arcis, and
his objective appeared to be Troyes. Schwarzenberg was at once
freed from all anxiety as regards his flank; he came to the conclusion that the Emperor was in a dangerous position, with a
river and marsh behind him, and he was suddenly infused with
energy. He stopped his retreat and determined not only not to
avoid a battle, but even to force one. At 9 p.m. he issued orders to
his corps commanders to mass their troops between Troyes and

Chaudrey and to march in concert at 11 a.m. the following day on Plancy and Méry, with a view to attacking Napoleon.

This manoeuvre was not really a bold one, because, after all, it only involved an attack by 100,000 men on a force of 20,000 which had a river in its rear, but nevertheless it evinced a certain amount of resolution on the part of the commander-in-chief. Now the allies were so little accustomed to any sign of energy on the part of their commander that this order caused the utmost astonishment throughout the army. It was even said that Schwarzenberg could not possibly have formed the idea himself and that he must have yielded to someone else's advice, and opinion was divided as to whether it was the Czar, Radetzky, Toll, Wrède, or the Prince of Würtemberg who had conceived the idea.

As a matter of fact, the Czar only learnt the change of plans during the night or on the following morning, and he was both displeased and frightened when he heard of it; neither Toll, nor Würtemberg, nor Radetzky, nor anyone else influenced Schwarzenberg in the matter. Schwarzenberg himself formed the resolution to attack, and he alone deserves the honour. As the majority of German and Russian historians have stated, the Prince of Schwarzenberg on this day rendered signal service to the allies. The retreat on Trannes would have seriously compromised the army of Bohemia and might very likely have resulted in disaster followed by a retreat to the Rhine.

Schwarzenberg's instructions were that the whole army was to be drawn up in line of battle at 7 a.m.; at about 11 o'clock the signal for the advance would be given by the firing of three guns and the lighting of a large fire on the heights of Mesnil, where the head-quarters would be. The preliminary orders for the concentration, however, were only received at a late hour during the night, and the various corps did not start till comparatively late in the morning and it was not till 9 o'clock that the 3rd, 4th, and 6th Corps began to issue out of Troyes.

Wrède alone was ready at an early hour in his position on the right of the line at Chaudrey, and he had sent forward some of

Frimont's squadrons as far as Arcis and the Barbuisse stream.

Sebastiani, with Colbert and Exelmans' cavalry divisions, formed the advance-guard of the imperial army, and left their bivouac at Bessy between 9 and 10 a.m. Colbert's lancers had no difficulty in driving Kaizarow's Cossacks and Frimont's Bavarians from the right bank of the Barbuisse; the allied cavalry retired at a gallop towards Troyes and Arcis, and Sebastiani continued his march and entered Arcis at 11 a.m. Very soon afterwards Marshal Ney arrived at Arcis by the left bank of the Aube with Janssen's and Rousseau's troops, while Defrance's Gardes d'Honneur and Mouriez's *cuirassiers* arrived by the right bank.

The movements of Frimont's cavalry, which indicated a retreat rather than an attack on the part of the allies, were not such as to alarm the French generals, who took up a position at Arcis and repaired the bridge. The Guard cavalry pushed reconnaissances along the Troyes and Brienne roads, and the Gardes d'Honneur and *cuirassiers* watched the roads on the right bank of the river.

Between 1 and 1.30 p.m. Napoleon arrived at Arcis by the left bank, with an escort of only one squadron. At this time Ney and Sebastiani were on the alert, for the peasants reported that large numbers of the enemy were approaching, and dispositions had been taken to hold the left bank of the river until the Emperor's arrival; Sebastiani deployed his cavalry in front of Arcis, and Ney occupied Torcy-le-Grand, a mile and a half east of the town, with Janssen's division in first line and Rousseau's brigade in reserve.

Napoleon believed that the enemy was retiring, and at first he refused to credit the reports of the peasants; but he sent one of his orderly officers with a squadron to reconnoitre along the Troyes road. If it were true that Schwarzenberg was preparing to attack, Sebastiani's cavalry and Ney's infantry had time to cross the river and destroy the bridge, and Napoleon could then have defied all the enemy's efforts. Unfortunately the young captain who was in charge of the reconnaissance did not push far enough forward on to the little plateau which rises gradually in front of Arcis, and which was broken enough to afford concealment to large numbers of troops; he soon returned, and reported to the Emperor that there were no enemy except a few Cossacks in the neighbourhood. This report agreed with the opinion which Napoleon had already formed, and he ordered Sebastiani to remain where he was, and he himself went to Torcy to inspect Ney's positions.

Sebastiani was less reassured by this reconnaissance than the Emperor had been, and he determined to find out the truth for himself. He took two squadrons and started at a gallop along the Troyes road, determined, if necessary, to break through the screen of Cossacks. He had hardly reached the top of the plateau when he saw large masses of cavalry within cannon-shot of him; these were the whole of Kaizarow's Cossacks and Frimont's fifty-six squadrons, who had waited for three hours for the signal for the attack, and were now beginning to advance.

The French occupation of Arcis was the cause of the delay; this movement forced the Comte de Wrède to draw back his right, and involved an extension of the whole front of the allied army. Schwarzenberg was disconcerted, and lapsed into his usual state of irresolution, while he found no encouragement in the anxious and reproachful demeanour of the Czar. Alexander was both surprised and displeased that the commander-in-chief had abandoned the retreat which had been decided upon on the 18th and was now marching against Napoleon. When he arrived on the plateau of Mesnil, with the King of Prussia, the Czar would not go near Schwarzenberg; he saluted him from a distance, and then dismounted and said in an angry tone to Generals Toll and Barclay de Tolly:

"I should like to know why the Prince of Schwarzenberg has once more altered all his dispositions? Why has not the army continued its retreat on Trannes?"

Toll replied: "If Napoleon had outflanked our right yesterday morning *via* Arcis, the army would have continued its retreat; but he has lost at least twenty-four hours by marching on Plancy, and has given us time to concentrate our troops between Troyes and Pougy. We have a chance of striking a good blow; we have the advantage of the ground, for we can manoeuvre freely, while the enemy has the marshy valley of the Aube in his rear."

Alexander was not convinced by these arguments, and replied: "Napoleon will keep us amused here with paltry demonstrations while the bulk of his army turns our position through Brienne."

Then, on the ground that Wrède's corps alone was not strong enough to hold the right, he ordered Barclay de Tolly to hasten the march of the Russian reserves.

The day wore on: Schwarzenberg was probably not less uneasy than the Czar, but he did not wish to show his anxiety, and he thought that, at any rate, it was too late to go back, and at last, at 2 o'clock, he gave the order for the attack. It was just at the moment when the Austro-Russians were moving forward that Sebastiani's reconnaissance reached the plateau. He knew that, especially for cavalry, attack is the best form of defence, and he returned at full gallop to Arcis and ordered forward his two divisions against the enemy. Colbert's division, which was in first line, was received by the fire of the light batteries ranged along the front of Frimont's squadrons, and at the same time Kaizarow's Cossacks, supported by a regiment of Austrian hussars, charged home against the right flank of the light cavalry of the Guard. The cry of *sauve qui peut* was raised in the ranks, and Colbert's horsemen fled in panic on to the front of Exelmans' division, which was in second line. The lancers and dragoons gave way under the shock, and in a confused mass the two divisions fled at full gallop towards Arcis, with the Cossacks in hot pursuit.

Napoleon was at Torcy when he heard the sound of the guns; he set off for Arcis at a gallop, followed only by a few officers and a small escort. As he reached the town he was met by the mixed mass of French and allied cavalry; he drew his sword and managed to take refuge in the square of the Vistula battalion. The bayonets of the Poles stopped the hussars and Cossacks, and their fire drove them back. As soon as the ground was clear the Emperor left the square and dashed into Arcis, which was crowded with the fugitive cavalry; he forced his way through the middle of the crowd and forestalled them at the bridge: there he turned suddenly, and cried in a loud voice "Which of you will cross before me?"

At these words the fugitives stopped. The Emperor rallied and re-formed them, and led them back against the enemy's squadrons.

Napoleon had only 2,600 sabres to place in line against more than 6,000, and Frimont and Kaizarow's horsemen were supported by a formidable mass of artillery, and they had a whole army behind them. The Emperor was in danger of being thrown back into Arcis and either captured or driven into the river. Ney's infantry could not come to his help, for they were engaged at Torcy with the whole of Wrède's corps. Seventy-two guns were firing against the front of the French, while on their left column after column was moving up to the assault.

The Austro-Bavarians drove Janssen's division out of Torcy, but Marshal Ney was not the man to lose a position so easily; he brought up Rousseau's brigade and drove the Austrians out of the village at the point of the bayonet, and pursued them to beyond Torcy-le-Petit. The strength of the enemy was momentarily increasing, and his artillery was making gaps in the French ranks which could not be filled. The danger was extreme, and it was doubtful whether the Old Guard would arrive in time to restore the situation.

At last the bearskins of the Guard were seen on the other side of the Aube; they crossed the bridge at a run and traversed the main street of the town. Napoleon sent one battalion of grenadiers and two battalions of *gendarmes* to reinforce Ney, then he himself led the Guard on to the bullet-swept battlefield and drew it up across the road to Troyes. While so doing a shell fell just in front of a company and some of the soldiers made an involuntary movement to the rear. Napoleon rode forward and halted beside the smoking projectile; the shell burst, killing the horse, which dragged the Emperor to the ground amid a cloud of dust and smoke. He got up without a wound, mounted another horse and rode off to align the other battalions. It has been said that the Emperor was in despair and was seeking death, but this is not the case. His dispatches show that he was full of hope, and his object was to set an example of courage to his veterans.

Desperate and bloody fighting continued at all points. Before Torcy the Austro-Bavarians made assault after assault; in front of Arcis a fierce cavalry combat surged to and fro with varying fortune, Frimont's and Kaizarow's cavalry hurling themselves in vain against the squares of the Old Guard. Meanwhile the 3rd, 4th, and 6th Corps of the allies were marching towards Méry and Plancy in accordance with Schwarzenberg's orders of the previous day, which were based on the supposition that the French army was concentrated between the Aube and the Seine.

As Napoleon was now at Arcis, this movement no longer served any useful purpose, and if, instead of marching towards Méry, these three corps had turned towards Arcis, Napoleon's small force could not have escaped. It was clear to Schwarzenberg that he ought to concentrate all his troops against the position occupied by the Emperor, but he sent no orders to the troops on the other side of the Barbuisse, and the Prince of Würtemberg, who had the supreme command over the three corps, did not march to the sound of the guns which he could hear to his right.

When the Prince of Würtemberg's advance-guards reached the heights of Premierfait, their scouts reported that a column of French cavalry was marching across their front along the main road; this was the 3rd division of Guard cavalry which had spent the night at Méry, and had not started till late in the day to join the army at Arcis. Generals Nostitz, Pahlen, and Bismarck, who commanded the cavalry of the allies, led forward their numerous squadrons. Three Russian regiments charged the head of the French column, while the flank was attacked by a division of Austrian cuirassiers and two regiments of Würtemberg dragoons, supported by two light batteries.

The French numbered only 1,600 against nearly 4,000 of

the allies, and to make matters worse they had with them the bridging train which had been captured the previous day. They made some gallant counter-charges, however, and gained time for Curély to arrive from Méry with his brigade of light cavalry and his horse battery. The numbers were even now not equal, and masses of the enemy's infantry were close at hand. The guard retreated across the Seine at Méry, covered by Curély. Some Russian squadrons made an attack on Méry, but were driven off by dismounted cavalry, and the enemy believed that Méry was occupied by infantry, and they retired towards Premierfait.

On the banks of the Aube the battle continued after nightfall. At Arcis, Frimont and Kaizarow's cavalry were held in check by the reserve artillery which arrived soon after Friant's division and gained a welcome respite for the Old Guard and the cavalry. At Torcy-le-Grand the Austro-Bavarian attacks were pressed with increasing vigour; twice they captured the outskirts of the place and twice they were driven out, and 3,000 dead and wounded were heaped around the burning village.

The Bavarian General Habermann was killed and General Janssen was seriously wounded, and the command of his division was assumed by General Lefol. At 8 p.m. Schwarzenberg made a last effort to capture Torcy and sent forward some of the Russian reserves. The first grenadier division, 4,400 strong, 500 *cuirassiers*, and two heavy batteries were brought up to reinforce the Bavarians. Ney's troops had lost heavily and were worn out by six hours of desperate fighting, but they refused to give way; and closing the gaps in their ranks they repulsed every assault, and shortly after midnight they were left in undisputed possession of the smoking ruins of Torcy.

In front of Arcis the battle finished as it had begun by a furious cavalry fight. Between 7 and 8 p.m. General Lefebvre-Desnoettes, leaving behind his worn-out infantry, reached the battlefield with his cavalry. The horses were given a rest, and towards 10 p.m. Sebastiani, in hopes of avenging his defeat of the morning, formed up his two divisions with Lefebvre-Desnoettes' 1,500 sabres and led them forward against the enemy's cavalry, who were posted between the Barbuisse and the Troyes road.

The French overthrew the Cossacks and hussars on the enemy's left, then wheeled to their left and fell on the flank of Frimont's regiments, who broke and fled in disorder. The flank of the allied infantry was exposed, and their situation was dangerous, but Sebastiani's cavalry were checked by the fire of a regiment of Russian grenadiers and a Bavarian battery; the allied horsemen rallied and returned to the charge, driving the French back behind the village of Nozay. The hostile cavalries spent the night within musket range of each other on either side of this village, and for fear of a surprise the men were unable even to lie down, and spent the night with their bridles over their arms.

This day should have witnessed the total destruction of the small army which was the last hope and resource of Napoleon, but, thanks to the magnificent tenacity of the French infantry, the allies were able to claim no advantage. They had killed and wounded 1,800 of the French, but had themselves lost more than 2,500 men. Napoleon at first could place in line only 7,500 against 14,000 of the enemy, then 13,000 against 20,000, and finally 16,000 against 25,000; for eight hours the French had fought in an unfavourable position with their backs to a river, and had not yielded an inch of ground.

CHAPTER 15

The Second Day of the Battle of Arcis-Sur-Aube

On March 20, owing to too great an extension of his front, Schwarzenberg had only been able to bring into action a quarter of his army; he had missed the opportunity of gaining a victory, but his error had the result of deceiving Napoleon. The Emperor thought that he had been opposed by only one corps, left behind by the army of Bohemia; he believed that after the failure of their attack these troops would retreat, and that the following day he would be quit of them. Instead of withdrawing his troops across the Aube during the night, and marching at once either on Vitry *en route* for the fortresses, or on Brienne to turn the enemy's right, the Emperor made up his mind to attack those of the Austro-Russians, who had been too slow in retreating. The Guard and Ney's division remained in their positions on the left bank of the Aube, and orders were sent to hasten the march of all troops who were within reach; Lefebvre-Desnoettes' infantry were at Plancy, Letort's and Curély's cavalry were at Méry, and the corps of Oudinot, Gerard, and Macdonald were between Boulages and Anglure, and these generals were all directed on Arcis.

Napoleon had been deceived by the vigorous but badly combined attack of the enemy, but Schwarzenberg was also misled by the obstinate defence of the French, and by their last cavalry attack; he credited the French with twice their real strength, and he was warned by his outposts that large numbers of bivouac fires could be seen on the right bank of the Aube near Plancy.

He considered it would be more prudent to await attack on the following day; if the French were to hurl themselves in vain against his positions he could launch his masses against them and crush them; but if, on the contrary, the situation seemed threatening, he had his troops well concentrated, and could retreat without being compromised by any ill-timed movement. Schwarzenberg's orders for the 21st indicated a defensive attitude; the 3rd, 4th, and 6th Corps were to recross the Barbuisse, and to deploy between this stream and the eastern slopes of Mesnil; Wrède's corps was to form the right wing, resting on the Aube and facing Torcy; the Guard and reserves were to be in second line on the heights of Mesnil. By 7 a.m. the troops had taken up these positions.

At almost the same hour Napoleon received some of his reinforcements, including Lefebvre-Desnoettes' infantry under General Henrion, the 2nd and 5th Cavalry Corps, and a division of Oudinot's corps. After deducting the losses of the previous day Napoleon's strength now amounted to 18,500 bayonets and 9,500 sabres.

As if to confirm the Emperor's rash assumption, hardly any of the enemy were visible. The outposts only reported a line of Cossack *vedettes* on the plateau, and the Emperor himself made a reconnaissance with one squadron on the Lesmont road, and saw nothing but a few cavalry pickets, which retired at his approach. Napoleon was more and more convinced that the corps which had attacked him the previous day was now in retreat, and he determined to surprise it by a sudden and strong attack. Leval's division and the Old Guard were held in reserve, and Sebastiani and Ney were ordered to advance on to the plateau with all the cavalry, and with Lefol, Rousseau, and Henrion's infantry. At 10 o'clock the cavalry moved forward.

As he watched the magnificent spectacle of 9,000 horsemen advancing to battle the Emperor might well have thought that victory was assured, but the sight which met the eyes of the

French when they reached the summit of the plateau was even more imposing and formidable. The whole of the allied army, nearly 100,000 combatants, was stretched in a semicircle, extending from the Aube on the east to the farther side of the Barbuisse on the west. Three hundred and seventy guns were in position in front of the troops; the infantry formed three lines of battalion columns, and the cavalry covered the flanks, and filled the intervals between the army corps. As far as the eye could reach sabres and bayonets glittered in the sun.

Without being disturbed by the sight of these masses, the horse artillery opened fire, and drew forth a crushing reply from the Austro-Russian guns, while the squadrons on the right gallantly charged Pahlen's cavalry and drove them back. During this engagement Ney and Sebastiani were in consultation. They came to the conclusion that the enemy was strong enough to hold them in front and to outflank their left, and they determined not to become seriously engaged without fresh orders from the Emperor.

When Napoleon learnt that the whole allied army was in front of him, he did not persist in fighting a battle which could only have ended in disaster, and he determined to retreat. The movement began at once. The reserve artillery and the Old Guard crossed by the bridge of Arcis, and the sappers began the construction of a temporary bridge below the town, which was finished by 1.30; the Emperor then ordered Ney and the 2nd and 5th Cavalry Corps to cross to the right bank, and directed Sebastiani to maintain himself on the plateau with the cavalry of the Guard until after dark, so as to hide the retreat of the army.

Sebastiani did not maintain his position until after dark, but by means of false attacks and unremitting activity he managed to impose upon the allies longer than could reasonably have been expected. The sudden halt of the French ought to have made Schwarzenberg move his troops forward, but the Austro-Russians remained on the defensive.

As was always the case, an excessive prudence and weak indecision held sway at the allied head-quarters. Reports were received of the march of a French column towards Saint-Thuise, and of the occupation of Méry by the whole of Macdonald's force. By general consent it was agreed that both flanks of the army of Bohemia were threatened, and it was dangerous to fight under such circumstances. According to a Russian military writer, the lack of initiative among the allies was so marked that Napoleon might have remained in his position the whole day and not have been attacked, and his retreat might have been carried out in perfect safety at night.

The allies first began to realize that the French were retreating when, from the heights of Mesnil, they saw the Guard on the farther bank of the Aube moving towards Vitry. If they had only marched straight on Arcis they would have crushed the Emperor's army while in the act of crossing the river. Instead of immediately giving the order to attack, Schwarzenberg summoned his corps commanders to Mesnil in order to have a "short conversation" with them as regards the necessary arrangements.

This short conversation lasted so long that when the Austro-Russians moved forward two-thirds of the French army were already on the farther bank of the Aube. At the approach of the cloud of horsemen which preceded the 3rd, 4th, and 6th Corps, Sebastiani retired his divisions in squares, and delayed the enemy's march by partial charges and by the fire of his artillery. Thanks to his firm demeanour, the cavalry of the Guard regained Arcis without having suffered heavy losses; one brigade alone was broken and lost some prisoners.

Sebastiani's squadrons crossed the river under the protection of Leval's division, which was the only infantry remaining on the left bank, and meanwhile the allied army advanced. From all points solid columns were converging on Arcis; from Torcy came Wrède's corps, by the Troyes road marched Gyulai and Würtemberg, and from the direction of Méry came Rajewsky. The temporary bridge was threatened by the enemy, and was destroyed by the sappers. Soon shells and cannon-balls were falling in the streets of the town, and Russians, Austrians, Bavarians, and Würtembergers rushed forward to the assault. But every house was loopholed and every entrance barricaded and the town was defended by 6,000 veterans of Spain.

The fighting was desperate, and assault followed on assault, till 50,000 of the allies were concentrated round Arcis. Almost all Leval's artillery was silenced, his infantry had run out of ammunition, and he had lost a sixth of his troops; he gave the order to retreat, but, taking advantage of the retirement of the French, three allied columns forced their way over the barricades; these three columns reached the market square and drove the infantry back to the bridge, which was still encumbered by Sebastiani's rear-guard and Leval's guns.

The confusion was terrible; Leval was wounded, and a panic began to spread. But General Chassé seized a drum and beat the charge; he rallied a number of veterans, who charged the enemy and cleared the approaches to the bridge. The French re-formed and drove off their assailants, and the crossing of the bridge was carried out in good order. At about 7 o'clock the sappers began to demolish the main bridge under cover of the sharp-shooters of Oudinot's 2nd Division, which had taken up a position on the right bank.

For a whole day 30,000 men had remained in contact with 100,000, who had only dared to attack when the French began to retreat. On March 20 the Prince of Schwarzenberg had failed to crush the French army; on the 21st he had allowed it to cross the river without moving a hand to stop it. Twice within thirty hours, owing to his faulty plans and his lack of resolution, the commander- in-chief had failed to win a decisive victory. With such an adversary Napoleon's cause was never hopeless.

CHAPTER 16

Operations of Blücher and Marmont

While Napoleon was manoeuvring against Schwarzenberg, Blücher at last made a move. On March 17 the Emperor had left Rheims, and on this day the Field-Marshal, who was still far from well, broke up his cantonments at Laon. As soon as Napoleon was at a distance the enemy were always ready to take the offensive; the allies were not afraid of Marmont, Augereau, Macdonald, or of any of the Emperor's lieutenants, they did not fear the bravery of his soldiers, but they were in dread of Napoleon himself. "Why cannot the Emperor be everywhere?" wrote Belliard.

Bülow's corps marched on Soissons, and the five other corps of the army of Silesia concentrated at Corbény. On the morning of the 18th the allies marched towards the Aisne in three columns; Czernischeff, with a strong body of cavalry and several battalions of infantry, crossed the river at Neufchatel above Berry-au-Bac; Kleist and York began a bridge at Pont-à-Vaire, and the bulk of the army moved towards Berry-au-Bac. It was thought that Marmont would abandon the bridge when he found he was in danger of being outflanked, but things did not turn out exactly as Blücher hoped.

The bridge was mined, and when the Russian columns advanced towards it Marmont gave the order to fire the charge. From Berry-au-Bac Marmont retired to Pont-à-Vaire; from there he went to Fismes, followed by the enemy's cavalry, and took up a position behind the Vesle. That evening he wrote to

Mortier, who was at Rheims, asking him to join him at Fismes. Mortier was always ready to meet his colleague's wishes, and left Rheims the following morning; but whether Marmont changed his mind or whether Mortier persuaded him that it was dangerous to abandon that town, Roussel's division, which formed the rear-guard, was ordered to re-occupy Rheims.

This division drove off a strong body of Cossacks and re-entered the town, which was surrounded by five or six thousand Russians. General Roussel dismounted two squadrons and sent them to man the walls, and he held out till 7 p.m. in spite of the enemy's attacks. A further order to retire was received, and the dragoons withdrew to Fismes without being molested.

The Emperor afterwards blamed Marmont for having made Fismes his line of retreat instead of Rheims, and this decision resulted in disaster. There is some excuse for Marmont, however, for on the 18th he had received an order to cover the road to Paris, and to do this he was bound to retire on Fismes, and not on Rheims. But Marmont had also been ordered to dispute the ground, and he could not do this unless he was able to appreciate the enemy's true objective.

If Marmont had not enough foresight to do this he ought not to have evacuated Rheims until the enemy's design had been more clearly indicated. Now Blücher had been cured of his love for adventures by the defeats which he had suffered in the middle of February and by the danger from which the capitulation of Soissons had saved him, and he had now no intention of marching on Paris, and was trying to effect a junction with Schwarzenberg.

On March 20 Marmont and Mortier were in position on the heights behind the Vesle, and expected, as Marmont said, to be able to induce the army of Silesia to expose itself to an attack; as a matter of fact they had only Kleist's and York's corps in front of them, and the main bulk of the enemy's army was marching from Rheims on Châlons. Napoleon's genius gave him from a distance a clearer view of the situation than Marmont was able to gain from close at hand, and it was a letter from the Emperor which tore the veil from Marmont's eyes.

"Blücher is about to join Schwarzenberg," wrote the Emperor on March 20, "and you are responsible."

As a result of this letter Marmont broke up his cantonments on March 21 with a view to marching on Châlons, but the enemy was holding the Rheims road, and the route to Epernay was impracticable for artillery. Marmont was obliged to march *via* Oulchy and Château-Thierry, and from there, as the Russians were already in Epernay, he had to go to Etoges. This was a long way round; he was followed by the Prussians and headed by the Russians, who marched parallel to him on his left, and his right was also threatened by a movement on the part of the Austrians; it was extremely doubtful whether the two marshals would be able to outstrip all the allies and save themselves from being surrounded.

While Marmont was compromising his army by these false movements, the procrastination and negligence of Augereau were losing the second city of the Empire. By leaving Lyons a fortnight too late, Augereau had lost the opportunity of cutting the enemy's communications, and he had returned to that town a fortnight before he should have done so. On the approach of the army of the Prince of Hesse on March 4, if the marshal thought that he ought to return to the lower Saone so as to protect Lyons, he ought to have concentrated all his troops at Mâcon.

In this position he could have stopped Bianchi's corps and imposed caution on the rest of the army of the South; he would thus have gained time for the numerous reinforcements which were on the way to him, and would have given Lyons an opportunity of putting itself in a state of defence. Instead of going to Mâcon he marched straight to Lyons, and arrived there on March 9. He then changed his mind and marched slowly towards Mâcon, with his troops scattered along the road to a depth of over thirty miles. The Austrians were already concentrated, and Augereau's leading division found itself opposed by the whole force of the enemy; it was driven back, and after another fight on March 18 the French army retired to Lyons and took up a position in front of the town at Limonest.

This position was almost impregnable against a frontal attack, but its flanks were in the air. The battle took place on March 20, and the French held their own everywhere until midday, when Augereau thought fit to return to Lyons to consult the civil authorities. Confusion resulted from the absence of the commander-in-chief, who had neglected to hand over the command to one of his subordinates. The defence was not co-ordinated, and the counter-attack failed for lack of support. When Augereau returned to the battlefield at 5 o'clock he found all the troops in retreat, and the army fell back into the town.

The erstwhile hero of Castiglione and Lodi, now for the second time summoned to the Town Hall the Commissioner Extraordinary, the *prefect*, the mayor, the Town Council, and the superintendent of police. He ingenuously asked them if he ought to hold out. For a Marshal of the Empire to ask such a question of a civil assembly was tantamount to dictating the answer.

This remarkable Council of Defence, which might more aptly have been termed Council of Surrender, gave it as their opinion that the inhabitants of Lyons ought to be spared the calamity of a useless resistance. Augereau agreed with the municipality, as he admitted in his report, and he gave orders for the evacuation of Lyons. On the following day, March 21, the Prince of Hesse reviewed his troops on the Place Bellecour. The Austrians were elated by the easy capture of Lyons, and had the keys of the city copied in gold and sent to the Emperor Francis.

Napoleon afterwards said that Augereau's desertion handed Lyons over to the enemy. Augereau did not desert in the proper sense of the word, but without actually committing treason to his country, he was false to his duty as a soldier. He had made many mistakes during the campaign, and he ought to have tried to make up for them by an energetic defence of Lyons. The disproportion of strength was not so great that defence was impossible.

After deducting losses and detached forces, the Austrians were only 30,000 strong and the French 21,500 men. In addition, 6,800 infantry of the army of Catalonia were expected on the 22nd, and 7,000 men from the armies of Tuscany and Piedmont were due to arrive about the 25th or 27th. Before the end of the month the garrison would have amounted to 36,000 men.

The population of Lyons was useless from a military point of view because there were no arms for them, but they were patriotic and would have bravely borne the trials of a siege and a bombardment. Certainly the fortifications were in ruins, and there were hardly any guns, but this was Augereau's fault; he had been at Lyons for two months, but had not brought up from Avignon the 80 guns intended for the armament of the place, and had not constructed a single work of defence. There was any amount of civilian labour available to construct earthworks, but it never occurred to Augereau to make use of it.

In this campaign Augereau seemed unable to make use of either men or material; his army was angry and ashamed at the way they were handled, and feeling ran very high.

"Under Suchet," said the soldiers, "we could have done a thousand times more than we have," and these veterans of the Spanish war were not boasting they knew by experience of what they were capable. At Castiglione Augereau, with one division, had routed 25,000 Austrians. The troops which he commanded in 1814 were as good as those of 1796, but Augereau was only the shadow of his former self.

CHAPTER 17

Napoleon's March Against the Enemy's Communications

Had the French army been commanded by a general less daring and resolute than Napoleon, the battle of Arcis-sur-Aube would have put an end to any idea of marching against the enemy's rear. The two days' fighting had ended without disaster to the French, and they had only lost 3,400 men, but the strategic situation was greatly altered. On March 16, 17, and 18 the allies were held in front by Macdonald and threatened on the flank by Napoleon; on the 19th they were in retreat, but by the evening of the 21st they had assumed the offensive against the French, who, it is true, were beginning to concentrate, but by that very act were uncovering the approaches to Paris.

Under these conditions the movement which the Emperor had intended was very dangerous. The roads were now open to Schwarzenberg and Blücher, and they could march rapidly on Paris by con- verging routes, leaving Napoleon free to cause them inconvenience but no actual danger, by manoeuvring on the line of operations of the army of Bohemia. Every political consideration demanded that the Emperor should be at Paris, and there was more than one strategic reason why his army should move there too.

If he were to retreat and take up a position in front of Paris the campaign would be back at the same point where it had been on February 3 after the battle of La Rothière, but the allies had now learnt by experience the dangers of eccentric marches and isolated movements, and they would certainly give Napoleon no more opportunities such as those which he had put to such good use in February. They would now advance on Paris by parallel roads in two columns each 100,000 strong, and this would require little science and no genius. Schwarzenberg and Blücher would only have to march straight ahead.

Their tactical objective, Napoleon, would be forced to coincide with their strategic objective, Paris, which was a fixed point. There was bound to be a battle in front of Paris, in which the French would be only half the strength of the enemy. On the other hand, if Napoleon were to march against the allies' lines of operations, he would give a fresh turn to the campaign, and the unforeseen would take a hand in the game.

It would have been easy for the enemy to follow the French army as it retreated on Paris, but it might well be beyond the power of the commander-in-chief of the allies to follow him in an unknown direction, where he could make play with the fortresses and develop to the full his unrivalled powers as a general. In such operations, and with such an adversary, the allies could scarcely avoid false movements, which would expose them to a lightning counter-stroke.

The Emperor, no doubt, considered the hypothesis that the allies might be bold enough to march upon Paris while he was threatening their lines of operations, but he rejected this idea as fanciful. He had no doubt that he would draw the enemy after him, and, as a matter of fact, Schwarzenberg was unnerved by the movement of the French army, and made all preparations for following it.

The Emperor made up his mind to continue his movement towards the fortresses, and on the evening of March 21 he was at Sompuis and had concentrated there the Old Guard, Ney's corps, and Letort, Berckheim, Saint-Germain, and Milhaud's cavalry. Sebastiani with Colbert, Exelmans, and Lefebvre-Desnoette's divisions were at Dosnon. Macdonald's three corps with Kellermann's cavalry remained along the right bank of the

Aube with their head at Le Chene and their rear beyond Plancy. On the 22nd Ney's infantry crossed the Marne at the ford of Frignicourt, and at daybreak Milhaud's dragoons and Defrance's Gardes d'Honneur marched on Vitry.

This town was held by 5,300 Russians and Prussians, under Colonel Schurchow, and had an armament of 41 guns. Ney drew up his troops as if for an assault and then summoned the town to surrender on condition that the garrison should retire with their arms and belongings. The commandant of Vitry was cut off from the head-quarters of the allies; he was surrounded by an army, and his means of defence were feeble; he was, then, in much the same situation as the commandant of Soissons had been on March 3, but Schurchow was not a Moreau.

He wrote a dignified and sensible letter to Ney:

> I beg that you will allow me to send an officer to the Prince of Schwarzenberg's head-quarters to ascertain where his Excellency is. If I learn that he has retired behind Vitry I will be ready to enter into negotiations in hopes of avoiding bloodshed.

Under the circumstances this proposal could not be accepted, and Ney opened fire. Schurchow was not frightened by the fire nor by demonstrations of attack, and he held inflexibly to the resolution which he had formed.

The possession of Vitry would have been useful to the French army, but it was not indispensable. The Emperor had foreseen that the garrison would make a serious defence, and had ordered the construction of two bridges below Frignicourt, and at this point, on the 22nd, the river was crossed by the Guard, the reserve artillery, and the 2nd and 5th Cavalry Corps. From Frignicourt the troops marched on Saint-Dizier. Towards 5 p.m. on the 22nd the advance-guard, composed of 400 cavalry under General Pire, reached this town in time to attack two Prussian battalions who were retiring by the Joinville road.

The Prussians were escorting an enormous convoy and a train of 80 pontoons. They formed up in two squares, of which one was broken at the first charge and forthwith surrendered, but the other made a stubborn resistance and succeeded in escaping after having burnt the pontoons. The French cavalry, however, captured 400 wagons of supplies and ammunition and between 400 and 500 fine horses, which were very welcome as remounts.

The Emperor reached Saint-Dizier during the afternoon of March 23, and he was now between the two main lines of communication of the allies the Strasburg road which the army of Silesia had followed, and the Bale road by which the army of Bohemia had advanced. The Emperor had no doubt that as soon as Schwarzenberg saw that his communications with the Rhine were threatened he would march so as to give battle to the French army, but he did not know which direction he would take. The Austro-Russians might follow Napoleon through Sompuis and Vitry or they might take the road through Brienne and Vassy.

The reports received from reconnaissances, spies, and peasants were at variance with each other. "The enemy is concentrating at Brienne he is retiring on Langres. The Czar spent the night at Montierender. Macdonald is being hard pressed in his retreat to Vitry by the whole allied army."

Among such conflicting reports it was not easy to arrive at the truth, and until Macdonald's three corps had at any rate crossed the Marne Napoleon could not neglect the enemy and march straight on the fortresses. At midday on the 23rd Piré's cavalry was in Joinville and Macdonald's rear-guard had only just left Dosnon, so the French army was stretched out along a front of nearly 50 miles. By sending forward the Guard and a portion of the cavalry so rapidly, Napoleon had intended to upset the enemy's equilibrium, but he would have risked a disaster if he had continued his march with such a long-drawn-out column.

Until his troops were concentrated on the right bank of the Marne, therefore, the Emperor found himself unable to undertake any serious operations. The most he could do was to scour the country round Saint-Dizier with his cavalry, who might pick up information while surprising the enemy's convoys and capturing isolated detachments. Piré's hussars were sent to Joinville and Chaumont, Saint-Germain's cuirassiers to Montierender, Defiance's Gardes d'Honneur to Void, Kellermann's Chasséurs and lancers to Bar-sur-Ornain, and Saint-Mihiel and Milhaud's dragoons to Châlons.

At the same time secret emissaries were sent off with dispatches for the commandants of the eastern fortresses and the mayors of the principal communes in departments of the Meurthe, the Meuse, and the Moselle. The commandants were ordered to take the field with their garrisons and to join the Emperor, and the mayors were instructed to collect the National Guards of the *levée-en-masse* and to fall upon the enemy.

Until he was certain of Schwarzenberg's movements, Napoleon held himself ready for all eventualities. He made all preparations for attacking the Austro-Russians, or for awaiting their attack, or for drawing them in his train towards the eastern fortresses. It would depend on circumstances whether he went to Metz or turned the enemy's right, or waited for him in a defensive position. The Emperor was not in a hurry to make his decision. "Twenty-four hours," he said, "make a great change in a military situation."

CHAPTER 18

The Council of War of Pougy

After the battle of Arcis Napoleon was uncertain as to what direction Schwarzenberg would take, and Schwarzenberg, with much less excuse, was quite in the dark as to where Napoleon had gone. On the evening of March 21, while fighting was still going on in Arcis, the Austrian commander-in-chief thought that the French army was retiring towards Vitry and ordered for the 22nd a concentration on the right bank of the Aube between Donnement and Dampierre, and during the night he wrote from Pougy to the Emperor of Austria announcing the success of the day's operations and telling him what had been ordered for the following day.

During the night, however, Schwarzenberg received a letter from the Prince of Wurtemberg, reporting that he had received definite information that Napoleon was retiring on Châlons. The orders were modified, and the troops were now directed to deploy between Corbeil and Herbisse preparatory to a march on Châlons. The crossing of the Aube caused great delay. Macdonald's three corps were in position on the right bank from Ormes to Le Chène, and they defended all the crossings and prevented the rebuilding of the bridge at Arcis. The Prince of Würtemberg saw that he could not cross the river at this point and moved some eight miles upstream and crossed by the bridge of Ramerupt.

When this movement was completed, during the afternoon of the 22nd, the 4th and 6th Corps were posted between Ramerupt and Dampierre, with their advance-guard at L'Huitre, the 5th Corps occupied Corbeil and Breban, with advance-guard at Le-Meix-Tiercelin, the Guard and reserves were near Donnement, and the 3rd Corps alone remained on the left of the Aube in observation before Arcis.

When we look at the map and compare the respective strength of the armies, we are surprised that Macdonald's small force should have escaped destruction. The Emperor had taken on with him the 2nd and 5th cavalry corps, leaving in their place two of Sebastiani's divisions and Pacthod and Amey's divisions, and the grand park had been delayed and had lost touch, so that Macdonald had only 20,000 combatants available; this small number of men was scattered from Ormes to Mailly and was opposed in front to the 3rd Corps, while their left was threatened by the bulk of the army of Bohemia, amounting to 80,000 men.

During the night Count Pahlen's cavalry marched from L'Huitre through Poivres to Sommesous, and thus crossed the line of retreat of the French. With their horde of light cavalry it is astonishing that the allied generals were ignorant of the road taken by the Emperor, and did not realize the critical position of Macdonald's army. They were in contact with the French rear-guard, and this alone should have enlightened them as to the situation; a vigorous attack was bound to have succeeded. Apparently Schwarzenberg's subordinates had imbibed their commander-in-chief's methods, and were content to allow their movements to conform to those of Macdonald; the marshal was left full liberty of movement at a time when nothing else could have saved him.

The allies remained without any definite news as to Napoleon's movements. During the evening of the 22nd Schwarzenberg received two letters, one from General Oscharowsky, saying "The Emperor is marching on Vitry," and the other from General De Wrède, who asserted "It is impossible that Napoleon is retiring on Vitry"; other reports were received saying that the French were retiring on Châlons, on Sézanne, and on Montmirail.

Schwarzenberg was more irresolute than ever, and this evening he wrote to the Emperor of Austria:

So far I have no certain information as to the direction taken by the enemy. I am expecting definite news at any moment, and I will then march at once.

Schwarzenberg had already written to Blücher:

Reports agree that the Emperor is moving on Châlons, but I do not feel quite certain. As soon as I have definite information, I will follow him with the whole of my army.

The best way to get information would have been to press the enemy in his retreat, but Schwarzenberg seems not to have thought of doing this. In order to occupy his spare time he spent the evening of the 22nd in drawing up three different orders for the following day to meet the three eventualities of Napoleon's retirement having been directed on Châlons, on Vitry, or on Montmirail. In each of these three cases Schwarzenberg intended to follow the French, and the only difference in the three orders was in the roads to be followed.

While Schwarzenberg was writing, Macdonald was acting. In spite of all risks he had carried out the Emperor's orders and had maintained his position behind the Aube during the whole day. When night fell he prepared to retreat, and collected his troops between Le Chène and Dosnon; at daybreak on the 23rd the army marched towards Vitry by Trouan and Sompuis. The Prince of Würtemberg was warned by his advance-guard of Macdonald's march and moved forward the 4th and 6th Corps towards Trouan, but he was still under the impression that the French were retiring on Châlons. A report from General Oscharowsky informed the Comte de Wrède that Napoleon was certainly retreating on Vitry, and De Wrède then proceeded to carry out Schwarzenberg's second alternative order and moved the 5th Corps towards Vitry.

The Prince of Würtemberg's cavalry encountered Macdonald's rear-guard at Trouan, and at Cour-de-Manges Wrède tried to intercept his retreat, and between these two points the armies marched on parallel routes and came into frequent contact with each other. Macdonald was attacked several times and lost some of his baggage and artillery.

> "I have been, so to speak, enveloped the whole day," he wrote to Berthier on March 24, "and fighting did not cease till 11 p.m. Your Highness can understand the state of disorder of my troops, who were worn out and had to march on a dark night over a desolate plain."

At last, thanks to the co-operation of Marshal Ney, who had occupied the heights of Cour-de-Manges, Macdonald's three corps were able to ford the Marne and establish themselves on the right bank. Fighting had begun earlier than Macdonald realized. Between 8 and 9 o'clock in the morning, Gerard, whose corps was heading the column, heard a violent cannonade in the direction of Sompuis; he hurried to that place and found that the grand park of the army was engaged with Oscharowsky's cavalry.

Macdonald had been afraid that the wagons and guns would be unable to cross the marshy ford at Saint-Saturnin, and had ordered the park to march through Pleurs, and unfortunately Amey's division, which ought to have formed the escort, misunderstood the orders, and had gone to Sézanne. Thus the park had arrived near Sompuis on the morning of the 23rd, and had no escort except ten troopers whom they had picked up on the way, and they formed a tempting prey for Oscharowsky's 1,700 horsemen.

The commandant of the convoy drew up his park in a square, and, with the 400 or 500 drivers, sappers, and gunners who were under his orders, endeavoured to keep off the enemy's squadrons. At first they were successful, and some mounted men even sallied out of the square and attacked the Russians, but Oscharowsky opened fire with his artillery and succeeded in blowing up some of the ammunition wagons; disorder ensued, and the enemy's cavalry broke into the square. At this moment the head of Gerard's troops arrived, and the infantry drove back the Russians; they could not, however, rescue the 200 prisoners and 14 guns which had been captured, and a still larger number of guns had been spiked.

During this affair a courier, carrying a letter from Berthier to Macdonald, was captured by the enemy. This letter, which was written at 3 a.m., urged Macdonald to hurry his march to the Marne, and told him that the Emperor was in rear of the army of Bohemia between Vitry and Saint-Dizier, and that the cavalry were already nearing Joinville, and had made many captures. Oscharowsky at once sent on this important dispatch to his chief, Barclay de Tolly, and he, thinking that this news necessitated immediate action, sent Diebitsch, his quartermaster-general, to Schwarzenberg.

The prince had left Pougy on a tour of inspection, and Diebitsch found him at Dommartin. He announced before the staff the success which the cavalry had gained, and then asked Schwarzenberg to come into a house with his chief of the staff in order to receive a secret communication. Diebitsch then produced the captured letter and tried to impress upon the commander-in-chief the gravity of the situation and the need for energy and resolution. The conference lasted for half an hour, at the end of which Schwarzenberg had come to no decision, and set off at a gallop for Pougy in order to summon to a Council of War the Czar, the King of Prussia, and the principal generals of the allied staff.

Fresh information had been received at the general headquarters. The army of Silesia was advancing from Rheims on Châlons, and the Prussian cavalry were already in touch with Count Pahlen's scouts. Further, Tettenborn's Cossacks had captured a courier who was bearing a letter from Napoleon to the Empress Marie-Louise, and Blücher had sent a copy of this letter to Schwarzenberg.

"*Mon amie,*" the letter ran, "I have been continually on horseback for the last few days. On the 20th I took Arcis-sur-Aube. The enemy attacked me at 8 o'clock in the evening. I beat him, killing 4,000 men and capturing four guns. On the 21st the enemy formed up his army to protect the march of his columns on Brienne and Bar-sur-Aube. I have decided to march to the Marne so as to draw the enemy away from Paris, and to bring myself nearer to my fortresses. This evening I shall be at Saint-Dizier. *Adieu, mon amie,* embrace my son for me."

The original of this letter is not in existence, and there is some doubt as to the exact wording; Rovigo says that the concluding words were, "This movement will either save me or ruin me."

This letter confirmed Berthier's dispatch which had been captured in the morning, and it was now certain that the Emperor was manoeuvring against the allies' line of operations. Schwarzenberg cannot have been surprised by this move of Napoleon's, because on the evening of the 21st he had believed that the Emperor would march towards Vitry, and during the 22nd he had issued provisional orders to meet that contingency. The commander-in-chief, however, was alarmed by the speed of Napoleon's march, and was much upset to find that he was already at Saint-Dizier and was in a position to threaten Chaumont, and to strike the right flank of the army of Bohemia.

A Council of War met at 3 p.m. To judge by the proposal which was first mooted, several generals had lost all heart.

"Napoleon," they said, "is already on our line of operations; he is two days ahead of us, and is threatening Chaumont. We must, therefore, recover our communications with Switzerland by a forced march through Vendeuvre, Bar-sur-Seine, and Châtillon. From there we must march either on Langres, or on Dijon and Vesoul."

This movement was nothing but a retreat, and would have been most dangerous from a military point of view, and fatal to the morale of the army. All the historians, German, English, and Russian alike, agree that the results of such a manoeuvre would have been incalculable; it would have involved a retreat to the Rhine or even beyond, and would have thrown away the results of two months of arduous campaigning; the army of Bohemia would have been demoralized, and Blücher would have been left alone and unsupported in the middle of his enemies; enthusiasm would have been aroused in France; convoys and magazines would have been pillaged, and the troops pursued by Napoleon and harried by a peasant rising: the result could only have been rout, disillusion, and disaster. Napoleon's move on Saint-Dizier was instinct with genius and admirable in its conception, and was justified in practice because it made the allies entertain for a moment the idea of an immediate retreat to the Rhine.

Unfortunately the dangers of this retreat, which strike us so forcibly after the lapse of a century, struck the majority of the Council in the same way. They next discussed a different plan which was suggested by the approach of the army of Silesia. This plan involved the abandonment of the lines of communication with Switzerland and the opening of a fresh line with the Netherlands through Châlons, Rheims, and Mons.

This would have been effected by a junction with Blücher's army, and the two armies would then march together against Napoleon and bring him to battle between Vitry and Metz. After a short discussion, the Council decided on this movement, but it seems that Schwarzenberg only reconciled himself to this course with difficulty and under the pressure of circumstances, and he thought it necessary to apologize to the Emperor of Austria for it.

> "I hope I shall gain," he wrote, "an increase of strength enough to compensate for what I lose in resources. The Emperor of Russia and the King of Prussia entirely agree with me and consider no other movement possible. In this important and daring decision their concurrence gives me great satisfaction."

Schwarzenberg described his march on Châlons as bold, but the epithet is not justified. Certainly this movement was sound, but it was prudent rather than bold. The Austro- Russians had driven back the small French army across the Aube, and this army was now extended over a depth of nearly forty miles and was carrying out a flank march across the front of the army of Bohemia.

Instead of directing their masses at once on Saint-Dizier, the allies were losing two days by moving to Châlons; they were gratuitously abandoning their line of operations and were handing over to the mercy of the French cavalry their detachments, convoys, and magazines. The Emperor had only 44,000 men, and Schwarzenberg had 100,000, but he dared not attack until he had been reinforced by Blücher's 80,000 soldiers. A superiority of two to one was not enough for the enemy. The name of Napoleon still inspired a superstitious fear in his enemies.

As the result of the Council, the troops were ordered to stop their move on Vitry, and to march on Châlons; the immense convoys of supplies and provisions which were massed at Brienne were to march by double stages through Breban.

Prince Moritz Lichtenstein was ordered to evacuate Troyes and to retire on Dijon, and the commandants of the garrisons, depots, and magazines at Chaumont and in its neighbourhood were directed to retire on Langres or on Vesoul.

The Emperor of Austria had remained in rear of the army and was now at Bar-sur-Aube; he thought he was perfectly safe here, but the march of the army towards Châlons and the retreat of the rear-guards towards Langres and Dijon would leave him at the mercy of the French cavalry. Unfortunately Schwarzenberg remembered the danger which threatened his sovereign and sent him respectful but pressing advice to leave Bar at once.

"I do not think," added Schwarzenberg, "that your Majesty can reach Arcis in time to take part in our march. I consider that your Majesty ought to go by the safest road to your army at Lyons, by Châtillon, Dijon, etc. In this way your Majesty will remain in any case in communication with Austria through Switzerland."

The words "in any case" show that Schwarzenberg was not convinced of the success of his movement on Châlons.

The commander-in-chief was exaggerating the danger when he advised the Emperor of Austria to go at once to Lyons. It is a question whether Schwarzenberg, in offering this advice, did not make himself an accomplice of the Czar and of those who were in favour of a fight to a finish with Napoleon. Doubtless the Russian and Prussian staffs should have been reassured against any attempted reconciliation by the rupture of the Congress of Châtillon, and by the anti-dynastic declaration with which the allied plenipotentiaries had broken off negotiations.

Doubtless also, the conduct of Francis I. since the conclusion of the quadruple alliance, had given no cause for suspicion. Nevertheless the feeling at the Czar's head-quarters was that Napoleon would, as a last resort, appeal to the Emperor of Austria, and consequently nothing but satisfaction could result from his absence from the army. The march on Châlons was a good opportunity to get rid of Francis I, and, consciously or no, Schwarzenberg was furthering the plans of the two northern sovereigns when he advised the Emperor of Austria to go to Lyons.

In any case, Schwarzenberg was right in urging the Emperor to leave Bar, and Francis was right in following this advice without delay; for if he had waited twenty-four hours longer he would have fallen into the hands of Saint-Germain's *cuirassiers*. If Napoleon had captured his father-in-law it would have been a fine revenge for Prague and would have afforded a comic relief to the tragedy which was in course of being played.

CHAPTER 19

The Council of War of Sompuis

It was the capture of dispatches which had decided the allies to march on Châlons; the capture of further dispatches was to cause them to alter this decision. At 8 p.m. on the 23rd, the Czar, the King of Prussia, and Schwarzenberg left Pougy to rejoin the army which was on the march towards Châlons. They crossed the Aube on a bridge of boats and reached Dampierre, where they stopped for several hours. During this halt they received a packet of dispatches which the Cossacks had taken from a courier on his way from Paris to Napoleon.

These dispatches were confidential letters from high officials of the Empire, and were all most despondent in tone. They spoke of the exhaustion of the treasury and of the arsenals, of the public ruin, and of the extreme anxiety and discontent which was spreading among the populace. One of these letters, written it is said by the Duc de Rovigo, reported that there were in Paris a number of influential people who were openly hostile to the Emperor, and who would be a source of the gravest danger if the enemy were to approach the capital.

Schwarzenberg thought himself as much a politician as a soldier, but he paid no special attention to these letters. The Czar, on the contrary, was much struck by them, but at first he said nothing of the great design which they suggested to him. At midnight they left Dampierre and reached Sompuis at about 3 a.m. On arrival there, Schwarzenberg learnt that the army of Silesia was just completing its movement towards the Marne.

Blücher was marching from Rheims on Epernay with Lang-eron and Sacken's corps; York and Kleist were in occupation of Château-Thierry; Winzingerode's infantry was at Châlons; the bulk of his cavalry was at Vitry, and his patrols at Sommesous and Soudé-Sainte-Croix. As the 6th Corps had reached Poivres, the junction of the army of Bohemia with that of Silesia might be said to be accomplished.

Now that his first objective had been obtained, the com-mander-in-chief did not wish to waste a moment in starting on a vigorous pursuit of the French army. At 4 a.m. he dictated fresh orders, stopping the march on Châlons, which was now unnecessary, and ordering for that day the crossing of the Marne in the neighbourhood of Vitry. In accordance with these orders the troops marched towards Vitry at daybreak on the 24th, and at 10 a.m. the King of Prussia and Schwarzenberg left Sompuis and accompanied the marching columns.

Thus Napoleon's anticipations were on the point of being re-alized and the allies were falling into the trap which he had laid for them; they were following him into Lorraine and towards the fortresses. As in so many victorious campaigns, the initiative was in the hands of the Emperor, and he was imposing his will on his adversaries and dictating the moves of their armies.

The Emperor of Russia, however, had not yet left Sompu-is. He had spent the night thinking over the letters from Paris which had been captured on the previous day. The news which they contained was certainly not altogether a revelation to him; a week before, the Baron de Vitrolles, who had been sent by the royalists, had been granted an audience and had painted a similar picture of the state of Paris.

"People are tired of the war and of Napoleon," he had said. "Consider politics rather than strategy, and march straight on Paris, where the true opinion of the people will be shown the minute the allies appear."

Although the Czar did not much favour the Bourbons, this language had flattered his dearest hopes, and he already imagined himself riding into Paris. But how much credence ought to be given to Vitrolles? Royalist emissaries had already assured the allies that the French would receive them enthusiastically, but the allies found the country everywhere rising in arms against them, and, instead of finding the gates of Paris thrown open to receive them, they might meet with a stubborn defence. But after reading these letters from high officials addressed to Napoleon himself, the Czar could no longer have any doubts as to Vitrolles' veracity.

It seems that on the morning of March 24 the Czar's mind was already made up, but before advocating his opinion he wished to submit the question to the officers in whom he had most confidence. While Schwarzenberg and the King of Prussia were on the way to Vitry, he summoned to the little house where he had passed the night his chief of the staff, Prince Wolkonsky, the commander of the Guard and reserves, Barclay de Tolly, and Generals Toll and Diebitsch.

When these officers had arrived the Czar showed them on the map the positions of the different corps; then he said, "Now that our communications with Blücher have been re-established, ought we to follow Napoleon in order to attack him with superior force, or ought we to march direct on Paris? What is your advice?"

The question was important, and each hesitated to be the first to give his opinion. The Czar turned impatiently towards Barclay, who was the senior, and he, after casting a rapid glance on the map, replied, "We must concentrate all our forces, follow Napoleon and attack him as soon as we overtake him."

The Czar made no remark, but turned to Diebitsch. This general was divided between his own opinion, which was that they should march on Paris, and the fear of openly opposing Barclay de Tolly, and in consequence he proposed a middle course; the army should be divided into two strong columns, one of which should advance on Paris, while the other crossed the Marne and pursued Napoleon.

This strange plan of campaign might have resulted in a double success, but would more likely have ended in one army being checked before Paris while the other was destroyed in detail beyond the Marne. General Toll could not contain himself when he heard this proposal, and as soon as Diebitsch had finished he exclaimed, without waiting to be asked:

Under the circumstances there is only one course to take. We must advance on Paris by forced marches with the whole of our army, detaching only 10,000 cavalry to mask our movement.

The Czar, who had hitherto listened without saying a word, could not help showing his pleasure. He expressed his approval of Toll's proposal and warmly praised the general. Diebitsch then said, "If your Majesty wishes to re-establish the Bourbons, the best course is to march on Paris with all our troops."

Alexander replied somewhat curtly, "There is no question of the Bourbons, our object is to overthrow Napoleon."

Barclay, however, was not convinced and raised several objections.

"Napoleon," he said, "will not be deceived by cavalry alone; he will retrace his steps and attack the rear of our troops as they march on Paris. Also, the garrison and the population of Paris may make a desperate defence, and finally, even if we capture the capital of France, what shall we gain? Will not the occupation of Paris mean the loss of the army? Have we not the example of Moscow before us?"

Toll and Diebitsch answered Barclay's arguments one by one, for the latter agreed with Toll now that the Czar had pronounced him to be right. Toll pointed out that the allies and the French would be marching in opposite directions, and each day they would be two days' march farther away from each other, so that even if Napoleon realized their movement and drove back the cavalry sent after him, the allies would have time to capture Paris before being attacked from the rear. Once they were masters of

Paris they would be covered by the Seine and the Marne.

Diebitsch added that the defence of Paris would not be a serious matter. "There is nothing but militia in the town, and imagine the effect which will be produced on the populace by the arrival of our armies, which Napoleon in his bulletins has claimed to have destroyed. We shall reap the greatest advantage from the occupation of Paris, which is the seat of government and the main centre of supply for the French army. Finally, think of the effect on the morale of our troops, who have been convinced by our hesitations that Napoleon is invincible. The example of Moscow is a mere bugbear; France cannot be compared with Russia as regards climate, distances, resources or national spirit. The occupation of the sacred city was a disaster for the French, but the occupation of Paris could carry with it no danger for the allies."

Barclay was at last convinced, and the Czar at once rode off to catch Schwarzenberg, whom he overtook an hour later halfway beyond Sompuis and Vitry. The two staffs dismounted, and the sovereigns and generals held a Council of War upon a hillock situated to the right of the road. Alexander ordered General Toll to open the map, and then he himself pointed out the positions of the armies and unfolded his plan of marching on Paris.

The King of Prussia warmly favoured the project, but there was marked opposition on the part of the Austrian generals and considerable hesitation on the part of Schwarzenberg. After the Czar had spoken, Toll, Diebitsch, and Wolkonsky, each in turn, pointed out the advantages and the necessity for the movement. Schwarzenberg at last gave way, and, although the Austrian generals were by no means convinced, he agreed to the newly suggested plan of campaign.

It was decided at once that the armies of Bohemia and Silesia should begin their march towards Paris on the following day, March 25, and that General Winzingerode, with his cavalry and light artillery and a small body of infantry, should follow Napoleon towards Saint-Dizier "endeavouring by all possible means to make him believe that the whole allied army was marching in pursuit."

It was past midday (on March 24), and the heads of the columns had reached the banks of the Marne. The troops were halted on the left bank between Pringry, Vitry, and Cour-de-Manges, while Winzingerode's advance-guard crossed the river and marched towards Saint-Dizier. Head-quarters were established at Vitry. In the evening Schwarzenberg dictated the order of march for the following day and wrote a long letter to Blücher to inform him of the decision which had been arrived at; he stated the route to be followed by the army of Bohemia, and urged Blücher to march by the most direct road so that the two armies might unite before Meaux on March 28. The Field-Marshal received this letter at Châlons. It is said that when he read it he exclaimed delightedly:

"I knew well that Schwarzenberg would come round to my opinion. We are going to finish this war, for now it is not here only, but everywhere, that the word is 'Forward!'"

It was all very well for Blücher to talk like this, but we may be excused for thinking that by his ten days' inaction after the battle of Laon he had forfeited his right to the glorious nickname of "General Vorwarts."

The news of the march towards Paris spread quickly through the army and roused the greatest enthusiasm. The army was tired of continual counter-marching; their spirits had been lowered by so-called indecisive battles which were followed by a retreat, and of so-called decisive victories which resulted in no forward move. Without troubling about political considerations, the soldiers understood that the capture of Paris was the aim and object of the war. There were also some who hoped for pillage, and others who looked forward to a triumphal entry into this famous city. But below these thoughts there probably lay a realisation of the fact that the nearer they went to Paris the farther they would be from Napoleon, whose strategic genius overawed the staffs and whose very name was enough to terrify the troops.

CHAPTER 20

The Two Fights at
Fère-Champenoise

Before daybreak on March 25 the main Austro-Russian army broke up its bivouacs on the banks of the Marne and marched in two columns. The main column was composed of the 3rd, 4th, 5th, and 6th corps, and moved along the main road from Vitry to Fère-Champenoise, the artillery marching on the road and the infantry in the fields on either side. The second column was formed by the guard and reserve, and moved across country through Cour-de-Manges, Sompuis, and Montepreux. The army of Silesia left Châlons at 6 a.m. and moved on Bergères. As far as Meaux the two armies were to march on parallel roads at a distance of ten to fifteen miles from each other, Schwarzenberg's troops passing through Fère-Champenoise, Sézanne, and Coulommiers, and Blücher's through Bergères, Montmirail, and La Ferté-sous-Jouarre.

Towards 8 a.m., when the cavalry under Count Pahlen and Prince Adam of Würtemberg, which formed the advance-guard, had just passed Coole, the scouts reported several thousand men drawn up in line of battle on the high ground near Soudé-Sainte-Croix. This was Marmont's small corps. We have related how Marmont and Mortier had delayed leaving Fismes to join the Emperor, and had been cut off from Rheims and Epernay and forced to make a wide detour. On March 24 Mortier arrived at Vitry, and Marmont at Soudé-Sainte-Croix; they intended to unite at the latter place at daybreak on the 25th and to march together on Vitry. The marshals were ignorant of the events of the last four days, and only knew that there had been fighting at Sompuis and on the Marne, and they supposed that the Emperor was on that river.

During the night of the 24th to 25th Marmont saw numberless bivouac fires on the horizon, and at first did not know whether they marked the position of the French or the allies. His reconnaissances reported that they belonged to the enemy, and he expected to be attacked on the following day either by one corps if the allies were marching on Vitry, or by the whole army if they were moving on Paris. Marmont had only 5,800 men, and it would have been wiser to have retreated at once. He did not think so, however, and held the peculiar idea "that he would be in any case in a good position to evacuate without loss the great plain which extends as far as Sézanne."

He did nothing except send an *aide-de-camp* to Mortier to ask him to hasten his march so as to reach Soudé before daybreak. The *aide-de-camp* lost his way, and towards 5 a.m. Mortier himself arrived, but he had left his troops at Vatry. The two marshals agreed to effect their junction at Sommesous, five miles in rear of Soudé.

Mortier returned to Vatry, and Marmont drew up his troops in order of battle, not with the idea of disputing the ground, but in hopes of imposing on the enemy and giving Mortier time to reach Sommesous. When the allied cavalry approached, Marmont retired in good order.

When Marmont reached Sommesous, Mortier had not yet arrived, and to abandon that place without waiting for him was to leave his troops at the mercy of the enemy. "It was better to die with them than to escape without them," as Marmont very truly said. He took up a position at the crossroads in front of Sommesous, and his 30 guns opened a hot fire, and kept the allied cavalry at a distance. Mortier at last arrived with his infantry and Belliard's cavalry, and took post on Marmont's left, with the artillery in first line, the cavalry in second, and the infantry in third. The enemy hesitated to charge, and commenced an artillery duel with 36 guns against the marshal's 60. The artillery fight lasted for two hours without result, but meanwhile the main body of the allies was approaching.

The French had 12,500 infantry and 4,000 cavalry, and were at present only opposed by some 7,000 cavalry, but they could see overpowering masses of the enemy advancing across the plain. The arrival of a fresh Austrian *cuirassier* division determined Marmont to retreat. Some disorder occurred among Mortier's artillery, which was horsed with stallions, and the enemy seized the opportunity; the Russian hussars charged, and overthrew Bordesoulle's *cuirassiers*, who were covering the retreat of the artillery. Belliard sent forward Roussel's division against the flank of the hussars; but the dragoons found themselves threatened in flank by Pahlen's second line, and they fled in panic. Luckily the infantry stood firm, and retired steadily in squares.

The marshals still hoped to avoid a disaster, but the treacherous spring weather played them false. The east wind suddenly freshened, and heavy dark clouds covered the sky and blotted out the sun; rain and hail fell in torrents, and the hailstones, driven before the wind, dashed in a blinding storm against the faces of the French and wet the priming of their muskets. The allies had the wind behind them, and were hardly affected by the storm, while the French infantry could neither charge nor fire, and could only defend themselves with the bayonet. The assailants had just been reinforced by more than 3,000 *cuirassiers* and dragoons of the Russian Guard, sent from Montepreux by Barclay de Tolly; they redoubled their efforts, charging the infantry in front and flank, and forced their way between the squares. Marmont made three separate attempts to move from one square to another, but was on each occasion forced to return at full speed.

While the storm and *mêlée* were at their height the French reached the ravine of Connantray, where the squares had to form into column in order to cross the defile. Some of the infantry fell into confusion, and one brigade was broken and entirely captured, while other troops abandoned their artillery. Thanks to a firm stand made by Ricard's division and by Christiani's division of the Old Guard, which formed the two wings, the army succeeded in crossing the ravine, and formed line behind Connantray, with the infantry in battalion columns on the left and the cavalry on the right, one echelon in line and the other in column of regiments.

Before long a force of 1,000 or 1,200 Cossacks, who had been sent the previous day to Pleurs, and had marched towards the sound of the guns, appeared from the direction of Oeuvy on the flank of the French. At this sight the whole of the French cavalry were seized with panic, and fled in wild disorder along the road to Fère-Champenoise. The infantry saw their flank exposed, and gave way; with cries of "*Sauve qui peut!*" they broke their ranks and fled after the cavalry, abandoning the guns and throwing away their knapsacks and muskets.

The whole army dashed pell-mell through the streets of Fère-Champenoise. Numbers of these fugitives did not stop until they had covered more than sixty miles; they passed through Sézanne, La Ferté-Gaucher, Coulommiers, and even Meaux, where they arrived during the afternoon of the following day. The fact seems incredible, especially when we remember that before taking to flight they had covered some thirteen miles, but it is beyond controversy.

The marshals were carried away by the flight of their soldiers, and despaired of being able to rally a solitary brigade; but luckily the 9th Heavy Cavalry, who were coming up from Sézanne, guided by the sound of the guns, arrived at a trot in Fère-Champenoise. Without being broken by the fleeing troops this regiment passed through the village in perfect order and formed in line facing the enemy, 530 men against 6,000. A force of 1,000 Cossacks advanced, but the *cuirassiers* charged and drove them back.

This vigorous charge and the magnificent attitude of this regiment imposed on the allied cavalry, who ceased to advance. The two marshals took advantage of the respite to restore some order among their troops and to form them up on high ground at Linthes, half-way to Sézanne.

It was now about 5 p.m. Suddenly the sound of guns was heard from the direction of Fère-Champenoise. A ray of hope set all hearts beating.

"They are the Emperor's guns: the Emperor is attacking," was passed down the ranks; cheers broke forth spontaneously, and the same men who an hour before had fled in panic now clamoured to be led forward against the enemy. The two marshals knew only too well what the guns portended, and restrained the eagerness of their men. Bordesoulle's *cuirassiers*, however, refused to be held back; in their eagerness to wipe out the disgrace of their previous conduct they drew their swords and dashed forward, but they were mown down by grape-shot and driven back.

The retreat continued towards Allemant, where the French took post between 6 and 7 p.m. The bulk of the pursuing cavalry had been drawn off, and the French were left almost unmolested. The guns which had aroused the enthusiasm of Marmont's soldiers were unfortunately not those of Napoleon. This cannonade marked the close of the heroic resistance made by the divisions of the National Guard under Generals Pacthod and Amey.

These two divisions formed part of the 11th Corps, and had been unable to rejoin Macdonald in his march towards the Aube and the Marne; they had gone to Sézanne, and had billeted there on March 23. A large convoy of 100 artillery ammunition-wagons and 80 wagons laden with baggage and with 200,000 rations of bread and brandy had also arrived at that town, escorted by four battalions and the 8th Regiment of cavalry, commanded by Colonel Noiset.

During the night of the 23rd-24th the two generals learnt that there was a French corps between Montmirail and Etoges on the march towards Sompuis, and they determined to get in touch with this column and to march in company with it. The supplies and the ammunition which had been sent from Paris seemed to be urgently required by the army, and Pacthod offered to escort them. He had sixteen guns, and the two divisions together amounted to 4,300 men, all of whom consisted, with the exception of one weak line battalion, of National Guards and conscripts who hardly knew their drill. In spite of the poor quality of these troops, the escort seemed to be sufficient, and Noiset's 1,600 men remained at Sézanne, where Napoleon had ordered all isolated detachments to assemble under command of General Compans.

On the morning of the 24th the column set off for Etoges, where they learnt that Mortier had left at daybreak for Vassy; the troops turned to the right and continued their march as far as Bergères, where they halted, worn out with fatigue. Pacthod sent an officer to Vatry to ask for instructions from Mortier. The marshal was in a difficult situation and was not quite sure what orders to give to his own corps, and he answered that Pacthod had better remain at Bergères.

This advice was bad, for at Bergères Pacthod would be left in the air whether Mortier advanced or retired. The officer lost his way and did not reach Bergères till the morning of the 25th, after the troops had left it, and rejoined them on the Vitry road near Villeseneux at 10.30 a.m. Pacthod halted his column, but before going back to Bergères he decided to give his men their midday rest. Arms had been piled for a quarter of an hour and the men were beginning to have their dinners, when General Delort perceived a large body of cavalry moving across the Bergères road. This was the advance-guard of the army of Silesia marching from Châlons on Bergères. Gneisenau had made a personal reconnaissance towards the left and had seen a large convoy moving towards Vitry; Korff, with 4,000 cavalry, 1,500 Cossacks, and a light battery, had in consequence left the road at Thibie and moved towards Germinon. Meanwhile the main body of Blücher's army, preceded by Wassilitschikoff's cavalry, continued its march on Bergères.

Pacthod imagined that they were only a strong party of foragers and made ready to receive them; he drew up his division with its right on Villeseneux, the infantry in battalion column and the three batteries in the front; Amey's division drawn up in one large square formed the left of the line, and the wagons were massed in rear.

On the approach of the enemy's squadrons the National Guards and conscripts stood firm and repulsed several charges. Pacthod maintained his position till midday, but seeing the enemy's forces increase, and fearing that he might be enveloped, he decided to retire on Fère-Champenoise. The column set off, the infantry in six squares surrounding the wagons. The march was very slow; the convoy was constantly falling into disorder and the infantry were continually halting to repulse the charges of Korff's cavalry. The Russian horse-artillery battery would come into action at three hundred yards from the French and open fire, and under cover of the grape the cavalry dashed forward against the squares.

In this way the column succeeded with great difficulty in covering four miles; the enormous number of wagons increased the danger and difficulties of the retreat, and General Pacthod made up his mind to abandon the convoy in hopes of saving his troops. He halted and ordered the teams to be unharnessed from the wagons, and the column then resumed its march under the fire of Korff's guns and amid the unceasing charges of the cavalry.

Towards 4 o'clock, as they were approaching Ecury-le-Repos, a section of artillery, supported by two regiments of dragoons, took post ahead of the column and brought it to a halt. At the same time 2,500 cavalry and two batteries under Wassilitschikoff arrived from the main army and appeared on the right flank of the French. The two divisions were surrounded and enclosed by a ring of sabres and guns. It was no longer a question of merely repulsing the enemy's charges, and the French had now to cut their way through the opposing masses. General Delort formed his square in column of attack and advanced with the bayonet against the troops who were blocking the road to Fère-Champenoise.

The enemy retired and the French column moved forward, but a mile farther on they found their way barred again by the same troops. Further reinforcements reached the enemy; Kretow's 1,600 *cuirassiers*, hearing the cannon on their right, gave up the pursuit of Marmont and arrived to join the troops who were attacking Pacthod. The six squares, however, resisted all attacks and continued their retreat through the middle of the dense swarms of the enemy's cavalry.

For more than four hours they had been exposed to the fire of the enemy's guns and the charges of his cavalry, yet not a square had broken and not a man had given way. The French generals were more surprised even than the Russians at the gallant behaviour of their young soldiers, fresh from the plough and still dressed in their *sabots* and blouses, and they hoped that they might yet reach Fère-Champenoise. When they came within view of the heights which overlook that town, they saw them to be occupied by a strong body of troops.

> "We thought at first," says General Delort, "that they were Mortier and Marmont's corps, and we rejoiced that we had effected a junction in a way which might reflect some glory upon us. But the illusion was short-lived. Our ranks were swept by the fire of a formidable artillery, and we knew that we were confronted by a fresh enemy."

These were the Russian and Prussian Guards commanded by the sovereigns in person. Alexander and Frederick William had left Vitry at 10 a.m., and the sound of the guns at an ever-increasing distance announced to them the success of their arms. They had passed Fère-Champenoise, and were following the cavalry, when they met an officer carrying a dispatch from General Kretow to Count Pahlen. Prince Wolkonsky opened the letter, and told the Czar and Schwarzenberg that Kretow reported the march of a French column on the right flank of the army. Schwarzenberg treated this news as imaginary; and Alexander said with a laugh to Wolkonsky, "You always see double when you are near the enemy."

At this very moment, however, the sound of guns was heard to the north of Fère-Champenoise; the sovereigns hurried back, and saw Pacthod's troops charged on the rear and on both flanks by the Russian squadrons. From a distance the National Guards took the staff of the allies for that of Marshal Marmont, and with one accord they raised the battle-cry of the French army, "*Vive l'Empereur!*" and even above the roar of the guns this shout of defiance reached the ear of the Czar.

Officers were sent in different directions to collect all the cavalry and artillery who were in the neighbourhood. The 23rd Horse Artillery battery arrived first upon the scene, and opened fire on the French, who were marching to their front full of confidence. Several shots passed over one of the squares, and fell upon Wassilitschikoff's hussars; and that general, thinking that a new French corps had arrived, had his guns trained against the Russian artillery, and some shells fell near the Czar, who was standing beside the battery. An *aide-de-camp* of Alexander's galloped off to put an end to the confusion, and all the batteries henceforward concentrated their fire upon the two small French divisions.

It was impossible to retreat on Fère-Champenoise. Pacthod determined to break his way out to the right towards some marshy ground where he would be able to defy all the cavalry attacks. The French had lost more than a third of their number, and were now formed in four squares only; they set off stoically in the new direction, and once more they cut their way through the mass of horsemen.

At each step the number of the enemy increased. Korff's 5,500 horsemen had been joined in turn by Wassilitschikoff's 2,500 hussars and dragoons and Kretow's 1,600 *cuirassiers*; there now arrived the three light cavalry regiments of the Russian guard, Pahlen's hussar division, Dépréradowitsch's *cuirassier* division of the Russian Guard, the cavalry brigade of the Prussian Guard, Nostitz's eight regiments of Austrian *cuirassiers*, and, finally, the Russian Life-guards under the Grand-Duke Constantine. There were now 20,000 horsemen surrounding the French, who were reduced to a strength of 3,000.

"Our troops," said General Delort, "only closed their ranks and marched the more proudly, as if their energy increased with the danger."

Under these conditions four miles were traversed. The enemy's charges were ceaseless, except when a pause was made to allow their batteries to open fire on these gallant battalions. After each salvo the infantry closed their ranks and received the Russian horsemen with their bent and bloody bayonets; as each charge was repulsed the march was resumed. One square was shot to pieces by the guns and broken; the men refused to surrender, and were almost all sabred. The other three squares were on the point of reaching the marshes when General Dépréradowitsch placed some reserve batteries across their front, and the fire of forty-eight guns brought the French to a standstill.

The Czar and the King of Prussia lost no time in sending staff officers to summon the French to surrender; it would be truer to say to implore them, for the sovereigns had been moved by the heroic defence. But the soldiers were exasperated by the ten hours' retreat, during every minute of which they had seen their ranks growing thinner and the enemy's numbers increase. They were drunk with noise and blood, and would neither give nor receive quarter; they bravely faced their fate, determined to sell their lives as dearly as possible. Colonel Rapatel, an orderly officer of the Czar's and a former *aide-de-camp* of Moreau's, fell, pierced by a musket-ball, as he advanced waving a white handkerchief.

The savage and desperate fight began again.

The soldiers did not wish to surrender; but Pacthod thought that after so long and gallant a resistance it was his duty as the commander to save the lives of the survivors of his men. He moved proudly out from his square, with his broken right arm hanging useless and bleeding by his side, and rode to meet a fresh flag of truce, Colonel Thiele.

"Surrender, I beg of you, General," cried Thiele, "you are surrounded on all sides."

"I will not discuss terms under the fire of your batteries," Pacthod replied coldly. " Cease your fire and I will stop mine."

The Russian artillery ceased their fire, and Pacthod gave up his sword. Shortly afterwards General Delort's square, swept with grape on all four faces, and having expended all their cartridges and repulsed several charges with the bayonet alone, laid down their arms. The last square still held out. A fresh salvo opened a breach in its living walls; the cavalry burst through and fell upon the soldiers, who defended themselves in groups, and tried to force their way through to the marshes.

Five hundred succeeded in escaping. Stirred by admiration, the Emperor Alexander galloped after his Lifeguards to stop the slaughter; his officers in vain tried to hold him back, and pointed out the dangers he would run in that terrible *mêlée*. "I wish to save these brave men," he said.

After the fight the captured generals were presented to the sovereigns Amey, Delort, Bonté, Janin, Thévenet, and Pacthod, the two last being wounded. The Czar warmly praised the generals for their heroic defence, and ordered their swords and their horses to be given back to them. All the prisoners were treated with the greatest humanity. Of the 4,300 men who had carried on a running fight for sixteen miles against overwhelming odds, 500 had gained the marshes, 1,500, of whom a large number were wounded, had surrendered after a desperate resistance, and more than 2,000 had fallen on the battlefield.

> "Everyone," said General Delort, "did more than honour demanded, but I cannot find words to describe the behaviour of the National Guards. The words 'brave' and 'heroic' are inadequate to give an idea of their conduct." And these were the very men who, a month earlier, Marshal Oudinot had been unwilling to put in line at Bar-sur-Aube, for fear that they might throw the army into disorder.

All the misfortunes of this day have been ascribed to Marmont. It has been said that if he had marched quicker when he left Fismes he would have been able to join the Emperor, and also that as he had lost so much time he ought to have gone to Sézanne instead of advancing to Soudé; at Sézanne he would have been reinforced by the 6,000 men under Generals Pacthod, Amey, and Compans, and he would very likely have avoided a battle with the allied armies. These reproaches are not well founded. On the one hand, Marmont could not know that there were three French divisions at Sézanne, and on the other hand his troops covered more than 75 miles between March 21 and 24.

It is on account of the wrong direction of his march rather than its slowness that Marmont deserves blame. That was his fatal error. If he had regulated his movements by those of the enemy instead of rigidly following an order of Berthier's. which, after all, was merely contingent, he would have gone on March 18 to Rheims instead of to Fismes. The advance-guard of the army of Silesia would have been held in front of Rheims until the 21st, and their subsequent advance on Châlons would have been delayed by Marmont and Mortier; they could not then have reached the neighbourhood of Sommesous until the evening of the 23rd.

The consequences would have been stupendous. The allied Council of War of March 23 would not have known of Blücher's approach, and would not have decided to move on Châlons. They would then have determined either to follow the Emperor across the Marne, which Napoleon desired, or to retire without fighting on Langres, a retreat which the Russian and German historians agree would not have stopped this side of the Rhine. In any case the march of the allies on Paris would have been delayed. Great results rarely spring from small causes, but in war a false movement is not a small cause.

On the evening of the fight of Fère-Champenoise Marmont and Mortier could no longer doubt that the allies were marching on Paris. The marshals were too weak to dispute the enemy's advance, but they should have been at the capital before him. Pacthod's gallant resistance had drawn against himself all the enemy's efforts and had relieved the pressure on the marshals' small army, which was able to continue its retreat without being seriously pressed. Unfortunately Marmont had not taken advantage of this respite to gain ground on the allies, and instead of marching straight on Sézanne, which was on the main Paris road, and which was occupied by General Compans with some 1,500 men, he made an excentric movement on Allemant.

When he arrived there Marmont changed his mind, but his troops had covered more than twenty-five miles during the day's fighting, and were not in a condition to go any farther that evening; he made up his mind to spend the night where he was, and sent an *aide-de-camp* to ask General Compans to remain in Sézanne till the following morning. Compans had been alarmed by the crowd of fugitives who had passed through the town during the evening, and was disturbed by the presence of Prussian cavalry on the Montmirail road.

His orders were that he was to retire if threatened, and he had already begun to evacuate Sézanne. He refused to stop his movement and answered that the most he could do was to leave a rear-guard in the town until 2 a.m. Marmont did not set off from Allemant until after that hour, and when his troops reached Sézanne at dawn they found it occupied by the enemy. It took several hours to capture the town, and the column then moved on, but it was found necessary to make the midday halt at Esternay.

These various delays gave time to Yorck's Prussians, who were advancing from Montmirail, to occupy La-Ferté-Gaucher, and enabled the cavalry of the army of Bohemia to overtake Marmont's rear-guard. The French found themselves opposed in front and threatened from behind. It was decided that Marmont should hold off Pahlen's cavalry while Mortier drove back the Prussians to the right bank of the Grand Morin stream.

After a brisk fight Marmont succeeded in delaying the enemy's pursuit, and he then started to rejoin his colleague on the Coulommiers road by moving over the high ground lying to the south of La-Ferté-Gaucher. He then received most disconcerting news from Mortier; this marshal, instead of confining

244

himself to occupying the high ground, had made a vain attempt to capture the town itself, and, finding that impossible, had retreated towards Provins. This incomprehensible movement was the crowning mistake among all those which the Emperor's two lieutenants had committed during the last ten days.

A retreat on Provins not only meant the loss of three marches, but it also made it impossible to join Compans at Meaux, and to defend the approaches to Paris in this strong position. This movement prevented the capital from having time to prepare its defence and deprived Napoleon of the opportunity of falling on the rear of the allied army.

Mortier's corps was committed to the Provins road and Marmont was bound to follow it. After marching all night the troops reached Provins on the morning of March 27. On the 28th they set off for Nangis, where Mortier took the road through Guignes and Brie-Comte-Robert and Marmont moved through Melun and Villeneuve-Saint-Georges. The two corps united again at the Charenton bridge on the afternoon of the 29th.

General Compans was nine hours ahead of the two marshals, and was able to pass freely through La-Ferté-Gaucher on March 26; he moved on Meaux by the main Coulommiers road. This town was occupied by General Vincent, who had retired there from Montmirail at daybreak with 200 infantry and 100 cavalry, and had succeeded in rallying 500 or 600 of Marmont's fugitives. The Prussian cavalry was in sight, and after a short halt Compans and Vincent continued their march towards Meaux, which they reached during the morning of the 27th.

The importance of the position of Meaux had been recognized for a long time; a large quantity of ammunition had been collected there, but no defensive works had been begun until the previous day. The armament consisted of seven guns, and the garrison was composed of 3,340 men. These were almost all conscripts and National Guardsmen, and they were not made of the same stuff as Pacthod's men. Their commander, General Ledru-Desessarts, described them in the following words: "The National Guards are a pitiable sight; they are slovenly and badly commanded, and do not know how to handle their muskets, which are disgustingly dirty."

Two days later the gallant Compans was forced to say: "I regret to have to state that it would be impossible to find worse troops."

Urgent letters from the Minister of War, however, announced the dispatch of reinforcements, and ordered Ledru-Desessarts to make a desperate defence.

"The safety of Paris depends on it," wrote Clarke.

Compans and Vincent brought with them eight guns, 1,000 infantry, and some 1,300 cavalry, composed of the 8th and 10th regiments and Marmont's fugitives. The garrison was thus raised to nearly 6,000 men, but this number was quite inadequate in view of the length of front to be held. The three generals nevertheless determined to dispute the passage of the Marne. Compans occupied Meaux and the suburb of Cornillon, Ledru-Desessarts took post at Trilport, and Vincent posted his cavalry on the left bank at St. Jean, where several hundred local National Guards voluntarily joined the troops.

Towards 4 o'clock in the afternoon the leading troops of the army of Silesia appeared on the road from La-Ferté-sous-Jouarre. Vincent resolutely attacked General Emmanuel's cavalry, but when his retreat was threatened by a movement of Horn's division towards Montceaux, he retired on Trilport and crossed the river. The enemy followed closely, and the National Guards, who were occupying Trilport, fled at the first shot without even attempting to sink the ferry boat. Before long the attackers had a footing on the right bank. Vincent attempted a charge, but the half of his cavalry, composed of Marmont's fugitives, turned and fled on the order to advance.

Neither words nor blows with the flat of the sword could stay the panic, and all the troops fled in disorder into Meaux. The night was falling; Emmanuel's cavalry and a portion of the Prussian infantry took post between the roads to La-Ferté and Soissons, while another Prussian column established itself in front of the suburb of Cornillon. Meaux appeared to be no longer tenable, and the generals determined to abandon the town during the night. At 10 p.m. the troops marched towards Claye and the rear-guard blew up the magazine, destroying a large number of houses.

On the following day, March 28, there was another fight and another retreat. During the morning the Prussians vigorously attacked Claye. Just as the village was being abandoned the reinforcements arrived from Paris, consisting of 3,000 infantry from the guard depots, three squadrons of Polish lancers, and 400 *cuirassiers* forming the 12th regiment of cavalry. Compans took post behind Claye, and when the Prussian infantry appeared on the plain they were suddenly charged by all the cavalry; 300 men were killed, 500 captured, and the rest of the enemy's column was driven back into the village. The Prussians were reinforced, and Compans continued his retreat from position to position as far as Ville-Parisis, which he was forced to evacuate after another fight. In the evening he bivouacked at Vert-Galant, within ten miles of Paris.

CHAPTER 21

The Last Victory

On March 23 the allied sovereigns and generals had been thrown into consternation by Napoleon's bold move against their line of operations; they had not yet thought of marching on Paris, and were discussing at Pougy whether to retreat towards Langres or to follow the French across the Marne. On this day at Saint-Dizier the Emperor was considering the relative advantages of various strategic plans. When Napoleon was trying to make up his mind between several alternatives, he often fixed his thoughts by committing to writing the different courses of action; in this way he was able to see them more clearly and judge better between them.

On this occasion he dictated a letter to the Duc de Bassano, in which he stated that there were four courses open to him: first, to march on Vitry during the night and attack the enemy there the following morning; second, to march on Saint-Mihiel and Pont-à-Mousson, collect the garrisons of the fortresses, and give battle with Metz as a base of operations; third, to march on Joinville and Chaumont; and fourth, to march on Brienne.

"The best of these courses," concluded the Emperor, "appears to be the one that avails itself of Metz and the fortresses, and which moves the theatre of war towards the frontier."

By the evening the Emperor had abandoned, or at any rate had altered, the course which had appeared to him best during the afternoon, and which agreed with his original plan. Numerous reports reached the imperial head-quarters, and it appeared that the allies were making no attempt to defend their line of operations, which they could have done by marching against the French army through Brienne; on the contrary, they had abandoned their line of operations, evacuated Troyes, Bar, Brienne, Chaumont, and Langres, and were advancing *en masse* on Vitry. Napoleon then evolved a fresh movement.

He would let the Austro-Russians commit themselves to a pursuit in the direction of Metz, and by a rapid change of front he would return to the Aube and would make Bar and Troyes his base of operations. Here he would be placed on the communications of the army of Bohemia and would be in touch with Paris; he would be able, according to circumstances, either to march against the allies or to await their attack in a strong position behind the Aube.

At 12.30 p.m. Berthier sent out orders to all the cavalry brigades which were marching towards Bar-sur-Ornain and Vaucouleurs, telling them to join the Emperor on the following day on the road from Saint-Dizier to Vassy. The same order was sent to Ney at Frignicourt and to Macdonald at Villotte.

"We are marching on Bar-sur-Aube," wrote Berthier, "but you should spread the rumour among your soldiers that we are marching on Metz."

These instructions were not forgotten, and the French wounded who were captured near Frignicourt told the allies that the Emperor was marching from Saint-Dizier on Metz.

During the evening of March 23 Caulaincourt arrived at Saint-Dizier. He had been deceived by Metternich's letters, and still believed peace to be possible. The plenipotentiaries had broken off the negotiations at Châtillon, but he hoped to be able to resume them with the Ministers at the allied head-quarters. After the closure of the Congress he had wished to join the Emperor without delay, so as to persuade him to the necessary sacrifices, but he had been detained at Châtillon until the 21st by formalities connected with his passport, and he had then been delayed during his journey by the ill-will of the enemy's outposts.

Caulaincourt was received by the Emperor as soon as he arrived, and gave a detailed account of the last sittings of the Congress; then, relying on Metternich's deceitful promises, he tried to inspire Napoleon with his own hope of being able to renew the negotiations and to bring them to a successful conclusion. The Emperor understood the thoughts of the allies better than his minister, and entertained no such illusions. He considered peace to be more impossible than ever. On the other hand, the latest information augured well for the success of his bold measure. He found no chance of safety except in victory, and Caulaincourt's entreaties were all in vain.

At 4 a.m. on March 24 the Old Guard, reserve artillery, and Letort and Lefebvre-Desnoettes' divisions set out on the road to Vassy. Ney's corps and the cavalry had orders to follow the movement, and on account of his position Macdonald was detailed as rear-guard. This duty caused him much uneasiness, for he imagined that he would be attacked by the whole allied army. As a matter of fact, the marshal's fears had no foundation, for the Austro-Russians had already been ordered to march on Châlons, but he was much alarmed.

"If the enemy pursues," he wrote, "there is bound to be a disaster. As things are I cannot hope for a success. ... A slight effort on the enemy's part will be successful. He can crush me, for neither men nor horses are fit for anything."

At 7 a.m., as the Emperor was about to leave Saint-Dizier, one of Ney's *aides-de-camp* arrived. The marshal had been moved by Macdonald's entreaties and not unaffected by his alarm, for fear is contagious, and he asked permission to remain on the Marne to support Macdonald, and asked for support in turn from the Emperor. Napoleon's dispositions had been already made, and since the beginning of this campaign he had been quite accustomed to receiving complaints from his subordinates. He refused to suspend his movement.

"The Emperor would have started at once to join you,"

Berthier told the *aide-de-camp*, "if his presence with the advance-guard had not been indispensable during the march on Colombey-les-deux-Eglises. The Emperor cannot direct the movement from here. He may find it necessary to alter the direction of the march according to information received on the way."

The movement was carried out as the Emperor wished. That evening the infantry of the Guard were at Doulevant; Saint-Germain's *cuirassiers* occupied Nully on the road to Brienne, and Piré's indefatigable light horsemen reached as far as Daillancourt and Colombey. Ney's infantry, Sebastiani's cavalry, and Defrance's division, were between Saint-Dizier and Vassy, while Macdonald's three corps and Kellermann and Milhaud's cavalry were between Perthes and Saint-Dizier. Contrary to his expectations, Macdonald had only been followed by a few squadrons, but when he saw that Ney did not remain close at hand, he invented an order from the Emperor by virtue of which he retained Sebastiani until 11 o'clock.

On the 25th the cavalry sent out parties to Brienne, Bar-sur-Aube, and Chaumont, while the Emperor remained at Doulevant, for he wished to gather further information before pushing on towards Bar and Troyes. The reconnaissances reported that the Austro-Russians were abandoning the country as far as Langres, that they were evacuating Troyes, that the Emperor of Austria was fleeing towards Dijon, and that a state of chaos prevailed on the allies' lines of operations.

On the other hand, however, Schwarzenberg had appeared on the previous day to be moving on Vitry, but this movement now seemed to have been stopped, or at any rate delayed; Macdonald's retreat had not been disturbed, and Ney reported that all was quiet towards Vitry, and that the allies appeared to be moving towards Brienne. The enemy was moving away from Vitry, and at the same time was evacuating Troyes and Langres; Napoleon could only conjecture what the allies' intentions might be, and, knowing Schwarzenberg's prudent strategy, it was impossible for him to believe that they were marching on Paris.

Nevertheless the Emperor was in doubt, and halted, sending orders to his corps commanders to remain where they were between Vassy and Doulevant.

"I shall not have a clear idea as to the enemy's movements for another four or five hours," he wrote. "It is necessary, therefore, that no one should move."

During the afternoon and evening fresh dispatches reached the imperial head-quarters. Macdonald wrote that he could hear the sound of guns, and Ney reported that 10,000 cavalry were advancing on the road from Vitry to Saint-Dizier, that they had entered this latter town and were crossing the Marne. It seemed, then, that the allies were not defending their line of operations by Brienne, and were not following the French army on the false scent to Metz. The Emperor did not know whether the 10,000 cavalry were a detached corps or a strong advance-guard, but whatever they might be these troops had the Marne at their back, and there was a good opportunity of attacking them. Macdonald was not optimistic, and was complaining of a dearth of rations, but he said that his position was quite tenable. At 9 p.m. the orders were issued.

"The Emperor," wrote Berthier to Ney and Macdonald, "intends to attack the enemy tomorrow morning and to drive him into the Marne. The enemy is scattered and everything points to a successful day."

In spite of Berthier's forecast of a successful day, the Emperor was very uneasy as to the enemy's movements, and the confidence which he had felt two days ago had now vanished. In addition, the arrival of Caulaincourt afforded a visible proof that the negotiations had been broken off, and had roused an unfortunate feeling at the imperial head-quarters. The soldiers and regimental officers were still actuated by hopes of revenge and victory, but the staff desired nothing but peace. The breaking off of the negotiations shattered their hopes, and their discontent could not be hidden. Napoleon could not help overhearing their discussions: "Where are we going? What will happen to us? If he falls, shall we fall with him?"

The Emperor pretended not to hear, but he was affected by the discouragement of his staff, and he authorized Caulaincourt to write to Prince Metternich with a view to renewing the negotiations. Where ill fortune had found him immovable, the disaffection of his comrades-in-arms affected him deeply. He consented to give up the left bank of the Rhine, and Caulaincourt's letters were dispatched during the night.

While awaiting possible diplomatic action, it was imperative to carry on the war without a pause. On the following day, March 26, the Emperor left Doulevant at 2.30 a.m., and reached Vassy at daybreak. He learnt from Macdonald that the enemy, who the day before had been pressing Gérard's rear-guard, had now halted, and that only a few *sotnias* of Cossacks were visible. Tettenborn, who formed Winzingerode's advance-guard, had acted with discretion.

So long as the French were retreating his function was to press them closely so as to make them think that they were followed by an army, but as soon as they showed an inclination to advance he was bound to avoid a serious engagement, which would have shown the Emperor that he had only a screen of troops in front of him. Tettenborn, therefore, halted at Eclaron, but in spite of these tactics he could not evade a fight. The French cavalry drove back the Cossacks to the Marne, and they crossed the river in disorder. From the plateau of Valcour the Emperor saw on the right bank of the river a mass of cavalry, supported by infantry and guns.

The squadrons were formed in two lines on either side of the Vitry road; their left rested on Saint-Dizier, which was occupied by 1.000 infantry, and their right extended to the wood of Perthes, which was defended by a battalion. Twelve guns were in action on the front, and thirty were in reserve, and a line of skirmishers were scattered along the river.

The Emperor ordered all his available troops to advance, so as to frighten the enemy by the rapidity of the attack and by an overwhelming display of force. Oudinot, with the 7th Corps, marched on Saint-Dizier, and all the cavalry, headed by Sebastiani, crossed the Marne at the ford of La Neuville. Macdonald and Gérard's troops and the Old Guard followed the cavalry, but they did not come into action. The cavalry repulsed Tettenborn's Cossacks, and moved forward to the attack as soon as they were formed up.

As generally happens, the enemy were more than half beaten by the mere sight of the vast mass of men advancing to attack them; in war this moral effect has a tremendous influence on the action of the combatants. The advance-guard of a large army has an irresistible strength, because the men which compose it, although they may be fewer than their opponents, feel that there are large numbers ready to support them. For this reason a general is not justified in saying, "The numbers were equal, for only half of my troops were engaged." More often than not the victory is decided by the half of the troops which have not been engaged.

So it was at Saint-Dizier. Before the battle had begun Winzingerode's cavalry were shaken, and at the first charges they were ready to give ground. Winzingerode ordered Tettenborn to retire on Vitry, while he himself retreated on Bar-sur-Ornain, and tried to take with him his infantry from Saint-Dizier. Sebastiani saw the Russians forming in column, and launched against their flank the dragoons of the Guard and the mounted grenadiers. Winzingerode's cavalry were soon broken, and took to flight, some towards the forest which lies to the north of Saint-Dizier, and some along the road to Bar.

During this time Leval's infantry entered Saint-Dizier almost without opposition. The two Russian battalions retreated towards Bar, but were overtaken by French dragoons, and were pursued almost into Bar. On the left a cavalry division drove back the Cossacks and skirmishers towards Perthes, and Lefebvre-Desnoettes, who was in support, was only opposed by a platoon of Mamelukes, among whom was the famous Roustan.

In two hours the plain was clear of the enemy, who lost 500

killed and wounded, and 2,000 prisoners, and eighteen guns captured. The dash of the French troops had been magnificent, and rivalled the tenacity they had shown at Arcis. The victory was comparatively unimportant, but there was much significance in the spirit of the troops, who had not been discouraged by hardships or fatigue. With such an army under his control, Napoleon was still to be feared.

The gravest anxiety damped the satisfaction which this brilliant affair gave to the Emperor. He had expected to fight a corps of Schwarzenberg's, and he had found himself opposed by some of Blücher's corps. A few days ago Blücher was threatening Soissons, and now he was on the borders of Lorraine. Schwarzenberg had been marching towards Vitry. and now he had suddenly disappeared and his whereabouts were unknown.

The Emperor did not know whether to place any trust in the reports of some of the prisoners that the allies were advancing on Paris. In order to clear up the situation, he pushed forward Oudinot's corps on Bar, while he himself with the rest of the army moved on Vitry. By resuming the offensive and vigorously pressing the scattered columns which were harassing his rearguard he would be able to learn where the bulk of the enemy was concentrated.

In the afternoon of March 27 the army was before Vitry. The Emperor was consulting with his marshals as to the possibility of capturing the place, when fresh information was received from various sources. Dispatches had been intercepted and the enemy's printed bulletins had been found, and these agreed with the reports of peasants and of escaped French prisoners in indicating that the allies were marching on Paris. The Emperor mounted his horse and dashed off to Saint-Dizier. He shut himself up with his maps and reports and concentrated his whole mind on deciding on his course of action. Never in the whole of his life had Napoleon been in such a difficult position. The crown and the army were still his, but the least false movement and they would be snatched from his hands.

Ought he to return to Paris by forced marches, and, if so,

would he arrive in time? The allies had three days' start on the imperial army; would he not find them already in possession of the capital? The garrison consisted only of the National Guard and a few troops from the depots; would they have been able to hold out for sixty hours?

Ought he, on the other hand, to take no more account of Paris than the Czar had of Moscow, and should he persist in the movement that he had begun? The allies had abandoned all the country from the Yonne to the Marne, and from the Seine to the Meurthe; for a fortnight he would be able to manoeuvre at his will. He might collect the garrisons of the fortresses, proclaim a *levée en masse* in Lorraine, Alsace, Champagne, and Burgundy, destroy the retreating columns, and retake the occupied towns Châlons, Vitry, Dijon, Vesoul, Langres, and Nancy.

Already Troyes, Bar-sur-Aube, Bar-sur-Ornain, and Chaumont were in possession of French troops, who were everywhere received with shouts of "*Vive l'Empereur!*" General Durutte had sallied out of Metz with 4,000 men; he had raised the blockade of Thionville, repulsed the corps of the Elector of Hesse, and was advancing down the Moselle. General Broussier was on the point of leaving Strasburg with 4,000 infantry and 1,000 cavalry; the garrisons of Schlestadt, Neuf-Brisach, and Phalsbourg had been warned and were ready to join Broussier. General Duvigneau was marching on Châlons with 2,000 men from the garrison of Verdun.

In front of Longwy, Montmédy, Luxembourg, Sarrelouis, and Landau were only a small number of the enemy, who would scatter at the first alarm. Souham was at Nogent with his division, and at Auxerre were collected 2,000 resolute men under the orders of General Allix, who was a host in himself.

In addition to the soldiers, Napoleon could now count upon help from the peasants. In the month of February a wave of patriotism had stirred the inhabitants of Champagne and the neighbouring country, and this had now spread to the whole of eastern France. The rural population had been surprised by the invasion, for Napoleon's lying bulletins had made them believe him to be invincible, and at first the frontier provinces offered no resistance to the enemy. Before long, however, they were roused to a state of exasperation by the foreign occupation, with its accompaniment of pillage, murder, and violation, and now the whole country from the Yonne to the Vosges was burning for vengeance on the invaders. Large numbers of peasants were in arms, and many more were ready to help the troops.

Napoleon himself said, "In the prevailing state of exasperation even the women are ready to take up arms," and this state of affairs was not confined to the eastern part of France, for bands of peasants were being organized in almost every department, and the people of Bordeaux were preparing a counter-revolution.

At Nancy, which was Blücher's main supply-depot, and at Langres, which was an important magazine on Schwarzenberg's communications, the inhabitants were only awaiting the arrival of a French squadron to rise and attack the garrison, and the governors of these two places had made preparations for retreat. From Toul to Chaumont, and from Saint-Mihiel to Bar-sur-Aube, every road was patrolled by bands of peasants armed with sporting guns, pitchforks, or clubs. In three days, between March 25 and 28, they brought in to head-quarters 1,000 prisoners, besides ammunition wagons, and even guns.

Oudinot wrote to Berthier, "It is incomprehensible that no advantage is taken of the eagerness of the peasants."

General Piré also wrote from Chaumont to say that the peasants were thronging to ask for arms and powder.

> They have seen immense columns of wagons carrying loot, and the peasants wish to recapture their cattle and their goods; they also wish to have their revenge for the wrongs they have suffered, and for the outrages committed on their wives and daughters. I propose to the Emperor that we should sound the alarm through all the parishes of the upper Marne. We will march on Langres and Vesoul, for the peasants know that they will find there plenty of booty and little resistance. The movement, once started, will spread to all the districts pillaged by the Cossacks. We

have few arms, but we will capture some from the enemy. I ask for nothing but orders and cartridges.

Thus everything was ready for that *levée en masse* which was the nightmare of the allies.

Since the beginning of the campaign Napoleon had constantly wavered between the policy of defending or abandoning Paris.

He had said, "If the enemy arrives in front of Paris the Empire is at an end."

He had written, "Paris will never be occupied while I live," and again, "We must not abandon Paris, it would be better that we should be buried beneath its ruins."

On the other hand he had more than once given definite orders as to the departure of the Empress and the Government. Also, on March 21, when he had continued his march towards the Marne, he knew that his movement might result in the loss of Paris. Finally, according to a trustworthy witness, Napoleon had continually borne in mind the possibility of the loss of Paris and had determined what he would do in that eventuality. It seems, however, that at any rate since March 15 Napoleon had made up his mind if necessary to sacrifice Paris, but he hoped that he would not be compelled to adopt such a dangerous course.

He now suddenly found himself obliged to make a definite decision, and he was not prepared to do so on the spur of the moment. The evidence tends to show that if Napoleon had consulted only his own feelings he would have abandoned the capital, but he was obliged to consider the effect which this decision would have upon his staff, whose discontent and despondency would be increased by such a desperate policy. There were Caulaincourt and the Duc de Bassano, who would look at the matter from a political point of view; there were Berthier, Ney, and twenty other generals whose homes and families were in Paris and who were tired of the war and realized that a move to Lorraine would prolong it indefinitely.

The Emperor gave way. At 11 p.m. Berthier issued his orders; the troops were to march the following day towards Paris through Bar-sur-Aube, Troyes, and Fontainebleau. This route was a little longer than the road through Sézanne, but it had the double advantage that it would not be necessary to force the passage of the Marne at Meaux and that the right flank would be protected by the Seine.

The movement began on the morning of March 28. At 10 a.m. the Emperor was sitting down to a meal before leaving Saint-Dizier when some peasants arrived with important prisoners whom they had captured on the road from Nancy to Langres. Among these prisoners was the Comte de Weissenberg, the Austrian Ambassador to London. The Baron de Vitrolles was travelling with him, but although he was very proud of having been received at Châtillon by the Comte de Stadion and at Troyes by the Czar and Metternich, he had thought it better to conceal his identity. He had the wit to understand that his mission as a traitor and a spy rendered him liable to be shot, and he had put on the livery of one of the ambassador's servants and succeeded in making his escape.

Possibly the Emperor saw the hand of fate in Weissenberg's capture. He invited the ambassador to share his meal, and after a long conversation he entrusted him with a confidential mission to the Emperor of Austria in which he no doubt undertook to agree to the allies' terms. Weissenberg set off in a carriage provided by the Emperor and carried a letter from Caulaincourt to Prince Metternich. The Emperor's message and Caulaincourt's letter received no reply. Ever since Prague Metternich had been conspiring for the fall of Napoleon, and from this time onwards he no longer concealed the fact.

Between 5 and 6 p.m. the Emperor reached Doulevant, where he was joined by a messenger bringing a letter from Lavallette, the Director-General of Posts. This was the only dispatch received from Paris for six long days; it described the intrigues of the enemy's *partisans* and ended with the words "The presence of the Emperor is necessary if he wishes to prevent the capital from being given up to the enemy. There is not a moment to be lost."

Napoleon agreed with Lavallette that there was not a moment to be lost, but he was obliged to march with military precautions; hostile detachments might still be between the Seine and the Aube, and the Emperor of the French could not risk being captured by Cossacks. He was obliged to spend the night at Doulevant and started early the following morning with the Guard. At the midday halt at the bridge of Dolancourt a whole troop of couriers were encountered. As the communications had been interrupted, several of these couriers had been obliged to wait for three days at Nogent and Montereau. They brought bundles of letters from King Joseph, the Minister for War, and Montalivet. These letters contained proposals, reports from the provinces, and requests for money; they included reports on the battle of Limonest, the occupation of Lyons, the fighting at Fère-Champenoise and the evacuation of Sézanne and Coulommiers. All this, however, was already ancient history, and the Emperor eagerly cast his eyes on the letters which were dated the previous day.

He learnt that the enemy had captured Meaux, that fighting was going on at Claye, and that Marmont and Mortier were moving on Paris. There was less time than ever to be lost. General Dejean, the Emperor's *aide-de-camp*, and a few hours later General Girardin, Berthier's *aide-de-camp*, were sent off posthaste to tell King Joseph that Napoleon was returning at once. The march of the troops was hurried forward, and during the night the Guard reached Troyes after having covered some thirty-seven miles since daybreak. The rest of the army followed as fast as it could; Ney halted at Dolancourt, Macdonald at Nully, and Oudinot near Doulevant. At Troyes the Emperor would hardly allow himself time to sleep.

On the morning of March 30 he handed over the command of the army to Berthier, and ordered him to march to Fontainebleau, and at 8.30 the Emperor started on horseback, escorted only by some cavalry. He intended to sleep at Villeneuvesur-Vanne, but he was mad with impatience. By posting it was just possible to reach Paris during the night. He put off his sleep, and leaving his escort behind he got into a wickerwork carriage with Caulaincourt. Drouot, Flahaut, and another *aide-de-camp* got into a second carriage; in a third were Gourgaud and Marshal Lefebvre, who was to organize the defence of the suburbs. The horses started at a gallop on the road to Paris.

CHAPTER 22

The Regency and the Defence of Paris

Since the departure of Napoleon to join the army the Government was nominally in the hands of the Empress, who was invested with the Regency by letters patent dated January 23; in actual practice, however, the Government was carried on by King Joseph, the Arch-Chancellor, and the Ministers of the Interior, of War, and of Police. As a matter of fact, however absorbed he might be by the duties of commander-in-chief, the Emperor rarely let a day pass without writing to Joseph, Clarke, Montalivet, and Rovigo on all sorts of military, administrative, and political questions.

The Emperor was absent from Paris, and his information was gathered from reports which were sometimes too optimistic, but more often unduly alarmist; he was only able to give advice and instructions in place of formal and definite orders. The result of this was that Napoleon was badly served in all matters except those which concerned reinforcements and stores to be sent to the army, or messages to be transmitted to detached commanders, or to the governors of fortresses. His orders were disputed, and were often altered or ignored.

"I am no longer obeyed," wrote the Emperor to Montalivet on February 26. "You all think you know better than me, and you oppose my wishes, and answer me with 'buts' and 'ifs'".

It is true that many of the measures ordered by Napoleon were very difficult to carry out; but the ministers did nothing to remove these difficulties, but merely reported them to the Emperor. If Joseph and the ministers rejected the majority of Napoleon's projects as being impracticable they ought to have suggested better alternatives.

This is what the Emperor wanted; he wrote, "You keep on sending me reports; that was all right when I was in Paris, but now it is not sufficient."

And again, "One would say that you were asleep in Paris. Only speak to me of indispensable things, let the Regency issue the necessary decrees."

Unfortunately Napoleon's system of forcing his ideas upon his advisers, and of making all wills bow to his own, had resulted in stifling all initiative. As Talleyrand said, he had governed too much. During the years of glory his subordinates had rested under the shelter of the Emperor's genius, and had carried out his orders blindly. The reverses had now shaken their confidence in Napoleon, and they no longer obeyed; but they had been so long unaccustomed to think or act for themselves that they had become incapable of doing anything.

Marie-Louise was a woman, and was only twenty-three years old; Cambacérès, the Arch-Chancellor, was a great jurist and a skilful politician, but he was enough of a philosopher to be always willing to accept an accomplished fact; Joseph was weak, and lacked initiative; he was devoted to his brother only so far as their interests coincided, and all his hopes were centred in peace; Montalivet, the Minister of the Interior, was a clever and trustworthy administrator; his brains were not of the first order, and he was opposed to any measure which was not strictly legal; Rovigo, the Minister of Police, lacked both sagacity and energy; Clarke, the Minister for War, was a scrupulous subordinate, and an indefatigable writer; he was a sort of inferior Berthier, more fitted to draft orders than to evolve them.

These personages were not capable of forming the Committee of Public Safety which circumstances required. Certainly the organization of the defence of Paris was an almost impossible task; zeal, intelligence, and energy would not have been sufficient to carry it out; nothing but faith and genius could have succeeded.

Since the end of December 1813 all recruits and all arms, ammunition, and supplies had been collected in Paris, and the town had a very military appearance; there were constant reviews and drills; the streets were full of soldiers, and echoed with the tramp of marching troops, and the sound of military music. Paris, however, was not so much a garrison town as a huge depot through which troops were constantly passing; each day numerous detachments arrived from different parts of France, and each day columns marched out to join the armies. Every afternoon the main boulevards were thronged with people watching the troops go by, and the wits used to say that the same troops were marched through the town time after time in order to inspire confidence in the Parisians.

It would have been well for the safety of Paris if the same troops had been marched again and again through the city, for the troops who left Paris were good, or at any rate passable, and those who remained were worthless. As soon as the conscripts had been clothed and armed, and had been taught to load their muskets, they were sent off to the army in response to the Emperor's urgent demands for reinforcements.

The daily departure of men who were just fit to march and fight explains why the daily states of the 1st Military Division show such a large number of ineffectives. On an average, in the infantry of the line, only one man in three was effective. In the depots of the Young Guard the proportion of men ready to march was even lower; the state of the 6th March shows 7,861 non-effectives out of a total of 10,721 men. In the big cavalry depot at Versailles matters were even worse, for the deficiencies of saddlery and remounts had to be taken into account; on the 10th March there were 18,577 officers and men in the depot, and of these 11,458 were either sick or not armed or drilled; to mount the 7,119 efficient men, however, there were only 3,615 horses, so only one man in six was available.

Although the depots were included in the 1st Military Division, it was only in an emergency that they could be counted upon as part of the garrison of Paris, and as things stood there was a chance that in case of attack there might be no effective men at all in the depots. For her defence, Paris could only rely upon 1,200 infantry and cavalry of the Old Guard who had been specially detailed by the Emperor for the protection of the Empress and the King of Rome, and on some 800 mounted *gendarmes*, and various companies of veterans, pensioners, and firemen, and finally on the National Guard.

The Parisian National Guard would have formed a real force if it had been organized earlier and if the recruiting had been less exclusive. This Guard had only been created by a decree of the 8th January, which was the last of all the decrees. This delay shows the prejudice which the Emperor and his minister felt against the Parisian militia, and demonstrates the distrust which it had inspired in those who had witnessed June 20, August 10, and *Vendemiaire* 13. Nevertheless the Emperor's original idea had been that the Parisian National Guard, like the provincial guards and the army itself, should be recruited from all classes of the population without distinction.

He is reported to have said,

In my present position I only find nobility in the riff-raff and riff-raff in the nobility which I have created.

These words seem prophetic if we remember the way many of this young nobility were to behave towards him. But the Emperor hesitated to arm those who had been guilty of the revolution; he summoned various dignitaries and officials to a private consultation and asked their advice. The reply was decided; they recalled the part which the National Guard had played during the revolution, and the Emperor agreed with their decision. It was settled that the militia should only be recruited from men whose position afforded a guarantee of good behaviour.

This measure was unfortunate, as are all those which are dictated by fear. The National Guard was composed of men who were the least fitted for the trade of a soldier, and at the same time were most hostile to the Government that is to say, men of property and shopkeepers who had been ruined by the war; and also, as recruiting was limited to a small class, the numbers were only a third of what they might have been.

At such a time it was a fatal mistake not to make use of some 40,000 work- men who had served in the army. According to calculations the National Guard as organized ought to have been composed of not less than 24,000 men; this was not enough to defend Paris and less than the half of this number were actually recruited; on February 11 the National Guard numbered 6,000 men; on February 27 8,000, and on March 16 11,500, of whom 3,000 were armed only with pikes.

The demands for exemption were numerous, and most ingenious methods were employed by the *bourgeois* to avoid "the ridicule of mounting guard," but nevertheless the lack of men was less serious than the lack of arms and equipment. The members of certain picked companies were obliged to arm and clothe themselves at their own expense, and they carried sporting guns or carbines and muskets of various calibres.

These found a small nucleus of combatants, but the greatest difficulty was found in equipping the remaining companies. Neither the town nor the Minister of the Interior had money available, and several loans were put upon the market in January and February. The sums realized were extraordinarily small when it is remembered that the clothing and equipment of each man cost 157 *francs* and the armament 100 *francs*.

The arsenals were empty, and it has been already said that in the majority of the depots there was only one musket for every three men. At the beginning of February there were in Paris 11,000 muskets in a serviceable condition, and Clarke was keeping these for the line and the Young Guard. There were in addition 30,000 muskets in the fort of Vincennes, but none were fit for use. Some workmen from the factory at Charleville arrived to repair them, escorting 800 wagons laden with material, and as soon as the muskets passed through the workshops the Minister of War distributed them to the depots. It was certainly more natural to issue the arms to the troops of the line who were only waiting for their receipt to go to the field of battle, than to keep them for the National Guard, whom every one, and no one more so than themselves, hoped to be destined never to see a shot fired.

The question of arming the militia was the constant pre-occupation of the officials, from King Joseph downwards, and every expedient was made use of to procure muskets. First of all they withdrew the drill muskets from the State colleges; then they wished to take those from the polytechnic school, on the grounds that the scholars were serving in the artillery and had no need of arms; the commandant of the school protested, how-ever, and the arms were not taken. Rovigo heard that there were guns in the merchants' warehouses at Nantes and Havre and he proposed to buy them, but they turned out to be trade guns, which were liable to burst if they were ever fired.

On February 13 the Emperor wrote to his brother that the peasants had picked up on the battlefields 40,000 muskets aban-doned by the enemy, and that commissioners should be sent to collect them. Napoleon was exaggerating as usual, and probably not more than five or six thousand muskets had been aban-doned, but on the following day a first commissioner, M. de Froidefonds, was sent to Champagne.

A few days afterwards, however, it was pointed out that the collection of these muskets would deprive the peasants of the means of resisting the Cossacks, and no more commissioners were sent. M. de Froidefonds returned on March 6, bringing 480 muskets, but these arms were not distributed to the Nation-al Guard, for Clarke seized upon them for the use of the army. In default of muskets, Joseph had 6,000 pikes manufactured.

A large number of the militia, however, refused to accept these obsolete weapons, although they had been most tastefully decorated with tricolour pennants, and although Joseph tried to increase the prestige of the pikemen by proposing to create a guard of honour for the King of Rome under the pompous title of Lancers of the National Guard.

The lack of arms prevented the carrying out of Napoleon's project of raising a further contingent of the National Guard from the populace of Paris, and especially from the unemployed workmen. The Emperor first of all wished to raise 30,000 men, but he gave up the idea on King Joseph's representing " that it would be impossible to double the National Guard without altering its nature, and further there is the insuperable difficulty of the lack of arms." Later, on March 10, 14, and 23, he raised the subject again, but reduced his demand from 30,000 to 12,000 men. Joseph consulted the *prefect* of police, whose usual sound judgment seems to have been upset by the panic which had reigned for the last few days. Baron Pasquier replied that the existing National Guard was not fit to bear arms of any sort; he said that at the least alarm they would refuse to do duty, and that they were in favour of a rebellion. Care should be taken, therefore, not to increase this militia, which was already very bad, by adding to it still worse material.

> "Above all," added Pasquier, "we must be most careful not to agitate the populace of Paris, for there is no knowing to what lengths they would not go. If they were once stirred up they could be easily led by any faction. The people are very unhappy, and it would be easy to drive them to take desperate measures against their rulers, and of this there are plenty of people ready to take advantage."

Pasquier should have confined himself to saying that, as they had not enough arms for the existing National Guard, it would be waste of time to raise a fresh contingent: that was the best, and, indeed, the only argument with which to oppose the Emperor's proposal. The other reasons given by the *prefect* of police were founded on cowardice rather than on clear judgment. It was not true that the National Guard was unfit to bear arms of any sort, or that on the least alarm it would refuse to do duty.

Although the method of recruiting was very objectionable, the Parisian National Guard was animated by a fairly satisfactory tone. It was certainly not at all inclined to sally out and attack the enemy, but it was determined to defend the walls stoutly. It was not true that the populace were ready to assist the invaders by a revolution. The secret police reports and Pasquier's own daily reports for the months of January, February, and March 1814 show that the working-class population had remained Bonapartist. The events of April were about to prove also that revolutions are not always made by the people. Napoleon was right when he wrote to King Joseph:

"The people have energy and honour. I am afraid that it is certain leading men who are unwilling to fight."

In the infantry there were men, but no muskets, but in the artillery there were plenty of guns, but no men. Vincennes contained 700 pieces of various calibres, mostly siege or fortress guns, and many of the field guns had no limbers; 342 guns were brought into Paris, but as soon as a battery had been organized it was sent off to the army; 28 batteries, comprising 156 guns, were sent off in this way, and 186 guns remained in Paris. This was more than could be made use of, for the outer defensive works had not been constructed and there were very few gunners available. At first they had counted upon having more than 20 companies of artillery, composed of coastguards, sailors, Dutchmen, pensioners, and pupils of the polytechnic schools and students of law and medicine.

The two Dutch companies, however, had been set apart for the garrison of Vincennes; the four naval companies had been incorporated in Arrighi's and Souham's divisions; and finally some of the students of law and medicine behaved in a disgraceful manner by hooting General Lespinasse, who had been put in command of them, and these companies were disbanded. There remained the coastguards, the pensioners, the polytechnic schools, and some volunteers from the National Guard, and the total numbered barely 1,000 men.

It would no doubt have been possible to have formed some

artillery from among the 12,000 National Guards, who were not properly armed, but as it is much more difficult to improvise gunners than infantry, it was not even attempted. Out of the 186 guns, 54 were mounted at the gates and the remaining 132 were parked on the Champ de Mars in anticipation of the building of fortifications and of artillerymen being somehow found to work them.

In the month of January, 1814, there were no fortifications round Paris except the *octroi* wall, and this did not completely encircle the town. The Emperor reverted to the idea which he had conceived at the beginning of the campaign of 1805, and proposed to make Paris a regular fortress; the engineer committee, in consequence, formulated its proposals: redoubts were to be built on the surrounding hills, and works were to be placed at the extremities of the suburbs, which were to be barricaded, loopholed, and connected by trenches.

The construction of these works would have needed plenty of time and money. The Emperor did not wish to frighten the Parisians with the prospect of a siege, and was unwilling to let it be thought that the conqueror of Europe was already in fear for the safety of his capital. He rejected the proposal, and suggested a simpler scheme. He thought it would be enough to barricade the outer suburbs, to make palisades where the *octroi* wall was unfinished, and to erect stockaded works at the gates with loopholes and embrasures to flank the wall.

These weak entrenchments would protect Paris from a cavalry raid, and in January the Emperor anticipated no more, or at any rate wished to give this impression. By February 3 the engineers of the National Guard had made the palisades and the stockaded works, but when the Emperor left to join the army the Committee of Defence was allowed to lapse and no steps were taken to fortify the suburbs.

In the beginning of March King Joseph inspected the defensive line, and his officers pointed out the inadequacy of the fortifications. The chief of Joseph's military office was consulted, and he recalled the fact that a more elaborate plan had been submitted to the Emperor. Joseph did not dare to order the works to be made without having consulted his brother, and he wrote on March 8 asking for authority to raise a new tax of 500,000 *francs* for the purpose, and suggesting that the money might be advanced at once from the treasury. On March 11 the Emperor replied that the redoubts at Montmartre ought to be begun, but he said nothing about the question of money. On March 12 Joseph reminded his brother that the Committee of Defence had prepared a plan, and that nothing but the lack of funds had delayed its execution.

"The plan is very complicated," replied Napoleon on March 13, but he still did not sanction any funds. On March 14 the engineer committee met again and drew up a second and more simple scheme; instead of redoubts there were to be open works, and the continuous trenches were to be replaced by short lengths of earthwork.

On March 15 Joseph sent this scheme to the Emperor and said, "In order that these works may be started at once, it is necessary first that your Majesty should approve the scheme, and secondly that you should authorize an advance of 100,000 *francs*."

The Emperor did not reply to this precise and urgent letter, for the successful battle of Rheims had made him hope that he would be able to attract against himself and away from Paris all the efforts of the allied armies.

On March 22 Joseph wrote again:

The president of the engineer committee is anxiously awaiting your Majesty's approval.

This last letter was either captured by the enemy or only reached Napoleon the day before the battle of Paris.

The behaviour of the inhabitants of Saint-Denis ought to have been an example to King Joseph. Since the beginning of February they had been left in an open town without any garrison and without an organized National Guard, and the townspeople of their own accord took steps to protect themselves against a Cossack raid. A National Guard was formed, and the members armed and equipped themselves at their own expense; they moulded their own bullets and made cartridges from some powder which had been left in the barrack magazine. A committee of defence was formed of militia officers and architects; works were erected at all entrances, and the town was surrounded with trenches, palisades, and obstacles.

It is surely not asking too much of the Council of the Regency to expect them to show as much initiative as a suburban municipality. In the month of February Joseph ought to have thought of the weakness of the fortifications, and he ought to have ordered the construction of the essential works, in spite of the delays and contradictory orders of the Emperor. He had written to the Emperor that he was stopped by want of funds, but many of the works could certainly have been put up without the expenditure of any money.

There was plenty of timber available in the Bois de Boulogne and at Vincennes, and the National Guardsmen would have been much more usefully employed digging trenches than doing sentry-go on the gates without arms or with guns whose ballistic properties were little better than those of a broomstick. Some of the militiamen might have found themselves unequal to handling a spade or pickaxe, and these might have been allowed to provide substitutes for this work only. This plan would have had the double advantage of fortifying Paris and of finding work for some of the unemployed. It seems probable even that if Saint-Denis had been held up as an example to the other suburbs, voluntary working parties would have been obtained.

With a little initiative there is no doubt that the Regency could have erected temporary fortifications round Paris, and it is worthwhile to consider whether they could by any means have raised enough money to complete the armament of the National Guard and of the 12,000 extra men whom the Emperor wished to enrol. The population of Paris was terribly impoverished and found the greatest difficulty in paying the taxes which were demanded of them; the majority of the townspeople were in misery, and even the best off were in great straits; manufacturers had no orders and their men were out of work; in the shops goods were sold at a loss if a customer ever appeared, and landlords had perforce to go without their rent. Since November 17, 1813, all pensions and civil salaries had been reduced by 25 *per cent.*, and they were paid in arrears and by instalments.

If large war taxes were to have been raised from the Parisians they would have had to be imposed at the beginning of January; during the first two months of the year direct taxation in Paris realized 70,000 *francs* a day, but in the month of March poverty in- creased to such an extent that the daily yield fell to less than 10,000 *francs*. When at last the Regency determined to impose a special tax for the defence of Paris it was too late.

The special contribution of 1,000,000 *francs* ordered on February 22 in order to provide 2,000 artillery horses was collected in five days, but the special demand for 750,000 *francs* voted on March 8 for the expenses of the National Guard yielded nothing, or practically nothing, and the tax of 120,000 *francs* for the defence of the town, which was approved by the Council of State on March 16, was not collected at all. The authorities in consequence found themselves unable to buy 3,000 sporting guns from the armourers or to start a factory which would turn out 500 to 1,000 muskets a day, or to start the fortifications by means of relief works.

This last proposal had been discussed by the Ministers on December 22, 1813. It had been postponed on account of lack of money, but the Emperor had ordered it to be undertaken on March 11. But, so far from their being able to start relief works, the lack of funds was so great that for want of orders the military con- tractors were obliged to dismiss their work-people wholesale. There was an absolute dearth of money. The Treasury had more than 400,000,000 *francs* in bonds and bills, but this was paper, not gold, and as King Joseph wrote, "Credit is no longer of the least use."

The Emperor alone, thanks to economies from his civil list,

had some cash, but the famous treasure in the cellars of the Tuileries was not inexhaustible. For the last three months the Emperor had paid out of his own pocket all the expenses of the Guard and of the main cavalry depot, and part of the cost of the War Office. The cellars of the Tuileries had contained 75,000,000 *francs*, but at the beginning of March there remained barely 24,000,000.

Napoleon expected the war to last some time, and was very chary of using what remained. The Baron de la Bouillerie, the crown treasurer, would not advance a penny without the express order of the Emperor, and his orders were often delayed. It frequently happened that General Ornano, commandant of the Guard depot, and General Préval, commandant of the cavalry depot, were forced, for want of money, to stop the equipment of battalions and squadrons. For this we have the evidence of letters written by Joseph and by General Préval, who in less than a month had mounted, equipped, clothed, and armed twelve regiments of cavalry.

"Although payments have ceased," wrote Préval to Clarke, "I have succeeded in getting a certain number of orders delivered. I managed today to get hold of 127 horses, and this, in spite of the fact that I am in debt at this moment for more than 800 horses, and that I owe the majority of contractors more than 500,000 *francs*. I believe that if payments had not ceased I would have succeeded in providing not 6,000 horses as I had undertaken, but 9,000 or 10,000. I have proof of this, because in spite of every obstacle I shall have provided 7,000 to 8,000 during March."

A few days later he wrote again;

I can send no more men because I have no money; the men must have boots and horses. I can only repeat to you, money, money, money.

If Napoleon was chary of spending his last millions on the army on which all his hopes were founded, he was certainly not going to deplete the treasure of the Tuileries to pay for the National Guard and the fortifications of Paris which he only occasionally believed to be of any use. Although the War Office was helped by grants from other departments, and from Napoleon's privy purse, it yet found itself unable to meet the enormous expenses of armament, clothing, ammunition, supplies, and pay. It certainly could not pay for muskets for the National Guard and for the relief works. Paris was bound to find the money for her own defence, but in the month of March Paris was bankrupt.

A few days before he left to join the army, at a meeting of the Council of Ministers, Napoleon had said aloud with his eyes fixed on Talleyrand, "I know well that I am leaving enemies behind me in Paris besides those whom I am going out to fight."

Murat had said of Talleyrand that if he were to be kicked from behind his face would show no sign, and on this occasion he had remained impassive. The Regency had not done all it might have in preparing for defence against the enemy; had it done its full duty towards checkmating the enemy within the walls whom Napoleon had denounced?

Certainly not. When initiative and energy are lacking in one direction, they are lacking everywhere. The responsibility for the moral anarchy which reigned in Paris under the Regency must be shared by six men: Pasquier, the Prefect of Police; Chabrol, the Prefect of the Seine; Montalivet, the Minister of the Interior; the Arch-Chancellor Cambacérès, the adviser of the Regent; and King Joseph, the Emperor's lieutenant-general, but the most to blame was the Minister of Police, the Duc de Rovigo. He ought to have known everything, but he did not know or did not want to know. He kept the Emperor informed of women's gossip and of miserable squabbles with his colleagues, but he did not tell him of the thousand and one plots which were being hatched.

He was at once sceptical and afraid of responsibility, and he took no steps to prepare for eventualities which he boasted to have foreseen. His brain was active and brilliant, but his self-confidence was over-weening and he amused himself by fencing with people cleverer than he, and as a result he became the tool of his opponents.

While the Emperor was fighting on the Aube and the Aisne, Paris had become a hot-bed of intrigue. An atmosphere of conspiracy seemed to have spread over the whole town, and even among the officials there were many who were working against Napoleon. Pasquier, the Prefect of Police, sent secret warning to the Comte d' Artois and the Duc d'Angoulme that their lives were in danger, and Jaucourt, King Joseph's chamberlain, took advantage of his position to learn the earliest news of the military operations in order that he might report to Talleyrand and his accomplices. Talleyrand was also kept in touch with the progress of negotiations at Châtillon by La Besnardière, a councillor-of-state who was on Caulaincourt's staff.

Since the month of November 1813 the malcontents, who were numerous, and the royalists, who still were few in number, had fixed their eyes on Talleyrand as their destined leader. He, however, was too prudent to accept this role definitely, but he wished to be able to take advantage of it should opportunity offer. He contented himself, therefore, with doing nothing to dash the hopes of the conspirators.

He had already for some time been at the head of the malcontents, but he was not yet a royalist; a common hatred of Napoleon, indeed, bound him to them, but his aims were different from theirs. He was not sure of the reception which he would receive from the Bourbons, and the prospect of being the First Minister under a king did not satisfy his ambition: he aimed higher. The King of Rome was three years old, and for fifteen years Talleyrand might govern France as President of the Council of Regency.

The Emperor's death would at once place him in this position. Although he did not believe in Providence, the death of Napoleon would have been described by Talleyrand as providential. He was charitable enough to hope that Napoleon would fall on the battlefield; but, failing that, he would have felt no repugnance had he been assassinated.

During the whole campaign of 1814 Talleyrand indulged himself in the dream of a Regency. The news of the proclamation of the King at Bordeaux, which delighted the royalists of Paris, surprised him, but caused him no anxiety, and he did not incline to the side of the Bourbons until the Empress left Paris for Blois. Up to that time, although he himself did not wish to see the Bourbons restored, he took care not to discourage the royalists. To him, as to the allied sovereigns, every agency was good which tended to overthrow Napoleon, and failing a Regency, a restoration was not to be despised; the important thing was Napoleon's fall.

The royalists, then, were well received by Talleyrand; without appearing to be doing so, he encouraged them by his comments on the news received from the army and from the Congress, and by his gloomy prophecies as to the result of the campaign. He gave them information and advice, but he was careful not to give them his open support. It did not suit him to appear as a conspirator, even in the eyes of his accomplices, and, in accordance with the method which he had always found to succeed, he avoided compromising himself before "the day after the event," as Chateaubriand puts it.

The liberals among the public men followed Talleyrand's example in not committing themselves and in waiting to see which way the cat would jump, but they were ready to form a government if occasion should offer. The royalists, however, were less reserved and more active. Numerous emissaries were sent to the allied head-quarters and the residence of the princes. The Abbé de Pradt regularly received the English papers through a lady in Brussels and distributed them from meeting to meeting, "which," as he said with satisfaction, "shattered the illusions with which the French papers entertained the public."

Illusions, no doubt, but illusions necessary for the defence of the country. Other royalists circulated violent pamphlets received from England and from the provinces occupied by the enemy; others, again, posted up by night in the streets royalist placards which promised to forget the past and to maintain vested rights, and foreshadowed a constitutional government and the abolition of conscription.

Rovigo knew all about the threatening attitude of the liberals and the royalist plots; or, at least, he afterwards pretended that he did. But it made very little difference whether he did or did not foresee the plots and know the names of the conspirators, because he was on principle opposed to all oppressive measures. When the Abbé de Pradt made treasonable overtures to him, he contented himself with answering, "Do not speak to me like that; I cannot listen."

Talleyrand often came to see him, and would constantly say: "France is in a deplorable state; what are we to do under the circumstances? It does not suit everyone to remain in a burning house. You should look after yourself."

To this sort of talk Rovigo used to answer nothing. One day, towards the middle of March, Rovigo entered Talleyrand's study without being announced, and found him closeted with Pradt. The sudden appearance of the Minister of Police was like a thunderbolt; neither of them could find anything to say, and Pradt's face clearly showed his discomfiture.

"This time," cried Rovigo, "I have found you in the act of conspiring."

Talleyrand and Pradt burst out laughing, and before long Rovigo was laughing too.

Rovigo acknowledges that he would have had grounds for arresting Talleyrand, but he said that, after all, there was nothing but prejudice against him. The Emperor was angry with Talleyrand, and distrusted him altogether; but he had refused to imprison him before he left Paris. Talleyrand was the Vice-Grand-Elector, and could only have been arrested with King Joseph's authority, and to do so would be to risk a revolution; also, he was only conspiring against the Emperor, and not against the dynasty; he made himself of use to the chief of police by informing him of what the royalists were doing; and finally, if all the conspirators were to be arrested, the prisons were not big enough to hold them. These were poor reasons and vain excuses.

The truth is that Rovigo was a dupe of the master diplomat, and he evaded the order to arrest Talleyrand which the Emperor gave after the battle of Montereau. Certainly Rovigo's devotion to Napoleon is beyond doubt; but his capabilities were limited, and he made himself unpopular in times of calm, but was of no use when a revolution was impending.

Rovigo was easily misled and he was unable to foresee events. It was unknown to him that in November 1813 the Duc de Dalberg's secretary had left for Frankfort with the message to the allied sovereigns that they were awaited in Paris with open arms; it was unknown to him that Vitrolles and ten other royalist emissaries left Paris to join the princes and the staff of the allies; it was unknown to him that the royalists received foreign newspapers, which they did through the agency of one of Rovigo's own subordinates. He shut his eyes to all the intrigues which were going on around him.

He did not know that the Bourbons' proclamations were being printed in Paris, or that Morin was spreading the royalist propaganda among the *bourgeoisie*, or that Chateaubriand was printing in Paris a most violent attack against Napoleon. He failed to expel the Germans who were publicly spreading alarm and he failed to stop the distribution and the posting up of royalist placards. He failed to prevent the escape of the two Polignacs whom he allowed to be on parole and whom he often received in his own house. Finally, in spite of formal orders, he failed to arrest Talleyrand or the Marquis de Rivière, who was engaged in furthering the royalist cause.

It is true that M. de Rivière had formerly told Rovigo that he felt himself to be under such an obligation to the Emperor that if the Comte d'Artois had appeared in front of Paris with 100,000 men he would be unable to join him, and this seems to have been enough to reassure the Minister of Police. Napoleon had been perfectly justified when he wrote to Rovigo on March 14, "Either you have been very clumsy or else you are no longer serving me."

While intrigue was busy among the politicians, a feeling of

alarm was gaining ground among the general populace. Until the beginning of March the Parisians were buoyed up by the confidence with which the battles of Champaubert and Montmirail had inspired them; they did not all believe in a successful issue of the campaign, but there were none who did not think that an honourable peace was near at hand.

Then came a lack of definite news, and this was followed in turn by the battle of Laon, the abandonment of the negotiations of Lusigny, the retreat of Napoleon on Soissons and of Macdonald on Provins, the events at Bordeaux, the rupture of the Congress of Châtillon, and finally the capture of Lyons. These events spread alarm and despondency broadcast through France. The newspapers were censored in accordance with the decree published at Troyes on February 4, and they only told such news as the Government wanted to be known; this was little or nothing, and if they mentioned bad news at all they did it in such a way as to minimize its importance.

The public, however, were not deceived; although the later bulletins followed the earlier ones almost word for word, and although salutes were fired in honour of victories, yet the public realized the difference between victories like Vauchamps and battles like Craonne. News leaked out through letters received from the army, and there were many people in Paris who made it their business to spread bad news.

There were also foreign papers which Pradt and his friends were never tired of circulating. According to the *Times*, the *Globe*, the *Courier* and the *Morning Chronicle*, the abandonment of the plateau of Craonne had been a clever manoeuvre designed to draw the Emperor into the plain of Laon; at Laon the French had been completely beaten? and had lost 70 guns and 60,000 men, besides a number of generals, among whom were Macdonald and Sebastiani; the Emperor was retiring on Rouen with an army reduced to 30,000 men; Blücher had routed Napoleon, and Schwarzenberg had defeated Oudinot, and they were marching in concert on Paris.

In February the alarmists had spread similar news, but then

these reports had been contradicted by private letters and by the Emperor's detailed bulletins, as well as by the presentation of captured colours and the convoys of prisoners who passed every day along the boulevards.

In the middle of March no one came back to Paris except the French wounded, who were carried in wagons or on boats on the river; there also arrived small groups of wounded men on foot, infantrymen using their muskets as crutches or cavalrymen with bloodstained bandages walking painfully beside their wounded horses. These men were refused admittance at the overcrowded hospitals; the barracks were not allowed to receive them, and they wandered through the streets begging for bread.

During the twelve years of the Consulate and of the Empire, victory was all that Paris had known of war; she had heard salutes and thanksgiving services, she had seen triumphant processions of victorious troops, thousands of captured cannons had been stored in the arsenals and numbers of colours deposited in the Invalides; she knew nothing of war but this. Now the war was at her gates; guns were firing in earnest within a few miles of Paris; every day convoys of wounded arrived in the town, and the Parisians could see with their own eyes the ghastly aftermath of battle.

The Government knew well the disastrous effect which the sight of the wounded was producing. On February 11 the Minister of the Interior had asked Clarke to have the convoys diverted to Normandy or towards Orleans, and it had been suggested that hospitals should be established outside the walls so that the wounded should not enter the town. King Joseph had wished to make a huge hospital either at the Invalides or at the barracks of Courbevoie, and Napoleon, who thought of everything, gave orders that the sick and wounded were to be sent to Versailles, Saint-Germain, Rouen, Evreux, and Chartres.

The administrative services, however, were in a state of chaos, and these proposals, in common with so many others, were not carried out, and the wounded continued to flock into Paris. The hospitals were full and even the passages, chapels, and bathrooms were crowded with wounded lying on straw. Between January 15 and March 10 the number of sick soldiers had risen from 1,685 to 8,375 and there was danger of an outbreak of typhus.

As if there was not enough real cause for anxiety in Paris, the Bureau of National Spirit, as it was called, seemed to be trying to conjure up imaginary terrors in the vain attempt to rouse a determination to resist the enemy. Everyday the newspapers and the police emissaries kept repeating that the allies had determined to mete out to Paris the lot which had befallen Moscow and that the city would be burnt to the ground.

It is true that the enemy's troops and the foreign newspapers gave utterance to such threats. The Prussians and the Cossacks spoke of the looting of Paris as having been promised to them. The Austrian general Colloredo said that the destruction of Paris would be a blessing for France; an article in the *Times* said:

> If Blücher and the Cossacks enter Paris what mercy will they show to the town? Why should they give any mercy? Will they spare the precious monuments of art? A thousand times no. These indignant warriors will believe that the hour of vengeance and destruction has come. A blow at Paris will be a blow at the heart of the French nation. Possibly at the moment of writing this famous city is already a heap of cinders.

The spiteful English papers advocated the burning of Paris, the allied generals pointed to this city as a prey for their troops, and their soldiers promised themselves an orgie of loot and violence; but this was no reason for reproducing these articles in the French papers, or for spreading these ideas broadcast in Paris. The spread of panic could only help the enemy and lower the courage of the Parisians. There is no doubt that the Government hoped to rouse their waning patriotism and inspire them to self-defence, but as there were no arms the effort was doomed to inevitable failure.

Presumably these appeals were addressed to the people, but

the Government of the Regency unjustly doubted the working-class population and asked nothing of them but to remain quiet. There were no muskets, and even if there had been, Joseph, Rovigo, Pasquier, and other cowardly persons would have hesitated to put them in the hands of the workmen.

It was the *bourgeoisie*, then, whose courage they hoped to stimulate, but they only succeeded in throwing them into a state of panic. The bourgeoisie could take no part in a war of extermination and would not consent to make Paris a second Saragossa. The papers were full of high-sounding phrases:

> The sacred soil which the enemy has invaded will become a devouring fire . . . the enemy will find his grave in the streets of Paris. . . . We must bury ourselves beneath the ruins of Paris.

These appeals were very badly received, and they were aptly compared with an article in the *Moniteur* on May 21, 1809, in which it was pointed out that the defence of a capital like Vienna is odious. (As a matter of fact it was the author of this article himself who recalled it, and after all no one had a better right to remember it than the author.) The National Guard contained a number of men who were determined to fight stubbornly, and it was childish to make such appeals to men who were actuated by honour, and the cowards and traitors had already made up their minds; they considered, in short, that the whole of Paris would not be burnt, and that those who exposed themselves most would be the ones to suffer most.

During the third week in March Paris relapsed into the same state of despair as during the early days of February; the situation was even worse, although hopes of peace remained, and people suspected that the enemy were between Napoleon and the capital. If Napoleon had been known to be near at hand the alarm would have been less, for though his subordinates no longer inspired any confidence, yet the Emperor was still believed to be capable of performing a miracle. People again began to leave Paris, business was at a standstill, the theatres were deserted and the shops closed, the rate of exchange rose and stocks fell. Crowds collected on the boulevards and in the public squares, anxiously awaiting the news of the day. The royalist proclamations increased in number and were distributed during the night, and other placards invited the citizens to assemble and urged the deputies to treat for peace in the name of the country.

On March 27 and 28 numbers of peasants arrived at the gates driving their cattle and bringing wagon-loads of household goods. This exodus augured the approach of the enemy, but the populace did not know whether it was merely an isolated column or a whole corps that was approaching. The Government, on the contrary, knew well that the whole allied army was near at hand.

On March 22 Joseph had been informed of the movement of Marmont and Mortier on Châlons, which uncovered the Soissons road, and of the march of the Emperor's army to Vitry, which in turn uncovered the Coulommiers road. Between March 23 and 28 no official news was received from the Emperor, but on March 24 Blücher, with the obvious intention of frightening the Regent, handed to the French outposts near La-Ferté-Milon the letter from Napoleon to the Empress which had been captured by the Cossacks on the night of the 22nd-23rd. This letter explained the Emperor's plans and announced his march on Saint-Dizier.

From the position of the armies and from the fact that the letter had been captured, it was easy to infer that the enemy's armies lay between Napoleon and Paris. On March 26 the news of Marmont's defeat at Fère-Champenoise and of Compans' retreat on La-Ferté-Gaucher served to confirm this supposition.

It was no longer possible to count on orders from Napoleon. Joseph had to act on his own initiative; he became flurried and issued numberless orders, but he still put off the construction of the redoubts "until the Emperor should approve of the plan which had been submitted to him."

Meanwhile the only works carried out were some stockades at the outer suburbs and some trenches across the roads. For these works the Minister of the Interior urgently opened a credit of 15,000 *francs* on the defence tax voted on March 15. Joseph ordered the director of artillery to put a certain number of batteries on the hills surrounding the town, and he decided that the National Guard should have sole charge of the *enceinte* so that the troops might be available to fight at the advanced posts.

He also ascertained the exact number of men without arms and of muskets remaining in the arsenals, and finally he ordered Clarke and Lavallette to send numerous couriers "to tell the Emperor what is happening and to recall him to the capital." In the opinion of everyone, and of King Joseph especially, the return of the Emperor was the most urgent necessity.

Clarke acted as if he still doubted the facts, and seems to have refused to understand that hence-forward everything must be sacrificed to the defence of Paris. He hesitated to allow artillery to be put in position, because, as he said, "no batteries will be left to send to the Emperor," and at the same time as he was urging the return of Marmont and Mortier he weakened the garrison of the town by sending to the Oise a column of infantry and a regiment of cavalry. Clarke seems also to have been more ready to urge others to heroic acts than to do them himself; he sent the following despairing appeal to General Ledru-Desessarts, who was in command at Meaux:

"In heaven's name, general, do not evacuate Meaux, which defends the approaches to Paris. Hold it with the greatest obstinacy; hold it as the Spaniards held Saragossa. That is the way in which Paris will be saved."

It was on March 27 that Clarke wrote this letter; on the 28th he learnt that Ledru-Desessarts and Compans had been driven back into Meaux and were retiring on Ville Parisis. There was no longer room for illusion; in two days the enemy would be before Paris.

Before dealing with the last arrangements for defence Joseph had to make the gravest of decisions. In these terrible circumstances should the Empress and the King of Rome remain in Paris? Joseph had Napoleon's explicit orders, but these orders were such that he would not take the responsibility of carrying them out without referring the question to the Council of Regency. On March 28 at 8.30 p.m. the Council assembled at the Tuileries under the presidency of the Empress. Joseph gave his reasons for summoning the Council and called upon the Minister of War to speak.

Clarke explained the situation without attempting to conceal the danger. He reminded the Council that the Emperor was on the farther side of the Marne, cut off from Paris by the enemy's army. He pointed out that the fortifications were hardly begun, that the National Guard consisted of 12,000 men, of whom 6,000 were armed with pikes or unserviceable muskets, and that the garrison amounted to 20,000 men, including the troops of Compans and Ledru-Desessarts who had behaved so badly the day before at Meaux. Marmont and Mortier's corps, which had lost heavily, were still on the Provins road, and it was doubtful if they would reach Paris before the enemy.

Taking things at their best, there were 43,000 soldiers and militiamen to oppose to the allied armies. Rovigo has given it as his opinion that if Clarke said nothing which might increase the anxiety of the Council, he certainly said nothing to allay their fears. Clarke was right to speak in this way; he was not making a proclamation to the people on the army, he was making a report to the Council of Ministers. He might doubtless have added, as his own opinion, that 40,000 men might hold out in Paris for two or three days, even against three times their own numbers, but as Minister of War it was his bounden duty to give the exact number of men available and to conceal nothing.

Clarke's words did not frighten the Council. Several of the members spoke in turn and gave it as their opinion that the departure of the Empress would give the impression that there was no hope, and would take the heart out of the defence; they insisted on the dangers which would be incurred by leaving the capital at the mercy of all the intriguers. The Government, the police, and the people agreed in thinking that if Paris fell the Empire would fall also, and Napoleon himself had several times said so. Rovigo, who seems to have repented rather too late of his prejudices, maintained that they could rely absolutely on the devotion and willingness of the working-classes. Talleyrand agreed, and declared that nothing could stop a revolution except the presence of the Empress in Paris.

The energetic Boulay de la Meurthe suggested that the Empress and the King of Rome should pass in procession to the Hôtel de Ville and call the city to arms. This would have been a good idea if there had been any arms; Marie-Louise had not the spirit of her grandmother, Marie-Therese, but she could at any rate have carried out the decorative part of the role assigned to her. She was a doll, and could have been used for anything, even for a great purpose. The sight of this young and beautiful woman with Napoleon's son in her arms, braving the bullets and the fire and summoning her people to the defence of Paris, would have roused the populace to enthusiasm.

When the votes were taken, all the members of the Council voted against the departure of the Empress, except Clarke, who was in favour of a retreat, and Joseph, who abstained from voting. Clarke knew of the existence of the Emperor's letter which Joseph would soon produce, and he now spoke again and said that the Empress and the King of Rome should not be exposed to the risk of capture, that the danger of leaving Paris had been exaggerated, that the power of the Emperor would follow them everywhere, and that as long as there remained one village where he or his son was recognized, that village would be the capital, and there all good Frenchmen would rally. The discussion broke out again, but a second vote showed the same result as the former.

Joseph then produced the Emperor's letter of March 16 which definitely ordered that the Empress and the King of Rome were to leave Paris as soon as it was threatened by the enemy.

"Bear in mind," wrote Napoleon, "that I would rather see my son drowned than in the hands of the enemies of France.

I have always looked upon the fate of Astyanax, the prisoner of the Greeks, as being the most miserable one which history records."

Joseph might have read several other letters expressing the same wish, but this one was enough. The members of the Council were astounded. They held to their own opinion, however, and said with reason that if the Council had had full powers the Empress would have remained in Paris, but that they were bound to obey the orders of the Emperor. They added that as the orders did not admit of discussion it had been merely waste of time asking them to consider the matter.

Cambacérès then announced that the Empress would leave at 8 a.m. on the following day and would go to Tours *via* Rambouillet and Chartres; he himself would accompany the Empress and the Crown Treasurer would follow with the treasure. As for the ministers and the dignitaries, they would remain in Paris until King Joseph ordered them to leave. The meeting broke up at 2 a.m.

Almost all the ministers remained in the ante- room, and spoke their minds freely. They all deplored the decision which had been arrived at, and one of them went so far as to say to Rovigo, "If I were Minister of Police, Paris would be in a state of revolt tomorrow morning, and the Empress would not leave."

Rovigo replied that he knew it would be quite easy to rouse the people to take such action, but that he was not ready to assume the responsibility for such a step when the Ministers in Council had agreed to let the Empress go. "I am as sorry as anyone else that such a decision should have been arrived at, but I will not undertake alone what you all have refused to do together." They all showed the same lack of initiative and fear of responsibility.

The ministers left for their homes, and an eye-witness says that each member said goodbye to his colleagues as if he was convinced that this was the last act of the Government.

"What a come-down," said Talleyrand, as he parted from Rovigo, "an adventurous journey instead of a deed of heroism!

. . . but it does not suit everyone to let himself be buried under the ruins of this edifice."

During the previous hour the cause of the Empire had become hopeless, and at the same moment Talleyrand had thrown in his lot with the Bourbons.

CHAPTER 23

The Allies Before Paris

The moment that the departure of the Empress had been decided upon, Joseph again found himself in difficulties. The Council of the Regency had wished the Empress to remain, and the danger of abandoning Paris had never before been so apparent to the Emperor's brother. His mind and conscience were assailed by doubts. The Emperor wished them to leave Paris, but if he allowed them to do so he would be false to Napoleon's cause. He did not feel that he was sufficiently relieved of responsibility by Napoleon's orders, and still less by the decision which the Council had so reluctantly taken, and he attempted therefore a last appeal to the Empress.

As soon as the meeting was over Joseph and Cambacérès followed Marie-Louise to her private apartments. They again put forward the arguments which they had just quashed by producing the Emperor's letter; they again pointed out the terrible consequences which might ensue if she left Paris, and they said finally that the Empress alone had authority to decide. Marie-Louise did not at all wish to leave the Tuileries, but they were really asking too much to expect her to take such a responsibility. She replied that the king and the arch-chancellor were her official advisers, and that she would not take upon herself to issue an order contrary to the instructions of the Emperor and the decision of the Council, unless they advised her to do so in writing.

This proposal was not at all to Joseph's liking, and it was decided that she should start at the hour named. The king, however, said he would leave Paris at daybreak to inspect the positions, and to try to get some news of Marmont and Mortier, and he asked the Empress not to start until he returned to the Tuileries. After some hours' sleep, Joseph went to the outposts, and he was either delayed or had no news to give the Empress, and he did not return to the palace, and sent no message.

The remainder of the night was occupied in preparations for the journey; at 7 a.m. the Empress was ready in her rooms with the King of Rome and her ladies, and in the adjoining rooms were waiting those who were to accompany her. An oppressive silence reigned; the least noise caused a flutter of excitement; they expected every minute to see King Joseph appear. At 8 o'clock the officers of the National Guard on duty in the palace asked to be admitted to the presence of the Empress; they begged her not to abandon Paris, and promised that they would defend her to the death.

Marie-Louise was touched to tears by their devotion, but pleaded that the Emperor wished her to go. She put off her departure from hour to hour, and, though she did not dare to admit it, she hoped that something would happen to oblige her to remain in Paris. At about 9 o'clock the carriages which were waiting were ordered back into the stables, but a few minutes afterwards Cambacérès arrived, and they were ordered out again. The Empress was urged by some to hasten her departure, and by others to put it off, and she still waited for Joseph's return. She went into her bedroom and threw her hat angrily on the bed, and sank down in an armchair; there she buried her head in her hands and burst into tears, and she was heard to repeat between her sobs, "*Mon Dieu*! I wish they would make up their minds, and put an end to this agony."

Joseph did not come, and Clarke had already sent an *aide-de-camp* to ask the Empress to start. At 10.30 a second *aide-de-camp* arrived, to say that there was not a moment to be lost, and that if they waited any longer there would be risk of their being captured by Cossacks. The Empress gave way and left the Tuileries, but they had to drag away the little King of Rome, who cried, and begged his mother: "Do not go to Rambouillet, it is not a nice castle. Let us stop here."

The child struggled in the arms of M. de Canisy, and clung to the doors and the bannisters, shouting at the top of his voice: "I don't want to leave my house; I don't want to go away. Now that father is away I am the master here."

The carriages moved slowly as if they still hoped for counter-orders; in front went ten heavy green *chaises*, crested with the imperial arms, then came the coronation coach, covered with cloth, and then the interminable column of wagons; 1,200 cavalry and infantry of the Old Guard formed the escort. Although it was already late in the morning, there were barely a hundred spectators opposite the Pont-Royal wicket gate, and they were as silent as if a funeral was passing; not a solitary shout or cheer was raised, and both those who were going and those who remained seemed equally depressed.

The carriages followed the quays along the wall of the palace garden; at the Champs Elysées the Empress leant out of her carriage to cast a last glance at Paris. She had arrived at the capital full of fear and dread, and had spent four happy years there; to leave it rent her heart and filled her eyes with tears, but she was destined to forget it in a short space of time.

When Joseph returned to Paris the departure of the Empress was an accomplished fact; the king was saved from his agony of indecision and his conscience was clear. Even if he had not done what he thought best, he had, at any rate, obeyed orders. On one point, however, Joseph had not conformed with the Emperor's instructions. Napoleon had intended that the departure of the Empress should be made simultaneously with the movement of the Government to the farther side of the Loire; the orders on this subject were definite. On February 8 he had written:

Send the Empress and the King of Rome to Rambouillet. Order the Senate and the Council of State to assemble on the Loire. Leave at Paris either the *prefect*, or a special commission, or a mayor.

On March 16 he had said,

If the enemy advances in force on Paris, send towards the
Loire the Regent, my son, the grand dignitaries, the ministers, the officers of the Senate, and the main officials of
the Crown.

Now, on March 28, it had been resolved that only Cambacérès and La Bouillerie, with the treasure, should accompany
the Empress.

The order of the Emperor was clear and formal and seems
to have been inspired by a vision of the future. Everyone, including Joseph, were to leave Paris. One can understand that
the king should take upon himself to remain, because he wore
the uniform of the grenadiers of the Guard and fighting was in
prospect. One can also understand that he did not nominate an
imperial commissioner, because the Emperor himself had not
been able to decide upon a man for the post, but it is not easy
to understand why Joseph delayed the departure of the Government.

Perhaps he thought that the danger was not very pressing and
that there was a chance of repulsing the enemy, but they had
moved the Empress, the King of Rome, and Cambacérès, and
they could quite well have moved the ministers and Talleyrand.
Must we conclude from this action of Joseph that he wished
to remain in Paris in order to treat with the allies in the name
of France, hoping thereby to confirm his title of Lieutenant-
General of the Empire under Marie-Louise as Regent?

To bring this about the presence of the ministers and of the
Senate was necessary. It is known that at the beginning of March
some of Joseph's entourage, and even some of the senators, had
made overtures in this direction, which they renewed when the
Empress left. But those who revealed these intrigues bear witness that the Emperor's brother would have nothing to say to
them, and during the twenty-four hours that Joseph remained
alone in Paris, the head of the Government and of the army, he
not only made no attempt to enter into negotiations with the

allies, but he refused to receive all flags of truce. At the Council of March 28 Joseph only sinned through want of forethought, but he none the less committed a serious mistake. By putting off till the following day what he could easily have done at once Joseph made himself responsible for the consequences of his action.

The news that the Empress had gone through Paris into a state of consternation. No hope seemed to remain now that the Government itself was in despair. The presence in Paris of the daughter of the most powerful monarch of the coalition had been felt to be a safeguard, but the flight of Marie-Louise abandoned Paris to pillage, fire, and destruction.

The sound of the guns could be heard in the direction of Bondy; the inhabitants of the north-eastern suburbs were flocking in panic through the gates, and an appeal to arms, which was distributed in the streets, began with the words, "Shall we let our city be pillaged and burnt?"

All this did not tend to allay the fears of the people. Numbers left Paris; the roads to Rouen, Chartres, and Dreux were thronged with carriages of every description bearing women and children and with wagons laden with furniture. Crowds assembled and expressed their indignation at the departure of the Regent.

"This was the first time I ever heard the people blame the Emperor," says a witness.

During the afternoon the following proclamation of Joseph's was issued:

Citizens of Paris, a column of the enemy is advancing from the eastward. The Emperor is in hot pursuit at the head of a victorious army. The Council of the Regency has provided for the safety of the Empress and the King of Rome. I remain with you. Let us take up arms in defence of the town. . . . The Emperor is marching to our assistance; let us help him by a short and bold resistance and let us save the honour of France.

This proclamation was not badly worded, for it was reassuring to the people to be told that only a column of the enemy was approaching and that the Emperor was arriving by forced marches, but unfortunately these statements were discounted by the fact of the Empress having been sent away. Joseph was not popular and his proclamation was badly received; those who still had the heart to joke composed ribald ballads at his expense and he was freely caricatured, in one instance being portrayed as disappearing at a gallop shouting out the words "Courage, I am going to fetch reinforcements."

The people were not all of one mind; some were angry while others were despondent, while patriotic men tried with some success to raise the courage of the crowds. Witnesses have said that these were police agents, and probably some of them were, but there were others as well. They pointed to regiments and batteries which were marching towards the northern gates and held them up as a proof that the Government intended to fight, and if they intended to fight, a successful resistance must be possible; the enemy were in small numbers and relief forces were on the way, and the Emperor himself would soon arrive with his Guards.

The result of this sort of talk was that numbers of people took up arms and energetically supported the army and the National Guard. The alarmists replied that Napoleon had been routed, Joseph was a coward and Clarke a traitor; a defence would only exasperate the allies, who as a matter of fact were liberators rather than enemies; the Parisians had everything to gain by the fall of the tyrant; there would be no more war, nor conscription, nor taxes, and they recalled the royalist proclamations which had been posted up on walls and left on doorsteps during the last few nights.

Though every shade of opinion was manifested, the great majority appeared to be dazed, and although the enemy were known to be close to Paris, no one seemed to expect that there would be a battle on the following day. The theatres opened as usual, and though some were nearly empty, others had fairly good houses.

Joseph and the Minister for War were informed of the approach of the allies both by letters received from Compans and by periodical reports from an engineer officer who was observing from the tower of Montmartre. They made their final arrangements, Joseph laying down the general lines and Clarke filling in the details. The Minister for War wrote sixty letters; he exhorted Compans to dispute the ground inch by inch.

> The safety of the State possibly depends on our being able to hold off the enemy for two or three days.

He hastened the return of Marmont and Mortier and sent them instructions from King Joseph; he recalled the column of infantry which was marching towards Beauvais; he ordered General Hullin to form six serviceable battalions from the depots of line, to arm a battalion of unemployed officers, to question the prisoners sent in from Ville-Parisis, to garrison Saint-Denis, and to send troops to the fort of Vincennes and to the bridge of Charenton. He ordered Ornano to organize all the men in the Guard depot and to post them in front of the suburbs; he told Fririon to send the students of Saint-Cyr to the bridges of Sevres, Saint-Cloud, and Neuilly, and he directed Préval to send to Paris every available man from the cavalry depot, adding, " It matters little whether the men are equipped or not as long as they are armed and mounted."

He filled the vacant commands; he invited Chabrol to hasten the raising of troops in the department of the Seine; he warned Daru that troops were being concentrated at Paris and that they would need supplies, and he told him that the pupils of the polytechnic school were bivouacking without greatcoats; finally he ordered General d'Aboville to place 84 guns in position on the high ground at Montmartre and Belleville and in the suburbs, and to organize eight reserve batteries.

Unfortunately Clarke turned his attention too late to the defence of Paris. It would have been possible to have held out for two or three days, even with the small number of troops available, provided preparations had been made in time; defensive measures should have been begun in the month of February, and they should have been completed before the end of March.

As it was, no one thought seriously of defending Paris until March 29, and then only twelve hours were available; they had to construct the works and mount 84 guns; they had to organize eight mobile batteries when hardly any trained men were available: they had to mount 3,000 cavalrymen, arm 1,200 infantrymen, and collect all the effectives from the depots at Havre, Rouen, Tours, and Orleans. The thing was manifestly impossible.

Whether from lack of time or from confusion or negligence, a large number of Clarke's belated orders were not carried out, and meanwhile the enemy were approaching. There had been some delay in the concentration of the various allied corps. After the fight of Fère-Champenoise, Blücher had regained his customary energy and had hurried on his troops, but the army of Bohemia had moved extremely slowly on the 26th and 27th. It was only on the 28th that the Austro-Russians reached the banks of the Marne, and on this day general head-quarters were established at Quincy, from which place Schwarzenberg issued his orders for the following day.

The allies had determined to attack Paris from the north, apparently for the reason that they would be protected by the Marne from a movement of Napoleon against their rear, and in case of a repulse they would have a secure line of retreat to the Netherlands. The allied generals considered there was not an hour to be lost if they were to capture Paris before the Emperor returned. They therefore made no preliminary reconnaissance, and decided that their troops should advance rapidly in three strong columns and force their way through any opposing forces. The right column was composed of the army of Silesia, which had crossed the Marne and driven back Compans and Ledru-Desessarts to the farther side of Claye.

This column was to move through Mory and Le Mesnil and to take post across the Lille road in the neighbourhood of

Saint-Denis. The centre column was composed of the corps of Rajewsky and Barclay de Tolly and was to cross the Marne at Meaux and march through Claye on Bondy. The left column was composed of the corps of Gyulai and the Prince of Würtemberg, and was also to cross at Meaux and to follow the river as far as Neuilly. In order to guard against an attack on the part of Napoleon's army, the corps of Sacken and Wrède were to remain at Meaux and Trilport with outpost towards La Ferté-sous-Jouarre, Rebais, and Coulommiers.

According to these orders, at daybreak on the 29th Rajewsky and Barclay's corps, accompanied by the Czar and the King of Prussia, crossed the Marne and moved to Claye; on their arrival, Kleist and York's corps, who were skirmishing with Compans at Ville-Parisis, moved off to their right towards Mory; Langeron and Woronzoff's corps were already on the march towards Le Tremblay.

During these movements Colonel Blücher rode forward under a flag of truce to the French outposts; he was received by General Vincent, and announced that he had been sent by the Czar to treat for the occupation of the capital and to propose terms of peace. Vincent referred to Compans, who ordered that the flag of truce was not to be received; Blücher then handed two letters to Vincent, one of which was a sealed paper for the Minister for War, and the other a proclamation issued by Schwarzenberg to the people of Paris.

This proclamation had been drawn up by Pozzo di Borgo, and was nothing more or less than a summons to revolution. In spite of their numbers, and even with Napoleon at a distance and Paris without a garrison, the allies did not feel themselves sure of victory; they needed the help of the French themselves, and appealed to treason and civil war.

"Under the present circumstances," said Schwarzenberg, "the city of Paris has it in her power to hasten the peace of the world. Her answer is awaited with the interest which accrues to such a momentous decision. At a word from her the army which is before her walls will be prepared to support her. Parisians, you know how Bordeaux has behaved; her example will show you how to bring the war to an end."

Compans indignantly handed back the proclamation to Colonel Blücher; he did not feel that he ought to refuse the letter addressed to Clarke, and he forwarded it without delay. It is not known what were the exact terms of this letter, nor who had signed it, but it does not afford grounds for accusing Clarke of having an understanding with the enemy. As a matter of fact, this letter was only an ordinary summons to surrender.

It is, no doubt, not easy to explain why the letter should have been addressed to the Minister for War and not to Joseph, but even if this mysterious letter had contained an invitation to commit treason, the fact of its having been received was no crime, and there is no evidence to show that Clarke made any reply.

During the conversation between Colonel Blücher and the French generals a second flag of truce arrived and requested an armistice for four hours. Compans only wished to gain time, and willingly agreed, subject to the usual condition that no movement of troops was to take place during the armistice.

Every step of the allies was tainted with treachery, and when they demanded an armistice it was in order to gain ground without having to fight for it. The fire had hardly ceased at the outposts when Vincent's *vedettes* reported a column of infantry advancing from Lagny on the right and a mass of cavalry moving towards Le Tremblay on the left; the French were afraid that they were going to be enveloped, and they consequently retreated. The allies who were in front of them advanced to the attack as soon as they saw them in movement. Compans' infantry retired on Paris, disputing the ground foot by foot, and Vincent's cavalry moved at a trot to La Villette, where they drove back 3,000 of General Emmanuel's cavalry who were preparing to attack that suburb.

Towards 5 p.m. the Czar and the King of Prussia, with the bulk of the Russian troops, reached the high ground at Clichy.

The wind was blowing from the north, the weather was clear, and there was not a cloud in the sky; Paris could be seen in the distance framed by the setting sun.

At this sight a cry of "Paris, Paris," was raised; the ranks were broken, and the soldiers pressed forward in disorder to see the glorious capital of France, which no hostile army had reached for four centuries.

"At the sight," says an officer of the Czar's, "all our fatigues, privations, and losses were forgotten. We were filled with an enthusiasm which we will always remember. If the officers and soldiers were transported with pride and joy, what must the two sovereigns have felt? Frederick William, who for six long years had borne the iron yoke of the conqueror, and our great Alexander, who has never recovered from the shock of the battle of Moscow."

During the evening Langeron arrived at Le Bourget, and Kleist and York at Aulnay, and their outposts occupied Drancy; Woronzoff's infantry occupied Villepainte, which Blücher chose as his head-quarters. Rajewsky's corps advanced as far as Noisy-le-Sec, and the guards and reserves were echeloned between Ville-Parisis and Bondy. The corps of Gyulai and the Prince of Würtemberg had had to wait till the bridge of Meaux was clear of troops, and instead of occupying Neuilly they bivouacked at Annet and Nanteuil.

The two sovereigns and Schwarzenberg spent the night at the castle of Bondy, from which place the orders for the following day were sent out. All the troops were to be on the move by 5 a.m. The right column was to attack the hill of Montmartre, the centre column was to capture the plateau of Romainville, and the left column, which was supposed to have reached Neuilly, was to advance between Charenton and Vincennes so as to occupy the bridges, mask the castle, and threaten the gate of Le Trône.

General head-quarters did not doubt that the fighting would be murderous, but they hoped that it would be short. Partly from humanity's sake and partly from fear of street fighting, Alexander hoped to be able to avoid having to force his way into Paris. He thought that an impetuous assault on Montmartre and Romainville would place the city at the mercy of his guns and would lead to a capitulation.

The coalition were in possession of Bordeaux, Lyons, Rheims, and half of France; Napoleon had been deceived by a daring manoeuvre, and had been left in Champagne with the remains of his army; the Czar was at Bondy, and from the windows of the castle he could see the last lights of Paris disappear and the numberless fires of the Russian bivouacs spring up all over the countryside. The following day would see the end of this terrible war, and would wipe out the memory of the capture of Moscow. But now that this long-hoped-for day was so near at hand the Czar could not look forward to it without the gravest anxiety.

No one knew better than Alexander I that a large city can become the tomb of an army. However well intrenched and armed the heights of Montmartre and Belleville might be, he did not doubt that they would be captured; even if it cost the allies 20,000 lives they would remain masters of the ground. He did not know, however, whether the people of Paris would defend themselves, and the possibility of desperate street fighting unnerved him. In this form of warfare the advantage of numbers is largely counterbalanced by the impossibility of deploying, and a single gun can command the only line of advance; the scattered columns of the assailants march at random beyond the power of control of the commander-in-chief; the courage of the soldiers ebbs away before a succession of barricades, and fire from the houses and cellars appals the bravest.

The Czar knew that he could not in any case hope to capture both the approaches to Paris and the city itself in the one day. If he should be obliged to force his way into the town, at least two days, and more probably three, would be necessary. Now the loss of three or even two days before the walls might lead to a disaster; the huge army might be cut off from its line of operations and left without supplies and without ammunition.

The whole country between the Seine and the Aisne was ruined and pillaged, and even if they might have been able to find supplies in the valley of the Oise there would be no possibility of their replacing the ammunition expended in sixty hours' fighting. Also if Paris could hold out even for two days, the garrison would be reinforced by the troops scattered in the neighbouring depots, and, what was much more to be feared, the delay of two days might give Napoleon time to arrive. For the last two days the allied staff had had no news of Napoleon's whereabouts, or rather, the news they had received was so contradictory that they could make nothing of it, but they did not doubt that he was marching rapidly towards Paris.

A prey to many anxieties, the Czar worked late into the night. While everyone else was asleep at Bondy and in the bivouacs, he was consulting with Nesselrode and Wolkonsky, and he took every possible measure to guard against the danger which he foresaw. Nesselrode was ordered to take advantage of the slightest pause in the fighting to. start negotiations for the surrender of the capital. In accordance with the Czar's instructions, Wolkonsky wrote ten letters. A dispatch addressed to Blücher contained the words:

> It is of the utmost importance to secure our line of communication with the Netherlands, which can only be done by occupying Compiègne and La Fère. You realize, then, the necessity of seizing Compiègne as soon as possible.

The same recommendations were made to the Prince of Saxe-Weimar:

> We are before Paris, and we hope to capture the city tomorrow, but it is nevertheless of the first importance that our communications should be made secure by opening the Compiègne road. General Bülow is charged with this task, but he has not enough men for the purpose. His Majesty desires that you will send him reinforcements at once.

Wolkonsky directed Sacken to leave one bridge only over the Marne, "and to protect the left bank by sending detachments far afield."

Similar instructions were sent to the commanders of all detached forces between the Marne and the Seine; they were to redouble their activity and vigilance, to take severe steps to stop the peasant rising, and to increase the number of their patrols and reconnaissances, so as not to let themselves be surprised by a march of Napoleon on Paris.

"That," wrote the Czar's chief of the staff, "that must be prevented before all else."

Thus during the night of March 29 Alexander's thoughts were fixed more on the dangers than on the triumphs of the following day. His eyes were not directed on Paris, but on the road from Troyes by which Napoleon was advancing, and on the road to La Fère, which might become the only line of retreat of the allied armies.

CHAPTER 24

The Battle of Paris

At 4 a.m. on March 30 the people of Paris were woken by the sound of drums; the alarm was being sounded at all points. In a few minutes crowds assembled in the streets asking for news, and they were told that the enemy were attacking. Groups of workmen, mixed with militiamen who had not yet received any muskets, assembled before General Hullin's house and clamoured to be given arms.

While the crowd was gathering in the Place Vendôme, the National Guardsmen, with loaves or rolls of bread fixed on the end of their bayonets, were hurrying to their alarm-posts, from which they were sent in organized bodies to the different gates. It had been considered that the National Guard should not be called upon to undertake any duty except the defence of the *octroi* wall, and those who went beyond the gates and helped the regular army, to the number of several thousand, were all volunteers. A certain number of the lower classes also went out to the battlefield and took part in the fight with the muskets of those who had been killed.

All the troops were in front of Paris, some already in position and others moving up. On the left the cavalry, under Generals Ornano and Vincent, were deployed between Saint-Ouen and La Chapelle, and commandeered cab-horses were dragging the guns on to the hill of Montmartre, under an escort of a detachment of firemen and some companies of the National Guard. In the centre, the two divisions of Michel and Boyer de Rebeval, which had been formed the day before from the depots of the Old and Young Guard, were in occupation of the ground between La Villette and the northern slopes of Belleville; they had pushed out strong advance-posts towards Aubervilliers and Pantin, the exits from which villages were covered by heavy batteries posted at Belleville and Le Rouvroy.

The divisions of Compans and Ledru-Desessarts were massed on the Beauregard hill. On the right, Bordesoulle and Merlin's cavalry protected the approaches to Charonne and the hills of Mont Louis and Fontarabie, which were crowned by 24 guns. The castle of Vincennes had a small but sufficient garrison under General Daumesnil. Mixed detachments, composed of National Guards, veterans, scholars, and linesmen, occupied Saint-Mandé and Charenton. Six grenadier companies of the National Guard and the pupils of the polytechnic school were at the gate of Le Trône.

Marmont's corps was marching rapidly from Saint-Mandé towards Romainville, so as to take post on the plateau and fill the gap in the line of battle, and Mortier's corps was leaving its cantonments at Picpus to take up its allotted position in the second line from Montmartre to the Ourcq canal. Including Marmont and Mortier's troops, the soldiers from the depots, the National Guard, veterans, pensioners, and scholars, Paris was defended by about 40,000 men all told, and the allies numbered 110,000.[1]

Joseph had himself reconnoitred the ground, and he considered that he ought, as the Emperor's lieutenant, to remain in command, but he left all initiative as regards the choice of positions to Marmont and Mortier. His orders were transmitted by Clarke, and indicated the general front to be defended between the Marne and the Seine, but they went into no details, for the king and the Minister for War deferred to the experience of the marshals. Marmont, who knew the importance of Romainville, had reconnoitred it during the night, and learning that it had not yet been occupied by the enemy, he moved his troops at

1 See tables end of chapter.

once towards the plateau. At dawn, as the head of the column arrived near the Château of Romainville, a brisk fire suddenly opened from the surrounding woods. Barclay de Tolly had also determined to occupy the plateau, and at 5 a.m. one of his brigades had taken its post in Romainville, while another brigade established itself at Pantin.

Marmont did not abandon his intention of occupying Romainville, which was one of the keys of the plateau, and without hesitation he ordered a vigorous attack. In the centre Lagrange's division, deployed on both sides of the road, with Ricard's division in support, advanced against Romainville; on the right Arrighi established his troops at the mill of Malassise, and threw two battalions into Montreuil; on the left Compans and Ledru-Desessarts reached the Romainville wood, while Boyer de Rebeval marched on Pantin. Between 6.30 and 7 a.m. fighting broke out on the plateau and in the valley; the Russians were surprised and outnumbered, and they gave way, abandoning the outskirts of Pantin, the Romainville wood and the approaches to the village.

At this moment, however, the enemy received reinforcements; Menzenzow's division advanced through Romainville and checked Lagrange, while Prince Eugène de Wurtemberg with two divisions drove Boyer de Rebeval's skirmishers out of Pantin. The success of the Russians went no farther. On the high ground Compans and Ledru-Desessart's infantry were strongly established in the wood and threatened the left of Romainville, while Marmont prepared a fresh attack against the front of the village; in the low ground Prince Eugène did not dare advance his troops beyond Pantin in face of the fire of the French guns; he left one brigade of infantry and a division of *cuirassiers* to hold Pantin, and took his two divisions to help the defenders of Romainville.

One division entered the village by the Noisy-le-Sec road, and the other, led by the prince in person, climbed the northern slopes of the plateau and attacked the wood in flank. The French resisted, and drove the Russians three times down the slopes and as far as the walls of the park of Romainville.

During this first phase of the fight Mortier, who had been delayed by the march of Marmont's columns, was moving up towards the scene of the fighting, According to Joseph's orders he should have taken post between La Villette and Montmartre, but he judged from the intensity of the fire that the enemy's whole efforts were directed on Romainville, and he determined to support Marmont's left. Curial's division reinforced the French troops at Les Maisonettes, and Charpentier's division took post in reserve at the foot of the plateau.

Mortier had now only Christiani's division with which to defend the north of Paris, and these troops took up their position at La Villette and La Chapelle in support of Robert's brigade at Aubervilliers and of Belliard's cavalry, which was deployed in the plain of Saint-Denis on the right of Ornano's squadrons.

It was already 10 o'clock, and although the situation was far from hopeless, yet, as a combatant puts it, "success appeared uncertain." Marmont and Compans were holding their own near Romainville, and in the valley of the Ourcq Boyer de Rebeval's young soldiers had succeeded in occupying Pantin. Four regiments of Russian *cuirassiers* had sallied out of the village, but had found themselves handicapped by ditches and enclosures, and exposed to heavy artillery fire; they had been unable to charge and had galloped back into Pantin closely followed by the French.

The enemy had met with no better success on the north side of Paris. The allied staff, in their anxiety and impatience to capture the capital, had ordered a general attack without taking the trouble to find out whether all their corps were concentrated, and some extraordinary delays had occurred in the transmission of the orders. The order to march on Montmartre at 5 a.m. had been sent off from Bondy at 11 o'clock the previous night, but did not reach Blücher till after 7 o'clock.

The Field-Marshal was enervated by fever and had lost all initiative, and his troops were still at some distance from Paris, except Langeron's corps, which was at Le Bourget, York and Kleist were at Aulnay, and Woronzoff at Villepainte. Langeron heard the sound of guns to his left and advanced towards Pantin without waiting for orders, but during this march an *aide-de-camp* arrived from General Blücher with orders to move on Aubervilliers. Langeron at once altered the direction of his march, but he did not arrive in front of Aubervilliers till 10 a.m., and he was received there by a hot fire. The left column of the allies was at this hour between Chelles and Neuilly. A grand attack had never been ordered in such a hurry or carried out so disjointedly.

At 6 a.m. Joseph, Clarke, Hullin, and their staffs were on the hill of Montmartre. They heard the sound of guns and musketry to their right and saw clouds of smoke rising over the Ourcq canal; in their front all was quiet.

"*Ma chère amie*," Joseph wrote to his wife at 8 a.m., "firing has been going on since the morning; no serious fighting has taken place yet, but the day is only beginning."

However, although "no serious fighting had yet taken place," the king warmly advised his wife to start without delay to join the Empress; at first she refused to go, and only consented when she received a formal order at about midday. Soon after sending off the above-quoted letter, Joseph saw a Russian column coming out of Le Bourget; from 10 to 11 a.m. they could see this column, which was composed of Langeron's troops, attacking Aubervilliers, while other masses of the enemy advanced from Blancmesnil and Aulnay. At this hour there arrived at Montmartre a man named Peyre, an architect employed under the *Prefecture* of the Seine and a captain of the fire brigade, a worthy man, but unsuited to be mixed up in such great events.

During the previous evening at the Pantin gate Peyre had met General Hullin, who was on a tour of inspection. The general had just learnt to his great annoyance that the commander of the outposts had twice refused to receive a Russian flag of truce; he directed Peyre to question that officer as to his reasons for refusing, and to try to overtake the Russian envoy and bring him back to the outposts. It seems that Hullin might have chosen an officer of his own staff, or at any rate of the army, for this extraordinary mission. Peyre started with one trooper, but he could learn nothing at the outposts, as they had just been relieved (it seems that in 1814 the outposts were relieved in the middle of the night !). The adventurous architect immediately passed through the French lines and rode on towards the enemy's outposts.

It turned out as might have been expected: Peyre fell in with a Cossack patrol, and as he had no flag of truce or written orders they refused to treat him as an envoy and made him a prisoner of war. He was taken first of all to Noisy and then, in deference to his protestations, he was sent at 6 a.m. to Bondy, where Danilewsky told him that he would take the orders of the Czar in the matter. Alexander was most anxious to get in communication with Paris and received Peyre in person in the main gallery of the castle.

In answer to the Czar's questions Peyre replied that the Empress had left Paris, and the preparations were being made for defence, but he refused to give any information as to the strength of the garrison. The Czar then told him to inform the French commander-in-chief that the troops in front of Paris were not merely a few thousand men, as had been said in the town, but they were the two main armies of the allies.

> "We shall always be ready to negotiate," he added, "even
> if fighting takes place in the suburbs; but if we are obliged
> to capture the *enceinte* we shall not be in a position to stop
> our troops and prevent pillage."

In conclusion, the Czar gave Peyre some twenty copies of Schwarzenberg's royalist proclamation.

Alexander summoned Comte Orlow and ordered him to accompany the French officer and to go with him to King Joseph as an envoy to hasten the surrender of Paris. "Goodbye," he said to Peyre, "the fate of the town is in your hands."

Then turning towards Orlow he solemnly spoke these moving sentences:

Go: I authorize you to sound the 'cease fire' whenever you may think fit. You may stop the most decisive attack, you may halt the troops even in the moment of victory, in order to save Paris. When God made me powerful and gave my armies success He wished me to secure the peace of the world. If we can do so without shedding any more blood we shall be glad, but if not, we shall carry on the fight to the end. . . . Whether it be in the palaces or on the ruins, Europe will sleep tonight at Paris.

Peyre started with his orderly, accompanied by Orlow and another officer with two flags of truce, and they arrived at Pantin in the thick of the fight at 9 a.m. At the sight of the flags of truce the fire ceased for a moment, but as the party were already between the lines, the French opened fire again. Peyre and his orderly pressed on towards Paris, but the Russians were charged by a party of French cavalry and galloped back to Pantin. Peyre went first of all to the Place Vendôme, and not finding General Hullin there, he went on to the hill of Montmartre.

The general led him to King Joseph and he delivered Schwarzenberg's proclamations and reported what he had seen and heard, stating the strength of the allies and quoting the words of the Emperor of Russia. As if to confirm Peyre's report, the plain was seen to be crowded with Prussian troops and Joseph's heart failed him. He had several times faced death on the battlefield, but he had not the high courage needed to assume responsibility.

He failed to imagine the heroic picture of Paris resisting to the end, of a retreat from the heights to the suburbs, from the suburbs to the gates; then street fighting in which the people would fly to arms and turn each house into a fortress; then the arrival of Napoleon with the Old Guard, raising the courage of all to the highest pitch and driving the enemy in headlong flight. Instead of this he saw the gates forced after a useless resistance; he saw the troops in rout, the militia throwing away their arms, the populace fleeing in terror; he saw the allies drunk with fury, giving way to pillage and massacre, and he saw himself cursed in history for having given Paris to destruction with a light heart.

The king immediately assembled the Council of Defence, probably in hopes of receiving advice to surrender. For the last month all, or almost all, the Council had been in despair, and the immediate danger did not raise their courage. With one voice the Council recognized the necessity for capitulation, and Joseph sent the following letter in duplicate to the two marshals:

> If Marshals Marmont and Mortier can no longer hold their positions they are authorized to enter into negotiations with the Prince of Schwarzenberg and the Emperor of Russia, who are in front of them. They will retire to the Loire.

A few minutes later the lieutenant-general of the Emperor left Montmartre and set out on the road to the Loire. He was the first to go.

No doubt Joseph had some cause for thinking that resistance was impossible, but he does not seem to have required much persuading. Before sending this demoralizing order to Marmont, he ought at least to have waited until the investment was complete on the north of Paris, and until the plateau of Romainville had been captured by the enemy. This battle was the end of the campaign, the supreme fight in which the destiny of France was to be decided; this being so, he certainly ought not to have given permission to negotiate after the first encounter when not an inch of ground had been lost.

The previous day Joseph had determined to defend Paris, and this defence ought to have been serious; to make it so, it was only necessary to resist until the following day, that is to say for a few hours longer, for night would probably put a stop to the fighting. Joseph was probably right in thinking that the French would be driven back to the enceinte before dark, but he ought not to have allowed himself to be frightened by the threats of the Czar. "If we are obliged to force the *enceinte* we shall not be in a position to halt our troops."

Whether it was done on purpose or whether he was carried

away by enthusiasm, the Czar certainly said more than he believed; the most precise and formal orders had been given to the corps commanders that they were not to attempt to force the gates the Emperor of Russia held them personally responsible "if a single one of their soldiers entered Paris."

While Joseph was sounding the knell of the Empire at Montmartre his gallant soldiers were fighting desperately. At midday the first of Barclay de Tolly's reserves reached the fighting line. Up till then Marmont had only been opposed by 13,000 men of Rajewsky's corps. Barclay sent to Romainville and Montreuil the 9,000 Russian grenadiers under Generals Tzokolow and Paskewitsch and directed the Royal Guard of Prussia on Pantin.

This magnificent corps, over 4,000 strong, had not been engaged since the crossing of the Rhine and was burning with eagerness. The Prussian Guard entered Pantin at the double and quickly drove out the French. General Aloberstern wished to follow up his success, and, although Prince Eugène warned him of the dangers he would meet with in the valley, he formed his troops into three columns which advanced simultaneously from the village. None of the columns went far; they were struck in front by a heavy musketry fire and enfiladed by the batteries at Le Rouvroi and Belleville, and the Prussians were brought to a stop by a hail of projectiles which struck down 700 men. The fire was so heavy that the trees along the road were cut down and the Prussians were driven back into the village. They tried a second attack, but were again forced to retire after suffering further loss.

On the plateau, between midday and 1 p.m., the enemy's attacks met with more success. Rajewsky's two divisions were reinforced by Tzokolow's 4,500 grenadiers and were able to resume the offensive, and drove back Lagrange's troops to the summit of the plateau; meanwhile Prince Eugène, with the other two divisions, got a footing on the slopes and drove Compans and Ledru-Desessarts' infantry out of the wood of Romainville. At the same time Paskewitsch's column moved along the Montreuil road and drove off the two battalions who were in occupation of that village; they then threatened the flank of Arrighi's division, which retired from Malassise to Bagnolet. To the south of Charonne Pahlen's cavalry worked round the flank of Bordesoulle and Vincent's squadrons, who had been brought up to this point at 8 a.m. by Marmont's orders; the Russians were about to charge when they were brought to a stop by the fire of the battery established on the hill of Fontarabie.

Marmont found his front hotly pressed and his right flank threatened, and he withdrew his troops to a position in rear. Arrighi moved to the park of Saint-Fargeau and to the outskirts of Ménil-Montant; Lagrange and Ledru-Desessarts retired through Ricard's division, which was posted in the park of Brière, and re-formed their troops on the Beauregard hill; Compans' division took post on the summit of Pré-Saint-Gervais, the slopes of which remained in occupation of Boyer de Rebeval's two brigades.

The majority of the French were deployed in lines of skirmishers and retired in small groups, and their retreat emboldened the enemy to a vigorous pursuit. Pischnisky's division and Kretow's *cuirassiers* moved forward to the charge at the same moment, and Marmont led forward one of Ricard's brigades in order to gain time for his troops to rally. A Russian battery opened fire at short range from near the Romainville wood and shattered the small French column.

All the French retired in disorder, mixed pell-mell with the Russian *cuirassiers* and infantry. Arrighi was wounded and General Clavier captured. Marmont himself was in danger of being surrounded, when Colonel Ghensener rallied 200 men in the park of Brière and fell with the bayonet upon the rear of the Russians, who fell into disorder and were driven back. Thus the five French divisions were saved by the resolution and courage of 200 men, and they succeeded in taking up their new positions without being further molested.

It was at this moment, at about 1 p.m., that Marmont received Joseph's letter authorizing him to enter into negotiations.

Although he had lost a good deal of ground since the king had written, Marmont had not given up hope, and thought that he could prolong the resistance until nightfall. He sent an *aide-de-camp* to Joseph, whom he supposed to be still at Montmartre, and pending further instructions from the King he made ready to carry on the fight.

The enemy gave him a slight respite. Marmont's new position was strong, and Barclay de Tolly thought that it could not be taken by a frontal attack without heavy loss; he decided, therefore, to postpone the attack until other troops should be in position to assail the two flanks. A lull followed, and from 1 o'clock till nearly 2 the fighting on this side was confined to an artillery duel, in which the batteries of the polytechnic school took a vigorous but quite ineffective share.

These twenty-eight guns had been parked on the Place du Trône, and formed a reserve ready to be sent to any threatened point. Since early morning Colonel Evain had heard the firing to his left, and he realized that the enemy were gradually gaining ground. Time was passing, and Evain received no orders, for in the prevailing confusion no one had thought of giving him any; Marmont did not know of the existence of this artillery reserve, Joseph was getting ready to leave Montmartre, and Hullin and Moncey were on the other side of Paris.

Evain rightly thought that his twenty-eight guns could be of some use, and he led them forward. When the head of the column reached the junction of the Vincennes and Charonne roads the Parisian artillery was seen by Count Pahlen, who had withdrawn his squadrons to a position between the village of Vincennes and the slopes of Montreuil. This large battery was escorted by only a troop of mounted men, and it seemed to Pahlen to be an easy prey. Evain thought he could keep the cavalry off, and opened fire with ten guns.

A Russian light battery replied, and a regiment of Uhlans moved at a trot against the flank of the French guns. Major Evain had had several guns dismounted, and when he saw the movement of the Uhlans he ordered a retreat; but, although the gunners were brave, the drivers, who were carters or cabdrivers, were quite unable to manoeuvre. Guns and wagons were overturned, and the Uhlans fell upon the column. They were about to carry off the guns and prisoners when Vincent's light horsemen and Ordener's dragoons arrived at a gallop, jumping the ditches and the garden enclosures, and drove off the Russians, who, however, succeeded in carrying away nine guns, six wagons, and some prisoners. After this unlucky move Major Evain's batteries returned to the Place du Trône.

Almost at the same moment the left column of the allies at last arrived on the scene, more than six hours late. The exploits of the Prince of Würtemberg on this day consisted in driving a few weak detachments out of Nogent, Saint-Maurice, and Charenton, and of surrounding the citadel of Vincennes at a respectful distance. The Austro-Würtembergers deployed between Bercy and Montreuil, covering the left of the Russians.

The Prince of Würtemberg had moved very slowly, but Blücher had been very little faster, and Barclay de Tolly was anxiously awaiting his arrival to deliver the decisive assault. Delay had been caused by the absence of instructions during the morning, and the deployment of 30,000 men advancing by one road was bound to take time. But there had also been orders and counter-orders.

Towards 11 a.m., when Langeron was engaged with Robert's brigade at Aubervilliers, he received an order direct from the Czar telling him to march at once on Saint-Denis and Montmartre. Langeron replied that his troops were in action, and he could not leave his position until he was relieved by another corps of the army of Silesia. York arrived at 12.30, just as Langeron was capturing Aubervilliers after three hours' fighting. The Prussians took possession of the village, and Langeron moved on towards Montmartre.

The other corps arrived, and Kleist deployed on York's right, and Woronzoff formed up in second line. York was preparing to attack La Villette and La Chapelle when he was ordered by Blücher to move his troops to the other side of the Ourcq canal so as to prolong the right of the army of Bohemia. Katzler and Prince William's divisions moved to the flank, and crossed the canal near Pantin, and drove the French out of the farm of Le Rouvroy, but the Prussians were checked by the guns in position near that place, and could advance no farther.

It was nearly 2 o'clock. The various corps had now taken up their positions, and Barclay de Tolly gave the signal for a general assault. The attack was pressed with vigour at all points. Prince Eugène's two divisions, supported by eight battalions of Russian grenadiers, advanced from the plateau of Romainville, and attacked Pré-Saint-Gervais and the parks of Brière and Saint-Fargeau. The ground was open, and rose in glacis-like slopes, and the Russians lost heavily from the murderous fire of the defence. Six times they forced their way into the parks, and were driven out again.

"To rally our soldiers," said Fabvier, "it was only necessary to point to Paris with one hand and to the enemy with the other."

This terrible frontal attack would probably have failed if it had not been supported by others directed against the flanks. On the left a column of two Russian divisions advanced from Bagnolet into the gorge of Charonne; they drove off Bordesoulle's cavalry, who attempted to charge them, and stormed the heights of Ménil-Montant, and captured the guns mounted on the summit.

On the right York's divisions advanced along the canal, while there moved forward along the main road from Pantin a column composed of the Royal Prussian Guard, and the two divisions of the Imperial Russian Guard, 9,000 picked men who formed the final reserve of the Russian army. The two French batteries mounted at Le Rouvroy and Pré-Saint-Gervais had been firing all day, and they now found themselves short of ammunition, or, rather, the fresh supplies of projectiles which they had received proved to be of the wrong calibre, and their fire was inaccurate.

The allies captured the guns at Le Rouvroy, and, neglecting the ineffective fire from the other battery, they pressed on to attack Les Maisonettes. General Michel was wounded, and the defenders were reduced by losses to the strength of a battalion. To make matters worse, Mortier, who was hotly pressed at La Villette, had summoned to that point Curial and Charpentier's divisions, which had hitherto been in reserve at the foot of the Chaumont hill.

After a short but gallant defence the conscripts of the Guard abandoned Les Maisonettes, and retired to the gate of Paris. The Prussians moved forward along the canal so as to take Mortier in flank at La Villette, and the Russians directed one column against the Chaumont hill, and another against Beauregard. Compans and Boyer de Rebeval's divisions were taken in reverse at Pré-Saint-Gervais, and found themselves between two fires; they cut their way out at the point of the bayonet, and reached Belleville, but they abandoned seventeen guns, which they were unable to bring away across the enclosed ground.

Marmont now found his right flank threatened from Ménil-Montant and his left from Beauregard and Chaumont. The Russian artillery and the captured French guns were trained upon his position, and columns of the allies were advancing to the attack. He could only hope to hold his ground for a short time, and a further resistance would contravene Joseph's instructions and expose Paris to the horrors of a sack.

It was now 4 o'clock and Marmont determined to make use of the authority which he had received several hours before. He sent three flags of truce to the skirmish line and at the same time withdrew his troops to Belleville. The position was no longer tenable, and if he had held out he would have risked being surrounded and forced to surrender. Marmont was watching the arrival of his decimated battalions when he was informed that the Russians were arriving on the Belleville Paris road from the direction of Chaumont.

The least hesitation or delay and retreat would be cut off. Marmont collected some sixty men, " whose small numbers," he says, " could not be seen by the enemy in such a defile," and placing himself at their head he charged the grenadiers of the

Imperial Russian Guard. The marshal's horse was wounded and his uniform torn by bullets; Generals Ricard and Pelleport were wounded beside him and twenty of his men were struck down, but the Russians fell back and Marmont's soldiers were able to establish themselves behind Belleville in line with the church. In this position the French were able to hold out until the return of the flags of truce.

In the other portions of the field of battle the success of the allies was no less decisive. At about 2 o'clock Mortier had been attacked at La Villette and La Chapelle by the corps of Kleist, York, and Woronzoff. At first the attackers were held in check by the artillery of the Guard, which was posted on the outskirts of the village and on the remains of the old redoubts of 1792; the French dragoons, however, were repulsed and pursued among the batteries, which were captured by the Prussians. Heavy artillery fire then prepared the way for the assault.

The cannon-balls enfiladed the streets in which the infantry were massed and made terrible gaps in the ranks. The cannonade ceased and the assaulting columns moved forward. Kleist moved against La Chapelle, and York, with Woronzoff in support, attacked La Villette, where Mortier commanded in person. The French made a heroic resistance, but a small body of veterans who were guarding the first bridge over the Ourcq canal were driven off by the Prussian Guard advancing from Les Maisonettes, and Mortier found himself taken in flank. He gave the order to retire on the wall of Paris and the movement was carried out slowly and steadily.

At one point the Prussians followed closely and a battalion of Christiani's division charged with the bayonet and captured four guns. During this fighting York is recorded to have uttered a sentence worthy of Ney or Napoleon: one of his soldiers fell struck by a bullet close beside his horse, "Why," said York, "did he come so close to me?"

At La Chapelle Charpentier and Robert resisted with equal stubbornness, and the streets of the village were piled with the French and Russian dead; they only evacuated their position when they were ordered to do so by Mortier, and Charpentier formed up his troops in front of the gate on the Saint-Denis road.

At the same time Langeron's infantry attacked Montmartre. After he had taken Aubervilliers, Langeron had moved on St. Ouen and Clichy-la-Garenne, so as to attack Montmartre from the west, which he thought was the only accessible point. During the march it occurred to him that he ought also to capture Saint-Denis, and Kapzéwitsch was ordered to do so. Saint-Denis was the only one of the suburbs which had made preparations for defence in the month of February; some entrenchments had been dug and the National Guard numbered 500 men; in addition, on the morning of March 30 General Hullin had increased the garrison by four guns and 400 infantry of the Young Guard under command of a Colonel Savarin. Kapzéwitsch had 6,000 men and 36 guns; his flag of truce was not received, and after a bombardment he sent his infantry forward to the assault.

The Russians were twice repulsed, and Kapzéwitsch then sent a second flag of truce, which also was not received. Savarin had used up all his ammunition, but he was determined not to surrender; a member of the municipality advised him to capitulate, as there were no cartridges left, and he replied, "We still have our bayonets, and as long as they are fit to use I will not surrender."

Kapzewitsch saw that he could do nothing with such a pigheaded opponent and he left a regiment in observation before Saint-Denis and hurried off with the rest of his troops to support Langeron's attack.

If Montmartre had been well armed and strongly occupied it would have been a very strong position, but as it was, it was not capable of resisting a formidable attack. When King Joseph went away the few companies of the National Guard who had been posted on the hill had also gone back to Paris, and there only remained 250 infantry and 30 guns which had only 60 gunners to work them. Langeron drove back the cavalry under Generals Belliard and Dautencourt, and he sent his infantry forward to the attack of the hill. The French guns fired over the heads of the Russians, who reached the summit almost without loss. Meanwhile Emmanuel's cavalry and some of Langeron's infantry drove the skirmishers of the National Guard back to the walls.

Moncey saw that the enemy were threatening the enceinte of Paris, but as long as he lived he would not retire on the town without fighting. He organized the defence and harangued the officers of the National Guard, who were greatly disheartened by the flight of Joseph and the success of the allies.

"We must defend ourselves," said the old marshal. "Even if we are compelled in the end to surrender to the overpowering forces of the enemy we must at any rate resist bravely so as to gain honourable terms."

Moncey's stirring words infused fresh courage into the militiamen, and numbers pressed forward to take part on the outskirts of Batignolles. So great was their enthusiasm that they refused to obey Moncey's orders to take cover in the houses.

"We are not afraid," they said, "we do not want to hide."

These were the words of brave men who had never seen war. "Do you think," cried Allent, "that the oldest of the marshals would advise you to do anything cowardly?" and at these words they took cover from the enemy's fire.

The gate on the Clichy road seemed to be the point of greatest danger, and Moncey himself took post there while he sent his *aides-de-camp* to the other gates to encourage the militiamen. The marshal's officers found the men everywhere in good heart, and the volunteers were skirmishing with the enemy's cavalry 500 yards in front of the enceinte. A detachment in occupation of the Montceaux gate, however, showed less determination. Moncey's *aide-de-camp* saw two French squadrons in the plain hotly pressed by the enemy and asked the National Guard to move forward to the rescue; the least demonstration would have been enough, but the men hesitated.

At last they were roused by the appeals and indignant reproaches of the officer, and were just setting off when the Duc de Fitz James stepped out of the ranks, and turning towards the company exclaimed, "The service asked of us is contrary to the constitution of the National Guard."

This argument appeared unanswerable and the militiamen piled arms. Another Fitz James, who was not the duke, was killed that day in the plain of St. Ouen after showing the greatest gallantry.

Meanwhile the National Guard were driven out of Batignolles by Langeron's leading battalions and fell back behind the Clichy gate. At that point all the troops were posted by Marshal Moncey; guns were run forward and sharp-shooters were stationed on the battlements and at the windows of the neighbouring houses, and the mass of the National Guard were formed up on either side of the Clichy road. Moncey was afraid that a very few rounds would demolish the stockades, and he ordered the construction of a second entrenchment in rear of the first.

Carts, logs, and paving-stones were piled up, and the spectators, including women and children, laboured at the work under the fire of the enemy's musketry. The enemy's troops were given a warm reception, and the men behaved in a way to please the heart of the veteran of Marengo and Saragossa, "who did not expect so much from the National Guard."

The Russian generals, however, had not been ordered to assault; on the contrary they had the Czar's formal order not to attack the gates of the town. Langeron and Rudzéwitsch themselves rode forward in front of their men and halted them, and the Russians took post in the houses of the suburb and exchanged shots with the militiamen.

The affair at the Clichy gate was the last episode of this battle, which really consisted only of a series of disjointed fights, lacking co-ordination on both sides. The battle of Paris had tremendous political consequences, but it conveys few military lessons. It must be remembered, however, that from the point of view of the number of troops engaged and the losses incurred, the battle of Paris was the most important and the most bloody of all those fought during the campaign, but unfortunately Napoleon was not in command. The losses amounted to about 9,000 men killed and wounded on each side.

The anticipation of danger is apt to cause more fright than the reality. Since the beginning of February the population of Paris had been panic-stricken at the very mention of the Cossacks, and on March 27, 28, and 29 it had shuddered at the idea of pillage and burning, but when the sound of the guns was heard people recovered their ordinary calmness. During the battle the main boulevards looked the same as usual except that shops were closed and there were very few carriages to be seen, and the crowd was larger and more animated than usual and its general appearance suggested a public holiday; pedestrians passed up and down, groups of people eagerly discussed the news and every chair was occupied and every café full.

The weather was cloudy and mild. Occasional prisoners were marched through the streets and large numbers of wounded passed by in wagons and commandeered cabs, while well-dressed people ate their ices and sipped their punch. The crowd did not seem to be at all alarmed; some were anxious and some curious, but the majority were quiet and even indifferent. National pride, or, rather, Parisian vanity helped the people to look upon the battle going on at Romainville as an affair of small importance. If anyone remarked that the noise of the cannon was approaching and indicated the advance of the enemy, someone was sure to reply with a knowing look, "It is only a manoeuvre."

The general calmness, however, was disturbed between 2 and 3 p.m.; a lancer galloped through the Faubourg Saint-Martin crying out "*Sauve qui peut!*" There was a sudden panic and everyone started running, but this false alarm soon passed away and the boulevards filled again.

In the northern and eastern portions of the town also people believed that the enemy would be defeated, but there was very great alarm and anxiety. The streets were crowded with people, although the National Guards had been ordered to let no one pass except those in uniform. At about 4 o'clock cannon-balls began to whistle overhead, but this had no effect on the crowd, and the fall of a projectile only caused a slight movement, and the children played with the cannon-balls, rolling them about the streets. In the neighbourhood of the gates all the shops were shut and the pavements were littered with cheap furniture, which the inhabitants in their panic had taken out of their houses without thinking how they were to carry it away.

Women were deafened by the sound of firing and panic-stricken at the thought of the violence with which they were threatened, and they ran madly up and down the streets. Wounded lay in every doorway and were cared for by the working-class population, whose chief feeling was anger at being unable to take part in the fight. The people had waited till 11 o'clock in front of General Hullin's house, and then, being unable to get arms, had returned in anger to their homes shouting "Treason!"

Even people near the gates knew no more of what was taking place than those on the boulevards. Every sort of rumour was current, and it was twice reported that the Emperor had just reached Paris. The people had no doubt of his arrival, and if some general was seen in the distance mounted on a white horse and surrounded by a group of officers the cry was raised, "It is he, it is he!"; there was no need to mention his name everyone knew who was meant.

The report of Napoleon's sudden return was not without some foundation. At about 1 o'clock General Dejean arrived post-haste from Troyes to warn the commander-in-chief that the Emperor was only half a day's march behind. He was too late, however, for the capitulation had been decided on, and Joseph had already left. The grand dignitaries and all the authorities had received the order to leave Paris at once, and the ministers and some councillors of State and senators had started on the road to Chartres; others, however, thought it was better to remain in Paris, and did not obey the order.

Talleyrand was less anxious to leave Paris than any one, but he did not dare disobey the order. He was the most conspicuous of the members of the Government, and he knew that he was under suspicion; a lack of obedience, which in any other would have been looked upon as neglect, would in his case have been treated as treason. No doubt he would have been risking little, because there seemed to be no chance of the Empire surviving; but still Napoleon was not yet disarmed, and the allied sovereigns had not yet given their decision.

If by any chance the Emperor were to remain on the throne Talleyrand would find himself more than compromised. He wished always to be on the winning side, and it was part of his nature to guard himself against every possible eventuality. In order to get himself out of the difficulty he went to his customary dupe, the Duc de Rovigo, and pointed out that the true interests of the Emperor, the dynasty, and the country demanded that he should stay in Paris, and he finished by asking the Minister of Police to authorize him not to rejoin the Empress.

On this occasion Rovigo showed some energy, and answered that, so far from authorizing him to remain in Paris, he ordered him to leave at once, and he added that he would take steps to see that the order was carried out. It was all very well for Rovigo to talk, but it would have been better if he had acted. Talleyrand pretended that he would obey; he went home, attended to some pressing matters, and at 5 o'clock he started for Rambouillet.

In Paris his carriage went very slowly, for it was important to let his departure be known to the public, and it was still more important to allow time for a messenger to reach the guard on the gate by which he was to leave the town. When Talleyrand's carriage arrived at the gate, the officer in charge of the guard had the audacity to ask the Vice-Grand Elector to produce his passport. Talleyrand might have produced the order of the Grand Judge, which was worth all the passports in the world, but he answered that he had no passport.

The officer then said he was afraid he would be unable to allow him to pass. Several men of the guard pointed out that the orders were not intended for Talleyrand; but he would not take advantage of their good offices, and returned home very pleased with the success of his stratagem. Once more he had attained his end without compromising himself.

Others still more highly placed than Talleyrand were to blame: Joseph, contrary to his brother's instructions, had put off ordering the Government to leave until the last moment; Rovigo, instead of ordering Talleyrand to obey, ought to have put him into a carriage and escorted him beyond the gates. Napoleon had to thank Joseph's lack of foresight and Rovigo 's weakness that the man who had become his most dangerous enemy was able to remain in Paris.

TROOPS ENGAGED IN THE BATTLE OF PARIS

French

(1) Garrison of Paris:

Troops under General Ornano, improvised from the Guard Depots:

Michel's Division	3,600
Boyer de Rebeval's Division	1,800
Dautencourt's Cavalry	800

Troops under General Hullin:

Improvised from the Line Depots	3,000
Parisian National Guard	12,000
Artillery of the National Guard	800
Various Artillery Companies	1,000
Gendarmes	800
Veterans	500
Total	21,300

(2) Garrisons of Saint-Denis, Vincennes, etc.:

About 2,500 men, half of whom have been included above, say	1,200

(3) Compans' Corps:

Compans' Division	1,200
Ledru-Desessarts	3,400
Vincent's Cavalry	1,400
	6,000

From these figures must be deducted the losses suffered
on March 27, 28, and 29, leaving about   5,100

(4) Marmont's Corps:

Ricard, Lagrarige, and Arrighi's Divisions	3,300
Merlin and Bordesoulle's Cavalry	1,400
	4,700

(5) Mortier's Corps:

Christiani, Curial, and Charpentier's Divs	4,600
Belliard's Cavalry	1,900
	6,500
Grand total	38,800

Allies

Army of Bohemia:

Guard and Reserve	26,000
Rajewsky's Corps	12,800
Prince of Würtemberg's Corps	15,000
Gyulai's Corps	11,500
	64,300

Army of Silesia:

York's Corps	10,000
Kleist's Corps	8,000
Langeron's Corps	17,000
Woronzoff's Corps	12,000
	47,000
Grand total	111,300

De Wrède's corps (20,000) and Sacken's corps (8,000) had remained at Meaux, and 6,000 Cossacks were between the Marne
and the Seine.

Bülow's corps (about 20,000) was in occupation of Laon and

La Fère and was besieging Soissons and Compiègne.

Winzingerode's cavalry (10,000) had been detached in observation of Napoleon.

The above figures show how the strength of the allies had been reduced during the two months' campaign.

CHAPTER 25

The Capitulation of Paris

When Marmont, at about 4 p.m., made up his mind to negotiate, cannon-balls and bullets were whistling around Belleville. Of the three envoys whom he sent, the first was seriously wounded, the second had his horse and his trumpeter killed, and General Lagrange's *aide-de-camp* alone succeeded in reaching the enemy's lines. He was immediately led to the Czar, who was on foot superintending the mounting of a new battery. The envoy asked for an armistice, which was as far as his powers extended. The Czar could not listen to such a proposal; if he had consented he would have surrendered the dearly-bought results of the day's fighting; he had not sacrificed 9,000 of his soldiers in order to allow the French to retire inside the *enceinte* and await Napoleon's return unmolested.

The Czar, however, was not less eager to occupy Paris than was Marmont to gain an armistice, and he was careful not to throw away the opportunity of negotiating. He ordered his favourite *aide-de-camp*, Count Orlow, to go back with the French envoy to Marshal Marmont. When the two officers arrived, under a hail of bullets, within 50 yards of the first French line, Orlow noticed a general standing among the skirmishers, who ordered fire to be stopped as soon as he saw the flags of truce.

"I am Marshal Marmont," he said, riding forward to meet Orlow.

"And I," replied Orlow, "am the Czar's *aide-de-camp*."

The conversation was short, for both were anxious to stop

the fight.

"His Majesty's wish," said Orlow, "is to preserve Paris for France and for the world."

"That is also our hope; what are your conditions?"

"Firing will cease at once. The French troops will retire inside the *enceinte*, and a military commission will meet as soon as possible to settle terms of capitulation."

"I consent," said Marmont. "Marshal Mortier and I will await you at the Pantin gate. We will give orders to ensure the fire ceasing everywhere. *Au revoir.*"

Orlow mounted his horse and started at a gallop. Then he came back again and said to the marshal, "Will your troops evacuate the hill of Montmartre?" (the allies were always afraid of Montmartre, which they considered to be the acropolis of Paris).

Marmont thought for a moment, and then answered, "Certainly, for it is outside the *enceinte*." Neither Marmont nor Orlow then knew that Langeron was on the point of capturing that position almost without striking a blow.

During these preliminary negotiations another flag of truce, General Lapointe, Mortier 's chief of the staff, crossed the enemy's lines. A little before 4 o'clock, when Mortier was in front of the La Villette gate, he was joined by General Dejean, who had wasted part of the afternoon looking for Joseph at Montmartre and in the Bois de Boulogne. Dejean announced that the Emperor was coming, and said that the enemy ought to be held off at all costs till the following day; the marshal replied by pointing to his troops, who had been driven back with heavy loss to the gates; but although by some extraordinary delay he had not yet received Joseph's order, he took upon himself to ask Schwarzenberg to grant an armistice.

Dejean had reported that Napoleon had made direct overtures for peace to the Emperor of Austria, and that they could not fail to be accepted, and Mortier relied on this statement when he asked for the armistice. General Lapointe delivered Mortier's letter to one of Schwarzenberg's *aides-de-camp*. The commander-in-chief justly thought that the allies would be extremely foolish to agree to an armistice which was not followed by the immediate surrender of the town, and he answered Mortier in the following words:

"The close and indissoluble union between the allied sovereigns convinces me that there is no truth in the statement that negotiations have been opened with one power alone. . . . The declaration of the allied powers which I have the honour to forward herewith is a certain proof of this."

While General Lapointe was returning to the Villette gate with this curt refusal, the commissioners nominated by the Czar were on their way to the Pantin gate to decide upon the terms of capitulation. The allied commissioners were Count Nesselrode, Colonel Orlow, and Count Paar, an *aide-de-camp* of Schwarzenberg's. They found Marmont alone, for although Mortier had been sent for he had not yet arrived.

After waiting for a few minutes, on Marmont's suggestion they went to the Villette gate, and from there to La Chapelle, where they at last found Mortier, and they assembled at an inn near the Saint-Denis Gate known as the "*Au petit jardinier.*" Nesselrode demanded that the town should be handed over to the allies, and that all the French troops should lay down their arms. Marmont and Mortier indignantly declared that rather than agree to such insulting terms " they would bury themselves under the ruins of Paris." Nesselrode pointed out in vain that the Czar wished to make their gallant troops prisoners so as to force Napoleon to make peace; this argument had little effect on the two marshals. At this point in the discussion the silence which had supervened on the noise of battle was suddenly broken by a hot cannonade.

The commissioners of the allies were stupefied for a moment, for they feared that it was the sound of the Emperor's guns; an officer, however, soon arrived to inform them that the firing had been occasioned by the capture of Montmartre. The order to cease fire had not yet reached Langeron, who was continuing his advance. The representatives of the allies next advanced the capture of Montmartre as a reason why their terms should be accepted, but Marmont replied that he had already agreed to evacuate that position; it mattered little in his eyes whether Montmartre had been surrendered or captured by assault.

The marshals considered that the surrender of Paris had been already agreed to, and they only continued the discussion in order to save their soldiers, and on this point they refused to yield. Nesselrode and his colleagues went to Bellevue to consult the Czar, and at 7 o'clock they came back with fresh proposals, which were certainly less humiliating, but were hardly more acceptable than the former ones. These proposals were that the troops should leave Paris with their arms and baggage, but that they should retire by the Rennes road. This was practically equivalent to a disarmament, for if the two marshals went in that direction they could be of no help to Napoleon. Marmont and Mortier protested that the allies had no right to lay down the road they were to follow.

> "Paris is not blockaded," said Marmont. "Even if you were to attack me tonight, I would defend the city street by street; I could only be driven back to the left bank of the Seine, and the Fontainebleau road would remain open to me. The conditions you propose wound the honour of two old soldiers; why do you wish to gain by such an armistice what you cannot win by force?"

Then, after a silence, the marshal continued in a voice shaken with emotion:

> Gentlemen, the fortune of war has been favourable to you; today your arms have gained a great success, which will have incalculable results. Be moderate, and do not drive Marshal Mortier and myself to a desperate resolution.

The Russian commissioners, especially Orlow, recognized the justice of these words, but they thought that their instructions did not allow them to yield the point. If the marshals had used their resistance as a pretext for breaking off the negotiations, they would perhaps have been well advised. They knew that the Emperor was near Paris, and now that the night had come they must have known that the assault would be put off till the following day.

It is true there was danger of a bombardment. A hundred guns were trained on the town, and the amiable Müffling in his impatience was already asking the Czar whether Paris should not be set on fire. Alexander replied in the negative, saying that he only wished to frighten the Parisians, but if Marmont had taken advantage of the three hours' armistice, and had evaded his moral obligation to surrender Paris, it is quite likely that the Czar's anger would have got the better of him.

The discussion lasted for more than an hour, and then Mortier retired, saying: "I leave Marshal Marmont to continue the negotiations, and to decide as he may think best. As for me, I am obliged to take steps for the defence of Paris."

The gallant Mortier was becoming a diplomat, and he said the defence of Paris when he really thought the evacuation of Paris. Orlow was now very anxious, and he pointed out to Nesselrode that the allied troops could not attack the town during the night, and that the French were in a position to retire by whatever road they chose. He concluded that they ought either to agree at once to the marshal's demands, or suspend the negotiations to consult the Czar again. Fearing, however, that Marmont might be so angry at the delay as to determine to defend Paris, Orlow announced that he would remain as a hostage until the armistice was ratified. Nesselrode left the marshal, assuring him that fire would not be reopened until Orlow reached the Russian outposts.

Marmont then took Count Orlow to his house in the Rue Paradis, where he found a crowd of people assembled. The mass of the inhabitants of Paris had remained in complete ignorance of the result of the battle, but in political circles people had drawn their own conclusions from the orders to leave which had been issued to more than two hundred people, as well as from Peyre's report to the Municipal Council, and the final instructions of the ministers to their subordinates. They knew that King Joseph and the members of the Government had left, they knew that the allies were victorious, and they knew that Marmont had been invested with full powers and was negotiating for the surrender of Paris, and they were most anxious to learn the terms of the capitulation. Thus all those who thought they had the entree to Marmont's house had assembled there in search of news, and among them was General de Girardin, Berthier's *aide-de-camp*, who had arrived from Troyes at 8 o'clock.

Marmont's uniform was torn and bloodstained, his boots were covered with mud, and his hands and face black with powder. When he entered he seemed the personification of battle, and all hearts were stirred with admiration for the gallant soldier. Everyone crowded round and heaped congratulations and praise upon him. Probably no conquering hero had ever had such an ovation, but the man who had been beaten that day was not Marmont, but Bonaparte; the name Napoleon was already falling into disuse.

Marmont had resisted long enough to save the honour of Paris, and had capitulated in time to preserve the town from the horrors of a sack; the company not only admired, but almost worshipped him. As a matter of fact, the surrender of Paris was Duc to King Joseph, but no one thought of him, except to accuse him of cowardice. Lavallette and General de Girardin were against the capitulation, and defended the cause of the Empire, but, with these two exceptions, everyone spoke openly of the inevitable fall of Napoleon and of the return of the Bourbons. Laffitte showed himself to be one of the warmest *partisans* of the royalists. Marmont pointed out to him that a restoration would involve great danger for the chiefs of the army, and the banker replied, "But, M. le Marechal, with written guarantees, and with a political order which will establish our rights, what is there to fear?"

The conversation was at this stage when Marmont hurriedly left the room. A very great personage, no less than Talleyrand himself, was asking for a private interview. Marmont received him in the dining-room, where he had had supper with Orlow. Talleyrand's pretext for coming was that he wished to know if communication was still open with Rambouillet; after this introduction he began to talk of the lamentable state of public affairs and the difficulties of the situation.

"I agreed with him," said Marmont, "but I did not say a word as to the remedies to be employed. Talleyrand was looking for an opportunity to make overtures. But although I foresaw extraordinary developments, it did not suit me to fall in with his plans."

Were these overtures really made, and was Marmont taken into Talleyrand's confidence? Between clever people the dotting of "i's" is not always necessary.

"The Prince de Talleyrand," said Marmont, "left me, after having failed in his attempt."

Marmont thought so, perhaps, but he was mistaken. At the close of this conversation his fidelity to Napoleon had been shaken, even if he had not been altogether won over to the cause of the Bourbons. The ovation he had received and Talleyrand's attempt were enough to turn the marshal's head. Marmont was a mass of vanity and envy; neither rank, titles, nor grants of money had satisfied his ambition, for his companions-in-arms remained his equals, and over them all towered Napoleon. He now saw a prospect of being second to none; he was becoming the arbiter of France; he held his master in the hollow of his hand, for Talleyrand had given him to understand, even if he had not actually said so, that the destiny of the Emperor depended upon him. The day of his defeat was the happiest day of his life.

On his way out Talleyrand passed through the reception-room, for he thought it advisable to address a few words to a person whom he knew he would find there. At the sight of Talleyrand, who was believed to be on the Rambouillet road, all those present thronged round him in the hopes of hearing his opinion of the situation, and Orlow found himself left alone at the end of the room.

Without deigning to reply to the silent interrogations of the crowd, Talleyrand limped towards the Russian officer, and said in his most courtly manner, "Sir, I beg of you to be so good as to convey to the feet of his Majesty the Emperor of Russia the expression of the profound respect of the Prince de Talleyrand."

"Prince," replied Orlow, who showed himself on this occasion to be no less diplomatic than Talleyrand, "rest assured, I will convey this blank cheque to his Majesty."

A suspicion of a smile crossed Talleyrand's lips as he saluted and left the room.

At 2 a.m. Comte Paar brought a letter from Nesselrode authorizing Orlow to agree to the marshal's conditions. The capitulation was drawn up without discussion in Marmont's study. The marshal went into the reception room, which was still crowded, and read out the terms of the treaty; at his request his two *aides-de-camp* signed in his name, and Orlow and Paar signed in the name of the Czar and Schwarzenberg.

The capitulation dealt with the evacuation of the city and the duration of the armistice. Marmont and Mortier had wished to insert some safeguards for Paris, but on the advice of Orlow, who had shown himself to be a sincere friend of France, the two marshals had been satisfied with a clause drafted by the Russian colonel "the city of Paris is recommended to the generosity of the allied powers."

Not only would there be no pillage or violence, but the Czar wished to spare the Parisians "even the humiliation of one day seeing the keys of their city in some European museum."

There remained to be settled the details of the entry of the sovereigns, of the billeting and feeding of their troops, and of the policing of the city. These matters would have to be arranged by the municipal magistrates, who were the only authorities remaining in Paris now that the Government had fled. The *prefect* of the Seine and several municipal councillors agreed to form a deputation to go to the Czar, and they started for Bondy under the guidance of Orlow. While they were on their way a bonfire was lighted in the court of the Invalides and 1,417 standards captured from the enemy by the soldiers of the republic and the

Empire were given to the flames.

At Bondy, Orlow took the Parisian deputation into the main hall of the castle, where it was received by Nesselrode, and he himself went up to the Czar's room. Alexander was in bed, but was not asleep. "What news do you bring?" he said.

"Sire, the capitulation of Paris," replied Orlow.

The Czar seized the paper which Orlow handed him and read it several times. "congratulate you," he said; "your name is attached to a great event."

He then asked for details of the mission which his *aide-de-camp* had fulfilled so well, and he finished by asking if he had seen Talleyrand.

Orlow repeated the conversation he had had with him in Marmont's house, and the Czar said, "At present that is only an anecdote, but it may become history."

Alexander put the capitulation of Paris under his pillow and slept soundly.

CHAPTER 26

Napoleon at La Cour de-France

During this night of March 30, at the hour when Marmont's vanity was being flattered by the congratulations and praises of the leaders of Parisian society, a man got down from a shabby carriage before the post station of La Cour-de-France, and, while a change of horses was being fetched, started impatiently to walk along the Paris road. This man was Napoleon.

He had left his horses and escort at Villeneuve and had continued his journey by post, and bad news greeted him at every stop. At Sens he was told that the enemy was near Paris, at Fontainebleau that the Empress had fled to the Loire, and at Essonnes he learnt that fighting had begun. A troop of cavalry arrived at a trot before the post station; the Emperor cried out "Halt," and the well-known voice was recognized by the commander of the troop, Belliard, who had been sent by Mortier to prepare cantonments for his troops. He jumped from his horse, and the Emperor led him alone at a rapid pace along the road.

Napoleon's questions tumbled from his lips in quick jerks, "Why are you here? . . . where is the enemy? . . . where is the army? . . . who is protecting Paris? . . . where are the Empress and the King of Rome? . . . where are Joseph and Clarke? . . . but Montmartre . . . but my troops . . . but my guns? . . ."

Amid a constant fire of questions Belliard gave a short account of the day's doings. He described the gallant defence of the troops, the honourable behaviour of the National Guard, the overpowering forces of the enemy, and finally the evacuation of the city in accordance with a convention which was then being ratified; but he also told how Montmartre had been left without defences or artillery, and spoke of the lack of ammunition and of the absence of Joseph from the field of battle.

Then Napoleon's anger burst out. "Everyone seems to have lost his head; that is what comes of employing men who have neither common sense nor energy . . . that idiot Joseph, who thinks he can lead an army as well as I can . . . and that fool Clarke, who is absolutely useless if you take him away from his office stool."

While talking the Emperor had covered nearly a couple of miles; he stopped and exclaimed to Caulaincourt and the other officers who had followed a short distance behind:

"You hear, gentlemen, what Belliard has just said. Come, we must go to Paris. Whenever I am away things go wrong. . . . Caulaincourt, bring up my carriage."

Belliard respectfully reminded the Emperor that it was too late, for by that time the capitulation must have been signed and Paris evacuated, and the troops could not re-enter the town which they had left under the terms of a convention. Caulaincourt supported the general's arguments, but Napoleon would not listen. He exclaimed excitedly that he would go to Paris, he would sound the bells, light up the town, and everyone would fly to arms; and he strode on towards Paris, repeating the order to bring up the carriages.

They had arrived near Athis when they saw a column of infantry on the road some distance ahead of them; it was Mortier's advance-guard, commanded by General Curial. Napoleon was astounded, but he did not give up all hope of going to Paris. He knew that Marmont's troops were still in the town and that the National Guard was under arms. Perhaps the capitulation had not been signed, and in that case Marmont should break off the negotiations and continue the defence; General Flahaut was mounted on a troop horse and sent off at a gallop with these instructions for Marmont.

Even if it should prove to be too late to fight, it was not too late to treat for peace, and as soon as he got back to the post-house the Emperor dispatched Caulaincourt to the allied sovereigns, furnished with full powers to negotiate and conclude a peace. Napoleon then shut himself up in a room at the inn and waited impatiently for news with his eyes fixed upon his maps.

At daybreak a messenger arrived from Caulaincourt, and reported that the capitulation had been signed and that the allies would enter Paris during the morning. Shortly afterwards General Flahaut returned, bringing the following letter from Marmont:

> Sire, General Flahaut tells me that your Majesty is at Villejuif. He asked me if I thought that the Parisians were inclined to defend themselves. I must tell your Majesty the whole truth. Not only have they no inclination to defend themselves, but they have very definitely decided to do nothing of the sort. It seems that feeling has entirely changed since the Empress left, and the departure of King Joseph and all the members of the Government has brought the discontent to a head. I have no doubt that with the best efforts in the world it would be impossible to make any portion of the National Guard fight. My troops are marching at 5 a.m. so as to escape the enemy's cavalry, who can cross the Sevres bridge at 9 o'clock to harass our march.

Marshal Marmont was exaggerating the state of feeling in Paris, but there was certainly a great deal of truth in what he said. The sudden arrival of Napoleon, even during the afternoon of the previous day, would have roused the soldierly spirit of the National Guards, to whom Belliard had done more justice than Marmont. The presence of the Emperor would have infused confidence into every one, but on March 31 the capitulation was generally known among the troops, and the National Guard had made up their minds to the necessity of a surrender, and it would have been asking too much of the militiamen to expect them to take up the arms which some had laid down with reluctance, but the majority with a feeling of relief.

The regular troops were on a different footing; they were inspired by Napoleon's personality, and would have responded to any appeal. After a stubborn defence of 10 hours against four times their numbers, they had looked forward to having their revenge in street fighting, in which the advantages of numbers would have been of little account. They had been ordered to abandon Paris, however, and they were sullen and angry; the soldiers grumbled against their chiefs, and the army blamed the National Guard. In his letter to the Emperor, however, Marmont had been careful not to mention the army, who were bound under the terms of the capitulation to evacuate Paris; he only spoke of the National Guard.

Napoleon was overwhelmed; he went back to Fontainebleau and took up his quarters in the small rooms on the first floor of the castle, beside the gallery of Francois I.

The anger which the Emperor had shown on hearing Belliard's story was not assumed as it had been on the day when he said to Bourrienne, as he tapped his chin, " My anger went no deeper than that," and in his rage he was unjust towards Joseph and Clarke. If the king and the minister had shown little energy and less initiative, the whole responsibility of the capture of Paris was not theirs; Napoleon was also to blame for this great disaster.

During the whole of January the Emperor had hesitated between the desire to fortify the town and the fear of alarming the Parisians. He had been persuaded by ministers who were afraid to arm the working-classes, and he had allowed the Parisian National Guard to be recruited on the most vicious basis. When he went to join the army on January 25 he had left Paris without any means of defence.

During the two months of his absence, he had been warned by letters and by the daily reports that things had remained in almost the same state; he knew that the National Guard had only reached half the required strength, he knew that there was a shortage of muskets and that there were no artillerymen to work the guns, and he knew that the works of defence could not be started without his orders, accompanied by a grant of money. So lately as March 13 the Emperor had written to King Joseph, "Before beginning the fortification of Paris I must know the design," and he had sent no answer to Joseph's letter of March 15 asking for his approval to the proposed works.

He knew well that the occupation of Paris would be the end of the Empire, and he had said, "If the enemy arrives at the gates of Paris the Empire is at an end."

Again he had written, "Paris must not be abandoned, it were better that we should be buried beneath its ruins."

Now, in spite of all, Napoleon had abandoned his capital to Joseph's weakness and Clarke's love of routine. He had withdrawn from Paris for the use of his army every effective man, horse, and gun. As if he was reconciled to the idea of the capture of Paris, he had issued definite orders for the departure of the Empress and the King of Rome, and when this desertion took place it gave the last blow to public confidence and sapped the spirit of the National Guard.

Finally, on March 20, Napoleon had summoned to him the corps of Marmont and Mortier which had hitherto been charged with the protection of Paris; these corps were to be involved with the whole of his army in a sublimely daring manoeuvre which might succeed, but which, in case of failure, would irrevocably cause his downfall.

The battle of Arcis-sur-Aube had shown the Emperor that Schwarzenberg was no longer afraid to attack him, and that he was not inclined to retire at the least movement of the French army as he had been in February. Under these conditions the chances of success of the march into Lorraine were less favourable. If Napoleon had retreated on Paris with all his troops on the evening of the second day of the battle of Arcis, he would have arrived there four days before the allies and he would have concentrated 100,000 men there.

In four days Napoleon could have worked miracles. The enemy would not have found the suburbs unfortified, the roads unblocked, and the hills without epaulements and guns. Clausewitz asserts that Napoleon did not wish to risk a second defeat of Leipzig under the eyes of the Parisians. As things turned out the French had 35,000 men engaged at Paris, the majority of whom had arrived the day before after a week's hard marching and fighting; the generals were discouraged and the troops fought without any general plan, yet for ten hours they held out against 100,000 of the enemy; if Napoleon had retired to Paris there would have been 100,000 Frenchmen opposed to 150,000 of the enemy; the French troops would have been rested and would have been posted in strong positions supported by a formidable artillery. With Napoleon himself in command and infusing his own spirit into the troops, we may be permitted to think that under these conditions the battle of Paris would not have been a second Leipzig.

CHAPTER 27

Entry of the Allies into Paris

As soon as he awoke on March 31, the Emperor of Russia received the Parisian deputation which had arrived at Bondy at daybreak; they had already had a long conference with Nesselrode, at the end of which Colonels Tourton and Laborde had returned to Paris. Tourton was accompanied by Prince Apraxine, and their object was to arrange for the handing over of the gates to the allied troops. Laborde's mission was of a different nature; Nesselrode had taken him to one side and questioned him on the political feeling in Paris, and he had replied:

"The more intelligent men are in favour of a Regency; the old nobility would like to see the Bourbons restored, subject to conditions, and the rest of the nation would be ready to accept them provided their power was limited. But no one knows the state of feeling better than M. de Talleyrand, and he is the man to consult."

The Russian minister thereupon sent Laborde to beg Talleyrand not to leave the capital.

"If necessary," added Nesselrode, "he should be detained by force."

We know that there was no need to arrest Talleyrand in order to make him remain in Paris.

The Czar received the deputation in a very friendly manner.

"Napoleon," he said, "invaded my states without any cause, and it is only a just decree of Providence that has placed me under the walls of Paris. I hope I have no enemies in this town; in the whole of the rest of France I have only one."

Baron Thibou asked for protection for the Bank of France.

"That is not necessary," replied Alexander, "because I shall take the whole town under my protection."

The deputation obtained all that they asked for; the Czar promised not to interfere with museums or public monuments, he undertook to respect the citizens, and allowed the National Guard and the police to be maintained. On more than one point, even, the Czar promised more than they had dared to ask, and he assured the deputation that the troops would not be billeted on the inhabitants and that Paris would have to supply nothing but rations.

Caulaincourt had to wait for the deputation to leave before being presented to the Czar. He had left La Cour de France before 2 a.m. and he had not reached the Castle of Bondy till after 7. It seems extraordinary that he should have been so slow; his papers were in order, and he ought to have reached the allied head-quarters before, or at least at the same time as, the deputation from the municipality.

Things might perhaps have turned out differently if the Czar's first impression had not been gained from the latter, who painted a picture of Paris as being deserted by the Government and conveyed the impression that the town councillors had forgotten that Napoleon was still sovereign of France. It is not certain whether Caulaincourt only reached the Hôtel de Ville after the deputation had left, or whether the members of the deputation refused to recognize the powers with which the Emperor had invested him.

At any rate Caulaincourt was only received by the Czar after all the details of the occupation of Paris had been settled. Alexander received him cordially, but he would listen to no overtures, and he declared that he and his allies would be little inclined to make peace with Napoleon in the future. The conversation lasted a short time, for the Emperor was in a hurry to start off for Paris; he said goodbye to Caulaincourt and invited him to come and see him in Paris. Caulaincourt was a French general and a devoted servant of Napoleon, and as he despondently left the castle he saw in the court-yard the Czar's horse standing ready saddled; possibly he recognized the splendid dappled-grey animal which he had himself presented to the Czar when he had been ambassador at St. Petersburg.

Meanwhile, during the earlier part of the morning, many people in Paris did not yet know that the city had capitulated. The previous day the cannonade at Belleville and Montmartre had ceased between 4 and 5 o'clock, but at some of the gates musketry firing had gone on till past 9, and the cessation of the fire had been ascribed to the darkness. The inhabitants of the northern part of the town alone were prepared for the actual state of things; they had seen the French troops marching despondently through the outer boulevards; they had seen the enemy's posts established within a few yards of the gates, and they had seen the Russian soldiers dancing in the suburban inns to the sound of their regimental bands.

In the other parts of Paris, however, people were in the most complete ignorance and they expected fighting to be resumed on the following day. The theatres, shops, and cafes were closed and shuttered, and during the night absolute silence prevailed in the town. People were surprised not to hear the guns open fire at daybreak, and the streets quickly filled with crowds asking for news. Towards 9 o'clock it was rumoured that a capitulation had been signed and that the Czar had given ample safeguards for the protection of persons and property, and that he had announced that he would take Paris under his protection.

Among the wild exaggerations of contemporary memoirs it is not difficult to ascertain the real feelings of the majority when this news became known. The royalists were indecently delighted and a few patriots were filled with dumb rage, but the great majority felt nothing but relief. The police had done their best to make people believe that the town would be methodically burnt to the ground; probably this was not generally believed, but there is no doubt that the populace was nervous as to what might happen. The papers had prophesied that Paris would be burnt, and the atrocities committed by the Cossacks and Prussians were well known, and for the last two months everyone had been haunted by a prospect of pillage and outrage. Suddenly every apprehension vanished, and the relief more than compensated for the disappointment caused by the loss of the battle.

The royalists were mad with joy, and they prepared a triumphal entry for the victorious enemy. During the battle they had waited anxiously for the defeat of the French, and in the evening they had been the first to know of the armistice and capitulation. A royalist emissary had made his way through the enemy's lines to Langeron's head-quarters and had returned with the reply that a royalist movement was necessary to influence the decision of the sovereigns. The leaders of the party immediately decided to organize a public demonstration in order to convince the Czar and the allies that the French were in favour of a restoration.

The first demonstration took place in the Place de la Concorde, where a small body of royalists assembled wearing white cockades and scarfs; they read Schwarzenberg's proclamation and called for cheers for the King. The crowd remained most apathetic, and when groups of royalists paraded the streets shouting "Long live the Bourbons, down with the tyrant!" their reception was not at all favourable, and in some places they were attacked and beaten by the mob.

The Government was on the road to Blois, the army was on the road to Fontainebleau, and the magistrates were occupied solely with the entry of the allies and the provision of rations and accommodation. The police had no orders and the National Guard were divided into two factions, one of which wore the white cockade and shouted "*Vive le Roi!*" while the other threatened to open fire on the royalists. Paris was in a state of absolute anarchy. Prudent people feared bloodshed and every imaginable disorder, and longed for the arrival of the enemy's troops to ensure order in the town.

At 11 a.m. there rode through the Pantin Gate the Red Cossacks of the Guard, formed on a front of fifteen men and preceded by a large number of trumpeters. After them came *cuirassiers*, hussars, and volunteer squadrons of the Prussian Guard and the dragoons and hussars of the Russian Imperial Guard. On the Czar's right was the Prince of Schwarzenberg, representing the Emperor of Austria, and on his left rode the King of Prussia, and behind the three came a staff composed of more than 1,000 officers of every nation and every arm. Behind the staff marched the infantry with the divisional batteries; first came two regiments of Austrian grenadiers, then the whole corps of Russian grenadiers and the Royal Prussian Guard, and lastly the two divisions of the Imperial Russian Guard.

The Russian Life Guards and forty-seven squadrons of *cuirassiers* closed the procession. Although almost all these men had been in action the day before, their uniforms and their arms seemed to be as clean as if they had marched straight out of the barracks in Berlin and St. Petersburg. For the most part they were men of tall stature, and they looked the picture of health and vigour. What a contrast to the poor Marie-Louises, whose squalid looks and pale faces had so often roused the pity of the Parisians! Alexander had only wished to show his picked troops, and their appearance was no doubt much more imposing than that of the Russian and Prussian troops of the line, who entered Paris with less pomp by the various gates and took post on the Orleans and Fontainebleau roads.

The allies had prepared the best of surprises for the royalists; they were all wearing white armbands. On the morning of the battle of La Rothière, in consequence of an English officer having been wounded by a Cossack, orders were issued that all officers and men of the allied army should wear white arm-bands so as avoid confusion among so many different uniforms. It is not known who suggested this idea, but whoever it was, it was not an enemy of the Bourbons.

It seems surprising that the allies should have waited till they were in France before adopting a distinguishing badge which they had not found necessary at Dresden or Leipzig. On January 28 at Langres the Czar had invited the French refugees not to hide their colours when they were in the allied lines, and it is astonishing that three days afterwards he should have made his army adopt the same colours. Jomini, who knew the Czar's hostility to a restoration, told him that the people of France would take this badge to be a royalist emblem, and the autocrat replied, "What is that to me?" Whatever may be the truth, the allies, and especially the Russians, wore the white arm-band during the whole campaign, and they were wearing it when they marched into Paris.

The white badge was not without effect. When the crowd on the boulevards saw that the allied soldiers had this badge on their arms, the opposition to the white cockades, which had been so marked in the morning, was much diminished. Many people spontaneously put on the royal colours, some adopting them as a safeguard against the brutalities of the Cossacks and others as an emblem of peace.

A Russian historian has remarked that although there was no political signification in the white arm-band worn by the troops, it nevertheless was of service to the royalist party by creating a two-fold confusion; when the Parisians saw the badges worn by the allied troops they jumped to the conclusion that Europe had taken up arms to help the Bourbons, and when the people adopted colours which they disliked at heart they gave the allies the impression that the royalist sympathisers were numerous.

In the Faubourg St. Martin, where the allies first entered, there were not many spectators, and the few who were looking on were silent and almost hostile. When the Russians entered the boulevards they were met by the same silence, and the crowd, which was considerable, showed no feeling except curiosity. After passing La Porte Saint-Denis, a few timid cries of "*Vive l'Empereur Alexandre, vive les allies!*" were raised.

At the first cheers the Czar saluted and said in a loud voice, "I do not come as an enemy, I come to bring you peace."

The crowd cheered and shouted, "*Vive la paix!*" and "*Vive Alexandre!*" the royalists joined in with repeated shouts of "*Vive les Bourbons, à bas le tyrant!*" and made themselves conspicuous by their enthusiasm. As the sovereigns approached the more well-to-do quarters of the town their progress began to be more like a triumphal procession. Cheers grew louder and windows and balconies were filled with women waving handkerchiefs and white cloths. The smartness and precision of the infantry and the splendid appearance of the cavalry horses evoked much admiration.

People were heard to say "They don't look so bad" and "This is the remains of the allied army which Bonaparte's bulletins told us about."

"How handsome the Emperor Alexander is!"

"He must stay in Paris or give us a sovereign who is like himself."

"He is going to give us back the Bourbons."

The officers smiled at the crowd and said, "You see' we are not man-eaters," and the cheers and enthusiasm increased with every step.

No doubt a large number of people watched the triumphal procession of the enemy's troops with sorrow and humiliation. Some dreamed of Napoleon's future revenge, while others ascribed the disgrace of the capture of Paris to his insatiable ambition. The patriots, however, could only keep silence; Paris was in the power of the allies and it would have been childish to shout "*À bas Alexandre!*" and that was the most they could have done.

The best thing was to remain silent and to stay at home so as not to increase the size of the crowd which added to the triumph of the enemy, but in 1814 the dignity of empty streets and closed windows was not understood, and curiosity gained the upper hand. According to royalist historians and foreign reports, the whole of Paris was enthusiastic; the enthusiasm was certainly very great, but it was not general.

A few thousand men cheering in the middle of a large crowd are capable of giving a very wrong impression of the feelings of that crowd. There were some Parisians who could not forget that the bayonets of these gorgeous troops were dyed with French blood, and that the corpses of the French soldiers killed on the previous day were not yet buried.

When they reached the Champs Elysées the two sovereigns and the Prince of Schwarzenberg took up their post on the right-hand side of the avenue and watched the troops march past amid the cheers of the crowd. In order to get a better view some women borrowed the horses of the staff officers, while others climbed up behind the Cossacks of the Guard, and among these was the beautiful Countess Edmond de Perigord, afterwards the Duchesse de Dino.

Everyone wanted to see Alexander, and the officers who were asked to point him out replied, "White horse and white plume." On that day white was certainly the fashionable colour.

After the review the Emperor of Russia went to Talleyrand's house in the Rue Saint-Florentin.

At 7 a.m. Nesselrode had sent an officer to tell Talleyrand that the Czar intended to honour him by staying in his house, and during the march past the Russian minister was discussing many important subjects with him. Nesselrode was strongly in favour of a restoration, and he found Talleyrand of the same opinion. During the whole of the campaign Talleyrand had dreamt of a Regency in which he would be President of the Council, but these secret hopes had gradually faded.

In the first place, the Emperor, who was the principal objection to a Regency, had not been killed; then the Empress by abandoning Paris had practically abdicated, and finally, during the previous day, Talleyrand had watched the royalist sentiments gaining ground in political and financial circles. Schwarzenberg's proclamation and Nesselrode's talk with Laborde had confirmed Talleyrand in the opinion that the allies wished to restore the Bourbons. This was quite enough to decide a time-server like Talleyrand, and when the Czar reached the Rue Saint-Florentin it seems that the main points for discussion had already been settled.

They assembled in the big reception room on the first floor where Talleyrand was afterwards to die; the King of Prussia and the Prince of Schwarzenberg sat down with Dalberg, Nesselrode, Pozzo di Borgo, and Prince Lichtenstein on their right and Talleyrand on their left. For some time the Czar walked up and down; at last he stopped and said that there were three courses to choose from: first to make peace with Napoleon with 29 suitable guarantees; secondly to establish Marie-Louise as Regent; and thirdly to recall the Bourbons. It has been said that Alexander also proposed Bernadotte or a republic, and this is not improbable. Talleyrand dreaded most of all that Napoleon should be allowed to remain Emperor; the Regency would have been the summit of his hopes, but while Napoleon was alive he was likely to gain little from it. He spoke next and found no difficulty in persuading his hearers that a treaty with Napoleon would afford no guarantee of peace.

"The Regency," he said, "would be hardly less dangerous for the peace of Europe, because the Emperor would reign under the name of Marie-Louise."

Talleyrand concluded that the most suitable course was to restore the Bourbons, who "represented a principle."

This phrase could not help impressing the Czar, who himself represented a principle, but nevertheless Alexander objected that he did not wish to do violence to the opinion of France which appeared to him to be unfavourable to the Bourbons, and he said that except among certain French emigrants he had seen nothing in France but hostility to a restoration. He did not forget the revolution of Bordeaux nor the white cockades which he had seen in Paris, but the impression which these had made on his mind was effaced by the memory of the National Guards who had shouted "*Vive l'Empereur!*" as they fell before the grape shot at Fère-Champenoise.

This heroic scene had made the greatest impression on him, and he said so to the Council. Talleyrand thought it well to bring up reinforcements, and he sent for Pradt and Baron Louis, who declared in answer to the Czar's questions that France was really royalist, but that uncertainty had hitherto prevented the people from showing their true feelings.

"Paris has begun today," they added; "her example will be

decisive and will be followed everywhere." The Czar was persuaded.

The course to be followed was decided upon, and there remained to be found the means of carrying it out. Talleyrand was equal to the occasion; he told the sovereigns that he had great influence over the Senate, which also contained many men who desired a change; this body would be ready to declare that Napoleon had forfeited the crown as long as the Senators were assured that the Emperor would never ascend the throne again. Talleyrand knew to what lengths the Senate would go, and that without written guarantees the upper chamber would not commit itself.

"Under those circumstances," said Alexander, "I declare that I will never again treat with Napoleon."

Talleyrand or Pradt pointed out to the Czar that this undertaking was not sufficient, because it did not guarantee the Senate against Marie-Louise being appointed Regent.

"Very well," replied the Czar, after obtaining Schwarzenberg's concurrence, "I will add, nor with any member of his family."

A declaration was immediately drawn up which stated that the allied sovereigns would no longer treat with Napoleon, and which invited the Senate to form a provisional government which should draw up a new constitution. It seems that the terms of this declaration had been agreed upon two hours earlier by Talleyrand and Nesselrode, for it would have been impossible to improvise such a masterpiece.

The declaration not only relieved the Senate of all fear, but also laid down the course to be followed. It was both a safeguard and an order. The assurance that the conditions of peace would be favourable if France had a stable government reconciled even the most hostile citizens to the change; the falsehood "that the sovereigns accepted the will of the people" humoured the French national pride, and the promise that the sovereigns would guarantee the constitution chosen by the French nation reassured the liberals against the encroachments of the *ancien régime*.

While the Czar, or more truly Talleyrand, was deciding the destinies of France by a few strokes of the pen, the allied troops were settling into their bivouacs in Paris, and their officers flocked to the boulevards, the Tuileries, and the Palais-Royal. In order to bring this day to a fitting close, the Vicomte Sosthene de la Rochefoucauld, the Marquis de Maubreuil and other noblemen determined to overturn the statue of the victor of Austerlitz. A cask of wine and a few small coins sufficed to collect willing workers.

They forced the door in the pedestal, in spite of the opposition of several people, and gained the summit of the monument and from the platform some attacked the statue with sledgehammers while others pulled at ropes fastened round its neck. The figure bent forward and the statue of victory fell from its hand, but in spite of all efforts Napoleon remained upright.

It remained for the Russians to awake a sense of shame in the French, and the Czar sent a battalion to clear and occupy the Place Vendôme. Two days later the Provisional Government ordered the statue to be veiled, and on April 8 the figure was removed from its high pedestal. It was afterwards suggested that it should be replaced by a statue of peace with the features of the Emperor Alexander.

During the evening of March 31 Paris was dull and gloomy. This is a proof that the outburst of royalist sentiment which had marked the entry of the allied troops was purely temporary and local. People were still anxious and not at all inclined to leave their houses after nightfall. The theatres and shops remained closed and the foreign officers, who believed the Palais-Royal to be the chief place of amusement in the world, were astonished to find its galleries dark and silent. Only the cafés and restaurants remained open, with the exception of the famous café Lemblin where the officers of the Guard were wont to assemble.

On the following day, April 1, the enemy had a better reception. The night had passed quietly and without any disturbances. The mixed patrols, composed of National Guardsmen and allied soldiers, found nothing more serious to do than to arrest a few drunken men and interfere in a few street brawls. The morning papers were full of the most reassuring declarations, and on the walls similar proclamations were posted up. In the working-class quarter the people remained sullen and angry, but the gay world of Paris resumed its ordinary life and all the shops were opened. Gold, which had been so scarce for some months, flowed from the hands of the allied officers, to the great joy of the shopkeepers, who showed their patriotism by raising their prices.

The cafés and restaurants were crowded, and in the evening a queue formed at the theatres two hours before the doors were opened. On April 2 there was a gala performance at the Opera in honour of the sovereigns. The theatre was crowded with ladies in their best dresses and finest jewels and with officers in brilliant uniforms. Royalists wore the white cockade in their hats, and from the boxes ladies threw down white rosettes and cried "*Vive le Roi!*" to which the stalls and the pit replied with "*Vive les Bourbons!*"

When the Czar and the King of Prussia entered, the whole audience sprang to their feet and there was loud and continuous applause.

"Down with the eagle!" cried someone who noticed the imperial emblem over Napoleon's box. The house took up the cry, and the offending bird was covered with a white cloth.

The climax was reached when the leading tenor came to the front of the stage and, to the air of the well-known Bourbon song, "*Vive Henri IV*," sang some verses composed in honour of the sovereigns and their gallant troops. The enthusiasm was unbounded.

It had not taken Paris long to forget the ruined villages, the widows and orphans, and those who had died for France.

CHAPTER 28

The Provisional Government at Paris

Talleyrand had begun well when he dictated to the Czar the declaration that the allies would not treat with Napoleon, but he had still to bring his work to a successful conclusion. He lost no time, and during the evening of March 31 he saw the most influential members of the Senate. Before summoning the assembly for the following day he wished to make sure that the Senators would be submissive; it was important that there should be no hesitation or discussion, and that everything should be arranged beforehand.

The same evening Talleyrand selected the members of the Provisional Government whom he proposed that the Senate should nominate in addition to himself. These were the Duc de Dalberg and the Marquis de Jaucourt, the two great friends of Talleyrand, who had faithfully followed him in his zeal and hatred for Napoleon; there was the Abbé de Montesquiou, a determined royalist and a born intriguer, and there was General Beurnonville, a Count of the Empire and a Senator, who for the last ten years had hated Napoleon for not having made him a marshal.

While Talleyrand was taking steps to bring about the revolution, the royalist *partisans*, chief among whom was Pradt, were preparing public opinion for what was to come. During the evening of March 31 they posted up the Czar's declaration and Schwarzenberg's manifesto, and then, in co-operation with Sacken, the new Governor of Paris, they appointed their own followers as editors of the newspapers in place of those who had been nominated by the Emperor. Morin was appointed director of the press, and he ordered that the following day's papers should be worded in such a way as to forecast the fall of the Empire and the recall of the Bourbons, in accordance with the will of the people. The order was carried out with military obedience. On April 1 the papers reproduced the proclamations of the allies, described the enthusiastic cheers which had greeted the sovereigns, and gave an important place to the royalist manifestations. When Napoleon brought the press into subjection he had fashioned a tool capable of serving any master.

At 3.30 the Senate met; the House was composed of 140 members, of whom some 90 were in Paris, and 63 assembled at Talleyrand's bidding. The sitting was opened by a short speech from Talleyrand, which was a rigmarole of platitudes, and was said to have been composed by Pradt. He spoke of "freedom of judgment," "a liberal allowance for difference of opinion," "enlightened patriotism," and "the re-establishment of the administration as the most urgent of all needs."

The subject to be discussed by the House was hardly indicated, but this would have been unnecessary, for the Senators had been instructed beforehand, and had already come to a decision. Without a debate the Senate determined to establish a Provisional Government with executive powers, and charged with the duty of framing a constitution; they appointed Talleyrand and the four members whom he had nominated. The new Government lost no time in putting its own friends into the different ministries with the title of Commissioners.

While the Senate was sitting the General and Municipal Councils held a joint meeting at the Hôtel de Ville, and discussed a motion of Advocate Bellart's, who, on the day of the battle of Paris, had sworn a solemn oath in the presence of his family that he would deliver France from the yoke of Napoleon. Bellart proposed a resolution which opened with a violent tirade against the Emperor, referring to him as a criminal and a public enemy, and ending with the following words:

The two Councils declare that they formally renounce all obedience to Napoleon Bonaparte, and they express the fervent hope that the Monarchy will be re-established in the person of Louis XVIII.

Only 14 members of the Council were present out of a total of 24, and at first they hesitated to make themselves responsible for such an announcement. The members of the Municipal Council were guaranteed against the Emperor's just resentment by the Czar's declaration, but the Czar's word was only guaranteed by 100,000 bayonets, and Napoleon's genius might still perform a miracle. Bellart's eloquence, however, carried the day, and the proclamation was signed by 13 members; the only one who refused to sign was Baron Thibou, the deputy governor of the Bank, who said that he sympathized with the resolution, but that in view of his personal obligations to the Emperor he could not associate himself with it. Chabrol, the *Prefect* of the Seine, also stated that his regard for the Emperor would not permit him to countersign the proclamation, but that he approved of it, and would authorize its printing and publication.

It was not until April 5 that Chateaubriand published his well-known pamphlet, *Bonaparte and the Bourbons*, in which, among other wild statements, the great writer said that Napoleon had degraded the art of war. Meanwhile Bellart's virulent resolution set the tone to the journalists and pamphleteers, and papers, songs, and handbills vied with each other in insulting the Emperor. Napoleon was described as a coward, an assassin, a charlatan, the most foolish of men and the worst of tyrants; he was compared with Robespierre, Cromwell, and Attila, and even his family were not spared in the coarsest of caricatures.

When the Senate instituted a Provisional Government, it had by that act declared an *interregnum*, but it did not necessarily imply that France could not remain under the imperial *régime*, with Marie-Louise as Regent. This gave an opening to the Bonapartists, and allowed them to bring influence to bear upon the people, and also upon Alexander, whose conversion to a Restoration had been sudden, and might be only temporary. A formal declaration that Napoleon and his family were deposed was necessary in order to bring the whole country into line and complete the revolution, and with this object the Senate was convoked by the Provisional Government on the evening of April 2. As soon as the sitting opened, Lambrecht proposed a resolution deposing the Emperor and his family.

Several Senators supported the motion, which was put to the vote and adopted without discussion, with the sole proviso that the act of deposition should be preceded by a preamble. The assembly charged Lambrecht to draw up this preamble, and adjourned for that purpose till noon on the following day. This progress was too slow to suit one of the Senators, who declared that in view of the importance of the step which had been taken, the President ought, that very evening, to invite the Provisional Government to announce that Bonaparte had been deposed, and a minute was therefore drawn up, and it was sent to the newspapers and printed during the night.

On the following day, April 3, Lambrecht read the preamble, which amounted to an indictment of the Emperor: Napoleon had broken his oath and infringed the rights of the people by raising men and money contrary to the constitution; he had destroyed the independence of the judiciary, suppressed the liberty of the press, arbitrarily adjourned the legislature, published the decrees of Fismes, "which gave the impression that the war was national, whereas in reality it was purely dynastic," and finally, had continually abused his power and brought his country to disaster. After a short debate the decree was passed unanimously.

For the last ten years the Senate had obeyed the Emperor implicitly; on the eve of the Russian campaign it had raised no voice of protest to Lacépède's words, "Conscription is no hardship," and Napoleon himself had said of the Senate, "A sign was as good as an order to the Senate, which always did more than was asked of it." Nevertheless there was not one man sensible enough to point out that if the preamble was true it was the condemnation of the Senate as much as of Napoleon.

Contemporary opinion agreed with posterity in its opinion of the Senate, and Talleyrand was fully aware of this. In order to give more authority to the deposition he thought it well that the measure should be passed by the legislative body, which was held in some esteem by the *bourgeoisie*. There were about 100 deputies in Paris, and 79 of them assembled on the invitation of the Provisional Government. The legislative body showed more dignity than the Senate, and it merely agreed to the deposition with the sole preamble that Napoleon had violated the constitution. Also the vice-president, Henri de Montesquiou, refused to sign the report, and the chair was taken in consequence by the second vice-president.

In spite of the decrees and manifestos, and in spite of the newspapers, Paris was in no hurry to side with the Bourbons, and in almost all parts of the town anyone wearing royalist emblems was insulted and ill-treated. Nesselrode had demanded that the National Guard should wear the white cockade. The chief of the staff consulted the commanders of battalions; six said that with few exceptions the men would obey, and six replied that it would be dangerous to attempt to take away the national cockade: as a result, the proposal was abandoned. During the evening of April 1 a body of a dozen armed royalists had publicly read Louis XVIII's proclamation in various parts of Paris; this reading had been greeted by a few cries of "*Vive le Roi!*" but by many more of "*Vive l'Empereur!*"

In the Senate and in the Government there was a lack of unanimity. They had agreed to overthrow Napoleon, but could not agree as to the form of government to be substituted. The liberals were ready to accept the Bourbons provided there were constitutional guarantees, but the royalists would not consent to the king being tied down in any way. Talleyrand had the greatest difficulty in conciliating everybody, and, for fear lest the high-flown language of the press in favour of the Bourbons might provoke a reaction, he ordered the newspapers to moderate their zeal.

The occupation of Paris by the allies had proved a boon to

the restaurants, theatres, and shops of the fashionable quarters of the town, but it had not increased employment, and the workmen remained discontented and threatening.

Politics were discussed in the streets according to the custom which the unemployed had adopted during the last three months. Every point of view was vented, and many people believed that Paris might yet prove the tomb of the allies. The mass of the population, however, had no thoughts beyond an early peace, and were prepared to support any one who was ready to sign a treaty. All those who considered the question calmly regretted that the allies were unwilling to treat with Napoleon, because their refusal seemed to postpone the conclusion of peace, and to expose Paris to fresh dangers.

To all appearances Talleyrand had only succeeded in putting off the end of the crisis by adding a revolution to a national struggle. There were henceforward two powers in France in addition to the invader. At Paris the Provisional Government was master of the town; it was in possession of all the administrative functions, and was supported by the Senate, the Chamber, and the Town Council, but it had been formed by means of a *coup d'état* carried out at the bidding of the enemy, and it was opposed by more than half the population of Paris, while it had no connection with the provinces, and its authority was entirely local. At Blois there was the Regency, which was in a state of dismay, but maintained an appearance of confidence; it was busy reorganizing the various services as if the future was assured, and it still held the whole of France that was not occupied by the enemy.

The Emperor's brothers and the ministers, who could be seen in full uniform in the crowded streets of Blois, had in reality lost almost all hope. They did not fail, however, to take every step to help Napoleon's last efforts. Even Rovigo seemed to have recovered zeal and energy, and owing to his activity all the Parisian papers and all the dispatches and manifestos of the Provisional Government were intercepted, and the emissaries of Talleyrand and the allied sovereigns were stopped; for this reason the existence of the Provisional Government was not known at Rouen until the evening of April 3, at Grenoble and Bordeaux until the 11th, and at Brest until the 15th. Montalivet ordered the *prefects* to hurry on the conscription of 1815; he drew up and issued a proclamation of the Empress-Regent to the French, in which Marie-Louise announced the occupation of the capital by the enemy, and the return of the Emperor towards Paris. The manifesto ended thus:

> The only orders which you can recognize will emanate from the residence which I have chosen. Towns in possession of the enemy are no longer free, and all publications that come from them are the work of the enemy. You will be true to your oaths. You will listen to the voice of a princess whose only pride it is that she is French. My son was less sure of your hearts in the days of our prosperity.

Clarke once more became an indefatigable writer, and the orders which he issued from Blois were bewilderingly numerous; he ordered the commandants of military divisions to send conscripts and details to Orleans; he ordered General Fririon, the commandant of the depots, to form all his available men into mobile battalions; the *prefects* of the Loire provinces were ordered to collect supplies; General Préval, who had retired from Versailles to Mantes with the 1,500 men of the main cavalry depot, was ordered to re-form the depot at Caen or at Saumur; the construction of field works was ordered at Orleans, Gien, and Montargis, and directions were issued that this line, which covered the communications between the Regency and the imperial head-quarters, should be defended to the last extremity.

The Emperor reached Fontainebleau during the morning of March 31, and took defensive measures while waiting till his troops should be sufficiently concentrated to allow him to advance against the enemy. Napoleon did not despair of the success of Caulaincourt's mission, but he acted as if it was bound to fail. If the Emperor was to make a treaty and retain his throne it was necessary that he should not appear to be disarmed, and he must impose on the allies by means of a concentrated and reorganized army. Those officers who were intimate with him, Drouot, Flahaut, and Gourgaud, advised him to retire to Lorraine, but he refused, saying that his presence near Paris would be a check on intrigue. Fontainebleau offered him a good position for his army, where the right and rear would be covered by the Seine and the Yonne, and the front and left by the Essonne, while at Essonnes there was a powder factory, and at Corbeil a storage depot of flour.

The first troops to arrive came from Paris and Versailles, and they were posted on March 31 behind the Essonne; Marmont was in first line at Corbeil and Essonnes; Mortier and Belliard in the second line between Essonnes and Fontainebleau, and Colonel Vertillac, with 2,250 men from the depots of the Seine-et-Oise, at Milly. The garrison of Fontainebleau was composed of two battalions of veterans, and a few miscellaneous detachments. On the following day some of the cavalry of the imperial army reached Fontainebleau; the three divisions of the Guard under Sebastiani took up their position at Moret, Saint-Germain's division was posted at Melun and Fossart, and Defrance's Gardes d'Honneur were stationed at Saint-Germain-sur-Ecolle. The concentration of the army would not be finished for three more days, for the troops were scattered over a length of fifty miles, from St. Liébault to Villeneuve-la-Guyard.

During the afternoon of April 1 the Emperor inspected Marmont's positions. He was talking with the marshal and praising the behaviour of his troops at Belleville when Fabvier and Danremont, the two signatories of the capitulation, arrived from Paris. They told the Emperor of the triumphal entry of the allies, and the royalist demonstrations, and they ended by reporting the declaration of the Czar that he would no longer treat with the Emperor. Napoleon was upset at this news, and he said to Marmont with some bitterness that as peace was now impossible for him he would have to continue the war at all costs. "That is the necessity of my position," he said.

When he got back to Fontainebleau he issued orders hastening the concentration and reorganization of the army, and he directed that the guns of the grand park should be divided among the corps which had not got their full complement of artillery.

Those who surrounded the Emperor noticed his sadness and despondency; he only regained his spirits when he saw his soldiers. On April 2 he was present at the guard-mounting parade at Fontainebleau; the two battalions received him with enthusiasm, and his face lit up, until, as an eye-witness tells us, he looked the same as he had done in the days of his prosperity at the Tuileries, at Schoenbrunn, and at Potsdam.

This same day Caulaincourt returned from Paris. After his short interview with the Czar at the Castle of Bondy, he had obtained two other audiences at Talleyrand's house, in spite of the efforts of the members of the Provisional Government; he had again offered to sign peace immediately on the conditions proposed by the allies at Châtillon, and accepted in principle by Napoleon on March 25. He had pleaded the Emperor's cause with warmth and emotion, and he had advanced his rights and those of the people and army of France in opposition to the claims of the few thousand *partisans* of the Bourbons.

The Czar had answered by his usual argument that a peace with Napoleon could not be permanent, and Caulaincourt had then suggested Napoleon II; Alexander's answer was: "But what shall we do with the Emperor. The father is an insuperable obstacle to the recognition of the son."

The Czar's mind, however, was somewhat unsettled; perhaps he did not regret his declaration of March 31, but he certainly confessed to himself that he had been in rather too much of a hurry. He was all-powerful, however, and he could undo what he had done; he promised nothing definitely to Caulaincourt, but he told him that if he could announce the abdication of Napoleon the question of a Regency would be considered. Caulaincourt repeated these words to the Emperor, and told him that the only thing to be done was to abdicate.

The Emperor had probably expected this, and at first he listened calmly, but he could not restrain his indignation for long;

he refused to listen to Caulaincourt's entreaties, and dismissed him. Napoleon had chosen his course of action, and had made up his mind to fight his last battle.

At 10.30 a.m. on April 3, Friant's division of the Old Guard and Henrion's division of the Young Guard, who had reached Fontainebleau the day before, were formed up to be reviewed by the Emperor. The troops waited under arms for more than an hour, and the officers noticed the disheartened appearance of the members of the Emperor's suite. At noon Napoleon appeared, accompanied by a large staff; the troops presented arms and the drums sounded, and when the Emperor rode round the ranks he was evidently worried and ill at ease.

He stopped before every man and questioned him as to his age and service, as if he wished to gauge his loyalty; his manner was so encouraging that he seemed to invite the men to ask for rewards, and he gave the cross to almost everyone who asked for it. During this inspection, which took a very long time, the Emperor was only followed by Berthier, Drouot, and two orderly officers, and the marshals and staff remained in a group in front of the castle.

When the inspection was over he assembled around him the officers and non-commissioned officers of the division, and said in a loud, clear voice:

Officers, non-commissioned officers, and men of my Old Guard, the enemy has gained three marches on us, and has occupied Paris. I have offered the Emperor Alexander peace, to be purchased by great sacrifices; I offered to renounce all our conquests and all that we have gained since the revolution. He refused; and not only that, but, by the treacherous suggestions of those refugees whose lives I spared and whom I have loaded with favours, he has authorized the wearing of the white cockade, and he will soon wish to substitute that badge for the national cockade. In a few days I shall advance to Paris to attack the enemy. I rely on you.

The Emperor paused for a moment, waiting for a reply from his veterans. A dead silence reigned; Napoleon was surprised and astonished, and hardly found strength to ask "Am I right?"

At these words a deafening shout arose, "*Vive l'Empereur, à Paris, à Paris!*"

They had remained silent, as General Pelet said, because they had thought it was unnecessary to answer.

The Emperor was reassured, and went on:

We will prove to them that the French nation knows how to be mistress in her own house, and that we are able to defend our colours, our independence, and the integrity of our country. Repeat what I have said to your men."

Another cheer, louder even than the last, greeted these words. The officers returned to their regiments, formed each company into a circle, and repeated the speech they had just heard. As each circle broke up, cheers and fierce cries of vengeance were raised; the soldiers in their enthusiasm swore that they would die under the ruins of Paris.

The ranks were re-formed, and the Old Guard marched past cheering loudly and shouting "*Vive l'Empereur, à Paris!*"

During the march past the band of the grenadiers played the "*Chant du départ*" and the Marseillaise, and these airs brought back to the minds of the veterans the glorious days of Zurich, of Marengo, and of Hohenlinden.

CHAPTER 29

Marmont's Defection

Napoleon was beaten, but he was far from powerless; he still had 60,000 bayonets, and the allies, in spite of their great numerical superiority, seemed to be in no hurry to beard the lion in his den. Instead of marching straight on Fontainebleau on April 1, and crushing the small body of men that Napoleon had with him, they had merely taken up a defensive line behind the Orge and had given the Emperor time to recover himself and concentrate his army. Alexander had become the sole arbiter in matters of policy and war, and he had made up his mind to fight if Napoleon attacked, but he was not at all inclined to provoke a battle; he stood to gain little by fighting, for if Napoleon were defeated he could still retire behind the Loire or to Lorraine, and if the allies had the worst of the encounter they would be driven back upon the guns of Vincennes, which was still holding out, and upon Paris, which in that case would probably rise against them.

The Czar was enjoying the sweets of triumph; he had gained his end and had ridden into Paris at the head of his Guard: he had brought the national war to a glorious termination, and he was not at all inclined to sacrifice his soldiers in a war which would be purely political and for a cause to which he had hitherto been indifferent. He temporized in the hopes that matters would arrange themselves without further bloodshed, and this had been the meaning of his words to Caulaincourt.

The Provisional Government was not deceived; it realized

that Napoleon's army was an obstacle to the restoration of the Bourbons and a danger to those who had dethroned the Emperor and seized the reins of power. In the month of March Talleyrand had thought and even written that the death of the Emperor would realize his dearest hopes and it is possible that in April he was still of the same opinion. In any case, in his immediate entourage there was a man, Roux-Laborie, the secretary of the Provisional Government, who had conceived the same idea.

On the day when the allies entered Paris Guerry de Maubreuil, the Marquis d'Orsvault, had made himself the most conspicuous of all the royalists; he had tied the cross of the Legion of Honour to the tail of his horse, and, with de la Rochefoucauld, had collected a number of scoundrels and tried to throw down the Emperor's statue. He was a brave man, but had come down in the world. He had been equerry to Catherine, the wife of Jerome Buonaparte, and had gained the Legion of Honour in Spain when a lieutenant in a Westphalian regiment; he had afterwards tried, without success, to be admitted into the French army; he had then ruined himself and lost all social standing by speculations in military supplies and by a life of debauchery. Maubreuil was now deep in debt and was the sort of man to whom any proposal might be made. Roux-Laborie knew his character, and on April 2 he wrote and begged him to come to Talleyrand's house.

In the evening Maubreuil arrived, and Roux-Laborie said, without beating about the bush. " I want to speak to you about the death of Napoleon. If he were put out of the way everything would be in our power. That is a task worthy of your courage, your character, and your ambition." He added that both in matters of money and of honours the reward would be proportionate to the service rendered. Maubreuil demanded an advance of money and a promise of promotion for the accomplices whom he expected to find in the army. Laborie promised everything and told him to come back the following morning. Maubreuil passed the night in looking for men of his own kidney, but on the following morning he had only got one recruit, a man named Dasies.

Laborie told him to come back that evening, and when he arrived he said: "My friend, we have great news. Your expedition must be postponed, but even if it does not take place at all we shall still be very grateful to you."

The assassination was no longer necessary, for it had been found that treason by itself was sufficient.

We have seen that during the night of March 30 Talleyrand had sounded Marmont, and the result had been promising; since the evening of March 31 Talleyrand and his friends had made it their business to complete the conversion of Marmont to their cause. They sent him copies of Schwarzenberg's manifesto and of Alexander's declaration, and on April 2 they conveyed to his outposts a number of copies of the address of the Provisional Government to the army.

> "Soldiers," it ran, "France has just thrown off the yoke under which she has suffered for so many years. You have always fought for your country; under the colours of the man who is your leader you can in future only fight against your country. You are no longer the soldiers of Napoleon; the Senate and the whole of France free you from your oaths."

Many officers received these proclamations as they deserved and treated them as treasonable documents, but unfortunately for the honour of the general staff, all the leaders of the army did not take this view. On April 2 Marmont received Schwarzenberg's proclamation and a copy of the *Gazette*, and forwarded these two letters to Berthier without uttering a word of indignation in his covering letter; he seemed to consider the events which had taken place in Paris as most natural.

On the following day, April 3, a former *aide-de-camp* of his, Charles de Montessuy, arrived at the head-quarters at Essonnes dressed in a Cossack uniform; he brought to Marmont a copy of the act of deposition and letters from Schwarzenberg, Pasquier, and various others, asking him to side with the true cause of France. These letters only appealed to the marshal's patriotism, but Montessuy had been directed to play upon his vanity and ambition. To save France and establish a secular dynasty would be a glorious achievement; an appeal had been made to him alone because he was the only one of the marshals who had the intelligence to see in which direction his true duty lay; if he secured peace for France he would secure the eternal gratitude of the country; if he gave the throne to the Bourbons he would reap all the rewards which fall to the lot of the man whom the king delighted to honour.

Marmont was still under the influence of the reception which had been given to him on the evening of the battle of Paris. He could still hear the murmurs of admiration which had greeted him, and could still see himself receiving Talleyrand and discussing affairs of State with him as with an equal. He was inflated with pride and believed that in a few days' time he might be the leading man in France, second only to the King, who would owe him a deep debt of gratitude. Marmont says that he accepted Schwarzenberg's proposals in order to save France; his enemies assert that his object was to retain his title of Duc de Raguse. As a matter of fact vanity alone was the cause of Marmont's treason.

Montessuy left Essonnes the same day with Marmont's verbal promise; the same evening or early the next morning the marshal wrote the following letter to Schwarzenberg:

I have received the letter which your Highness has done me the honour to write and also all the accompanying papers. My conduct has always been guided by public opinion. The decree of the Senate has released the army and the people from their oaths of fidelity to the Emperor Napoleon. I am inclined to co-operate in an understanding between the people and the army, which should prevent any chance of civil war and stop the effusion of French blood. In consequence, I am ready to withdraw my troops from Napoleon's army on the following conditions which

I require to be guaranteed by you in writing.

Marmont's conditions were, firstly, that the troops should retire in freedom to Normandy with their arms, baggage, and ammunition; secondly, "If in consequence of this movement Napoleon should fall into the hands of the allies, his life and liberty shall be guaranteed to him within an area to be selected by the allied powers and the French Government." Marmont was not only ready to abandon his post, but he even contemplated handing over the Emperor to his worst enemies, subject to the above condition. There seems to have been a certain amount of irony in the following reply of Schwarzenberg's:

> I appreciate the delicacy of the condition which you stipulate with reference to Napoleon's person. Nothing could be more typical of the generosity which is natural to all Frenchmen and which distinguishes your Excellency above all others.

At Fontainebleau nothing was known of these negotiations. During the morning of April 4 Macdonald's three corps arrived and were posted as follows: the 11th at Chailly, the 7th at Fontainebleau, the 2nd at Pringy, and the cavalry along the Ecolle river. Marmont's corps was in occupation of Essonnes and Corbeil; Mortier's corps was at Menecy; Lefol's division at Milly; the Old Guard with Henrion's division and the reserve artillery at Tilly; the cavalry of the Guard at Auvernaux and Nainville; Defrance's division at Fontenay-le-Vicomte; the light cavalry of the second corps at Melun and the heavy cavalry at St. Germain-sur-Ecolle. All the Emperor's troops were now concentrated and he was ready to advance; orders had already been issued to move the imperial head-quarters to the castle of Tilly, and at midday the Emperor was present at the mounting of the Guard and was received with the cheers of the troops.

The soldiers, the regimental officers and the younger generals were full of enthusiasm, and the reverses had filled them with grim determination. The marshals and divisional generals, however, were tired of the war, and could hope for no further honours; they had nothing to gain from further fighting and they only wished for peace in which to enjoy the high rank and rewards which had been showered upon them.

Many of them, like Marmont, had only spent three months in Paris during the last ten years; at Prague in 1813 the Emperor had questioned Belliard as to the feelings of the army, and the general had been bold enough to reply, "Your generals wish for peace in order to enjoy your Majesty's bounty, for up till now you have never given them time to do so."

Formerly they had loved war and had been most anxious to be given high commands, but this war gave them only danger and fatigue without either success or pay, and the numbers of troops were so reduced that the high commands did not amount to much. During the whole of the campaign Ney had had only a brigadier-general's command, and his young troops had so little training that he had to do the work of a non-commissioned officer. In their state of depression they took a gloomy view of the prospects of the campaign: the idea of a victory was almost as distasteful to them as defeat, for it involved street fighting and would probably mean the pillage and burning of Paris, which sheltered their homes and families. Even after this victory they did not know where they would stop; the Emperor might push on as far as the Niemen, and there seemed no prospect of the war ever coming to an end.

However discontented and despondent the generals might be, they were not willing to go over to the side of the enemy, however, as Marmont was doing; for they did not at all like the idea of a restoration of the Bourbons, which would mean retirement, or possibly exile, for them. The Emperor had been so imprudent as to discuss with his staff the suggestion that he should abdicate in favour of the King of Rome, and this proposal was eagerly discussed at head-quarters; this would have suited every one, for a Regency would mean peace, with the existing institutions and without loss of their rank or their pensions. They had, however, to reckon with Napoleon's decision, and his orders and preparations showed clearly that he did not wish to abdicate.

During the guard mounting parade the marshals and generals indulged in a warm discussion within a few paces of Napoleon, and while the soldiers were shouting "*Vive l'Empereur!*" Marshal Ney exclaimed, in a voice which could have been heard above the roar of a battle, "Nothing but abdication can save us!"

Napoleon did not hear, or pretended not to hear, and went back to his quarters; but the marshals were excited, and Ney, Lefebvre, and Moncey followed the Emperor and burst into his study, where he was engaged with Berthier, Bassano, Caulaincourt, and Bertrand. When he found himself face to face with the Emperor, Ney lost some of his confidence; but he was supported by the other two marshals and by the thought of the crowd of generals who had remained in the court of the palace and to whom he had given a promise that he would bring about an abdication.

Screwing up his courage, he asked Napoleon if he had any news from Paris. The Emperor knew as much as Ney did, but he answered that he had no news. Ney thereupon announced that the Senate had decreed the deposition of the Emperor. Napoleon remained calm; for during this campaign he had become accustomed to his marshals' attempts to lay down the law, and he replied that the Senate had not the power to do this and that the nation alone could depose him.

"As to the allies," he added, "I am going to rout them at Paris."

At these words Ney and Lefebvre exclaimed, "The situation is desperate; you should have made peace before now; abdication is the only course!"

The Emperor calmly began to argue with the marshals; he enumerated the troops which were collected between the Essonne and the Yonne, and the reinforcements who were coming from the depots and from the other armies; he pointed out the faulty position of the allies and explained his plan of attack, and said that the slightest success at Paris would change the whole complexion of affairs. His words had no effect, and he looked round in vain for a sign of encouragement or loyalty; he was met with a stony silence.

The three marshals had gone too far to withdraw. Berthier was tired of war and had lost all hope, and the most that he could do for Napoleon was to say nothing; Bassano knew that his voice would only irritate the soldiers, and Caulaincourt had already told the Emperor that an abdication was the only way to save his dynasty. This terrible silence must have wrung Napoleon's heart with pain and humiliation. In *L'Expiation*, Victor Hugo has told us of the Beresina and of Waterloo, but he forgot Fontainebleau.

At this moment an orderly officer introduced Macdonald and Oudinot, whose corps had just reached Villeneuve-le-Guyard. The Emperor hoped to find a supporter in Macdonald, and went forward to receive him. Four days before, Macdonald had been anxious to sacrifice himself and his army in a last battle, and had written to Berthier to suggest the plan which the Emperor had just outlined; since that time, however, he had changed his mind, and the object of his visit was to ask the Emperor to make peace.

He replied: "I assure you we are not willing to expose Paris to the fate which overtook Moscow. We have made up our minds, and are determined that the war must end."

The Emperor, however, pretended to be confident, and declared that, whatever his marshals might think, he was determined to attack the enemy. At these words Ney lost all self-control and exclaimed that the army would not march on Paris.

"The army will obey me," said Napoleon in a loud voice.

"Sire," replied Ney in the same tone, "the army will obey its generals."

Napoleon knew that his control over his marshals was enough to prevent open disobedience, and he knew that his soldiers had not changed. An order from him would have immediately placed under arrest the marshals who had dared to threaten him, and he knew that he could have replaced them by junior officers. There was a limit, however, even to his energy; for the last three months he had continued the war in spite of his ministers and generals, and now he himself was becoming weary. When on the point of marching on Paris, he hesitated to sacrifice the remains of his army in a battle which might perhaps result in disaster. On the previous day his head-quarters had been established at Tilly, but the Emperor himself had remained at Fontainebleau.

One word of encouragement, however, from his old comrades, and he would have moved forward; but this word did not come, and in its place they showed themselves to be despondent and mutinous. Napoleon was always lenient towards his marshals, and he was not at all anxious to take vigorous measures which would have dishonoured them, while it would have been a very serious step to change all his corps commanders and many of his divisional generals in the presence of the enemy.

On the other hand, Caulaincourt, the most devoted of his servants, had not wasted all his trouble when he urged an abdication in favour of the King of Rome. A Regency would have given Napoleon a chance of seizing the reins of power at some future time, and it would in any case have saved his dynasty. The Emperor suddenly made up his mind. Without deigning to reply to Ney's outburst he coldly dismissed the marshals, who left the room rather astonished at their own boldness. The Emperor was left alone with Caulaincourt, and after a short discussion he wrote an act of abdication, conditional on the Empress being Regent and on the recognition of the rights of Napoleon II.

Caulaincourt was Minister for Foreign Affairs; he had been the Emperor's plenipotentiary at Châtillon, and he was a personal friend of the Czar's; he was, therefore, the natural person to take the act of abdication to Paris, but Napoleon wished that he should be accompanied by two marshals. The army was the main support of the Empire, and it was of importance, therefore, that two leading generals should go with Caulaincourt in order to demonstrate their loyalty.

The first marshal to be selected was Ney, who had behaved so rudely to him a few minutes before, and this proves that the Emperor was incapable of showing spite; he next thought of Marmont, his former *aide-de-camp* and the most trusted of his comrades, but it was pointed out that it would be better to employ Macdonald, for he was known to have had less personal intercourse with the Emperor, and he would for that reason have more influence on this mission. Napoleon decided that Macdonald should be his third plenipotentiary, but he wished that Caulaincourt and the marshals should tell Marmont what had taken place as they passed his head-quarters at Essonnes. Marmont was to be given the choice of remaining at the head of his corps or of carrying out the mission for which the Emperor had originally chosen him. After receiving these last instructions, Caulaincourt, Ney, and Macdonald started in a coach accompanied by two secretaries.

Meanwhile matters were developing at Essonnes. During the morning Marmont had received Schwarzenberg's guarantees and he had decided to start his movement that evening, for he wished to take advantage of darkness in order to deceive his troops as to the object of their march. He could not deceive his generals and it was necessary to make them his accomplices; Marmont interviewed them one by one and made them give their word of honour that they would reveal nothing of what he was going to say to them. Fabvier was the first to be told of the proposal which the Provisional Government had made, and when Marmont asked him his opinion as to what answer should be given to the messenger, he pointed to a large branch of a tree in the garden and said, "I think that would be the proper answer."

Marmont changed the conversation. His chief of the staff, Meynadier and Generals Digeon, Souham, Merlin, and Ledru-Desessarts, were surprised, but were easily convinced. Marmont did not speak to Lucotte, for he knew the honesty of his character. There was a lively scene with Bordesoulle. Marmont made him give his word of honour that he would reveal nothing, and then announced that, as a Government had been established in Paris, and as the Senate had deposed Napoleon, he had made an agreement with Schwarzenberg to allow his corps to pass through the allies' lines and to go to Normandy, and he added that when there his troops would have no dealings with the allies and would receive no orders except from the Provisional Government. Bordesoulle could contain himself no longer.

"What," he exclaimed, "you have made a treaty like that!"

Marmont reminded the general that he had given his word.

"I will keep my word," said Bordesoulle, "but you must not count upon my cavalry."

"You can do what you like," replied Marmont, "but I have decided that the troops shall be under arms at 6 o'clock under pretext of a review, and I will then pass through the enemy's lines."

Bordesoulle broke out again: "You are going to leave the Fontainebleau road open, and you will put the Emperor at the mercy of the enemy. And what is going to happen to Mortier's corps which you will uncover?"

Marmont answered that he had stipulated for Napoleon's safety, and untruthfully said that Mortier had been informed of the movement.

"Think it over," he concluded, "and come back at 4 o'clock and tell me what you have decided to do."

Marmont, who apprehended some danger from the direction of Fontainebleau, said to Bordesoulle as he was leaving, "If a couple of hundred cavalrymen were to come to arrest me, would you protect me from them."

"Marshal," replied Bordesoulle, "you did not consult me before doing what you have done and you ought not to apply to me now if you have done anything to fear."

Towards 4 p.m. the Emperor's plenipotentiaries reached Essonnes. They told Marmont what had happened at Fontainebleau and repeated the friendly and flattering messages which Napoleon had sent. Marmont was very much troubled: he could not help being moved by the thought that, at the very time he was engaged in betraying his sovereign, Napoleon, overlooking his defeats at Salamanca, Athies, and Fère-Champenoise, was giving him a unique proof of his confidence and affection.

Marmont had justified his defection by specious arguments

based on the fear of civil war, the good of his country, and the safety of France, but these all fell to the ground now that Napoleon had abdicated. The marshal found himself on the horns of a dilemma; there was now no possible excuse for carrying out his proposed movement, and it would also irretrievably compromise him, for if the Czar were to agree to Napoleon's proposals his position under the Regency of Marie-Louise would be an impossible one.

It was equally dangerous to break his agreement with Schwarzenberg and remain at Essonnes with his corps, for at any moment the Emperor might hear of his negotiations and place him under arrest. Again, he could not go to Paris as a plenipotentiary, for it was impossible for him to appear before the Czar to defend a cause which he had undertaken to abandon.

In his perplexity he could not make up his mind how to reply to the Emperor's envoys, but finally he decided to confess his negotiations with Schwarzenberg. Caulaincourt and his two companions were astounded and said that the least division in the army would be the downfall of France, but they calmed down when Marmont told them that he had not committed himself, and he was prepared at once to break off his personal negotiations.

They again asked if Marmont was ready to go with them to Paris, and he warmly consented. In his *memoirs* he says that he did so because his word would carry great weight with the allies, but his real reason was that he wished as soon as possible to place the enemy's army between himself and the Emperor's Provost Marshal; the proof of this is that he did not wait to get his credentials from Fontainebleau, and when they got to Paris he took no part in the negotiations. Caulaincourt and the marshals understood the delicacy of Marmont 's position and did not insist on his getting his credentials, but they wished to get him to Paris as soon as possible, so as to prevent him carrying out his project.

Before he left Essonnes Marmont handed over the command to General Souham; he told him why he was leaving, and ordered him to make no movement until he returned. He gravely exceeded his duty, however, by ordering his chief of the staff to assemble the troops at once and to inform them that the Emperor had abdicated.

The abdication was conditional and should have been kept secret until it had been accepted by the allies, and to make it known was an act of treason, and was enough to demoralize the army. Marmont's remorse was not sincere, and he had only suspended his movement without renouncing it; even if the Emperor were to withdraw his abdication, the fidelity of the troops would be much shaken, and they would be ready to abandon his cause. Marmont was determined that in any case Napoleon should be unable to count on the 6th Corps.

Marmont's extraordinary order was immediately issued to the generals and was communicated by them to their troops. The only one who refused was General Lucotte, who had succeeded to the command of Arrighi's division. He assembled his troops, and said to them, "Soldiers, the Emperor will consent to every sacrifice in order to bring peace to France. You will obey him in everything."

The soldiers replied with shouts of "*Vive 1'Empereur.*"

The plenipotentiaries left Essonnes at 6 p.m. and stopped at Schwarzenberg's head-quarters, near Chevilly. Caulaincourt, Ney, and Macdonald had to tell the commander-in-chief the object of their mission and to ask to be allowed to pass through his lines; Marmont had a much more difficult task, which was to escape from his written undertaking. He saw Schwarzenberg in private, and in his memoirs he says "that he had no difficulty in withdrawing from the negotiations which he had begun, and Schwarzenberg appreciated his reasons for changing his mind and fully approved of his resolution."

We may be permitted to doubt whether the matter was really so easily arranged. Certainly Schwarzenberg could not have sent Marmont back to Essonnes under an escort in order to force him to bring his corps to Versailles, but he probably did not fail to remind the marshal of his written undertaking, and to tell him that the Czar and the Provisional Government had already been informed. If the negotiations were to fail, the publication of his letter would bring his treason home to Marmont, and his military honour was henceforward at the mercy of a Talleyrand or a Roux-Laborie.

It was about 9 p.m. when Talleyrand learnt that the Emperor's emissaries were on the way. He summoned to his house the members of the Provisional Government and the ministers, and when they learnt that the marshals were bringing an act of abdication in favour of Napoleon II they were frightened out of their wits. They were admitted to the presence of the Czar and assured him that France wished to see the Bourbons restored, that a peace with Napoleon could only be temporary, and that a Regency would only be the Empire in disguise, and they added that the Czar could not go back upon his declaration of March 31, for they all relied on his word and would be in great danger if the Regency were proclaimed. Many of them began to regret having compromised themselves, and they were pleading much more for themselves than for the Bourbons. General Dessolles insisted so strongly on the Czar's responsibility towards those who had sided against Napoleon, that Alexander haughtily replied, "Whatever happens, no one will have cause to repent of having trusted in me."

Caulaincourt and his companions arrived soon after midnight and were introduced to the Czar. They read the act of abdication, and then each in turn warmly pleaded the cause of the imperial dynasty. Ney and Macdonald laid stress upon the will of the army, which had lost none of its devotion for the Emperor, and was ready to continue the war; they pointed out the advantages of a Regency, which would ensure peace and would meet the wishes of the majority of the population of France. Caulaincourt reminded the Czar of his proclamation, in which he had promised that France would be free to choose its own form of government. Macdonald took a leading part in the discussion, and his words carried a special weight, because he was known to have received fewer favours from Napoleon than the other marshals; he once more described the feelings of the army in the following words;

The army cannot but be dismayed at the prospect of .the return of the Bourbons, who are strange to its services and strange to its glories.

According to almost all accounts, Alexander was very much disturbed, and in view of his situation and his character this is very likely true. On April 4, at Paris, Alexander was much more inclined to treat with Napoleon than he had been at Châtillon on February 10. The other allied powers could not be satisfied with a Regency; the policy of England was far-seeing, and took more account of the future than of the present; Austria was bound by monarchical traditions, and Prussia was vindictive even after victory, but Alexander resembled rather the visionary hero of an epic poem, and he had already attained his end: he had ridden into Paris at the head of his Guard and he had avenged the insult to Moscow.

The Czar had refused to place Bernadotte on the throne, but he had no more preference for the Bourbons than for Marie-Louise. During the whole campaign he had been far from cordial to the royalist *partisans*, and on March 31 he had raised grave objections to a restoration; he had certainly signed the declaration that he would not treat with Napoleon, but he had been inveigled into doing so by Talleyrand and Pradt. During the last five days the promises and assurances of Talleyrand and the royalists that a lead from the allies would make the whole of France show its devotion to the Bourbons had signally failed of realization.

The cause of the former dynasty had made little progress; the National Guard refused to wear the white cockade, the population showed no enthusiasm, the proclamations to the army produced no result, and the Senate and royalists were quarrelling with each other; finally, behind the Essonne there were 60,000 soldiers whose devotion to the Emperor was likely to prove a very serious complication. The Regency of Marie-Louise would have put an end to all these embarrassments and would have been very acceptable to Alexander's chivalrous character. In addition, he had promised to listen to the will of France, and here were Macdonald, whom he respected, Ney, whom he admired, and Caulaincourt, whom he loved, all assuring him that France was in favour of a Regency.

The evidence of these three men was worth more than that of Talleyrand and his associates, for whom Alexander could feel no respect. In spite of all, however, the Czar was far from being ready to fall in with the wishes of Napoleon's representatives. Personally he was inclined to favour a Regency, but in the other scale must be put his undertakings with the royalists, the declaration which he had signed, and the clearly expressed views of his allies. Certainly Alexander had not made up his mind to abandon the Bourbons, but he was wavering.

The interview lasted for more than two hours, and the marshals began to think that their mission would be successful.

"Gentlemen," said the Czar at last, "I will inform my allies of your proposals, which will have my support. I am anxious to have the matter settled, for there is a peasant rising in Lorraine, and one of my columns has lost 3,000 men there without having seen a single French soldier. Come back at 9 o'clock, and you shall have your answer."

The members of the Provisional Government and the ministers were anxiously awaiting the end of the conference in an adjoining room. When Napoleon's envoys appeared they came forward to speak to them, but they were very coldly received. Caulaincourt almost assaulted the Abbé de Pradt, who made second-rate jokes in the worst taste about the position of the Emperor, and was obliged to escape down a back staircase. General de Beurnonville offered Macdonald his hand, but the marshal refused, saying, "Your conduct makes me forget a friendship of thirty years' standing."

During this heated interview one of Schwarzenberg's *aides-de-camp* came out of the Czar's room; he had just reported to Alexander the news that the whole of Marmont's corps was marching into the Austrian lines.

This move had been brought about by chance. The news of the Emperor's abdication had caused great excitement among the troops, and between 6 and 7 p.m. an order from Berthier arrived at Essonnes directing Marmont to report himself at once to the Emperor, and in his absence it was given to General Souham.

As a matter of fact there was nothing personal to Marmont in this order, for similar instructions had been sent to all commanders of corps and independent divisions. The receipt of the order, however, made Souham rather nervous, and his nervousness was changed to terror when he learnt that one of the Emperor's orderly officers wished to speak to him; he was so frightened that he forgot that orders were always sent from head-quarters in duplicate, and he refused to receive the officer. The general's secret was so dangerous that he did not feel safe, and he imagined that the treason of Marmont and his lieutenants was known to everyone, and especially to the Emperor, who was sending for him in order to put him under arrest.

"He will shoot me," he said to the generals whom he summoned to his head-quarters. The generals, all except Lucotte, who had not been summoned, felt that they were Marmont's accomplices equally with Souham, and they decided that they ought to follow Marmont's example and put themselves beyond Napoleon's reach. The generals might have fled, but they chose to abandon Napoleon rather than to desert from the army. Orders were issued for the whole of the corps to stand to arms, and an officer was sent to Schwarzenberg, warning him that the proposed movement was about to be carried out.

Fabvier knew of the plan which Marmont had formed, and which he had apparently abandoned, and when he saw the troops getting under arms he realized that Souham was disobeying the marshal's counter-order. He briskly questioned him and the other generals, and implored them to remain at Essonnes until Marmont should return, or at any rate until he sent further orders, and he offered to go himself and ask for the marshal's instructions. His superiors would not listen to him, and ordered him to be silent, and he thereupon sprang into the saddle and started at full gallop to warn the marshal. He had no difficulty in crossing the enemy's lines, for Marmont was already so well known there that his *aide-de- camp* was allowed to pass freely.

The troops started at about 11 p.m. At first they had no suspicion, and thought they were going to occupy fresh positions; the officers were ordered to keep their places in the column and to maintain the strictest silence in the ranks, and this precaution prevented the men from discussing where they were going. The enemy's *vedettes* and outposts, also, withdrew to either side of the road as the column approached. One or two officers, however, had their suspicions, and left the column and returned, and at the rear-guard a squadron of Polish lancers also turned back.

When they got near Juvisy the soldiers were astonished to hear the rattle of arms and the sound of horses to their right and left, but they imagined that the noises were made by French cavalry. When day broke, however, they were astonished to find themselves in the enemy's lines. Russian *cuirassiers* were marching on either flank of the column, and Austrians and Bavarians were standing to arms beside their bivouacs and saluting the French as they passed. The men began to murmur, and raised cries of "Treason," and the generals who tried to calm them were hooted.

The troops, however, were in column of route, surrounded by the enemy, and they were unable to form a concerted plan of action. The soldier also is as credulous as a child, and they imagined that they were going to unite with the Austrians to keep the Emperor on the throne. The unfortunate men continued their march towards Versailles. The cause of the Bourbons had triumphed; the defection of the 6th Corps disarmed Napoleon physically and morally. He could not now fight a last battle before Paris, and Ney and Macdonald's assertions as to the feeling of the army fell to the ground now that a whole corps had deserted.

The Czar no longer hesitated. "You see," he said to Pozzo

di Borgo, "the will of Providence is made manifest. There can be no further doubt or hesitation." Alexander had made up his mind that the empire was at an end.

The same day, April 5, at about 9 a.m., Caulaincourt, Ney, and Macdonald were again received by the Czar, who was accompanied by the King of Prussia. Frederick William, in his best German manner, began by apostrophizing the marshals and saying that the French were the cause of all the ills of Europe.

Alexander cut him short. "Brother," he said, "this is no time to rake up the past."

He then broached the subject of the conference, and stated definitely that he and his allies could not accept the abdication of Napoleon in favour of his son; they demanded an abdication pure and simple.

As to Napoleon, he would preserve "the title under which he is generally known," and would be given the sovereignty of the Isle of Elba. Caulaincourt and the two marshals expected an answer of this nature, for they also knew that the 6th Corps had abandoned Essonnes; they had learnt the news from Marmont himself, while they were having an early breakfast at Ney's house. Marmont had been much distressed, and had exclaimed, "I would give one of my arms to prevent it having happened."

"An arm!" replied Ney curtly; "if you said your head it would not be too much."

Possibly Marmont felt a certain amount of remorse, but the pricks of his conscience rapidly disappeared before the congratulations of the Provisional Government. If he had realized the indelible shame with which the defection of the 6th corps would cover him, he would not have lost a moment in rejoining his troops and leading them back to the French lines by the Rambouillet road, which was still open. If he was afraid to expose his corps in an action with the masses of hostile cavalry which would have been sent in pursuit, he could have gone to Fontainebleau and offered his head to Napoleon, as he had promised to do the previous day. Napoleon without doubt would have pardoned him, and so would posterity.

Marmont, however, was too proud to humiliate himself; he considered that he had saved France by a brilliant action. He arranged that his correspondence with Schwarzenberg should be published in the *Moniteur*, and he issued the following order to his corps:

"Your actions must be guided by public opinion, and in deference to this opinion I have saved you from useless dangers."

After issuing this order, Marmont left Paris to review his troops, who had arrived at Versailles in a state of anger and dismay. The sight of the white cockades which some civilians were wearing had roused the temper of the troops, and the officers knocked off the royalists' hats with their swords. The men, however, were tired out. They had had hardly any sleep during the night, and had covered thirty miles. They went to their cantonments, and there officers and men discussed the situation, and it was realized that the generals had handed over the corps to the enemy. Suddenly an order was issued that the troops were to get ready for a review.

The soldiers, who knew that Versailles was occupied by Russian cavalry, thought that they were going to be disarmed, and they assembled in a crowd on the Place d'Armes, shouting "Treason," and uttering threats against their generals; officers tore off their epaulettes and soldiers broke their muskets. Souham, Bordesoulle, and several other generals tried to calm the men, but their presence only increased the exasperation of the troops; at first they were received with hoots, but as they did not go away, muskets and pistols were fired, and the generals fled to Paris. Groups of infuriated soldiers ran through the empty streets; the inhabitants barricaded themselves in their houses, and the Russian *cuirassiers* remained in their quarters.

The officers succeeded in collecting their men on the Place d'Armes, and a proposal that they should rejoin the Emperor's army was received with cheers; the command was given to Colonel Ordener, of the 30th regiment of dragoons, and the column set out on the Rambouillet road, shouting "*Vive l'Empereur*! Down with the traitors!"

Souham had sent several messages to Marmont to tell him of what was happening, and these reached the marshal as he was on his way to the review. The generals had assembled in great alarm at the Versailles gate, and Marmont told them that they must rejoin their troops.

"Do no such thing, Marshal," cried one of them, "the soldiers will shoot you."

Marmont was not afraid of being shot, and his conscience was so blunted that he was quite ready to show himself to the troops whom he had handed over to the enemy.

"You may stop here if you like," he replied. "My mind is made up, and in a quarter of an hour's time I shall either have asserted my authority or I shall be dead," and he galloped off to overtake the column.

For some time, however, he followed at a distance behind the troops; he was not afraid for his life, but he considered that the soldiers were so exasperated that they would not listen to him. After having followed the troops for a couple of miles, Marmont sent on *an aide-de-camp*, who reported that they appeared to be calmer; he waited for a short time longer, and then sent on two other *aides-de-camp*, the first of whom announced that he was coming, and the second ordered the officers to halt the column and to assemble on the left flank of their brigades.

He then rode on, and dismounted before the first group of officers. Probably the marshal was badly received at first, but he knew how to speak to the men; he showed them his wounded arm, and reminded them of the battles they had fought together and of the dangers they had shared.

"Since when," he asked, "have you been authorized to defy me?"

The officers were confused, and it did not occur to them to reply that his treason was sufficient authorization. Marmont continued by assuring them that the troops would not be disarmed, and he told them that they were the honour and the safeguard of the country, and that, as Napoleon had abdicated, they were bound to obey the Government of France.

"Your honour," he cried, "is as dear to me as my own."

Without being frightened by the threats which arose from the ranks, the marshal uttered the same fine sentiments to each group of officers. The commanders were convinced, and calmed their soldiers, and the troops silently marched off to take up fresh cantonments.

Full of pride at having brought his treason to a successful conclusion, Marshal Marmont returned at a gallop to announce the good news to the Provisional Government, which was in a state of the greatest alarm. The revolt of the troops threatened to throw everything into the melting-pot, for such an example of loyalty to Napoleon would have had the greatest effect on the allies and throughout the whole country. Marmont was given a triumphal reception.

"I can still see the marshal," says Bourrienne, "arriving at Talleyrand's house just as everyone had finished dinner. I can see him seated alone before a small table in the middle of the room, while we each went up in turn to congratulate him. He was the hero of the hour."

His triumph was the matter of a day: the expiation lasted for more than thirty years. Among the people, in the army, and at court, no insult and no outrage was spared him. Under the first restoration a word "*ragusade*" was coined to signify treason, and the company of Life-Guards which Marmont commanded was known as the company of Judas. In 1815 Napoleon branded his old comrade as a traitor, and crossed his name off the list of marshals. In 1830 the Duc d'Angaulême said of the unfortunate commander of the army of Paris, " He betrayed us as he betrayed Napoleon."

The clamour of public conscience pursued Marmont beyond the frontiers. At Venice, as the aged marshal walked sadly along the quays thinking of France, where he would fain have returned to die, children used to point at him and shout, " There goes the man who betrayed Napoleon."

CHAPTER 30

The Abdication

The marshals had compelled Napoleon to abdicate in favour of the King of Rome, but having been compelled, he honestly made up his mind to the step. As soon as his plenipotentiaries had started, he wrote a letter to the Empress, authorizing her to appeal to the Emperor of Austria to intervene in the negotiations. Although he did his best by these means to facilitate the mission of his envoys, he was nevertheless not sanguine of success.

He did not, however, think that, even if the negotiations failed, he would be at the mercy of the enemy, for when he signed the abdication, the thought lay at the back of the Emperor's mind that if the allies refused to accept his conditions the chiefs of the army would be reconciled to his cause. By making the marshals the bearers of the act of abdication he forced them to make common cause with himself; he knew that they were hostile to the Bourbons, and if his offer to abdicate were refused they would have no alternative but to fight.

On the supposition that his proposals would be rejected, the Emperor ordered the commanders of 500 corps and independent divisions to assemble at the palace at 10 p.m. on April 4. Napoleon was sure of the devotion of the troops, but he was less certain of the generals, and he wished to obtain from the army a statement of its opinion which would bind every one. At the hour named the generals were received by the Emperor, who described the position of affairs, and asked if they wished to abandon the tricolour cockade and serve the Bourbons. There is no doubt that they all assured him of their fidelity, and it was decided that an address should be signed in the various corps.

The Emperor had received a letter from General Lucotte, telling him that, in accordance with Marmont's instructions, the abdication had been announced in orders, and had caused the greatest excitement among the troops; shortly afterwards his orderly officer reported verbally that Marmont had left for Paris, and that General Souham was not at his quarters. These reports had begun to make the Emperor uneasy, but he was not seriously alarmed, for he ascribed the events at Essonnes to a misunderstanding. Napoleon could not think that a marshal of the empire would desert his post and go over to the enemy with 11,000 soldiers.

Between 1 and 2 a.m. there arrived at Fontainebleau several officers who had left Souham's column. They were received by the *aide-de-camp* on duty and brought to the Emperor without delay. Napoleon was walking up and down with his hands behind his back, and his manner was extraordinarily calm as he questioned them. At first he would not believe that Marmont had gone over to the enemy, and at last when there was no further possibility of doubt, he sat down in silence as if stunned; then, after a long pause, as if finishing a sentence, he said in a low tone, "the ungrateful wretch, he will be more unhappy than me."

The line of the Essonne was now uncovered and there was danger of being attacked. The Emperor sent Belliard to the outposts with all the cavalry he could collect, and he ordered Mortier to move his head-quarters to Essonnes. Before long he received a letter from General Krazinski, which showed that the Emperor was not abandoned by the whole army.

"Sire," wrote the general, "some of the marshals are betraying you, but the Poles will never do such a thing; their devotion is unalterable. Our life is necessary for your safety, and I am leaving my cantonments without orders, so as to assemble some reliable battalions around your person."

The following day, April 5, or perhaps during this night, Napoleon wrote an order to the army, in which he allowed his bitterness and discouragement to be plainly seen, and which seems to be an appeal to posterity, rather than a proclamation intended to rouse the enthusiasm of his troops. At noon he reviewed the remains of the 7th Corps in the court of the palace, and Leval's veterans of the Spanish wars cheered him as the Guard had cheered him the day before. Marmont's defection, however, had taken away 11,000 men, and had so seriously reduced his army that he could no longer fight a battle before Paris if his proposals were rejected.

He made preparations therefore to retire behind the Loire. At 3 o'clock the Old Guard, which was bivouacked at Tilly, were ordered to return to Fontainebleau and to take post on the Orleans road. This was only the beginning of a general movement, for Napoleon had formed his plan of retreat, but was waiting for news from Paris before carrying it out. He felt a strong presentiment that Marmont's treason would result in the breaking off of negotiations, and towards evening he issued his orders. The Guard, with Gérard's corps, were to start for Malesherbes at daybreak on the 6th, and the rest of the troops were to follow the movement during the morning; Mortier's corps was to form the rear-guard, and was to march from Menecy to Fontainebleau and bivouac there. On April 7 the head of the army would be at Pithiviers, and the rear-guard between Fontainebleau and Malesherbes.

Between 9 and 10 p.m. the Emperor's three envoys returned to Fontainebleau and reported the result of their mission. The defection of the 6th corps had decided the question. Alexander would not accept an abdication in favour of the King of Rome, and the Senate was about to proclaim the Comte de Provence under the title of Louis XVIII. The Czar guaranteed to Napoleon the sovereignty of the Isle of Elba.

Since the occurrences at Essonnes the Emperor had been prepared for a refusal. He declared that he would appeal to arms, for, as he said, "war can bring nothing worse than peace."

Then, with the utmost calmness, he described his plan of retreat behind the Loire and enumerated the forces which he still had at his disposal. There were still 50,000 men in the imperial army, and there were also the armies under Augereau, Soult, Suchet, Maison, and Prince Eugène; in addition there were the depots and the fortresses and the possibility of a general rising.

The Emperor finished with the words, "All may yet be saved."

Napoleon hoped that the marshals, in their dislike for the Bourbons, would be only too eager to fight, but this was a vain illusion. After having tried to secure a Regency in place of the Empire, the marshals had determined to side with the Bourbons; one day at Paris and two interviews with the Czar had been enough to persuade them. Napoleon was tired of arguing with people who would not listen, and he gave way, or at any rate pretended to do so. He dismissed his three envoys, and put off till the following day the drafting of his act of abdication.

It is not easy to know whether Napoleon was in earnest or not; he had foreseen the rejection of his proposals, and had made all preparations, and it is very doubtful if he gave way so quickly to the wishes of his marshals, and abandoned the idea of retreating on Pithiviers. It is not known whether he suddenly lost all energy and cancelled his orders, or whether he intended resolutely to carry them out. What is certain, however, is that the orders were sent out, no written counter-orders were issued, but the movement did not take place.

The utmost uncertainty prevailed. The army was indignant at the defection of the 6th Corps, and Marmont was stigmatized as a traitor and deserter, but, although they condemned his action, the generals discussed the motives which had influenced him. Further resistance seemed impossible, and it was admitted that Marmont wished to save the army from destruction, and to avert civil war. The speech which the Emperor had delivered on April 3 had roused the enthusiasm of the troops, but it had had no effect on the staffs, and the subsequent news from Paris had increased their despondency.

It was known that the marshals had compelled Napoleon to abdicate, and this had had a bad effect on discipline; those who were responsible for this act were the pride of the army: Ney, the bravest of the brave, Macdonald, the personification of strictness, and Oudinot, the former commander of the corps of Grenadiers, whose wounds out-numbered his years of service. Although the abdication had been conditional, it nevertheless deprived the Emperor of his authority, and his tenure of the crown henceforward was also conditional. It was doubtful how far he could still command. Even Lucotte seemed to waver in his obedience to the Emperor.

In the energetic order in which he blamed Marmont's conduct, he wrote, "France is now represented by the Government. We will serve our country under whatever Government the majority of the nation shall choose."

During the evening of April 5 the generals held a secret meeting. Several among them, notably General Pelet, considered the meeting illegal, and refused to attend. We can only guess at the decisions which were come to; at 2 a.m. no less a person than General Friant, who commanded the 1st Division of the Old Guard, warned Pelet that the Corps Commanders had determined to make no movement, and that no further orders would be received from the Emperor, and finally, during the morning of April 6, Ney, Macdonald, and Caulaincourt ordered Berthier to transmit no orders which Napoleon might give as regards the movements of troops.

On the same day, April 6, the Emperor assembled his marshals for the last time; he made a final appeal to them, and urged them to continue the war behind the Loire. The marshals refused to be convinced, and there was a repetition of the scenes of the last two days. Ney, Oudinot, Macdonald, and Lefebvre showed less heat than they had done before, but they were equally determined. They coldly pointed out to Napoleon that there was nothing left but the debris of his armies, and that, even if he did succeed in reaching the Loire, his last struggles would only bring about a civil war. The marshals had determined to force an abdication; the Empire had been tried and condemned by its chief officers.

For the last five days Napoleon had seen around him nothing but despondency and treason. His appeals had not been listened to, nor his orders obeyed. He had given up his conquests, and his Empire was crumbling to pieces, but what affected him more than this was the fact that those who had now turned against him were his old comrades-in-arms. The Emperor had drunk to the dregs the cup of humiliation and bitterness, and the last sacrifice was now demanded of him.

"You wish for rest." said Napoleon to his marshals. "Well, then, you shall have it," and he wrote the act of abdication.

> "The Allied Powers having announced that the Emperor Napoleon is the only obstacle to the peace of Europe, the Emperor Napoleon, faithful to his oath, declares that he renounces for himself, and for his heirs, the thrones of France and Italy, because there is no personal sacrifice, not excepting even that of his life, which he is not ready to make in the interests of France."

When the great news became known at the various head-quarters, all the senior officers began to desert. Everyone found an excuse to go to Paris; one did so in the interests of his troops, a second wanted to get some money, and a third went to see a sick wife. The Palace of Fontainebleau, which the day before had been full of officers, was gradually emptied. The Duc de Bassano and a few *aides-de-camp* and generals alone remembered that the Emperor was still alive.

"One would have thought," says General Pelet, "that his Majesty was already in his grave."

On April 6, when Ney was returning to Paris in triumph with the Emperor's abdication, the Senate proclaimed Louis XVIII. At once each general hastened to be the first to give his public approval to the acts of the Provisional Government, and to protest his loyalty to the King. The *Moniteur* was unable to print the proclamations which were issued by Jourdan,

Augereau, Maison, Lagrange, Nansouty, Oudinot, Kellermann, Lefebvre, Hullin, Milhaud, Latour-Maubourg, de Sgur, Berthier, and many others. On April 7 the Minister for War sent a circular to all general officers, inviting them "to make their personal adhesion known as early as possible." Belliard, by some mistake, did not receive this circular, and he was very much troubled that he had been passed over. He did not waste an hour in writing to the minister.

"Yesterday your Excellency addressed a letter to all the divisional generals of the army, asking for their adhesion to the new order of things. I did not receive this letter, and I think it must have been by mistake. I hasten, then, to assure you of my adherence to the new Government."

This is the last letter to appear in the register of Napoleon's correspondence, which Belliard had kept for so many years.

The soldiers were less ready to forget their Emperor and their colours than the generals. The announcement of the abdication filled the army with astonishment and anger. On April 7 the regiments of the Guard came out of their quarters at night, carrying arms and torches. They paraded the streets of Fontainebleau, and marched round the Palace, shouting, "*Vive l'Empereur!* Down with the traitors! To Paris!"

When the Emperor said goodbye to them these old soldiers did not shout "*Vive l'Empereur!*" but their silence and their tears bore eloquent testimony to the feelings of the army.

At Orleans the troops took possession of the town, and forced the inhabitants to join them in cheering the Emperor; on April 9, when the Empress entered the town, and again on the 13th, similar scenes were repeated. At Clermont-Ferrand the mayor proclaimed the Bourbons, and marched through the town carrying the white flag, but the garrison broke out of the barracks, dispersed the procession, and burnt the flag on the main square.

The following day a *Te Deum* was celebrated with the white flag on the altar, when some cavalry rode into the church, seized the flag, and dragged it through the streets. At Briare a division of infantry terrorized the whole countryside by its threats against the *partisans* of the Bourbons. At Lyons fighting took place every day with the allied soldiers, and these affairs threatened to develop into a pitched battle. Augereau's corps was inclined to mutiny, and as it was feared that the passage of the Emperor would bring things to a head the regiments were all cantoned in towns and villages at a distance from the main road.

In many towns the troops refused to take the oath of allegiance to the king, and in some places they burnt the white flag. In Paris the soldiers vented their anger on the foreigners; they pulled off the leaves with which the Austrians ornamented their helmets, and the medals which the Russians wore on their breasts. Every day there were quarrels and fights, and on April 29 there was a serious affair in the gardens of the Palais-Royal, and several people were wounded. On May 8 some Cossacks were sabred in a public- house.

Chateaubriand relates that "when the King passed, the grenadiers of the Guard bared their teeth like tigers. When they presented arms they did so with a movement of fury, and with a noise which filled the onlookers with terror."

At Antwerp, Metz, and Mayence the garrisons attempted a rising. At Lille the troops were in open revolt for three days; during the night of April 13 the cry of "*Vive l'Empereur!*" was raised in the barracks, and on the 14th they assembled in a mass on the Place d'Armes; they fired on their officers, and then broke open the gates of the town, saying they were going to join the Emperor.

At Douai and Thionville there were similar risings. At Landau soldiers nearly cut to pieces the delegates who came to announce Napoleon's downfall. Almost everywhere the soldiers showed the same outbursts of anger; they threw away the new cockades, they burnt the white flag, insulted the name of Louis XVIII, and ill-treated the royalists; they mutinied against their officers, and declared that they would fight for no one except their Emperor.

Among the civil population the new Government was accepted without displeasure, but without the unanimous expressions of joy which have been described by royalist writers. At Paris the middle classes were still under the influence of the imperial regime, and were lukewarm or almost hostile to the royalists. The working-classes egged on the soldiers against the allies, and sided with them in the frequent brawls; they used to amuse themselves by tying white cockades on to the tails of stray dogs, and whipping them through the streets, and sometimes in the evenings groups of workingmen would parade the streets singing songs in honour of the Emperor.

The Comte d'Artois and Louis XVIII entered Paris on April 12 and May 3. They were received with cheers; the newly raised Mounted National Guards, who were at the head of the processions, led the cheering, and waved their swords, and some worthy people wept for joy, but everyone was not deceived as to the share taken by the bulk of the citizens in these ovations; an English officer, who was a prisoner in Paris, was sceptical as to the real feeling of the French, and a Prussian is related to have said that he did not think the Bourbons could remain in France for six months after the allies had left.

The day after the solemn entry of the king two caricatures were surreptitiously sold; one represented a troop of fat geese solemnly walking up the steps of the Tuileries while an eagle was flying away from the Palace, and the other showed the fat Louis XVIII mounted behind a Cossack, galloping over the corpses of French soldiers, with a burnt village in the background.

In the provinces the municipalities presented addresses, and the royalists illuminated their houses, but the mass of the people exhibited more surprise than enthusiasm. There was much dislike of the new king, and while the soldiers kept the tricolour cockade in their haversacks, many working-men and peasants remained faithful to the memory of Napoleon. In April and May the *prefects* of thirty departments reported considerable discontent. White flags were torn down, royalist emblems trampled underfoot, official notices were defaced, and seditious manifestos posted in their place.

At Nemours, Montargis, and Nevers, and in all the towns and

villages as far as Moulins, Napoleon was greeted with cheers as he passed on his way to Elba, and the commissioners of the allies were insulted. At Lyons the population had remained devoted to Napoleon, and huge crowds waited in the streets during the whole of April 23 to see him pass. In the south-east of France, however, the Emperor was jeered at and hooted, and this reception bears witness to the feelings which were beginning to divide France.

In the west there were highly placed royalists, but the workmen of the towns were hostile to the Bourbons, and in the country districts the royalists were in a minority, and on May 8 the police reported that there was danger of civil war.

The Abbé de Pradt had told the Czar that the whole of France wished to see the Bourbons restored. The whole of France ardently longed for peace, but a very small number of people even thought of the Bourbons, who were complete strangers to the country and to the younger generation. France was ruined and worn out by war, and she was ready to accept any Government which would ensure peace and promise a reduction of taxation, but the former dynasty could not suddenly become popular, for the circumstances under which it had returned were degrading to the national pride.

No doubt Napoleon had been responsible for the invasion, but in his last campaign he had been fighting in a national war, and he was now being sent into exile after having made a magnificent resistance. The Bourbons, on the contrary, had sided with the enemy; they had followed the invaders into France and had taken advantage of their victories. The arrival of the Bourbons was identified with the triumph of the allies, and it must be admitted that the royalist manifestos had tended to encourage this idea.

The allies were not deceived as to the true sentiments of France. On March 31 Alexander had opposed Talleyrand's arguments, because he realised that the royalist agitation was merely superficial. On April 10 Metternich said that the war would break out again within two years, and he had come to this conclusion because he knew that public opinion was still in a state of flux. A restoration, however, was in the interests of Europe, and the allies were only too ready to let themselves be persuaded that the French wished to have the Bourbons back again.

The Czar had written that when they had captured Paris the allies would treat with Napoleon unless the nation declared against him, or that they would summon representatives of the people, who would be free to decide upon the Government to be set up. After the victory, however, Alexander merely consulted Talleyrand, Pradt, and Louis, and he then proclaimed that the sovereigns would no longer treat with Napoleon or his family.

During the night of April 4 the Czar had been so affected by Macdonald's words that he was on the point of agreeing to a Regency. The news of the defection of the 6th Corps was received just in time to prevent a decision which would have bitterly deceived the allies. Napoleon II was 3 years old, and Napoleon I only 45. The Regency could only have been an interregnum or a pretence, and the peace could not have been permanent.

Now, Europe was as tired of fighting as were Napoleon's marshals, and she desired, as Metternich expressed it, "a lasting peace, founded upon a balance of power." A restoration of the Bourbons was the most simple and certain solution of the problem, and at the same time it conformed more closely than any other to the principles of the allied courts. A restoration of the former monarchy was not the object of the war, but it was bound to come as the result of the victory, because no victory could be final which failed to outlaw Napoleon.

CPSIA information can be obtained at www.ICGtesting.com
Printed in the USA
BVOW07s0212120813

328410BV00001B/13/P

9 781846 777738